UNITED STATES MILITARY ALMANAC

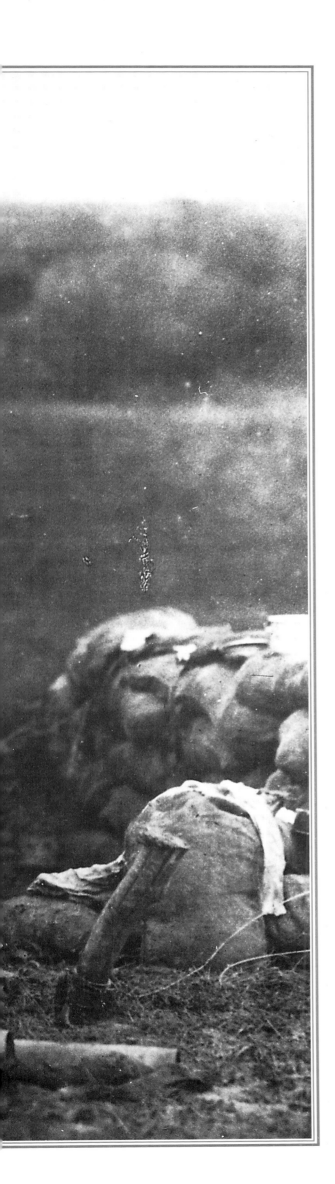

UNITED STATES MILITARY ALMANAC

A chronological compendium of over
200 years of American history

WALT LANG

PUBLISHED BY
SALAMANDER BOOKS LIMITED
LONDON

A Salamander Book

Published by
Salamander Books Ltd.
8 Blenheim Court
Brewery Road
London N7 9NT
United Kingdom

© Salamander Books Ltd. 1989, 1998

ISBN 0-517-16092-7

9 8 7 6 5 4 3 2 1

Distributed by
Random House Value Publishing, Inc.
40 Engelhard Avenue
Avenel, New Jersey 07001

A CIP catalog record for this book is available from the Library of Congress.

Credits

Revised edition by: David Miller
Project manager: Ray Bonds
Editor: Tony Hall
Designers: Philip Gorton, Rod Teasdale
Picture research: Military Archive and Research Services
Colour artworks: Ray Hutchins, Tony Gibbons, Pilot Press Ltd
Filmsetting: The Old Mill, SX Composing DTP.
Colour reproduction: Scantrans PTE Ltd., Emirates Printing Press
Printed in Spain

Contents

23.80

Foreword

Military history is laden with the dramatic fare of heroic exploits; battles and campaigns, analyses of how mankind has been affected on the field of battle

This is not a dramatic book. Nor will it provide major insights into the course of military history. It is simply an attempt to provide a useful chronological reference to more than 1,000 events in US military history so that the reader will have quick and easy access to the information in a way that had not perhaps been available before now.

These events are not all of equal weight; nor are they meant to be all-embracing. Every effort was made to ensure the inclusion of the major events in US military history — if there are oversights, they are mine and certainly not intentional.

The events share one thing in common: they explain details about US military history in a quick and understandable fashion. Hopefully they will prove interesting to the reader and useful to the student.

No work such as this, of course, is ever created in a vacuum. The effort started off as a large pile of index cards and evolved into a manuscript that required verification, cross-checking and additional research.

Many, many people helped with this effort. But special thanks are owed to Bill Heimdahl, Chief of the Reference Services Branch, Office of Air Force History; Kim Holien, historian, US Army Center of Military History; John C. Reilly, Head, Ships' Histories Branch, US Naval Historical Center; and Dan Crawford, Head of the Reference Section, History and Museums Branch, US Marine Corps. Each took the time to review the script and offer criticism and corrections

Two people whose contributions are measured in another way are Harry Zubkoff and Ben Schemmer. Harry Zubkoff, now retired from his post as head of the Current News and Analysis Branch in the Pentagon, did much work along these lines for the US Air Force. It is fair to say the work he did — and the counsel he so freely gave — were the inspirational origins of the product.

Ben Schemmer, editor of *Armed Forces Journal International*, provided help of another kind. His book, *The Almanac of American Liberty*, was the best chronology on American military history I ran across during the early research efforts for the book. It is equally fair to say his efforts were just as inspirational and served as a model for my similar albeit different approach.

Additional research for the book came from Christy Carter; my daughter Heidi and my son Kurt, who had the patience of maturity to help them dig out impossible information they were asked to dig out. They also had the energy of youth when it came to keeping up the pace of the research. Yet another son, Eric, was instrumental in helping put together the database that made it easier to compile and sort through the mountain of available information.

Of course, my wife Paula displayed the most patience as the book took shape step-by-step. To her, my grateful thanks appreciation and love.
Walt Lang

7 October 1636 The General Court of the Massachusetts Bay Colony orders the organization of that colony's militia companies in three groups: the North, East and South regiments. That division greatly increased the effectiveness of the militia and is generally recognized as the root of the American tradition of Minutemen — citizen soldiers standing ready to serve at a moment's notice.

18 April 1637 Colonial conscription legislation is enacted at Boston, Massachusetts. Theoretically, all able-bodied men can be called up for service under this legislation, but its enforcement leaves something to be desired. Any steps that are taken in this direction are done sporadically and are largely ineffective.

3 February 1690 The first paper money in America is issued by the colony of Massachusetts. The currency will be used to pay soldiers fighting a war against Quebec and, later, during the French and Indian wars. It would be far more accurate to call the "money" bills of credit, since the bills were receipts for loans made by citizens to the government to help finance the war effort.

5 March 1770 The "Boston Massacre" takes place. It comes as the climax to rioting in front of the Custom House in the city. British troops under the command of Capt. Thomas Preston of the 29th Regiment of Foot fire into the mob — killing five and wounding six others. Preston is later tried and acquitted for the murder of civilians, but the event helps stir anti-British feeling.

16 December 1773 Dressed as Indians, a group of Americans board English ships in Boston Harbor and destroy 342 tea chests — value $90,000 — by throwing them into the harbor. The action was organized by Samuel Adams and becomes known to history as "The Boston Tea Party". It also prompts the passage of the British Coercive Acts of 1774, which are called the Intolerable Acts by the colonists.

20 October 1774 The Continental Congress says theater should be at a standstill during the Revolution. It orders the colonies to "discountenance and discourage all horse racing and all kinds of gaming, cock fighting, exhibitions of shows, plays and other expensive diversion and entertainments". The colony of Pennsylvania will be among the first to fall in line with the order.

14 December 1774 The first military encounter of the American Revolution occurs. On the report (the news was carried by Paul Revere) that the British intend

to station a garrison at Portsmouth, N.H., Maj. John Sullivan leads a band of militia to Fort William and Mary, breaks into the arsenal and carries off a store of arms and ammunition. Neither side suffers casualties.

23 March 1775 The Virginia Provincial Convention, in a daring move for the times, resolves that the colony ought to prepare her defenses against possible attack. During debate, Patrick Henry utters his famous words "... give me liberty or give me death". An ardent supporter of the idea of individual liberty, Henry will become the governor of the Commonwealth (twice) and will play a major role in the passage of the Bill of Rights.

18 April 1775 Paul Revere makes his famous "midnight ride" from Charlestown to Lexington, Massachusetts, warning colonists along the way that the British are coming. Gen. Thomas Gage had sent 700 men from the British garrison in Boston to capture arms and ammunition stored by the colonists, who in turn began gathering their "minute" companies (known better as "Minutemen") in response.

19 April 1775 American Revolution begins with opening shots at the Battle of Lexington and Concord. Known as

Above: "The Boston Massacre" as originally engraved by Paul Revere. John Adams handled the legal defense of the British troop commander and eight of the men who fired on the mob. Six (and the commander) were acquitted.

"the shot heard round the world", it came from Capt. John Parker's company (no one knows who actually fired the shot) of 70 assembled men at Lexington Common and brought British volleys in response. The Americans scattered and left some eight dead and ten wounded in their wake.

19 April 1775 Chaplain William Emerson responds to the call for help at the Battle of Lexington and becomes the first chaplain to serve in the Revolution. He is credited with encouraging a timid Minuteman by saying "Don't be afraid, Harry; God is on our side." Ralph Waldo Emerson, poet, essayist and easily the best known member of the family, was his grandson.

3 May 1775 The existence of American Marines is established by the payroll for the *Enterprise* of 1 July which starts

Right: Engraving showing the Battle of Concord. Concord was actually one of two battles fought on the first day of the Revolution. The other battle, where the first shot of the war was fired, was actually at Lexington.

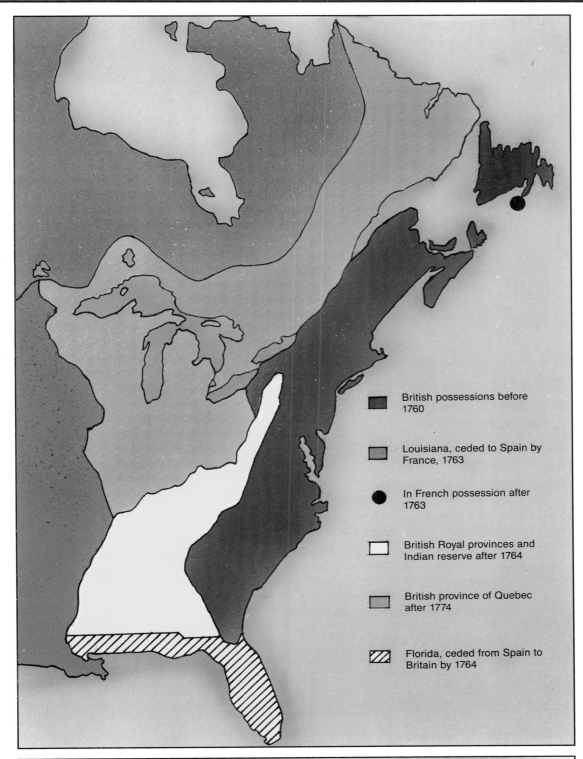

British possessions before 1760

Louisiana, ceded to Spain by France, 1763

In French possession after 1763

British Royal provinces and Indian reserve after 1764

British province of Quebec after 1774

Florida, ceded from Spain to Britain by 1764

with this date. Lt. James Watson is the first Marine Officer, at least as far as can be identified from the ship's payroll.

10 May 1775 Col. Ethan Allen and his Green Mountain Boys capture the British-held fortress at Fort Ticonderoga, New York. The garrison was surrounded and was called upon by Allen to "surrender in the name of Jehovah and the Continental Congress", and promptly did so. Allen was helped in the effort by a certain colonel who was to become infamous before the end of the Revolution; his name was Benedict Arnold.

27 May 1775 A committee is appointed by the Continental Congress to consider ways and means to supply the colonies with ammunition and military stores. It authorizes Gen. George Washington to appoint an officer known as the Commissary General of Artillery Stores, the nucleus around which will grow a corps of officers and civilians assigned exclusively to ordnance duty.

12 June 1775 Led by Jeremiah O'Brien, about 40 men board and capture the British armed schooner *Margaretta* at Machias Bay, Maine. It is considered the first naval action of the Revolution. The people of Machias had heard about Lexington and Concord; O'Brien and his men, armed with guns, swords, axes and pitchforks boarded the *Unity*, set out after the *Margaretta* and took her at sea in a fierce fight.

14 June 1775 Birthday of the Army. On or before this day, the Continental Congress secretly adopted New England forces besieging Boston and New York forces that were guarding strategic postions; they openly appointed a committee to draft regulations for the Continental Army and authorized the addition of 10 companies to be drawn from Pennsylvania, Virginia and Maryland.

15 June 1775 Washington is appointed by the Continental Congress to "command all the Continental forces raised, or to be raised, for the defense of American liberty". Moving swiftly to support him, the Congress next day appoints two Major Generals, eight Brigadiers, an Adjutant General, Quartermaster General and deputy, a Commissary General of Stores, as well as other positions.

The American Revolution (1775 — 1783)

The population of the 13 colonies at the start of the American Revolution was around 2.5 million — about 20 percent of whom were slaves. Ranged against them was a developed empire with an established and professional Army and the first-ranked navy of the world.

The colonies were dealing with what they felt was oppressive taxation and the forced quartering of British troops. Early protests and demonstrations against these — most notably the Boston Tea Party on 16 December, 1773 — led to the imposition of even more coercive measures.

This atmosphere boiled over on 19 April, 1775 when 700 British regulars left Boston to seize colonial military stores at Concord, Massachusetts. This force was met by militiamen at Lexington, and a

US Army Campaign Streamers Revolutionary War

Lexington	Apr 19, 1775
Ticonderoga	May 10, 1775
Boston	Jun 17, 1775 — Mar 17, 1776
Quebec	Aug 28, 1775 — Jul 1776
Charleston	Jun 28-29, 1776
Long Island	Aug 26-29, 1776
Trenton	Dec 26, 1776
Princeton	Jan 3, 1777
Saratoga	Jul 2, 1777 — Oct 17, 1777
Brandywine	Sep 11, 1777
Germantown	Oct 4, 1777
Monmouth	Jun 28, 1778
Savannah	Dec 29, 1778; Sep 16, 1779 — Oct 10, 1779
Charleston	Mar 29, 1780 — May 12, 1780
Cowpens	Jan 17, 1781
Guilford Court House	Mar 15, 1781
Yorktown	Sep 28 — Oct 19, 1781

shot was fired.

The British force marched onto Concord, but by then the countryside had been roused. Militia units and the Minutemen assembled along the route of the British march. They fired behind cover, refusing to present the formations the British had been trained to combat.

First American Flags

Right: The first official American flag known as the Cambridge or Grand Union Flag.

Left: An American merchant flag of the sort in use until the 1790s; the color could vary.

Right: The first Stars and Stripes, adopted by the Continental Congress, 14 June 1777.

AN APPEAL TO HEAVEN

Left: The ensign of Washington's Cruisers, a candidate for the official American flag.

Right: The flag of John Paul Jones's prize ship *Serapis*, as seen after her capture in October 1779.

Left: Naval flag as flown by the US Navy ship *Alliance*, in European waters, October 1779.

This unorthodox method of warfare proved unsettling and it set the pattern for the entire Revolution. It forced the British to operate in an area measuring 1,000 by 600 miles (1,600 by 480 km), 3,000 miles (4,825 km) away from home with no key center of resistance that could be subdued and occupied.

Notwithstanding the success of the militiamen, the colonies needed a standing army and on 14 June, 1775, the Continental Congress obliged by passing legislation forming one. General George Washington was appointed its commander-in-chief.

On paper, the Continental Army looked impressive. Congress authorized 88 battalions with 60,000 men; an additional 22 battalions were authorized later.

In fact, the Continental Army never came even close to these numbers. The entire Army never numbered much more than 30,000 men and Washington seldom commanded as many as 15,000 effectives in the field. Throughout the struggle, the Continental Army had to rely on the state militia is to fill out its ranks.

British strength on the other hand was considerable. In mid-1776 — when the colonies declared their independence — they had more than 30,000 soldiers.

Another source of manpower for the British should not be overlooked. Loyalist support was considerable — with nearly 50,000 Americans fighting for the Crown.

On the maritime side, British superiority was clearcut. The Continental Navy was not even formed until 13 October, 1775. By 1776, it had 27 ships against Britain's 270. Corresponding figures at the end of the Revolutionary War were 20, a net loss for the Americans, and close to 500 for the British.

The Continental Navy was augmented by privateers sailing under state auspices. American ships swarmed over the seas and by the end of 1777 had captured 560 British vessels; that figure climbed to 1,500 by the end of the war.

Washington and other American leaders recognized the need for command of the seas and looked to Europe for help. It came largely as the result of

Below: Less than a month after their official formation, men of the Marine Corps sail with John Paul Jones's ship, *Alfred*. Their role will include fighting from the tops of the masts onto the enemy's deck below.

the most decisive land battle of the war at Saratoga, New York.

This prompted France to recognize American independence, which brought with it the soon-to-be-realized promise of French soldiers, money and the French fleet.

The alliance with France — and later Spain and the Netherlands — proved decisive. This was particularly true in 1781 when British forces under Maj. Gen. Lord Charles Cornwallis were driven to the coast at Yorktown, Virginia.

His force of about 10,000 surrendered to about 11,000 Americans and 9,000 French soldiers and sailors.

The American nation had been forged at a cost of 4,435 battle deaths and another 6,188 wounded. The toll to disease would place that number at more than 13,000.

In 1783 the Treaty of Paris was signed. The first war in the young history of the United States of America was over.

16 June 1775 Col. Richard Gridley, the designer of the defense works at Breed's Hill (known as Bunker Hill), is appointed chief engineer of the Continental Army. He will build the fortifications on Dorchester Heights that will help force the British from Boston. Gridley was a civil engineer and studied military engineering; in fact, he planned the fortifications for Boston in 1746.

17 June 1775 The Battle of Bunker Hill is fought. More than 2,500 British regulars launch an attack on about 1,400 Minutemen under William Prescott. Considered the first battle of the Revolutionary War, the British win a costly tactical victory. The battle is actually fought at an American redoubt called "Breed's Hill". Casualties are 226 British and 140 Americans.

3 July 1775 Washington takes command of the Continental Army at Cambridge, Massachusetts. It forms the core of American military forces for the Revolutionary War, although the number of regulars in the army is uncertain. Less than 100,000 men bore arms under repeated enlistments, and only half served in the Continental Army. By 1778, the number of regulars altogether may be only 10,000.

5 July 1775 Special insignia denoting army rank is instituted in Massachusetts by Washington. Under the system, generals, field officers, captains and subalterns are to wear different-colored ribbons and cockades. It will not be until 1780 that a system of epaulets on one or both shoulders will be adopted, including the first of the modern insignia — silver stars for generals.

Below: A young George Washington as a member of the Virginia militia. He consistently sided with his native country as tensions grew with Britain. The vote to make him Continental Army commander was unanimous.

Above: A Gilbert Stuart painting of Gen. Horatio Gates. His 1775 order barred blacks from serving in the Continental Army; after the Revolution he freed his slaves and moved to a farm on Manhattan Island.

6 July 1775 After hostilities begin against the British, it does not take too long for discipline to begin to exert itself in the Continental Army; the first general court martial held in the Revolution is ordered on the heels of action at Bunker Hill. John Lemsy, John Batcheler and William Crostin are charged with "desertion and theft". They are all attached to the artillery regiment of Col. Richard Gridley.

10 July 1775 An order excluding blacks from serving in the Continental Army is issued by Horatio Gates, who holds the post of Washington's Adjutant General. Seeking to take advantage of this, Lord John Murray Dunmore, who is the deposed Royal Governor of Virginia, pledges full freedom to all slaves who will fight with the British.

27 July 1775 Action by the Congress in setting up a "hospital" or medical service for an army of 20,000 headed by a "Director General and Chief Physician" marks the establishment of an Army Medical Department. It is headed by Dr Benjamin Church of Boston, who stays at the job a brief time, when it is shortly discovered that he is in treasonous correspondence with the British.

29 July 1775 Congressional action authorizes $20.00 in monthly pay for chaplains then in Continental service, which is the earliest official recognition of the chaplaincy in the army. Washington in his order directing that chaplains are to be procured, says: "The blessings and protection of heaven are at all times necessary, but especially is it in time of public distress and danger".

Above: Battle of Bunker Hill. At this battle, Maj. Gen. Israel Putnam, ranking American officer, issued his famous order: "Men, you are all marksmen — don't one of you fire until you see the white of their eyes."

5 September 1775 At Beverly, Massachusetts, the *Hannah* becomes the first regularly commissioned warship of the USA. On the same day as she is commissioned, the schooner sails and within two days captures the British ship *Unity*, which is the first prize taken in the Revolution. *Hannah* is the first ship in "Washington's Fleet", and a forerunner to the Continental Navy. She will soon be joined by five schooners and a brigantine.

5 October 1775 The Continental Congress uses the word "Marines" for the first time when it directs Washington to secure two vessels on "Continental risque and pay", and to give orders for the "proper encouragement to the Marines and seamen" to serve on the two armed ships.

7 October 1775 In Rhode Island a small fleet of British ships operating out of Newport arrives at Bristol and bombards it until the natives give

13 October 1775 Birthday of the United States Navy. Congress this day directs the fitting out of two vessels to intercept ships carrying warlike stores and other supplies to the invading British land forces. Silas Deane, John Langdon and Christopher Gadsen are the individuals officially appointed to fit them out. Because "Washington's Fleet" had enjoyed such great success in the past, the Congress had been considering forming a Continental Navy.

20 October 1775 Agents throughout the colonies are solicited on their views about adopting an official American flag. Col. Joseph Reed, Washington's military secretary writes to them: "Please decide upon some particular colour for a flag and a signal by which our vessels may know one another. What do you think of a flag with a white ground and a tree in the middle with the motto 'An Appeal to Heaven'. This is the flag of our floating batteries."

4 November 1775 On this day, a resolution of the Continental Congress sets up the statutory ration for the enlisted soldier. The ration is issued uncooked and includes, among other things, 1 lb (0.45 kg) of beef, or 0.75 lb (0.34 kg) of pork, or 1 lb of saltfish per day. The fighting man also gets 1 lb of bread or flour, 1 pint (0.47 litre) of milk and 1 quart (0.95 litre) of spruce beer or cider. Bathing is a different matter: there will be 6 lb (2.72 kg) of hard soap made available per 100 men weekly.

up 40 of their sheep for consumption by the army. It is one of many marauding attacks that will be made on islands and shores in and around Naragansett Bay, and that will lead in their turn to the virtual extinction of any loyalist support for the British occupying forces in the area.

voluntarily enlisted myself as a soldier in the American Continental army for one year, unless sooner discharged, and do bind myself to conform in all instances to such rules and regulations as are or shall be established for the government of the said army."

10 November 1775 Birthday of US Marine Corps. Though the American colonies and the Continental Army had used marines since the spring of the year, this action by the Congress directing that two marine battalions be raised and appropriately officered is marked

12 October 1775 Washington sends a letter to Congress advising it not to reduce the pay of soldiers. Carefully worded, his letter is succinct and to the point on the question. It reads: "With respect to the Reduction of the Pay of the men, which may enter into the consideration of their Support; it is the unanimous Opinion of the General Officers, that it cannot be touched with Safety at present".

12 October 1775 The enlistment form for any person who joins the ranks of the Continental Army is adopted. It reads: "I_____have this day

Right: Depiction of the first Marine recruits. Marines were provided to man the infant fleets of the Continental Navy. Soldiers detailed for sea service, they were to fight aboard but not sail the ships they were assigned to.

as the official beginning of the Corps. The senior officer is Capt. Samuel Nicholas, now considered by historians to be the first Marine commandant.

17 November 1775 Col. Henry Knox is appointed to command of the Continental Regiment of Artillery, which marks the formal establishment of artillery in the army. He orders the 55 cannons that were captured from the British at the battle of Ticonderoga, New York, to be hauled overland to help the fight at Boston, Massachusetts. The guns when they eventually arrive will have a decisive effect on operations there. By 1777, there will be four artillery regiments.

28 November 1775 President John Hancock of the Continental Congress signs a commission making Samuel Nicholas of Philadelphia a Captain of Marines, the first commission issued for service in the Continental Navy or Marine Corps. With subordinate officers, he proceeded with enlistment and by the end of December, five companies of Marines will be organized to serve Congress and country.

28 November 1775 Written by John Adams, the first regulations for the Navy are issued. Called ''Rules for the Regulation of the Navy of the United Colonies'', they also establish a chaplain corps. They state: ''The

Above: Sailors and Marines land at New Providence, Nassau, in the first amphibious landing in US military history. They took Ft. Nassau and completed their mission (to sieze military stores) within two weeks.

Commandants* of the US Marine Corps

Samuel Nicholas	1775-1781
William Ward Burrows	1798-1804
Franklin Wharton	1804-1818
Anthony Gale	1819-1820
Archibald Henderson	1820-1859
John Harris	1859-1864
Jacob Zeilin	1864-1876
Charles G. McCawley	1876-1891
Charles Heywood	1891-1903
George F. Elliott	1903-1910
William P. Biddle	1911-1914
George Barnett	1914-1920
John A. Lejeune	1920-1929
Wendell C. Neville	1929-1930
Ben H. Fuller	1930-1934
John H. Russell	1934-1936
Thomas Holcomb	1936-1943
Alexander A. Vandegrift	1944-1947
Clifton B. Cates	1948-1951
Lemuel C. Shepherd, Jr.	1952-1955
Randolph McC. Pate	1956-1959
David M. Shoup	1960-1963
Wallace M. Greene, Jr.	1964-1967
Leonard F. Chapman, Jr.	1968-1971
Robert E. Cushman, Jr.	1972-1975
Louis H. Wilson	1975-1979
Robert H. Barrow	1979-1983
Paul X. Kelley	1983-1987
Alfred M. Gray, Jr.	1987-

*The term Commandant was not used until 1800. Nicholas was the senior officer of the Continental Marines.

commanders of the ships of the 13 United Colonies, are to take care that divine service be performed twice a day on board and a sermon preached on Sundays...''

3 December 1775 Lt. John Paul Jones, aboard his ship *Alfred*, hoists the Grand Union flag — 13 American stripes with the Union Flag in the field — thus unfurling a flag for the first time ever aboard an American man-of-war. He was later to write about the flag: ''We cannot be parted in life or death. So long as we can float, we shall float together. If we must sink, we shall go down as one.''

13 December 1775 The Continental Congress authorizes the building of 13 ships for the Continental Navy — only seven of which will ever be completed and all of which will be lost during the war. The frigates that are authorized are: five of 32 guns, five of 28 guns and three of 24. It is also specified where they are to be built, with the work spread among seven colonies.

22 December 1775 Esek Hopkins is appointed commander-in-chief of the newly-established Continental Navy. His rank corresponds to that of Washington's in the army. The first Continental fleet consists of four ships that are quickly supplemented with four converted merchant vessels. Hopkins's command proves to be short lived; within two years, he is cashiered for failure to follow orders from Congress.

1 January 1776 The first American submarine, which carries a crew of one, is built by David Bushnell, a 34-year old Yale University graduate. Propulsion of the ship, named the *American Turtle*, is by means of a screw on a hand crank.

1 January 1776 The first American flag with seven red and six white stripes is raised to recognize the reorganization of Continental forces at Cambridge, Massachussetts. Called the Continental Colors Flag, it was also know as the Cambridge or Grand Union Flag. Prior to this date, Americans had fought under many different flags — but the Cambridge Flag will be the unofficial American flag until 1777.

5 January 1776 First fleet of the Continental Navy receives sailing orders. Congress orders Commodore Esek Hopkins to clear the Chesapeake Bay and the coasts of the colonies of Virginia and the Carolinas of British raiders. Hopkins sails from Delaware with a squadron of eight vessels in February and attempts to carry out the orders; however, he loses contact with two of the ships in his fleet and heads for the Bahamas instead.

6 January 1776 The oldest regular army unit still on regular service is authorized. Battery D, 5th Artillery is constituted as Alexander Hamiltons's ''Provincial Company of Artillery of the Colony of New York''. Today it is the 1st Battalion, 5th Field Artillery Regiment-- assigned to the 1st Infantry Division (Mechanized). Organized by Hamilton when he was 19, its motto is ''Faithful and True''.

10 January 1776 Washington asks the Massachusetts legislature for recruits. In his letter to the solons he says: ''Troops raised in the other Colonies are more complete...'' He estimates the strength of the Continental Army at 14,500, and that the need is for at least 22,000. The British, he points out, believe we have more soldiers than we do, "an Error which is not our Interest to remove".

10 January 1776 Thomas Paine's pamphlet *Common Sense* is printed in Philadelphia, and urges an American declaration of independence. The 47-page tract reflects his knack for putting into layman's terms what John Adams and others have been saying in the Congress. The final page of the document carries a single statement in black letters that says: The Free and Independent States of America.

26 January 1776 Father Louis Eustace Lotbinière, although more than 60 years of age, is appointed the first Roman Catholic chaplain in the Continental Army. He is appointed chaplain in a Canadian regiment then being organized by Benedict Arnold. Lotbinière incurs ecclesiastical censure and discipline from his superiors for administering the sacraments to the troops.

17 February 1776 The first regularly organized expedition of the Continental Navy puts out to sea. Although its original objective is to wreak havoc with British ships along the Atlantic coast, its mission is ruined by foul weather.

3 March 1776 Sailors and Marines attack New Providence (which is now Nassau) in the Bahamas, capturing 100 cannon and mortars and large quantities of other useful military stores. This action was the first amphibious landing by American Marines as an organized unit. The island was defended by a handful of militia, who preferred capitulation to resistance, and the marines left in high spirits.

17 March 1776 The British evacuate Boston. Gen. Lord Howe had decided earlier to abandon his initial plans to attack American fortifications on Dorchester Heights, all the while realizing it made the British

position in the city untenable. Howe decided on March 7 to abandon Boston and left 10 days later with 1,000 loyalists, sailing with them to Halifax, Nova Scotia.

23 March 1776 Privateering is made legal by the Continental Congress through issue of letters of remarque and reprisal against the British. In fact, most of the actions of sea-going patriots in the first year of the war were in this particular direction, (55 ships were seized in all) because the British ships were too heavily armed for the Americans — and transports and merchantmen carried supplies and ammunition.

4 April 1776 On her return from the Bahamas where she helped in the first operation of the Continental Navy, the 24-gun armed ship *Columbus*, under Captain Abraham Whipple, captures the British schooner *Hawk* off Block Island, Rhode Island. It is the first engagement with an enemy warship in the Revolution. *Columbus* will capture five prizes before being run aground and burned in 1778.

28 June 1776 Massed spectators watched the hanging of Thomas Hickey near Bowery Lane, New York City. He was the first American soldier executed by order of a military court. Hickey belonged to Washington's personal guard and was executed for "sedition and mutiny" after being discovered to have been involved in a loyalist-inspired plot that allegedly included a plan to assassinate Washington and other generals.

4 July 1776 The Declaration of Independence is signed in Philadelphia. As drafted by Thomas Jefferson and approved by other members of the committee which had been appointed to draw it up, the declaration "solemnly

Above: The signing of the Declaration of Independence of the United States of America. It declared the US was now "free and independent . . . absolved from all allegiance to the British Crown".

published and declared that these United Colonies are, and of Right, ought to be Free and Independent States". It is sent to printer John Dunlop, who publishes it as a short broadside.

4 July 1776 The first habor defense of the new American nation, which came into being this day, inflicts damage and casualties on HMS *Asia*. The defense is mounted by a battery on the site of present-day Fort Hamilton, in Brooklyn, New York.

8 July 1776 Col. John Nixon gives the first public reading of the Declaration of Independence to a crowd of people in the state house yard in Philadelphia. Within days the Congress will order the Declaration engrossed (written in script) on parchment and that all its members sign the engrossed copy. Fifty-six members eventually did.

Continental Currency Printed (1775-1779)*

Year	Amount
1775	$6,000,000
1776	$19,000,000
1777	$13,000,000
1778	$63,400,000
1779	$124,800,000

*By 1779, the amount of Continental paper money it took to buy $1.00 in gold started to climb. By 1781, the ratio relative to specie was 150:1; hence the term "not worth a Continental".

The Size of the Continental Army (1775-1783)*

Year	Size
1775	27,443
1776	46,891
1777	34,820
1778	32,899
1779	27,699
1780	21,015
1781	13,292
1782	14,256
1783	13,476

*As compiled and reported to the Congress by Secretary of War Henry Knox.

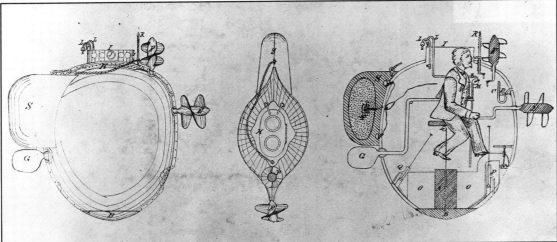

Above: A painting and plan of the American *Turtle*. This ingenious one-man craft was designed by David Bushnell and used against HMS *Eagle* in New York Harbor. The plan of the submarine was drawn long afterwards in 1885 by Lieutenant Commander F.M. Barber, who based it on a description left by Bushnell himself.

27 August 1776 The Continental Congress passes an act offering a land grant — 50 acres (20.23 hectares) of land in certain states — to British officers as a way of encouraging them to desert from the invading forces. It offers to make them (both British and Hessians) citizens of the nation and provides the land to the deserter, his heirs, or to be held by them in absolute property.

28 August 1776 The Continental Congress authorizes a quality mark on all gun powder containers. Inspectors, it says, must approve any gun powder purchase and ensure it proper as "to its quickness in firing, strength, dryness, and other necessary qualities". Once that approval has been given, inspectors are to stamp the letters "USA" on every cask received.

5 September 1776 Standardized uniforms are adopted for the Navy by the Marine Committee of the Continental Congress. Sailors are to have green coats faced with white, round cuffs, slashed sleeves and pockets, with buttons around the cuff, a silver epaulet on the right shoulder, shirt collars turned back, buttons to match the facings, waistcoat and breeches edged with green black gaiters, and garters.

7 September 1776 Sgt. Ezra Lee of the Continental Army takes the first one-man submarine, the *American Turtle*, out to attack HMS *Eagle* off Staten Island. The plan was to bore a hole in the hull of the ship and to attach a time bomb; but the drill is not strong enough to penetrate the ship's copper sheathing, and so the mission was a failure; albeit a historic one.

9 September 1776 The Continental Congress formally renames the colonies "the United States". It resolves that in the future all of its commissions and other instruments will be issued in the name of the United States instead of the "United Colonies" as had previously been the case.

15 September 1776 Under protection of their warships, British troops from Long Island cross the East River and rout the patriot forces at Kip's Bay (now 34th Street) on Manhattan Island. This is accomplished almost without a shot being fired. The British proceed to occupy New York as Washington withdraws his troops — but not before fighting a holding action that helps boost troop morale.

16 September 1776 It is resolved by the Continental Congress that 88 battalions of troops be enlisted for the Continental Army as soon as possible for the duration of the war. Their numbers, declares the resolution, should be apportioned by population among the colonies. The action is essential since existing forces in the army were enlisted only through the end of the year.

22 September 1776 Capt. Nathan Hale of Connecticut is hanged by the British as a spy. Disguised as a Dutch schoolmaster, Hale had undertaken a reconnaissance mission on Long Island behind enemy lines and was returning to his regiment when captured. His brief speech on the gallows — "I only regret that I have but one life to lose for my country" — makes Hale a martyr to American independence.

11 October 1776 The first Battle of Lake Champlain is fought in the Revolutionary War. The 17-ship flotilla under Col. Benedict Arnold — whose largest ship has 12 guns — meets a vastly superior British force. The flagship of the British fleet, with its 18 guns, devastates the Americans. Arnold returns to Fort Ticonderoga with 3 ships and 200 survivors, but slows down British forces advancing from Canada.

30 October 1776 The Continental Congress resolves that the rank and titles of Marine officers should be the same as the rank and titles of similar commissions in the army. At the same time, it goes on to spell out details about how "commanders, officers, seamen, and marines in the continental navy" will be entitled to prizes they might take, including all privateers authorized by the King.

13 November 1776 Capt. John Paul Jones and the brig *Providence* capture the British transport *Mellish* with its 10,000 suits of winter uniforms and other military supplies for the Redcoats. While escorting eight prizes to port later, Jones meets the frigate HMS *Milford* and tricks her into running in the opposite direction while the prizes head to shore. Jones then escapes.

16 November 1776 The first salute of the American flag by a foreign power is rendered by the Dutch at St Eustatius, West Indies, when the brig *Andrew Doria* enters port to purchase supplies for the Continental Army. The incident does not occur without repercussions, however. The British protest so strongly to the Dutch that they not only dismiss the governor of the port but completely disavow the salute.

24 November 1776 Pvt. Harry Hassen becomes one of the first men known to have been court martialed on charges of desertion from the Marine Corps. He will plead guilty to the charges and is sentenced to 50 lashes for desertion and 21 lashes for "quitting his guard" without being properly relieved.

29 November 1776 The brig *Reprisal*, under Captain Lambert Wickes, enters Quiberon

Above: Battle of Princeton. Coming swiftly on the heels of his victory at Trenton, George Washington and his Continental Army achieved another victory here — liberating all but the eastern part of New Jersey from the British.

Officer Ranks US Armed Forces (1776-1800)

ARMY
Ensign
Lieutenant
Captain
Major
Lieutenant Colonel
Colonel
Brigadier General
Major General
Lieutenant General

NAVY
Midshipman

Sailing Master
Lieutenant
Lieut. Commanding
Master Commandant
Captain
Commodore
Rear Admiral
Vice Admiral

MARINES
Lieutenant
Captain
Major

Below: After crossing the Delaware River, Gen. Washington surprised the Hessian troops and took Trenton. He crossed it a second time and reoccupied the city six days later after taking his prisoners to Philadelphia.

Bay, France, carrying three diplomatic commissioners — Benjamin Franklin, Silas Deane, and Arthur Lee — sent by the Continental Congress to meet with the French government. Franklin had just been appointed Commissioner to France, which will join with the US as an ally during the Revolutionary War.

12 December 1776 A regiment of light dragoons is formed and Col. Elisha Sheldon of Connecticut is appointed its commander, marking the establishment of the cavalry. Gen. George Washington had asked for a "Regiment of Horse on the Continental Establishment", and promptly received it. Manning it was another question: by June 1777, Sheldon was able to send only 16 complete dragoons to Washington.

25 December 1776 Washington crosses the Delaware with his troops prior to attacking

the British at Trenton, New Jersey. With a force of 2,400 Continentals, he pushes off at 5:00 in the afternoon in the first boats and the last arrives on the New Jersey shore at 4:00 the following morning. The surprise at Trenton is complete — and the victory encourages more Americans to join the Revolutionary cause.

2 January 1777 John Rosbrugh becomes the first army chaplain to be killed in action. The Presbyterian minister is chaplain of a regiment to which his company from Philadelphia is attached. In a skirmish near Trenton, New Jersey, he falls into the hands of a party of Hessian troops, who kill him as he kneels, praying for his family and his friends. A parishioner has him buried in Trenton.

3 January 1777 Washington side-slips the British force under Gen. Lord Cornwallis, then attacks and defeats the British rearguard at Princeton, New Jersey. About 275 Redcoats and 40 Continentals are killed in the battle. The victories here and at Trenton, New Jersey, eight days earlier, do much to fan the dying embers of Revolution.

5 January 1777 The first use of "mines" (torpedoes) in US military history occurs on this date as a score of mines are floated on the Delaware River in a fruitless attempt to sink British ships. Patriots from New Jersey carry out the abortive attempt with what are believed to be oaken-staved contact mines with flintlock detonators. The event is captured later in a mock-heroic song, "The Battle of the Kegs".

24 February 1777 The Continental Congress orders all government arms and accoutrements stamped or marked with the words ''United States''. All arms already made are to bear the new impression, as will those to be manufactured — ''United States'' is to appear on all parts. The Congress also recommends that states enact legislation to punish those who unlawfully ''take, secret, refuse, or neglect to deliver'' arms.

7 April 1777 Army nurses — whose mission it is to attend the sick and obey the matron's (supervisor's) orders — receive a raise in pay. They had started the war at $2 per month and one ration per day; this is now to be increased to $8 per month and one ration per day. Matrons, on other hand, will now receive $15 per month with the raise, and one ration per day.

4 June 1777 The Continental Congress receives proceeds of the loan it negotiated with the French for the purpose of financing the Revolution. The $181,500 loan is to be used to buy supplies and for the building of cruisers. although it is made for an indefinite period of time (the rate of interest was five percent), it is finally paid off on 31 December, 1793.

14 June 1777 The Continental Congress adopts a resolution which states: ''Resolved, that the flag of the thirteen United States be thirteen stars, white in a blue field, representing a new constellation''. The day on which the resolution is adopted, a muggy Saturday morning in which the

Below: Fighting at Saratoga. The American victory here not only drew a great deal of French support for the US cause, but it prompted the Congress to begin work on the Articles of Confederation for the new nation.

Service and Casualties in the Revolutionary War (1775-1783)

	Battle Deaths	Wounds Not Mortal
Army	4,044	6,004
Navy	342	114
Marines	49	70
Total	4,435	6,188

order of business is so routine that debate is not recorded, becomes known to Americans everywhere as Flag Day.

2 July 1777 Marine Capts. Matthew Parke and Edward Arrowsmith were ordered by Captain John Paul Jones to help man the Continental Navy sloop *Ranger* by recruiting with the aid of ''a Drum, Fife, and Colors''. They managed to recruit 21 men in Providence, Rhode Island.

4 July 1777 The first ''Stars and Stripes'' flag is unfurled on a Continental warship by John Paul Jones at Portsmouth, New Hampshire as it goes to sea for the first time. There is little doubt the Navy fought under the ensign regularly.

31 July 1777 The Marquis de Lafayette is commissioned a Major General in the Army. The young marquis agrees to serve without pay and without a specific command. He distinguishes himself at the Battle of Brandywine and is with Washington at Valley Forge and Yorktown. His spirited generalship and the key role he plays in securing French help for the colonists contribute to the American victory.

6 August 1777 Gen. Nicholas Herkimer, a commander of the colonial militia forces, is ambushed and killed by Indian and Tory forces during the Battle of Oriskany during the Revolutionary War. The Americans successfully fight off the attack, but in further fighting the relief column loses nearly half its strength. On a man-to-man basis, this battle is considered the bloodiest of the Revolutionary War.

16 August 1777 In the Battle of Bennington, American forces led by Gen. John Stark overpower a detachment of British forces. The battle, considered a turning point in the Revolutionary War, featured the first time during which the Stars and Stripes flew in a land battle. Fought on the border of the states of New York and Vermont, the date of the battle is now celebrated as a legal holiday in Vermont.

3 September 1777 After debarking at Elk Ferry, Maryland, British and Hessian troops proceed toward Philadelphia, Pennsylvania, and are attacked by Gen. William Maxwell's marksmen and cavalry. The attack takes place from Cooch's Bridge, Delaware, with the British forced to retreat after three hours.

20 September 1777 The first American warship to be captured overseas surrenders after a sharp action in which her rigging is seriously damaged and she runs out of powder. The *Lexington*, originally the *Wild Duck*, is taken off Ushant, France, by the British cutter HMS *Alert*, which is under the command of Lt. John Bazley.

21 September 1777 Five British regiments launch a surprise early morning attack (the men had been ordered to march with unloaded muskets to avoid accidentally firing them and thus alerting the Americans) on Gen. ''Mad Anthony'' Wayne and 1,500 troops near Paoli Tavern, Pennsylvania. Wayne loses about 150 men, and the British move on to Philadelphia after what became known as the ''Paoli Massacre''.

17 October 1777 At Saratoga, New York, Americans win a battle of the Revolution that has far-reaching consequences. Gen. John Burgoyne, surrounded by 17,000 troops and under intense artillery fire, surrenders his army of 5,728 officers and men to Gen. Horatio Gates. The victory cements American determination to win full freedom and encourages the French to come into the war on the side of the colonies.

18 December 1777 A General Order of this date begins the business of ''hutting'', (hut building) at Valley Forge, Pa. The Continental Army is in winter quarters, and the 12,000 troops

Right: Hoisting the American flag over Fort Nassau, the first time it had flown over a foreign stronghold. A landing party from the brig *Providence* captures the seat of British government in the Bahamas.

will be tested in their loyalty to the American cause in the most severe fashion. They cannot get much food or warm clothing — Congress can't afford it — and more than 2,000 will lose their lives during the winter months.

8 January 1778 Gambling is prohibited in the Army. In general orders, Washington observes that the vice of gambling is again becoming prevalent and he therefore directs "exemplary punishment" of any officer or enlisted man caught gambling, or playing with cards and dice in any way. This order is but one of many that will be issued during the course of the war to curb gambling.

25 January 1778 Washington orders the fortification of West Point, New York, which is now the oldest American military post in continuous occupation by US troops. First occupied because of its strategic importance in controlling the Hudson River against the enemy during the Revolution, it will later become the site of the US Military Academy, which will be established there on 16 March 1802.

27 January 1778 Americans capture Fort Nassau, Bahamas. Marines and bluejackets from the sloop *Providence* landed at New Providence Island, seized the forts there and used the opportunity to haul away supplies for the American war effort. At dawn the next morning, the "Stars and Stripes" flies proudly over a foreign stronghold for the first time.

6 February 1778 Entering its only military alliance until the North Atlantic Treaty Organization pact of 1949, the United States signs a treaty with France to "maintain effectually the liberty, sovereignty, and independence" of the US. The US agrees to be France's ally in any war with Britain and France gives its consent to the conquest of Canada and Bermuda.

14 February 1778 In Quiberon Bay, on the Atlantic coast of France, the Continental sloop-of-war *Ranger*, with 18 guns, under its captain (John Paul Jones) exchanges salutes with the *Robuste*, flagship of French Admiral Lamotte-Picquet. This act represents the first official salute rendered an American warship in European waters.

23 February 1778 Baron von Steuben arrives at Valley Forge and begins organizing,

disciplining and training Gen. George Washington's army. He proves to be highly effective and brings the colonial citizen army a discipline and effectiveness it had lacked before this. This brought him an appointment as Major General and the army's first Inspector General. Prussian-born, he became a US citizen in 1783.

26 February 1778 Congress requests that the states institute drafts from their militia for nine months of service with the Continental Army in order to fill out their regiments. Though it was a request, some consider it the first national draft in American history.

7 March 1778 It will not be until Pearl Harbor that the Navy will suffer a disaster as great as the one that befalls the frigate *Randolph* on this date when more than 300 Americans are killed. She had engaged the 64-gun British ship-of-the-line HMS *Yarmouth* and seemed to be on the verge of victory when some unknown cause — perhaps a chance spark — blew up her magazine. She disintegrated in a blinding flash.

28 March 1778 The Congress authorizes the raising of a corps of 68 cavalrymen and 200 light infantry that will ultimately be called "Pulaski's Legion". Named after and commanded by Count Casimir Pulaski, a Polish nobleman who fought during the Revolution, they are welded into three troops of cavalry, a rifle company, two of infantry and one "supernumerary" company.

27 May 1778 A resolution of the Congress establishes the post of "Provost" in the Continental Army. The new force, which is to be mounted as

light dragoons, is to consist of a captain, four lieutenants, one clerk, a quartermaster sergeant, two trumpeters, two sergeants, five corporals and 43 provosts. Last, but by no means least, the force is also authorized four executioners.

4 July 1778 The court martial of Maj. Gen. Charles Lee begins at the White Hart Tavern, Brunswick, New Jersey. Lee was second in rank in the Continental Army only to Washington and the charges were that he failed to attack in spite of orders to do so at the Battle of Monmouth and had shown disrespect in two insulting letters to Washington. Lee is convicted and suspended from command.

8 July 1778 The first direct French military reinforcement of the Americans arrives with Admiral Jean Comte d'Estaing and his fleet of 16 ships and 4,000 soldiers off the Delaware Capes. The British naval forces in the area are chased away, which permits the dying American seaborne trade to be reestablished as an important part of the American war effort.

11 November 1778 British Loyalists and Indians attack Cherry Valley, New York, at the northern end of the Susquehanna Valley — easily one of the most vividly remembered of the atrocities of the Revolution. In what is now known as the Cherry Valley Massacre, houses were burned and victims were scalped. Several soldiers were killed as well as 30 non-combatants, and 71 prisoners were carried off.

4 February 1779 John Paul Jones takes command of the *Bonhomme Richard* — French for "Poor Richard" and named in honor of Ben Franklin. It is

Above: The defeat at Penobscot River. The largest American amphibious operation of the Revolutionary War also became one of its greatest disasters. In all 474 Americans lost their lives out of a landing force of 3,000.

actually a frigate built for France and placed at America's disposal. Refitted with 42 guns, it takes 16 prizes before meeting HMS *Serapis* in September.

11 March 1779 Congress resolves that military engineers in service of the US should be formed into a Corps of Engineers. It declares that "the Engineers in the service of the United States shall be formed into a Corps and styled the Corps of Engineers". It will not be until 1803, however, until the first enlisted men of the present Corps of Engineers will be authorized.

16 July 1779 The first silent attack — a bayonet charge — of the Revolution is mounted during the battle of Stony Point, New York. Gen. Anthony Wayne leads 1,350 Continentals in a surprise attack in which the British lose 94 killed and wounded and nearly 550 captured or missing. The successful attack recaptures the post and ends a threat to West Point, a key American fortress on the Hudson River.

19 July 1779 The largest American amphibious operation of the Revolutionary War begins on a Penobscot River base in Maine. The naval force is made up of six ships and 13 privateers;

the landing force is made up of 3,000 Massachusetts militia in 20 transports. Their brave and ambitious effort turns into a disaster — with 13 British and 474 Americans killed. Captain Dudley Saltonstall, the commander, is court martialed and dismissed.

26 July 1779 The first decoration to a foreign national is made by the Congress to Lt. Col. François Louis Teisseidre de Fleury, a Frenchman. He is presented with a silver medallion for his part in the attack on the fort at Stony Point, New York, where he commanded part of the American attack forces and captured the British flag.

23 September 1779 The *Bonhomme Richard* engages the 50-gun HMS *Serapis* of the British fleet, which is at the head of a convoy. One of the most bitterly fought engagements during the age of sail, the ships pound at each other with unremitting fury. John Paul Jones, asked to surrender at the height of battle, replies "I have just begun to fight". The *Serapis* is captured, but the *Bonhomme Richard* sinks two days later.

9 October 1779 A combined force under Benjamin Lincoln of 1,500 Americans, supported by more than 5,000 Frenchmen from a fleet offshore, lays siege to 3,200 British troops in Savannah, Georgia. During the first major attack, Gen. Pulaski — the Polish nobleman who rendered such great service to the cause of the American Revolution — is mortally wounded. The campaign is abandoned 10 days later.

4 May 1780 The first Navy seal is adopted by the Continental Congress. John Witherspoon, Governor Morris and Richard Henry Lee were members of a committee that came up with the official seal, which was recommended for the Board of Admiralty. The Board was a forerunner of the Department of the Navy, which did not become officially established until 30 April 1798. It used a new seal, which was of unknown origin.

12 May 1780 Charleston, South Carolina, falls to the British in what will be the costliest American defeat of the Revolution. After a six-week siege, 17,200 British troops and seamen force the surrender of the garrison, which has 5,500 defenders. During the siege, combat losses for the Americans were 230 while the British lost about 265. The British were then able to overrun most of South Carolina.

3 August 1780 Benedict Arnold is given command of West Point, New York. It is part and parcel of the treasonous negotiations he is engaged in with the British. The intent is to make it

Right: Oil painting of the engagement between the *Bonhomme Richard* and the *Serapis*. The battle, fought off Flamborough Head, England, reduced both ships to wrecks before the *Serapis* struck her colors.

Above: Benedict Arnold, whose name became synonymous with the word "traitor" after his plot to turn over West Point was uncovered. Four months after the plot was revealed, he was leading British raids against Americans.

Above: Storming the redoubts at Yorktown. Assailed by a joint Franco-American force twice its size and cut off by a French fleet, the British garrison could do nothing but accept inevitable defeat and surrender.

Above: The surrender of the British under Lord Cornwallis at Yorktown, which effectively ended the Revolutionary War. Sporadic fighting continued on for another two years, but the new nation became a reality on this day.

easier for them to capture the post. Arnold had known since June he was to be appointed as commandant and in July he proposed to betray the fort to British Maj. Gen. Henry Clinton for the sum of £20,000.

16 August 1780 In a battle 7 miles (11.3 km) north of Camden, South Carolina, Cornwallis and the British annihilate the army under Gen. Gates, the most crushing defeat for the US on a major field of battle during the Revolution. The estimates of American killed, wounded and captured approach 2,000; British losses totalled about 325 of the 2,240 engaged.

23 September 1780 Maj. Gen. Benedict Arnold's plot to surrender West Point to the British is revealed. Major John Andre is captured on this date and reveals the plot in full detail. Andre, who is serving Sir Henry Clinton, goes to the gallows on 2 October. Arnold escapes. He receives £6,315, a

commission as a brigadier general, and a pension of £500 annually for his wife Peggy.

1 January 1781 Approximately 1,500 Pennsylvania Continentals, principally from regiments under Maj. Gen. Anthony Wayne, mutiny at their winter quarters in Morristown, New Jersey. They march to and occupy Princeton, claiming their three-year enlistments are up and they are due back pay. After 10 days of tense negotiations, about 1,300 are discharged, but many reenlist.

5 January 1781 A British raiding expedition under the command of Benedict Arnold occupies the Virginia state capital of Richmond after a brief skirmish with the 200 militiamen defending

it. His force will burn tobacco warehouses and some private and public buildings before withdrawing. Arnold will lead other marauding expeditions before he is withdrawn and sails for England in December.

17 January 1781 The Battle of Cowpens, South Carolina, is fought. One of the most brilliant tactical operations ever mounted on US soil, it has been called the American "Cannae", the battle in which Carthaginians led by Hannibal decimated the Romans. Cannae is considered to be the most perfect example in the history of warfare of the double envelopment of an opposing army.

1 March 1781 The colonies ratify the Articles of Confederation and on the next day the Second Continental Congress becomes "The United States in Congress Assembled", and thus the governing body of the new nation. The articles had been approved three years earlier — on 15 November, 1777 — but they did not become effective until they were ratified by all 13 states.

19 October 1781 Military operations in the Revolutionary War come to an end as a British force numbering about 10,000 men under Lord Cornwallis surrenders to about 11,000 American and 9,000 French soldiers at Yorktown, Virginia. When the news reaches London, Lord North, first minister to the King, says, "O God, it's all over". Funding for the campaign is stopped and a treaty signed.

Key Battles: Revolutionary War

Lexington and Concord	1775
Fort Ticonderoga II	1775
Bunker Hill	1775
Boston	1775-1776
Great Bridge	1775
Quebec III	1775
Saint Johns	1775
Moores Creek Bridge	1776
Charleston I	1776
Fort Moultrie	1776
Long Island	1776
Valcour Island	1776
White Plains	1776
Harlem Heights	1776
Fort Washington	1776
Trenton	1776
Princeton	1777
Danbury	1777
Fort Ticonderoga III	1777
Hubbardton	1777
Fort Stanwix	1777
Oriskany	1777
Bennington	1777
Cooch's Bridge	1777
Brandywine Creek	1777
Paoli	1777
Germantown	1777
Saratoga	1777
Freeman's Farm	1777
Bemis Heights	1777
Fort Clinton and	1777
Fort Montgomery	1777
Fort Mercer and	1777
Fort Mifflin	1777
Carrickfergus	1778
Monmouth	1778
Ushant I	1778
Newport	1778
Savannah I	1778
Port Royal Island	1779
Kettle Creek	1779
Vincennes	1779
Briar Creek	1779
Stono Ferry	1779
Grenada	1779
Stony Point	1779
Paulus Hook	1779
Newton	1779
Savannah II	1779
Flamborough Head	1779
Gibraltar II	1779-1783
Saint Vincent Cape I	1780
Charleston II	1780
Waxhaw Creek	1780
Camden	1780
Fishing Creek	1780
Kings Mountain	1780
Cowpens	1781
Guilford Courthouse	1781
Praia	1781
Hobkirk's Hill	1781
Ninety Six	1781
Dogger Bank I	1781
Chesapeake Capes	1781
Eutaw Springs	1781
Yorktown I	1781
Minorca II	1782
Madras III	1782
Trincomalee I	1782
Sainetes, Les	1782
Cuddalore I	1782
Trincomalee II	1782
Cuddalore II	1783

Above: Presenting the Badge for Military Merit, the first American military medal to be awarded. It was designed by Charles L'Enfant, the architect who was also responsible for planning the layout of the nation's new capital.

20 June 1782 Congress approves the Great Seal of the United States. On 16 September, 1782, it will be used for the first time on a document granting Washington the authority to consult with the British about exchanging prisoners. In 1789, Congress declares it the official seal of the US. The legend carried on the Great Seal is "E Pluribus Unum", or "From many, one".

7 August 1782 The Badge of Military Merit is established to recognize "singularly meritorious action". Only three men of the Continental Army are known to have received the award, which was instituted by Washington. The award generally came into disuse after the Revolutionary War but was revived in February 1932 as the Purple Heart.

11 September 1782 In what has been described as last "battle" of the American Revolution, Fort Henry, Virginia, withstood a three-day attack by 250 Indians and 40 loyalists. Fort Henry, on the site of modern day Wheeling, West Virginia, was at that time a frontier outpost on the Ohio River and had already been attacked earlier in the war by Indians. After substantial losses to both sides, the attackers were driven off by garrison reinforcements.

4 February 1783 Britain declares a formal cessation of hostilities with the US. The declaration caps a series of moves, including a preliminary treaty of peace which had been signed four months earlier that recognized American independence and provided a cessation of hostilities would occur when the UK and France signed similar preliminaries. These were signed on 20 January.

10 March 1783 The final naval action of the Revolution is fought between the 36-gun *Alliance* and three British ships, HMS *Sybil, Alarm* and *Tobago*. Even though the preliminary peace treaty was signed by this time, word had not been received at sea. The *Alliance* loosed a broadside against the *Sybil* and mauled her badly. She then limped off to join her sister ships, who had not joined in the fight.

15 April 1783 All naval prisoners of war are ordered released by the Continental Congress. As is the custom in these types of arrangements, they are released since the preliminary peace treaty ending the Revolution had already been signed. It comes on the eve of Washington's announcement that an order proclaiming the end of hostilities be read to the troops.

18 April 1783 George Washington orders that the cessation of hostilities between the US and Britain be publicly proclaimed. This is to be done at noon on 19 April to every regiment and corps of the Continental Army then encamped around headquarters at Newburgh, New York. He times the announcement so it will come eight years to the day on which the Revolutionary War started.

3 September 1783 The Treaty of Paris is signed, which ends the Revolutionary War. Under its terms, the boundaries of the US extend from the Atlantic Coast to the Mississippi River and from the Great Lakes and Canada southward to the 31st parallel. Congress

Below: Secretary of War Henry Knox. In 1786, the civil military administration of the entire US consisted only of Knox, three clerks and a messenger. Expenses for running his office and staff for the year were $176.

agrees to ''earnestly recommend'' to states that the property taken from Loyalists be restored. The last British troops leave New York in November.

3 December 1783 Washington completes the demobilization of the Continental Army. He orders reduction of the infantry to a strength of 500 rank and file, and a reduction of artillery to the minimum strength needed to guard the stores at West Point and elsewhere. The following day he delivers his farewell address to his officers at Fraunces' Tavern in New York City and by 23 December resigns his post.

23 December 1783 Washington resigns his commission and retires to Mount Vernon. He appears personally before the Congress in Annapolis and says, ''... I retire from the great theatre of Action; and bidding an Affectionate farewell to this August body under whose orders I have so long acted, I here offer my Commission and take my leave of all the employments of public life''.

2 June 1784 Congress disbands the army with the statement that in time of peace it is ''inconsistent with the principles of republic government''. The only vestige of the Continental Army still in service is a group of 80 artillerymen guarding the stores at West Point and at Fort Pitt. The short time that follows is the only time when the US has no regular infantry.

2 February 1785 The Congress officially condemns the counterfeiting of Army pay certificates. In a proclamation it issues this date, it says the certificates ''have been counterfeited by some fraudulent and wicked persons, by erasing the sums for which they were first given, and inserting others to a much greater amount''. A reward of $500 is offered to help bring offenders ''to condign punishment''.

8 March 1785 Henry Knox is appointed the nation's Secretary of War by the Congress. Involved with Washington in many of the key battles of the Revolution, Knox was the youngest major general in the Continental Army. He will resign from his post in 1794 to return to private life, but not before he lays the goundwork that would help reestablish a US Navy.

2 June 1785 The *Alliance*, a 36-gun frigate and the only ship left in the Continental Navy, is ordered sold. She is not only the last ship in the Navy, but also the last ship to have engaged the British on the seas during the Revolution. It will not be until a full nine years later — on 27 March, 1794 — that a naval arm will be

reestablished as an important part of the nation's defenses.

25 July 1785 The American schooner *Maria* is seized by Algerian pirates, the first in a series of captures that leads to the Barbary Wars. The four Barbary powers on the coast of North Africa — Morocco, Algiers, Tunis and Tripoli — had demanded and received tribute from foreign nations for not attacking their ships. Another generation will pass before this practice is stopped by the US Navy.

13 May 1787 Washington arrives in Philadelphia, Pa., to participate in the Constitutional Convention and is greeted by a large, enthusiastic gathering of well-wishers. A troop of horsemen, the City Light Dragoons, rides out to the pike to south of Chester to escort Washington into the city. Bells are rung and an artillery salute is fired as the procession moves along the crowded streets.

18 August 1787 The Constitutional Convention — which is meeting in Philadelphia, Pennsylvania — proposes giving the Congress of the new United States the power to raise and support armies and to provide and maintain a navy.

23 August 1787 Delegates to the Constitutional Convention consider giving Congress the ''power to make laws for organizing, arming & disciplining the Militia, and for governing such parts of them as may be employed in the service of the U.S., reserving to the States

Below: John Paul Jones, naval hero of the Revolutionary War. Within six weeks of being commissioned a captain in the Continental Navy, he captured eight British vessels and destroyed eight more.

Above: George Washington in later life. He died at Mount Vernon, Virginia, in 1799. In the words of Henry Lee's famous eulogy, he was ''first in war, first in peace, and first in the hearts of his countrymen''.

respectively, the appointment of officers, and authority of training the militia''.

19 September 1787 The US Constitution is first published in a newspaper — the *Pennsylvania Packet and Daily Advertiser*, at Philadelphia, Pennsylvania. This remarkable document has proved to be one of the most effective instruments of government ever written.

3 October 1787 Congress resolves the following: that the US require that a corps of 700 troops be stationed near the frontiers to protect the settlers from the Indians and to prevent unlawful intrusion on public property; that troops will serve for a three-year period; and that the US will retain troops already on the frontier rather than recruit other inexperienced men.

15 April 1788 Catherine the Great, Empress of Russia, offers a commission to John Paul Jones, the ''Father of the American Navy''. He accepts and becomes a rear admiral in the Imperial Russian Navy. Within two months, he is in command of a Russian squadron fighting the Turks. The victim of intrigues, he is dismissed in 1789 and retires to Paris where he dies in 1792.

7 August 1789 The US War Department is created, with Gen. Henry Knox chosen by Washington to become the first Secretary of War. At this time, the regular Army could count a grand total of 840 men. Knox will actually assume the office on 12 September and will serve through the end of 1794. Among other things, Knox was the first to embrace the idea of a national military academy.

11 September 1789 Henry Knox is appointed the first Secretary of War. He thus maintains under the constitutional government of 1789 the same position he occupied under the Articles of Confederation.

29 September 1789 The first legislation authorizing pensions for disabled veterans is enacted. It actually takes up an obligation established by the Continental Congress and authorizes a pension to those made invalids as a result of being wounded or disabled in the Revolutionary War. There will be several changes to the law; the first universal disability pension legislation will not be enacted until 19 years later.

30 April 1790 Congress votes to increase the Army to 1,216 enlisted men, while cutting a private's pay from $4 to $3 per month. The Army is reorganized. The infantry regiment is now three battalions of four companies, each consisting of a captain, lieutenant, an ensign, 4 sergeants, 4 corporals, 2 musicians and 61 privates.

4 August 1790 A US naval task force known as the Revenue Cutter Service is established. It becomes the United States Coast Guard, with this date considered the birth date of that service. Revenue cutters were invaluable during the formative years of the "new" Navy, reinforcing the small fleet against pirates in the Caribbean and the Seminoles in Florida.

18 October 1790 In the first expedition against Western Indians, US troops led by Gen. Josiah Harmar are whipped in three engagements on the Maumee River (which is near present-day Fort Wayne, Indiana) by Miami Indians under Little Turtle. Harmar is criticized for his conduct of the expedition, but a court of inquiry later exonerates him on the basis that his troops were largely untrained.

21 March 1791 The first commission issued by President George Washington to an officer afloat is issued to Capt. Hopley Yeaton, master of the revenue cutter *Scannel*. The Continental Navy had been disbanded and the sole maritime defense of the nation was the revenue cutters. As an added footnote to this bit of history, it was not until 1934 that Coast Guard officials could find positive evidence of this act.

Above: Launched in 1797 and still with us today; the frigate *Constitution* saw action as a flagship during the war with Tripoli and won legendary fame in the war of 1812. She was saved for posterity in 1828.

4 November 1791 Gen. Arthur St Clair, a 55-year old officer who fought well in the Revolution, but knew nothing of the subtleties of Indian warfare, blunders into an ambush with the entire 2,000-man army. Northern Indians succeed in wiping out half the army and St Clair, who survives the battle, spends the rest of his life knowing he was in charge of the worst disaster in the history of the Indian wars.

8 May 1792 Congress passes a national conscription act to require "each and every free able-bodied white male citizen of the republic" to serve in the US militia. Known as the "Militia Act", it allows the states to draft all able-bodied men between 18 and 45 and is a clear attempt to raise troops to counter Indian hostilities.

13 November 1792 For the first time, troops of the Federal government are used to put down domestic agitation when they are brought in to put down the Whiskey Rebellion in Western Pennsylvania — which came about because settlers resented an excise tax imposed on whiskey. It is bloodless and the troops take 20 prisoners. The troops were sent, at least in part, to demonstrate the power of the new government.

2 January 1794 Congress passes a resolution to provide for a navy to protect the nation's commerce against attacks by Algerian pirates. The resolution, however, is not without its opponents. They feel a navy will be ruinously expensive, aristocratic in

its bent, subversive of democratic ideals and larded with glory-hungry officers who will drag the nation into unwanted wars overseas.

27 March 1794 Congress passes an act to construct six frigates of 44 guns each, and three of 36 each. It is, however, stipulated that the order will be cancelled in the event that peace is made with Algiers prior to their completion. This is widely viewed as the foundation of the US Navy.

2 April 1794 An Act of Congress establishes the nation's first national armories at Springfield, Massachusetts, and Harper's Ferry, Virginia (now West Virginia). An initial appropriation of $340,000 is made, with part of it to be used for the purchase of military muskets from private gun makers and the rest for lands, buildings and equipment for the two armories.

5 June 1794 Reinforcing Washington's call of 1793 for neutrality, Congress passes legislation that forbids American citizens to join the military service of any foreign power and bans the fitting and provisioning of any foreign armed vessels in US ports.

28 June 1794 A prominent Philadelphia shipbuilder, Joshua Humphreys, is engaged by the Navy to build two classes of frigates authorized by the Navy Act of 27 March, 1794. Appointed by Knox as master builder at an annual salary of $2,000, he constructs the first of the naval war vessels for the country, including the *Constitution*, *Constellation* and the *United States* among others.

3 August 1795 The Treaty of Greenville is signed by a mixture of Indian tribes. They cede the southeastern corner of the Northwest Territory together with enclaves beyond (Detroit and the future Chicago) for $10,000 in annuities.

2 March 1796 A treaty is ratified by Congress with the Dey of Algiers. It halts the construction of warships and pays out nearly $1 million in ransom and tribute. This represents a low point in the naval fortunes of the US. Negotiations on the treaty had begun in September 1795.

22 February 1797 Washington confers the first US Navy commission under the constitution on Captain John Barry. The successful merchant had been in command of the brig *Lexington* in March 1776 and captured the British tender *Edward* in the Navy's first successful engagement at sea.

10 May 1797 The frigate *United States*, designed by naval architect Joshua

Humphreys and Captain Thomas Truxtun, is launched at Philadelphia, Pennsylvania. Revolutionary War naval hero Captain John Barry is the first to command the *United States*, the first American warship to be launched under provisions of the Constitution. She will render distinguished service to the nation until 1864.

21 October 1797 The *Constitution*, third of the original six ships of its type (frigate) is launched in Boston with the copper bolts and spikes in her supplied by Paul Revere. She receives her famous name, "Old Ironsides", from her engagement with the British ship HMS *Guerriere* during the War of 1812. Her crew cheered as shots fell harmlessly from the hull. She is still in commission today.

30 April 1798 The Navy Department is established under a Secretary of the Navy. Within days, the Congress will authorize President John Adams to buy or build 10 vessels for defense of the US, "galleys or otherwise"; and commanders of armed public vessels are authorized to make reprisals upon French commerce.

18 May 1798 Benjamin Stoddert is appointed the first Secretary of the Navy by President John Adams. During the next two years, some 50 vessels are added to the US fleet and by early

Below: Captain Stephen Decatur's capture of the French ship *La Croyable* enriched not only the US Navy but also its captain and crew. Prizes and prize money created a powerful incentive for the 'unofficial' naval war of the 1790s.

1799 a strong naval presence is established in the privateer-infested West Indies. Within months of taking office, Stoddert drafted the legislation for the organization of the Marines.

7 July 1798 During the undeclared naval war with France, the *Delaware* captures the French privateer *La Croyable* just off Great Egg Harbor in the Delaware Capes. This leads to the first award of prize money by the US Navy — it goes to crew of the *Delaware* and her commander, Captain Stephen Decatur, Sr.

11 July 1798 President John Adams approves an act to establish and organize a Marine Corps. Legislation for this purpose had been introduced by Samuel Sewall, chairman of the House Naval Committee. William Ward Burrows is appointed as Major Commandant and the strength of the Corps is set at 33 officers and 848 "noncommissioned officers, musicians and privates".

11 July 1798 The Marine Corps Band is authorized by law. Known as "The President's Own", it is not only the oldest military band in the US, but it is the only musical organization whose primary duty is to provide music for the president.

22 July 1798 The *Constitution* leaves Boston to provide convoy service for merchant ships. She leaves with 48,600 gallons (183,970 litres) of water and some 79,400 gallons (300,560 litres) of rum aboard. Several stops and battles later, *Constitution* has taken on nearly 200,000 gallons (757,080 litres) of spirits. In mid-1799, she returns . . . with 48,600 gallons of stagnant water.

Above: A view of the battle between the American ship *Planter* and a French national privateer during the "Quasi-War" with France. During the undeclared naval war, the number of US fighting ships reached a total of 45.

9 February 1799 The frigate *Constellation*, 48 guns, becomes the first US ship to gain a victory over an enemy warship and the first to capture an enemy ship after the Revolutionary War. During what historians have dubbed the "Quasi-War" with France, she catches the frigate *L'Insurgente* in the Caribbean and hits her with deadly raking fire. The French ship hauls down her colors after receiving heavy structural damage and losing 29 men killed.

28 March 1800 The frigate *Essex* sails around the Cape of Good Hope, thus becoming first US ship of war to enter the Indian Ocean. Under the command of Captain Edward Preble, she achieves another first by also being the first US warship to cross the equator — a feat she accomplished on 7 February.

12 June 1800 The Navy buys its first official shipbuilding yard after it formally becomes a military service. The Yard is bought from William Dennet and his wife for $5,500. The property is about 60 acres and had previously been used to build men-of-war, so it already had a naval connection. The yard, located in New Hampshire, will become known to future generations as the Portsmouth Navy Yard.

1 January 1801 The Marine Band plays for the first New Year's Day reception ever held at the President's house in Washington, D.C. Due to the limited amount of space in the Oval Office, only six musicians are used for the first major social event held there.

War of 1812 (1812 — 1815)

The War of 1812 has often been called the Second War for Independence . . . and justly so. Even though the nation had gained formal recognition of its freedom nearly three decades earlier, it remained a negligible player in world affairs.

When war was declared in 1812, it was the product of resentment at various British actions of the time that, in effect, challenged American sovereignty on land and sea.

The impressment of American seamen into the British Navy was a major problem. While this normally consisted of stopping and seizing men from American merchantmen, there was at least one occasion (it provoked a bitter outcry in America) when four seamen were taken from a US warship. The seizures were viewed as tantamount to insults to flag and country.

Added to this was the perception that the British were stirring up the Indians in the Northwest Territory to attack American outposts and settlements. Western politicians felt the only solution was to drive the British out of Canada.

These grievances culminated in a declaration of war on the UK on 18 June, 1812. At the time, the entire US Navy consisted of 20 vessels — including three large 44-gun frigates and three smaller

Key Battles: War of 1812

Fort Dearborn	1812
Detroit	1812
Queenston Heights	1812
Frenchtown	1813
Sackets Harbor	1813
Chesapeake vs. *Shannon*	1813
Stony Creek	1813
Lake Erie	1813
Thames River	1813
Chateaugay River	1813
Chrysler's Farm	1813
Chippewa River	1814
Lundy's Lane	1814
Fort Erie	1814
Bladensburg	1814
Lake Champlain, Plattsburgh	1814
Fort McHenry	1814
New Orleans I	1815

38-gun frigates. Ranged against this were more than 600 fighting ships of the Royal Navy, the most powerful fleet in the world.

Fortunately for the US, the Royal Navy was fighting France in the Napoleonic Wars and had only 11 ships of the line, 34 frigates and 30 plus smaller vessels in the western Atlantic area.

The US Army had 6,686 officers and men, spread mostly along the frontier; this did not count 5,000 recruits who had been authorized by the Congress earlier in the year. It would not be until September 1814 that the regular Army would hit its peak strength of 38,186 men. Estimates are that the US called up 450,000 militiamen, but that only half that number actually saw combat.

But the matchup was far more even than the numbers might indicate. Most of the British Army of nearly 100,000 men was fighting in Europe and the governor of Canada could call on only about 7,000 British and Canadian regulars. The population of Canada was so small that contributions of the militia (about 10,000) was negligible. The Canadian alliance with the Indians was a plus, with 3,500 warriors available to help with the fighting.

There were 18 states in the Union at the time. The military forces of these states fought several battles at sea and 86 skirmishes, engagements and battles on land. The regular Army fought in 72 engagements.

The small US Navy brought lasting glory to itself and significantly boosted morale among Americans. Perhaps the most famous engagement it fought squared the *Constitution* off against the *Guerrière* on 19 August, 1812. It was the first in a series of single-ship engagements in which Americans took the measure of their opponents.

The British fleet became increasingly effective as the war progressed. At war's end, only the *Constitution* and four smaller ships were still in operation for the US. Privateers, on the other hand, were extremely active and captured nearly 1,000 British vessels.

The land war got under way in-

auspiciously for the US. In 1812 Detroit and a large area of the American Northwest Territory fell to the British and a three-pronged attack against Montreal failed miserably.

American military fortunes recovered somewhat the following year. Captain Oliver Hazard Perry defeated the British on Lake Erie, Detroit was recaptured and Gen. William Henry Harrison broke up the Indian Confederacy at the Battle of the Thames.

In 1814, the military picture changed. Napoleon surrendered, which freed British ships and soldiers for campaigns in America. No longer did Americans think of taking Canada, but rather of protecting their own territory.

The British took the offensive, but were stopped for good at Plattsburgh, New York, in what turned out to be their major military effort of the war. Some 11,000 British troops under Gen. Sir George Prevost invaded New York at the foot of Lake Champlain and headed toward Plattsburgh.

It was here that the naval squadron covering the British flank was annihilated by an American fleet under Master-Commandant Thomas Macdonough. The importance of the battle: it convinced the British government, weary of war on both sides of the Atlantic to seek peace.

Meanwhile, a British expeditionary force of 4,000 men landed at Chesapeake Bay, Maryland, and proceeded to Bladensburg on 24 August, 1814, and then on to the nation's capital. Undefended since the Army had fled, Washington fell to British torches. The White House and other government buildings were burned.

The British hoped to repeat this victory with a sea-land assault on Baltimore, but it was not to be. They were repulsed by the Maryland militia, and the British fleet, which bombarded Fort McHenry at Baltimore Harbor, was forced to call off its assault. Inspired by the defense of the harbor, eyewitness Francis Scott Key wrote the ''Star Spangled Banner'', which in time became the national anthem of the US.

In the south, meanwhile, General Andrew Jackson crushed the British-supported Creek Indians. But his greatest victory was yet to come. Fought after the war was officially over, the Battle of New Orleans matched British Peninsula War veterans against a motley collection of American regular Army regiments, militia, pirates and battalions of free Negroes. At the end of the battle more than 2,100 British soldiers had been killed or wounded. The American losses were 6 dead and 7 wounded.

Records of the time were far from accurate, but the best estimates are that a total of 286,730 Americans served in the War of 1812. Of these, 2,260 died in battle (1,950 Army, 265 Navy and 45 Marine Corps). Death by disease and accident were not recorded, but a figure of 6,500 Americans is probably not out of line. A total of 4,505 Americans were wounded in action.

The war essentially ended with a return to the status quo. Indian power in the Midwest and south was broken; there were no further disputes over blockades or impressments and the way was paved for the US to purchase Florida from Spain.

If the young nation gained anything from the war, it was the feeling it had successfully defended its rights as a sovereign nation and was entitled to a renewed spirit of national unity and patriotism.

3 February 1801 Congress ratifies the Treaty of Paris, which ends the ''Quasi-War'' with France. An undeclared naval war that had been going on for some years, it saw French ships raiding American commerce in the mid-1790s. The US had not begun to retaliate until 1798. The war had a profound influence on the Navy, which built 45 ships; 85 French vessels were captured.

14 May 1801 The North African state of Tripoli declares war on the US in a dispute over safe passage of merchant vessels through the Mediterranean Sea. The Pasha, Yusuf Karamanli, states that the amount of tribute he is receiving is insufficient. The first action in the war will occur by 1 August off Malta when the *Enterprise* will capture the Tripolitan ship *Tripoli* after a three-hour battle.

4 July 1801 President Thomas Jefferson reviews the Marine Corps, led by the Marine Band, on the grounds of the White House in the then newly-founded capital, Washington, D.C. It is the first time in the country's history that a body of regular troops is reviewed by the president, in his capacity as commander-in-chief, at his official residence.

6 February 1802 Congress recognizes that a state of war exists with Tripoli. The war resulted from the pirate activities of the four Barbary states — nations had found it more practical to pay them tribute for protection of commerce. US punitive expeditions to the area resulted in a cessation of ransom payments, but US participation in the Barbary Wars did not really end until 1815.

16 March 1802 Congress authorizes the establishment of a US Military Academy at West Point, New York. The 16,000-acre (6,480 hectare) area was first occupied because of its high strategic importance in controlling the Hudson River. Fortifications were built on the site, the remains of which can still be seen.

4 July 1802 The US Military Academy officially opens at West Point, New York, beginning its life as a school for military engineering and the first technical school in America. It is an outgrowth of a school begun with 11 enlisted men at Valley Forge on 9 June, 1778. George Washington had directed that the school be established to train ''artificers'' — or craftsmen.

5 July 1803 The Army organizes the Lewis and Clark Expedition. A band of about 40 soldiers and civilians, loaded with supplies and gifts for Indians, will set out on the celebrated geographical and scientific expedition on 14 May, 1804. The men will leave St Louis, Missouri, and go up the Mississippi River, across the Rocky Mountains and down the Columbia River to the Pacific Ocean before returning (1806).

16 February 1804 Lt. Stephen Decatur leads the first Marine Corps commando raid. Dressed in Maltese costume, he and 80 volunteers sail into Tripoli Harbor at nightfall in the *Intrepid* to burn the frigate *Philadelphia*. The disguise holds until the last minute, when guards recognize the Americans. It is too late and Decatur and his men overcome them and set the ship ablaze.

14 May 1804 The Lewis and Clark Expedition leaves St Louis, Missouri with about 40 men. It is headed by Meriwether Lewis, President Thomas Jefferson's private secretary, and William Clark, an army officer. The three-year expedition plays a major role in obtaining scientific information

Above: British troops shown burning public buildings in Washington, D.C. It was viewed as retaliation for the burning of public buildings in 1813 by American troops (contrary to orders) in York — now Toronto.

about new areas; as Theodore Roosevelt later wrote, it ''opened the door into the heart of the Far West''.

27 April 1805 Marines raise the American flag for the first time over a fort in the Old World at Derna, Tripoli. Lt. Presley O'Bannon, the seven Marines in his detail, and Midshipman Mann do the honors after a 600-mile (965km) march across the North African desert from their starting point in Alexandria, Egypt. The action, however, does not solve American shipping problems; they will continue until 1816.

9 August 1805 Army Gen. James Wilkinson, as governor of the Territory of Louisiana with headquarters in St Louis, Missouri, dispatches Lt. Zebulon M. Pike (of ''Pike's Peak'' fame) to explore the Mississippi region of the Louisiana Purchase in an effort to find the source of the Mississippi River. He does not, but on a second expedition in November 1806, discovers the peak that bears his name.

23 September 1805 Lt. Zebulon Pike, representing the Army, purchases a 9-sq mile (23.3km²) tract of land at the mouth of the Minnesota River for $2,000 in wares. Fort Snelling, a miltary post, will ultimately become the first US government presence in the region.

22 June 1807 In one of the most serious incidents in a number of events that would ultimately lead the US to war with the UK in 1812, the frigate HMS *Leopard* engages the US frigate *Chesapeake* in the waters off Norfolk, Virginia. Three Americans

Ships in US Navy At the Outbreak of the War of 1812

Name	Classification	Guns	Tonnage
Adams	Corvette	28	560
Argus	Brig-sloop	16	298
Chesapeake	Friagte	38	1,244
Congress	Frigate	38	1,268
Constellation	Frigate	38	1,265
Constitution	Frigate	44	1,576
Enterprise	Brig	12	165
Essex	Frigate	32	860
Hornet	Ship-sloop	18	480
Nautilus	Brig-sloop	14	185
President	Frigate	44	1,576
Syren	Brig-sloop	16	250
United States	Frigate	44	1,576
Viper	Brig	12	148
Vixen	Brig-sloop	14	185
Wasp	Ship-sloop	18	450

lose their lives and another 18 are wounded. The question of reparation is not settled until 1811, but even then it remains an important issue.

26 February 1811 Congress passes an act to provide Navy hospitals. It will not be until 1827, however, until the $50,000 appropriation will bear fruit; then, a cornerstone is put into place for the naval hospital at Norfolk, Virginia. A wing of the new hospital was ready to be occupied in 1830, but it was not completed until 1833.

14 March 1812 The Congress authorizes the issue of the first US War Bonds, which are valued at $11,000,000. They will be the first of six war loans that will be floated by the government to underwrite the costs of the War of 1812.

1 June 1812 President James Madison asks both houses of the Congress for a declaration of war against the UK. To become known as the War of 1812, it caps a situation that has been brewing for some time, as Americans are aware of efforts by the British to incite Indian tribes to attack American settlers. Adding fuel to the fire is the British declaration that they have a right to impress American seamen.

18 June 1812 The US declares war against the UK. As of this date, the US fleet consists of 17 seaworthy ships; the Royal Navy has some 1,048. The US appears to enjoy an immense advantage on land with its regular army of 6,700 men and state militias numbering several hundred thousand. The British garrison in Canada at the start of the War of 1812, on the other hand, numbers 4,500 men.

15 August 1812 Just slightly more than 10 years after the first graduates of the US Military Academy at West Point were commissioned into the regular forces, Capt. Nathan Heald becomes its first graduate to fall on the field of battle. He is killed fighting in a battle during the War of 1812 near Fort Chicago, Illinois. Heald is struck down following a hand-to-hand fight against a vastly superior force of Indians.

25 October 1812 The frigate HMS *Macedonian* is captured singlehandedly by the frigate *United States* during the War of 1812 in a spectacular victory. Ironically, Captain Stephen Decatur of The *United States* had met Captain John Carden of the *Macedonian* in 1810 while at Norfolk — and Carden wagered a beaver hat the *Macedonian* would win if it ever came to a battle. She suffered 104 casualties and he lost his bet.

5 March 1813 The frigate *Essex*, under the command of Captain David Porter, sails around Cape Horn and thus becomes the first US warship to enter the Pacific Ocean. She will dock in Chile on 15 March. The first prize she takes on her voyage is *Nereyda*, a Peruvian cruiser; she takes 13 additional prizes over the next five months.

30 May 1813 John Gamble takes command of a British prize vessel, the *Greenwich*, and then directs it in action against the British vessel HMS *Seringapatam*. He becomes the first Marine officer to command a naval

---

Below: Commodore Oliver Hazard Perry points towards the distant British squadron, as the two forces close for battle. The American victory at Lake Erie destroyed British ambitions in the Northwest.

vessel in battle. The ship's guard commander will go on to perform many heroic deeds during the historical voyage of the *Essex*, the ship to which he is assigned.

4 September 1813 Marines participate in the action when the US brig *Enterprise* defeats the British brig *Boxer* in the Atlantic. Lieutenant William Burrows, son of the second Commandant of the Marine Corps, was the commander of the American vessel. Both he and the captain of the *Boxer* were mortally wounded during the fierce battle.

10 September 1813 An American naval force under Commodore Oliver H. Perry defeats the British in the Battle of Lake Erie in the War of 1812. Reporting on the victory Perry says, ''We have met the enemy and they are ours''. The victory represents a turning point in the war in the Northwest. The Americans lose 27 killed and 93 wounded and the British suffer 41 killed and 91 wounded.

19 November 1813 The Marquesas Islands in the South Pacific are taken over by the Navy. Captain David Porter and his ship, the *Essex*, needed repairs so badly that he stopped there, made a treaty with the natives and built a fort at Nukahiva. A hostile tribe of natives, the Typees, did not want to do business and a small war started. The stone-throwing enemy were subdued in two days.

2 April 1814 Dr James Tilton, Physician and Surgeon General of the Army, directs hospital surgeons to record the weather. It marks the beginning of systematic observations.

9 August 1814 Half the holdings of the Creek Indians — or about 23 million acres (9.3 million hectares) comprising most of present day Alabama and part of Georgia — are ceded to the US under the Treaty of Fort Jackson. The terms of the treaty were put together by Gen. Andrew Jackson (''The Indian Fighter''), who had been in the middle of the fighting in the Creek War since it began in 1811.

24 August 1814 Washington is invaded and burned during the War of 1812 — the

Capitol, White House and several other public and private buildings are gutted. The American government had already fled before the burning started. American War Secretary General John Armstrong is ousted from his post as a result and replaced by future American president James Monroe.

25 August 1814 President James Madison becomes the first chief executive to face gunfire while in office and the first to exercise the presidential prerogative (that of commander-in-chief of the nation's armed forces) on the field of battle. Madison assumes command of Commodore Joshua Barney's battery just north of Bladensburg, Maryland, as the British drive on the nation's capital.

13 September 1814 Francis Scott Key, a lawyer, writes the words to the ''Star Spangled Banner'' as British warships bombard Fort McHenry, near Baltimore, Maryland. His song is first printed as a handbill and will appear in the *Baltimore Patriot* one week later. Long considered the national anthem of the United States, it did not gain official status until legislation makes it so on 3 March, 1931.

29 October 1814 First steam warship, *Fulton*, is launched in New York. With center-wheel propulsion she drew 8 ft (2.44 m) of water and carried 30 32-pound cannon and two Columbia 100-pounders. Known officially as the *Demologos* (*Fulton I*), she had been designed by Robert Fulton for use in harbor defense.

8 January 1815 American forces under Jackson defeat the British at the Battle of New Orleans, the final engagement of the War of 1812. American sharpshooters behind earth, timbers and cotton bales piled along a canal, pick off the attackers who approach twice. There are 2,100 British killed or wounded; American losses are 7 dead and 6 wounded.

8 February 1815 A colonel of the Ordnance Department is authorized by legislation to ''direct the inspection and proving of all pieces of ordnance, cannon balls, shot, shells, small arms and side arms, and equipments procured for use by the armies of the United States, and to direct the constuction of all cannon and carriages and every implement and apparatus for ordnance''.

17 February 1815 The US Senate ratifies the Treaty of Ghent, which officially ends the War of 1812 and restores the situation to that which existed prior to the war. Interestingly, the treaty does not even mention the question

Above: US President James Monroe. Monroe had served as Secretary of State and had illegally directed troops at the Battle of Bladensburg (Maryland) prior to the time the British occupied and burned Washington, D.C.

of forcing American seamen to serve on British ships, one of the causes of the war, and it marks the beginning of a period in which the British and US will settle disputes peacefully.

31 March 1815 Company Book 569 lists Pvt. John Johnson of the US Light Infantry Regiment as being discharged from duty ''on account of being a Negro and unfit to accompany American soldiers''. In March 1955, almost precisely 140 years later, Army Sgt. C.H. Chalton receives the Medal of Honor posthumously for action in Chipo-ri during the Korean War. He is black.

10 May 1815 A squadron of 10 ships under Commodore Stephen Decatur sets sail for the Mediterranean from New York to settle once and for all the question of paying tribute to the Barbary States. Decatur quickly captures the Algerian flagship *Mashouda* and sails into the harbor at Algiers. He exacts a treaty and secures the release of all prisoners, marking an end of American troubles in this area.

20 November 1817 The Seminole Wars begin in Florida. Without doubt one of the most nagging and exhausting military efforts in US history, it begins when Gen. Edmund P. Gaines is ordered into Spanish-owned Florida in pursuit of Indian raiders. The determined Indians will keep the army at bay for years

— more than 30,000 soldiers will be involved, the cost will be $20 million, and 1,500 Americans will be killed.

18 March 1818 Congress authorizes lifetime pensions of $20 per month for officers who served in the Revolution and $8 per month for privates. The authority is given as part of the first universal service pension act that was not limited to those who could prove their disabilities to be of service origin.

14 April 1818 The Army Medical Corps is organized. Congress approves an act that provides for an Army Medical Department to be headed by a Surgeon General. Dr Joseph Lovell is appointed to that postion, which he will hold for the next 18 years. Among other advances, he presides over the collection of the first public health statistics generally compiled.

27 May 1818 The fall of Pensacola, Florida, ends the First Seminole War. Jackson, with 1,200 men, occupies the Spanish capital and the Spanish post of St Marks as well. In the meantime, other American columns are destroying Seminole Indian villages and otherwise breaking up their power. The net result of these actions is the occupation of Spanish Florida — and a start to negotiations.

4 July 1818 The Congress decides the official flag of the US should consist of 13 red and white stripes to represent the original colonies, with a new star to be added for every new state in the Union. The star is to be added for each state on the Fourth of July after admission. Congress will not approve any significant flag legislation for the next 100 years.

3 March 1819 Congress authorizes war on pirates who are looting hundreds of merchant ships annually. President James Monroe signs the law to ''protect the commerce of the United States, and to punish the crime of piracy''. Pirates were swarming all over the Caribbean at the time and the law gave the Navy authority to convoy American ships and to recapture those unlawfully seized.

3 March 1819 The first law is passed governing the naming of Navy ships of the line. Ships of the line were to be named after states, frigates after rivers, and sloops after cities. The nomenclature of a ship will be spelled out — i.e., sloop-of-war — until 17 July, 1920, when classification symbols are also used to identify warships. A battleship becomes therefore, USS _____ (BB ____) and so on.

3 March 1819 Congress passes an act authorizing the president to use the Navy to suppress American participation in the West African slave trade. To carry out the patrols needed to enforce this legislation and to support the colonization of Liberia by American blacks, who had begun to settle in that West African county, an African Squadron is later established. It is at deactivated three years later, but then reestablished under the Webster-Ashburton treaty.

16 September 1819 Patent Number 3131X is issued to Thomas Blanchard by the US Patent Office for "T. Blanchard's Turning Machine", a special purpose lathe designed to produce gunstocks. Its goal is to reduce the labor requirements of US armories. It proves a benchmark in the manufacture of interchangeable precision parts, and models of it work so well that they are adapted so also produce other goods besides gunstocks.

27 March 1821 Blue is specified as the national color for Army uniforms under an order issued by the service. Congress had passed legislation making it official on 2 March. "Making it official" is the key here since Army troops could be found garbed in several different colors. In practice, blue was the order of the day before the Army — and Congress — chose to make it official.

14 February 1823 Lieutenant William H. Watson assumes command of the *Sea Gull*, the Navy's second steamship and its first to serve actively as a warship. She had originally been purchased by the Navy in December 1822 for use as a shallow water vessel operating against pirates along the coast of Cuba. Hundreds of American merchantmen had been plundered by pirates in the Caribbean.

1 August 1823 An unofficial Navy medical school opens at the Navy Yard in

Flags of the Union

The second United States Flag, 1795-1818. This was the flag that was the inspiration behind the "Star-spangled Banner."

The Third United States Flag, 1818. From 4th July 1818 until today, each new state has been represented by a new star.

Philadelphia, Pennsylvania. Under the direction of Dr Thomas Harris, who teaches naval hygiene, military surgery, customs and usage of the naval service, among other things, it is supported by a $400 appropriation from the Navy, with all other expenses related to the school coming from Dr Harris. It closes in 1843.

4 May 1824 Legislation authorizing a civil works program by the Army Corps of Engineers is passed. In fact, construction to meet army and other national needs is the largest single mission of the corps. It is unique in that it handles an immense volume of nonmilitary work — stemming from this law — in the areas of navigation, flood control and other public activities.

10 July 1826 Jefferson Barracks, Missouri, is founded as the first permanent military reservation west of the Mississippi River. During the westward expansion of the 1840s, it was the largest post in the country. It occupied 1,400 acres (566.5 hectares) and could house 22 companies. It served as a training center, and ultimately as an important recruiting area; but it became outmoded and was deactivated in 1946.

3 September 1826 The sloop *Vincennes*, one of 10 of its kind whose construction was authorized in 1825 by the Congress, departs from New York City. It will become the first US naval vessel to circumnavigate the globe. Under Captain W. B. Finch, her voyage will take her around Cape Horn, through the Pacific, to China, South Africa, and St Helena. *Vincennes* will return to New York on 8 June, 1830.

2 February 1827 The president has final authority to call out the militia, says the Supreme Court in a unanimous decision handed down in Martin v. Mott. That decision is not subject to judicial review and is binding on state authorities. As a result of the congressional delegation of power

to the nation's chief executive, that decision, says the court, belongs to the president, whose decision is final.

26 May 1827 Poet Edgar Allen Poe enlists in the army under the name Edgar A. Perry. By the time he is honorably discharged in 1829, Poe has attained the rank of sergeant major. This is not to be the genius' last contact with the army. In 1830, he will be admitted to West Point; however, during the year, he deliberately breaks regulations (for personal reasons) and forces his dismissal.

14 November 1827 An incident occurs that will result in a US Navy flag officer resigning and accepting a commission as commander-in-chief of the Mexican Navy. A landing party of sailors and Marines goes ashore at Fajardo, Puerto Rico, under orders of Adm. David Porter. Porter will be court martialed over the incident (a Navy officer had been arrested and jailed) and sentenced —, but will choose to resign.

4 June 1829 The *Fulton* is totally destroyed in Brooklyn Navy Yard when her magazine explodes, killing some 30 men and wounding many others. The catamaran steam frigate had made successful trial runs in the summer of 1815. With the close of the war of 1812 it was decided not to fit her out for service and, instead, to use her as a receiving vessel.

8 June 1830 The *Vincennes* arrives back in New York City after successfully circumnavigating the world. A 16-gun sloop-of-war of 700 tons, she had left New York heading for the Pacific by way of Cape Horn. The ship was 127 ft (38.71 m) long and 34 ft (10.36 m) in beam, and was captained by Commander William Bolton Finch.

6 December 1830 The Navy establishes the Depot of Charts and Instruments to store charts, sailing directions, and

Service and Casualties in the War of 1812 (1812-1815)

	Army	Navy	Marines	Total
Number Serving	—	—	—	286,730
Battle Deaths	1,950	265	45	2,260
Other Deaths	—	—	—	—
Wounds not Mortal	4,000	439	66	4,505

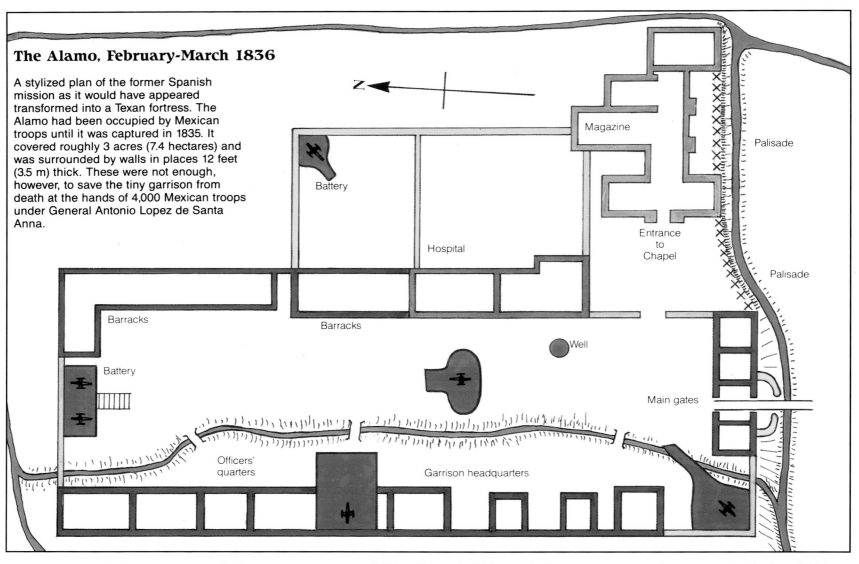

The Alamo, February-March 1836

A stylized plan of the former Spanish mission as it would have appeared transformed into a Texan fortress. The Alamo had been occupied by Mexican troops until it was captured in 1835. It covered roughly 3 acres (7.4 hectares) and was surrounded by walls in places 12 feet (3.5 m) thick. These were not enough, however, to save the tiny garrison from death at the hands of 4,000 Mexican troops under General Antonio Lopez de Santa Anna.

Magazine

Palisade

Battery

Entrance to Chapel

Hospital

Palisade

Barracks

Barracks

Well

Battery

Main gates

Officers' quarters

Garrison headquarters

navigational instruments for issue to Navy ships. In 1854 it is designated the US Naval and Hydrographic Office and then redesignated in 1862 as the US Naval Oceanographic Office. Its Superintendent, Lieutenant Matthew Fontain Maury, gains acclaim in the ocean sciences.

8 December 1830 The regular issue of whiskey — each soldier has received a daily gill (0.47 litre) with his rations — is stopped by Order No. 72 of the Adjutant General's Office. The daily ration ends because "the habitual use of ardent spirits by the troops has a pernicious effect upon their health, morals and discipline". A sum of money replaces the ration, and two years later that is replaced with sugar and coffee.

30 June 1831 Brig. Gen. George H. Steuart, First Division of the Maryland Guards, and 100 troops are transported to Sykes Mill (present-day Sykesville), Maryland on the Baltimore and Ohio Railroad. It is the first time a railroad is used to transport troops, who are taken there to quell a riot of railroad workers on strike for back pay. About 50 of the workers are arrested.

10 August 1831 The US flag is nicknamed "Old Glory" by a sea captain named

William Driver. At 21, he received his license to command his first ship and was given a United States flag as a gift. He called it "Old Glory" and flew it aboard the *Charles Doggett* during his voyages around the world. The flag was kept carefully hidden during the upheavals of the Civil War and donated to the Smithsonian Institution in 1922.

1 May 1832 Capt. Benjamin L. E. Bonneville, disguised as a fur trader, and 110 enlisted men of the 7th Infantry set out to study western Indians in the Rocky Mountains. They will remain in the West for several years and return with much valuable information on the Nez Perce and Flathead Indians.

3 August 1832 Some 1,300 Army regulars and volunteers catch up with Indian leader and chief Black Hawk at the Mississippi River. The troops set upon the Sauk and Fox Indians and after the massacre goes on for eight hours — the steamboat *Warrior* hits them with her 6-pounders as well — it is all over. The youthful Abraham Lincoln and Jefferson Davis will play very small roles in the Black Hawk War.

2 March 1833 Responding to the need for a mounted corps of some sort, the

Congress creates the United States Regiment of Dragoons. Commanded by Henry Dodge, who is promoted to colonel and put in command, its authorized strength is fixed at 10 overstrength companies totalling 34 officers and 715 men. In the view of some, the establishment of this unit is the birthdate of the US Cavalry.

17 June 1833 The Navy's first dry dock opens to receive the ship-of-the line *Delaware*, at the Charleston Navy Yard at Boston, Massachusetts. She will have a rather uneventful naval career, serving as a flagship and carrying out goodwill visits in the Mediterranean. She is in Norfolk,

The Alamo Flag, 1836

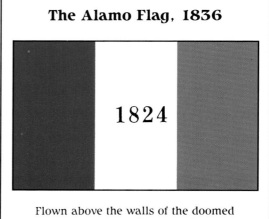

1824

Flown above the walls of the doomed fortress throughout the siege, this was a modified Mexican National Flag.

Virginia, after being decommissioned and at the outbreak of Civil War is burned to prevent her use by the rebels.

14 June 1834 Leonard Norcross of Dixfield, Maine, obtains a patent for the first practical diving suit for submarine diving. Called a "water-dress", it consists of an airtight rubber dress to which a brass cap or helmet is attached that rests on the shoulders. The cap is connected to an air pump on the boat by means of a rubber hose. Heavy lead shot completed the outfit — to weight the feet down.

30 June 1834 Congress authorizes the expenditure of $5,000 for experiments with shipboard steam engines and at the same time passes legislation "For the Better Organization of the Marine Corps". The Marine Corps commandant, Archibald Henderson, is promoted to the rank of colonel, the Corps' strength levels are increased and it is clearly established that the Marine Corps is part of the naval service.

27 January 1836 Col. Commandant Archibald Henderson brevetted a brigadier general, the first in the Marine Corps. The basis for the promotion was his service in the Second Seminole war for which he volunteered. Before leaving, he had tacked a sign on his door that read: "Have gone to Florida to fight Indians. Will be back when the war is over". Marines will continue to operate in Florida until 1838.

23 February 1836 The siege of the Alamo begins. The garrison at the Alamo, near San Antonio, has 187 Texans under the command of Col. William B. Travis. He is faced with 3,000 Mexican regular troops under the command of Gen. Antonio Lopez de Santa Anna. Ten days later, after a heroic stand, the Alamo will fall. The Texans were seceding from Mexico so they could set up a country of their own.

25 February 1836 Samuel Colt is issued Patent No. 138 for his new invention, the revolver. The principle of the invention occurred to him as he observed the wheel of a ship. It spun in either direction, but it locked into position when still (was "fired"). This, he felt, could be incorporated into a firearm, and he began whittling a model of a rotating cylinder intended to hold six balls and charges.

6 March 1836 The Alamo falls. Among its fallen defenders are famed knife inventor James Bowie and storied frontiersman Davey Crockett. Every Texan in the fort except a mother, child and servant were killed.

Above: This lithograph shows the army of Mexican Gen. Santa Anna during their brutal attack on the Alamo. The tiny garrison was slaughtered by the 4,000-man army and their oil-soaked bodies subsequently burned.

18 May 1836 Congress authorizes a naval exploring and surveying expedition that comes to be known as the Wilkes Expedition. Lt. Charles Wilkes is placed in command of the effort, which leaves Hampton Roads, Virginia, with a fleet of six ships to explore hundreds of islands of the Pacific Ocean; a large sector of the continent of Antarctica, a portion of which Captain Wilkes claims for the US; and the American coastline.

19 January 1840 Wilkes, sailing the ship *Vincennes*, sights and claims parts of Antarctica for the US; the region in which he lands becoming known later as Wilkes Land. Some of the charts produced by the expedition will be used a century later during World War II. Wilkes went on to have a checkered career. He was the officer responsible for the Trent Affair during the Civil War, and was court martialed for insubordination in 1864.

14 February 1840 Several officers and the mascot dog from the *Vincennes* make the first arrival in the Antarctic regions on floating ice. The sloop is flagship of what was known as the US South Sea Surveying Expedition to the Antarctica and South Pacific. She had tried to land but was blocked by the ice floes.

7 August 1840 During the Second Seminole War in Florida, Chief Chakaika makes the only amphibious assault by Indians known to history. Chakaika heads a war party of about 135 Seminoles, who paddle across 30 miles (48 km) of open water after nightfall and attack at Indian Key, Florida. Part of the "Mosquito Fleet" (Navy ships fighting in the swamps) opens fire in response. Unfortunately the guns recoil overboard, ending the action.

1 February 1841 The Navy issues its first official regulations governing enlisted uniforms. Called "Regulation for the Uniform and Dress of the Navy of the United States", it contains the first device for Navy petty officers. Their insignia is a spread eagle, perched on the stock of a foul anchor. It had been a common practice for men to decorate their frocks according to their fancies.

4 July 1842 In the first test of an electrically-operated underwater "torpedo", the gunboat *Boser* is sunk. The device, actually a mine, was invented by Samuel Colt. Lesser known was his work with torpedoes, to which he introduced electricity as the agent for igniting the powder, thus aiding its development.

19 October 1842 A landing force of Marines and sailors captures the town of Monterey, capital of the Mexican province of California, in the mistaken belief war has been declared. Two days later, the town is returned with profuse apologies from the US Commodore Thomas ap Catesby Jones, who led the foray. He is cashiered. In 1846, during the Mexican War, the town will be recaptured.

1 December 1842 In the only case of mutiny in the Navy, three men take part in an uprising aboard the naval training brig *Somers*. They will be hanged. Midshipman Philip Spencer, son of the US Secretary of War and two enlisted men were found guilty of planning the mutiny. They were tried and ordered executed by

The Mexican War (1846 — 1848)

The Mexican War was one of a very different stripe for the young US. The first offensive war undertaken by the nation, it was relatively unconfused by world issues.

Its causes, in essence, were the refusal of Mexico to accept the 1845 annexation of Texas with its boundaries and the expansionist tendencies of the US as it moved inexorably westward.

Texas had proclaimed its independence from Mexico in 1836, asserting that its boundary with its neighbor to the south was the Rio Grande River. When she was admitted to the Union in 1845, its boundary claim became that of the US.

But the US wanted not only to ensure that this claim stood; it also wanted Mexican California and other areas strung across the present-day Southwest US. The cry was "manifest destiny" and many Americans felt that the Pacific was the preordained western boundary of the country.

Mexico obviously did not. In fact, she had declared that the annexation of Texas would be the equivalent of the declaration of war. When that occurred, she did not react immediately; however, Brig. Gen. Zachary Taylor was sent to the disputed area with 4,000 troops. When diplomatic means failed to solve the problem, he was ordered to the Rio Grande. After a series of moves, American troops were attacked by Mexicans and the war was under way.

The regular army at the time was 8,600 men strong — with less than half of them present for duty. When war was formally declared on 13 May, 1846, the army had already fought and won two battles with Mexican forces (Palo Alto and Resaca de la Palma) in the Rio Grande area.

In the meantime, President James K. Polk called for 50,000 volunteers to serve for the term of one year or the duration of the war. The army increased steadily in numbers and hit its peak strength at 47,319 just prior to demobilization in 1848.

Estimates of the total number who served in the war are approximately 79,000, including the Navy — which at first had the missions of blockading the east coast of Mexico and providing support for efforts to capture California. Later, this was changed to add support for operations at Vera Cruz during the first army amphibious assault in US history.

Mexico, for its part, had a regular army establishment of 15 infantry regiments, 15 light cavalry regiments, 4 artillery brigades and several other units. In all, 32,000 men were under arms and Mexican soldiers and their leadership were considered highly experienced.

The objective in the war was to seize all of Mexico north of the Rio Grande and Gila Rivers — all the way to the Pacific Ocean. It was a war in which the US would not sustain a single defeat in battle. In part, this turned on superior leadership and training, but perhaps even more so because of the modern equipment and materiel in the arsenals of the US.

For example: Mexican artillerists still employed old-fashioned bronze 4-pounders and 8-pounders. Their range was so short they did little actual damage; American troops could simply dodge shots because they ricocheted so slowly. Outgunned by the Americans, Mexican troops were slaughtered in battle after battle by devastating artillery fire.

After the victories at Palo Alto and Resaca de la Palma, Taylor went on to capture Matamoros and then Monterrey after a four-day siege. His most significant victory of the war, however, came at Buena Vista in February 1847. With an army of less than 5,000 men and faced by 20,000 Mexican soldiers, his organization, skill, arms and equipment carried the day.

Above: US President James K. Polk. His war message to the Congress declared in May 1846: "War exists by act of Mexico herself." Within two days Congress had voted to appropriate $10 million for it.

US Army Campaign Streamers Mexican War

Palo Alto	May 8, 1846
Resaca de la Palma	May 9, 1846
Monterrey	Sep 21, 1846
Buena Vista	Feb 22-23, 1847
Vera Cruz	Mar 9-29,1847
Contreras	Aug 18-20, 1847
Churubusco	Aug 20, 1847
Molino del Rey	Sep 8, 1847
Chapultepec	Sep 13, 1847

Artillery once again provided the edge. Before it was over, the Mexicans had suffered between 1,500 and 2,000 killed or wounded against American losses of 264 dead, 450 wounded and 26 missing. The heroics, which ended the northern campaign of the war were not lost on the American public and Buena Vista is said to have made Taylor an irresistiable candidate for future US president.

On another war front, meanwhile, Santa Fe was captured by Colonel Stephen

Key Battles Mexican War

Fort Texas	1846
Palo Alto	1846
Resaca de la Palma	1846
Monterrey	1846
San Pasqual	1846
Buena Vista	1847
Chihuahua	1847
Vera Cruz	1847
Cerro-Gordo	1847
Contreras-Churubusco	1847
Molino del Rey	1847
Chapultepec	1847
Puebla I	1847

Kearny and New Mexico was secured with almost no loss of life; Kearny linked up with Commodore Robert F. Stockton in the west and, after minor skirmishing, occupied Los Angeles in January 1847. In effect, all the territory the US desired from the conflict, including California, was in the possession of its armies by this time.

However, Mexico itself was unconquered. Commanding General of the Army, Maj. Gen. Winfield Scott, was about to change that. With an army of 13,660 men, he launched a drive on the central part of Mexico when his troops landed at Vera Cruz on 9 March.

Scott swiftly moved through victories at Vera Cruz, San Juan de Ulua, Cerro Gordo, Jalapa, Perote and Puebla. On 10 May, he moved within sight of Mexico City. After two more victories (Contreras and Churubusco), he captured Molino del Rey — and a victory at Chapultepec yielded Mexico City itself.

On 14 September, 1847, Scott and 6,000 soldiers took the capital and, for the first time in its history, the US flag flew over a foreign capital. The war ended with the ratification of the Treaty of Guadalupe Hidalgo on 30 May, 1848.

Battle deaths for American forces during the war were 1,733 (army 1,721, navy and marines 11). In addition, there were 11,550 non-battle deaths — mostly caused by disease. A total of 4,152 were wounded in action.

The American Continent 1830-1848

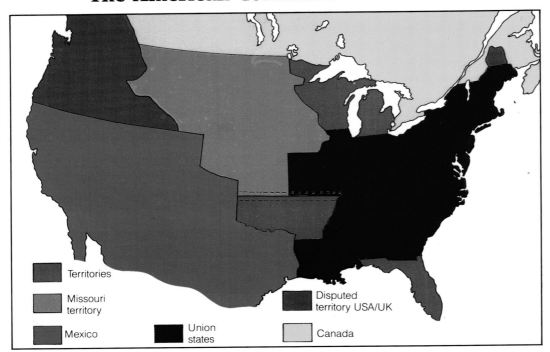

Legend:
- Territories
- Missouri territory
- Mexico
- Disputed territory USA/UK
- Union states
- Canada

The map shows how much land the United States had to gain from the successful prosecution of the Mexican War. The huge areas of land won for the Union in the far west, however, would bring the whole question of slavery in the new territories to a head.

Alexander S. McKenzie, commanding officer, who was later court martialed and acquitted.

12 October 1843 The *Princeton*, the first American warship with her propulsion machinery below the waterline, makes a trial trip in the Delaware River. Launched in September at Philadelphia, she had two vibrating lever engines built by Merrick & Towne of that city and three tubular iron boilers. The latter burned hard coal and drove a six-bladed screw that was 14 in (356 mm) in diameter.

5 December 1843 The first prefabricated ship — it is also the first iron ship — is launched at Erie, Pennsylvania. The *Michigan* operates from that port throughout her career. She was built by the Navy for the defense of Lake Erie. Navy Secretary A. P. Upshur selected iron for her hull to use that "immense resource of our country" and to ascertain how practical its use would be in ships.

28 February 1944 A 12 in (305 mm) "Peacemaker" gun explodes on the navy's first screw steamer, the *Princeton*, and cuts a deadly swath through bystanders invited to cruise on the ship. Eight are killed and nine wounded. Among the dead are Secretary of State Abel P. Upshur (a former Navy Secretary), Secretary of the Navy Thomas W. Gilmer, a US senator and a navy captain. The gun's inventor is among the wounded.

29 September 1844 The frigate *Constitution* seizes the entire Buenos Aires naval squadron blockading Montevideo. A petty officer on board the *Constitution*, Thomas E. Atkinson will be cited for his efforts in this action and others, such as his bravery during the Battle of Mobile Bay. The dates in Atkinson's citation (1842-1846) are the earliest found in any citation for the Medal of Honor.

10 October 1845 The Naval School — which is now the United States Naval Academy — opens at Annapolis, Maryland. Its first superintendent is Commander Franklin Buchanan and it has a student body of 56 and a staff of 7. The site at Annapolis is where an obsolete army post, Fort Severn, once stood. All midshipmen entering the Navy attend the school for two years, with three-year apprenticeships at sea in between.

18 February 1846 For the first time, the now familiar markings of "port and starboard" are used in Navy general orders in place of the traditional "larboard and starboard". The "load board" (larboard) was the left side of the ship, in contrast to the right side "steer board" (starboard). The two terms were confused and the term "port" or loading entrance was finally officially adopted to help solve the problem.

23 February 1846 The Liberty Bell, being used to celebrate George Washington's birthday, is rung for the last time. As bells go, several in world are larger than the one in Philadelphia, but few mean so much to so many people. Cast in London, England, in 1752, it heralded the closing of the port of Boston, the start of the Revolution, and the convening of the Second Continental Congress. It was hidden in a church during the Revolution to protect it from marauding British.

8 May 1846 The Battle of Palo Alto, Texas. Gen. Zachary Taylor with 2,200 men and Mexican Gen. Mariano Arista, with about 4,500, square off in the first regular engagement of the war with Mexico. American artillery proves decisive on the flat, open ground, causing severe casualties to the Mexicans, who lose 200 men. This is four times as many as the Americans.

Officer Ranks US Armed Forces (1800-1850)

ARMY
Coronet
Second Lieutenant
Captain
Major
Lieutenant Colonel
Colonel
Brigadier General
Major General
Lieutenant General

Lieut. Commanding
Master Commandant
Captain
Commodore
Rear Admiral
Vice Admiral

MARINES
Second Lieutenant
First Lieutenant
Captain
Major
Lieutenant Colonel
Colonel

NAVY
Midshipman
Master
Lieutenant

Organized Militia (National Guard) Units Participating in Mexican War

	Regiments	Separate Battalions	Separate Companies and Batteries
Alabama	1	2	4
Arkansas	1	—	2
California	—	1	—
Florida	—	—	2
Georgia	1	2	1
Illinois	5	—	4
Indiana	5	—	—
Iowa	—	1	—
Kentucky	4	—	—
Louisiana	7	4	1
Maryland and D.C.	1	1	1
Massachusetts	1	—	—
Michigan	1	—	—
Mississippi	2	1	1
Missouri	4	6	9
New Jersey	—	1	—
New York	2	—	—
North Carolina	1	—	—
Ohio	5	—	3
Pennsylvania	2	—	1
South Carolina	1	—	—
Tennessee	6	—	1
Texas	7	2	1
Virginia	1	—	—
Total	58	21	31

13 May 1846 War with Mexico is declared. President James K. Polk, in asking the Congress for the declaration of war two days earlier, had said, "Mexico has passed the boundary of the United States, has invaded our territory and shed American blood on American soil". Congress, suitably impressed at his words, authorizes $10 million and the recruitment of 50,000 soldiers when it approves the request.

29 July 1846 During the war with Mexico, the city of San Diego, California, is captured by a naval detachment under the command of Lieutenant Stephen C. Rowan. He is followed by Capt. John C. Fremont and a battalion of California volunteers who had sailed there on the sloop *Cyane* from Monterey. It is an important step in preparing for the bloodless capture of the Mexican city of Los Angeles, which occurs within two weeks.

18 August 1846 Brig. Gen. Stephen W. Kearny enters Santa Fe, New Mexico, unopposed during the war with Mexico. He was heading a group of 900 irregular volunteers and was part of a two-prong drive against the Mexicans in New Mexico and California.

22 September 1846 Brig. Gen. Kearny announces a code of US law for occupied New Mexico. After a march of hundreds of miles — during which Kearny was forced to put his men on half rations — the old dragoon manages to occupy the capital, Santa Fe, without having to fire a shot. He stays only long enough to set up his code and win the inhabitants over, then heads for California.

10 December 1846 Balloonist John Wise submits a formal plan to the War Department to use large balloons, 100 ft (30.48 m) in diameter and loaded "with percussion bomb shells and torpedos" to capture the Castle of San Juan de Ulua in the war with Mexico. The War Department have doubts and his proposal for this airborne assault is rejected.

11 February 1846 The Congress passes legislation giving military rank to medical officers for the first time. Although it was changing, army medicine up to this time was one of simple wartime expediency. During the Revolution, for example, only a small percentage of doctors had MD degrees and most were either apprentices or self-trained. Between 1784 and 1789 there was no formally organized Medical Department.

19 February 1847 Gen. Winfield Scott issues General Order 20 at Tampico, Mexico, which declares martial law on foreign soil for the first time in the nation's history. The order authorizes the establishment of military commissions to try offenses committed by and against his men while they are operating beyond the territorial limits of the United States.

9 March 1847 Scott lands on beaches south of Vera Cruz with a force of 10,000 troops. It is the first large-scale amphibious operation in US military history. The troops land without any casualties near the Mexican fortress of San Juan de Ulua, which some Mexican naval officers had sworn could "sink all the ships in the world". The besieged city of Vera Cruz surrenders on 29 March. The army moved inland and seized Contreras and Churubusco on the way to Mexico City.

13 September 1847 Marines and soldiers, after hacking their way through the walls around Chapultapec, the gateway to Mexico City, raise the American flag over the "Halls of Montezuma". This action will ultimately become enshrined in Marine legend — along with "the shores of Tripoli".

14 September 1847 For the first time in US history, the American flag is raised over a foreign capital, Mexico City. It is put there by Winfield Scott's troops during the war with Mexico. It was the major campaign of the war

Above: Zachary Taylor during his days of command in Mexico. His victory over the numerically superior forces of Santa Anna at Buena Vista secured northern Mexico for the United States. Taylor became president in 1849.

Service and Casualties in the Mexican War (1846-1848)

	Army	Navy	Marines	Total
Number Serving	—	—	—	78,718
Battle Deaths	1,721	1	11	1,733
Other Deaths	11,550	—	—	11,550
Wounds not Mortal	4,102	3	47	4,152

and led to the surrender of forces under the command Gen. Antonio Lopez de Santa Anna.

2 February 1848 The war with Mexico ends with the signing of the treaty of Guadalupe-Hidalgo, a settlement successfully negotiated the American side by Nicolas Trist. US casualties in the war include 1,733 dead and 4,152 wounded. Under treaty terms, Mexico cedes what are now Nevada, Utah, California and most or all of three other states in exchange for a payment of $15 million. US forces evacuate Mexico City and Vera Cruz and the treaty is ratified on 10 March.

12 June 1849 In the first of two related incidents that will gain even more importance during World War I, Lewis Haslett of Louisville, Kentucky, receives patent number 6,529 for an "inhaler or lung protector" (gas mask). Within one year, Benjamin Lane of Cambridge, Massachusetts, receives his patent for a "respiring apparatus", the first gas mask with a self-contained breathing system.

28 September 1850 The Congress restricts the practice of flogging in the Navy. It was the second time the Congress had placed restrictions on the practice. (The Department of the Navy said it would be "utterly impractical to have an efficient Navy without this form of practice".) Notwithstanding, the Congress will ban it forever by legislative fiat on 17 July, 1862 even though sailors petitioned for no change.

8 January 1851 In an effort to relieve the enormous strain on its budget, the Army issues orders that military posts are to begin large-scale farming. It is hoped this will reduce the need to ship food and turn a profit for the Army from the sales of produce. In fact in following this policy, two posts on the northern Great Plains are proposed for closure — on the grounds that farming is not possible at either location.

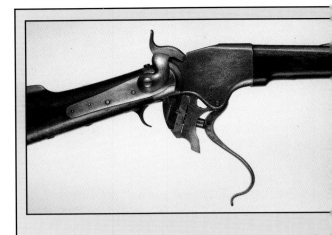

1 July 1851 Although he was later to be discharged for being incompetent in chemistry, James Abbott McNeill Whistler enters the United States Military Academy at West Point. Later to become one of best-known artists in the world and the creator of "Arrangement in Gray and Black" ("Whistler's Mother"), he comments, "Had silicon been a gas I would have been a major general".

5 February 1852 The first chapel to be built on naval property is dedicated at Annapolis, Maryland. Built like a Greek temple, it proves inadequate and by July 1866 an appropriation of $25,000 is made to erect an impressive-looking Gothic structure with a high thin spire. This gives way to the structure that is a main part of today's Chapel at the Naval Academy, dedicated in 1908.

3 March 1853 The War Department is voted an appropriation of $150,000 to pay for a survey of the various routes for a transcontinental railroad. The best route will be recommended by the surveyors. This magnificent dream becomes a certainty when President Abraham Lincoln signs a bill in 1862 that provides a government subsidy to the Union Pacific Company that will permit it to build the first transcontinental railroad.

3 March 1855 The Congress appropriates $30,000 for the purchase of camels to be used by the Army in the Southwest US. The "camel experiment", as it was to become known, results in the Army assembling a group of 75 camels at Camp Verde, near Bandera Pass, Texas. The plan is to small mount howitzers on their humps and use them to fight hostile Indians. The project fails in 1857 for lack of interest — and experienced camelteers.

3 March 1855 What will ultimately become the first American military units that carry the title of "cavalry" are authorized. The two regiments of horse become the 1st and 2nd United States Cavalry at Fort Leavenworth, Kansas, and Jefferson Barracks, Missouri, respectively.

Among officers selected to serve with the new units are Capt. George B. McClellan and Lt. Col. Robert E. Lee.

22 September 1855 Marines and sailors from the US sloop-of-war *John Adams* go ashore at Viti Levu, Fiji Islands, and capture King Tui Viti. The king, who abrogated a treaty with the US, was brought aboard the *John Adams* while 300 of his followers stayed in their canoes alongside. Tui Viti was detained on the sloop-of-war until he agreed to a new treaty.

13 December 1855 The first turreted frigate in the navy, *Roanoke*, is launched. This, however, did not occur until her conversion to an ironclad in 1863 when she was given three turrets with covered platforms. The North and South built ironclads during the Civil War, but they were designed for inshore operations. The *Roanoke* was the first attempt — it did not work due to structural problems — at a seagoing ironclad.

8 July 1856 Charles E. Barnes is officially issued patent number 15,315, which is for an "improved automatic cannon". Barnes, of Lowell, Massachusetts, had devised a crude machine gun, operated by a crank, with the rate of fire depending upon the speed with which the crank was turned.

16 August 1856 A patent is received by Gail Borden for a process that will work on the "concentration of milk". It was originally intended to recognize the plight of mothers and their children on long sea journeys. However, the surveyor's and farmer's invention will become widely adopted during the course of the Civil War and then popularized by returning soldiers.

2 October 1857 The *Independence*, one of the most venerable ships in the Navy, puts in to Mare Island Navy Yard, where she will serve as a receiving ship for the next 55 years (she will actually stay on the Navy's rolls for 98). While there, she will also become the site for the newly-established (1862) Marine Corps barracks at Mare Island, the oldest permanent Marine Corps installation in the West.

5 October 1857 The rumblings of civil war are being heard on the horizon. Federal troops are called up to supervise the balloting in territorial elections in Kansas. Gov. Robert J. Walker had thrown out thousands of fraudulent ballots that had been cast by the pro-slavery party. The Army's presence prevented a phony victory and gave the Kansas free-staters large majorities in the legislature.

18 October 1859 Marines commanded by Brevet Col. Robert E. Lee storm the Federal arsenal at Harper's Ferry, Virginia (now West Virginia) and capture radical abolitionist John Brown and four of his men. This was part of Brown's vague plan to establish a "country" for fugitive slaves. Two Marines were shot and one killed; the leathernecks returned to base having spent $62 for rations and one coffin.

6 March 1860 Christopher M. Spencer patents a multi-shot rifle bearing his name that will have a profound effect on the outcome of the Civil War. Although the carbines (and rifles) were available at the outset of the war, substantial quantities did not come on the scene until 1863. With it came the inevitable demise of the single-shot muzzle loader — 200,000 Spencer carbines were used in the war.

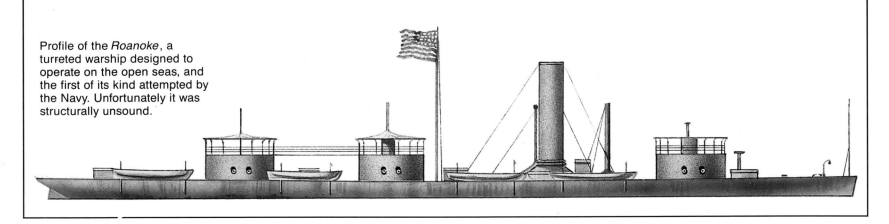

Profile of the *Roanoke*, a turreted warship designed to operate on the open seas, and the first of its kind attempted by the Navy. Unfortunately it was structurally unsound.

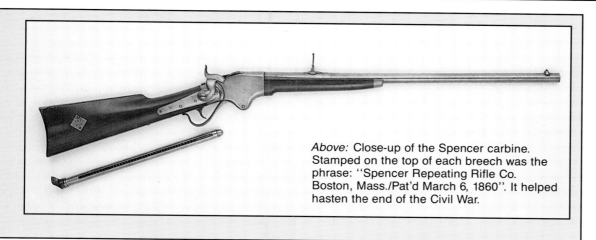

Above: Close-up of the Spencer carbine. Stamped on the top of each breech was the phrase: "Spencer Repeating Rifle Co. Boston, Mass./Pat'd March 6, 1860". It helped hasten the end of the Civil War.

Above: Painting of a Tree Signal Station (about 1861), one of the visible signal towers set up during the Civil War. It was part of a line of fixed relay stations for the operation of flag telegraphy. These were superceded by wire telegraphy.

21 June 1860 The official birthday of the Army Signal Corps. Maj. Albert J. Myer, who previously had obtained War Department approval for his flag signalling — or wigwag — system, is appointed the first Signal Officer. The US Army was the first in the world to establish the position of Signal Officer, as well as the first to create an independent and separate Signal Corps.

1 November 1860 The Navy announces plans to convert seven of its sailing ships into steam-powered warships. The cost of the conversion is estimated at $3,064,000.

9 January 1861 Forces in South Carolina, including cadets from its military school — The Citadel — fire on the chartered steamer, *Star of the West*, as she tries to enter the harbor with reinforcements and supplies for Fort Sumter. They are the first

Confederate shots fired at a vessel flying the flag of the US. The vessel turns around and returns to New York City.

4 February 1861 The Confederate States of America are organized in Montgomery, Alabama. Proclaims Howell Cobb of Georgia, one of the 37 delegates to the convention that organized the meeting: "The separation is perfect, complete, and perpetual. The great duty is now imposed upon us of providing for these states a government for their future security and protection".

9 February 1861 Jefferson Davis is unanimously elected President of the Confederate States of America. Alexander Stephens joins him as Vice President. Both men are considered moderates and it is hoped that they will please the border states and encourage those who have not seceded to do so. Interestingly, Stephens will be sworn into office (11 February) before Davis, who takes the oath a week later.

20 February 1861 The Confederate States establish a Department of the Navy. In addition, the Provisional Congress empowers Davis to contract for the manufacture and purchase of war goods. Among the innovations used by the Confederates to balance the odds against the North were the water mine, the torpedo, the submarine and the ironclad warship.

4 March 1861 An official Confederate flag, the "Stars and Bars", is adopted by a convention at Montgomery, Alabama. The flag has seven stars and three stripes, and is raised over the Confederate capitol. (Richmond, Va., becomes the capitol on 20 May). Later, after the similarity between Union and Confederate flags creates confusion at First Bull Run, the "Stars and Bars" is changed to a flag with a red field and the blue cross of St Andrew, with 13 stars.

7 March 1861 Samuel Cooper resigns as adjutant general of the US Army and is quickly appointed Confederate adjutant general. What has not been generally recognized is that Cooper, and not Robert E. Lee as one would expect, was thus the

The Confederate States of America, 1861

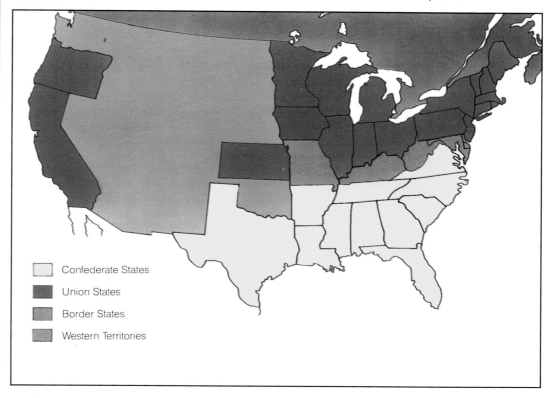

Confederate States

Union States

Border States

Western Territories

This is how the states divided during those tense months of secession in 1860-1. Not all slaves States joined the Confederacy: Delaware, Maryland, Missouri and Kentucky backed the Union after various struggles, and Virginia split itself in half in its attempt to appease the political factions then arming in both North and South.

The Civil War (1861-1865)

There were no great standing armies in the United States on 12 April, 1861, as the North and South squared off at Fort Sumter, South Carolina, at the start of what would become known to history as the American Civil War.

The entire US Army at that time consisted of 16,350 officers and men spread across the nation's seacoasts and frontiers. The US Navy consisted of 90 wooden ships — only 42 of which were in commission; the Confederacy had no ships at all.

With its 22 states and a population of about 22 million, the industrial North had a manpower advantage. The 11 seceding Southern states were mostly rural and had a population of 9 million — including 3.5 million slaves. In terms of men available to fight, the North enjoyed a 5 to 2 advantage.

Because it came to resemble World War I in many respects, America's Civil War has at times been called the first of the "modern wars". Indeed, if the dimensions of the conflict — at least those that can be captured in statistics — are any measure at all, then the characterization is apt.

Those dimensions are staggering. Approximately 2.2 million men served the Union cause — 364,511 were killed in battle or otherwise died in service. There were 281,881 men wounded in action. Confederate military statistics are hard to come by since the archives in Richmond, Virginia (capital of the Confederacy) were destroyed by fire. But the best estimates are that between 600,000 and 1.5 million wore Confederate gray — and at least 133,821 of them were killed.

In fact, more Americans were killed during the Civil War in just three Virginia counties than were killed in the Revolutionary War, the War of 1812, the War with Mexico and the Indian Wars *combined*.

Something in excess of 10,400 military actions were fought — 76 of them considered full-scale battles. Among them: Antietam, which to this day remains the engagement that took a toll in American lives that has never been exceeded on any other single day in the nation's history.

The Confederates captured 211,411 Federals during the war. A total of 16,668 were paroled on the field and more than 30,000 died in captivity. Union forces captured 462,634 men. About 250,000 were paroled on the field and 25,976 died in captivity.

While combat was deadly, disease was far more lethal. For every Confederate soldier killed in battle, three more died from disease. For his Union counterpart, the odds were 1 in 13.5 that disease, and not battle, would claim his life. Some 44,558 Unionists fell victim to diarrhea and dysentery; 40,656 to "camp fever" (typhoid, typhus and so on); and 19,971 to pneumonia . . . to name some of the more common diseases.

War itself was not only taking a toll in sheer numbers, but it was also getting to be a much more deadly business. The means with which to wage war, and the tactics that accompanied them, changed.

One such major change was the conversion from smoothbore to rifled muskets, which not only provided much greater accuracy to the shooter, but made traditional massed formations closing at short distances a perilous operation.

Service and Casualties in the Civil War* (1861-1865)

	Army	Navy	Marines	Total
Number Serving	2,128,948	84,415**	—	2,213,363
Battle Deaths	138,154	2,112	148	140,414
Other Deaths	221,374	2,411	312	224,097
Wounds not Mortal	280,040	1,710	131	281,881

*Authoritative statistics for the Confederate forces are not available. Estimates of the number who served range from 600,000 to 1,500,000. The Final Report of the Provost Marshal General, 1863-1866, indicated 133,821 Confederate deaths (74,524 battle and 59,297 other) based upon incomplete returns. In addition, an estimated 26,000 to 31,000 Confederate personnel died in Union prisons.

**Includes Navy and Marines.

In Defense of Washington, D.C. 1865

At the close of the Civil War, there were 68 enclosed forts and batteries, with perimeter of 13 miles, around Washington, D.C. In support of this were 807 guns and 98 mortars mounted, and emplacements for 1,120 guns, 93 unarmed batteries for field guns, 35,711 yards of rifle trenches, and 3 blockhouses. The entire extent of the front of the lines was 37 miles; 32 miles of military roads, besides those previously existing in the District of Columbia, formed the means of interior communication.

A charge of this kind became suicidal. Union infantrymen at Cold Harbor, for example, wrote their names and addresses on paper and pinned them to their uniforms. They knew they had little chance of surviving the assault they had been ordered to mount against Confederate fortifications.

Railroads played a crucial role in battle for the first time, indeed many of the major engagements took place along the lines of the railroad. During the First Battle of Bull Run, for example, reinforce-ments rushed to the battlefield by train proved critical to the Confederate victory that followed.

The Civil War witnessed a number of firsts in military history, including: the first battle between ironclad naval vessels; first use of a balloon for an aerial observation mission; first use of the machine gun in battle; the first employment of land mines; the first electrically-fired torpedoes (today we would call them sea mines); the first successful attack by a submarine; the first telegraphic control of artillery; the first use of wire as a defensive measure; conscription became yet another first as it became necessary to resort to the draft for the first time in American history.

The American Civil War was monumental in scope, long lasting in its effects and is easily the most studied war in American history. But of all its many consequences, it settled two major issues: slavery and the question of the Union. The house, although divided against itself, did not fall.

Left: The Stars and Bars fly proudly over a defeated Fort Sumter, and war has begun. Federal forces in the South Carolina stronghold were restricted to serving only six cannon during the Confederate bombardment because they were short of powder bag cartridges. The garrison was forced to surrender on 14 April.

highest ranking general in the Southern armies. The name of the West Pointer headed the first list of full generals confirmed by the Confederate Congress.

16 March 1861 The Confederate Congress creates a Confederate States Marine Corps with an authorized strength of 46 officers and 944 enlisted men. Actual numbers never approach this, as the Confederate States Marine Corps reached its maximum strenth of 539 officers and men in October 1864. Confederate Marines saw their first action aboard the *Virginia* (*Merrimack*) off Hampton Roads, Virginia.

12 April 1861 The Civil War begins when the garrison at Fort Sumter, South Carolina, is shelled. The Federal fort is manned by 85 officers and men and 43 other workers. Outnumbered by 4,000 Confederates with 70 or more guns, the issue — on this day at least — is never in doubt. Union officer Abner Doubleday, who fires the

Below: President Abraham Lincoln's order to blockade Southern ports was the largest blockade ever attempted by any nation. More than 3,549 miles (5,711 km) of coast were involved, with 180 openings for commerce.

first shot at the attackers, is the same Doubleday who invented baseball in 1839.

12 April 1861 The *Nashville*, a Confederate ship even though she flies no colors, takes a shot across the bow from the revenue cutter *Harriet Lane*, which had left New York City four days before. The incident is the first naval attack of the war and takes place in Charleston (South Carolina) Harbor. The ship is allowed to proceed on her way.

14 April 1861 The first recognized act of valor for which the Medal of Honor is awarded goes to 1st Lt. Bernard J. D. Irwin for service this date. An assistant army surgeon, he rescued 2nd Lt. George N. Banscom, 7th Infantry, and his 60 men, who were trapped by Apaches under Cochise at Apache Pass, Arizona.

19 April 1861 President Abraham Lincoln establishes a naval blockade of the South, thereby elevating the struggle from a domestic insurrection to a full-fledged war since, under international law, a blockade could be established only against another state. Lincoln had thus inadvertently given recognition to the statehood of the South in the eyes of Europeans and the world.

19 April 1861 During riots in Baltimore, Maryland, at least four men of the 6th Massachusetts Volunteers and nine civilians are killed in clashes between the troops and pro-secessionist sympathizers, becoming the first Civil War casualties. The 6th was heading toward Washington and had been forced to detrain. American Red Cross founder Clara Barton organized care for the wounded in Washington.

10 May 1861 Confederate Naval Secretary Stephen R. Mallory suggests — as part of his government's purchase

of warships and munitions — that ironclads will make logical additions to the small Confederate Navy. Such ships could challenge the Federal blockade. Within a month, Lieutenant John M. Brooke begins working on the design for an ironclad that can operate both inland and on the open sea.

18 May 1861 In their first offensive against the South, Union forces engage rebel batteries at Sewell's Point, Virginia. It is a brief engagement in the Norfolk area involving two Federal vessels, notable only for the fact that it is one of many "firsts" to be recorded in the war between the states.

22 May 1861 Bailey T. Brown, Company B, 2nd West Virginia Volunteer Infantry, is the first Union soldier to be killed in action during the Civil War. Some Confederate pickets at Fetterman, in western Virginia, shoot him dead as he tries to get recruits for Federal service. A monument to him will be put up in 1928 by the Betsy Ross Tent Daughters of the Union on the spot where he was killed.

24 May 1861 As Federal troops move across the Potomac River to occupy Alexandria, Va., 24-year old Col. Elmer Ellsworth, 11th New York Infantry, becomes the first Union combat fatality of the Civil War. He had removed a Confederate flag from atop a hotel in the city; while descending from the stairs, the colonel ran into the proprietor, who blasted him with a shotgun.

26 May 1861 Montgomery Blair, the Postmaster General in President Abraham Lincoln's cabinet, announces that postal connections with the Confederacy will be cut from 31 May. Blair organized the postal service in the army, introduced the idea of compulsory payment of postage by the sender and free mail delivery in the cities. He left his post in the cabinet in 1864.

1 June 1861 Capt. John Q. Marr, during a minor skirmish in northern Virginia at Fairfax Court House, is the first Confederate to be killed in combat during the Civil War. Outnumbered by seven to one, federal forces — 60 US Dragoons — entered the village, made three charges through the streets, and retreated. Seven prisoners, seven horses and a number of rifles were captured by the bluecoats.

Right: The capture of Capts. James B. Ricketts and Simon G. Griffin at First Bull Run. Ricketts commanded an artillery battery and was shot four times before he fell into Confederate hands. The Union retreat from the field nearly turned into a rout as troops and civilian bystanders rushed back to Washington D.C.

10 June 1861 Secretary of War Cameron appoints Dorothea Dix as superintendent of nurses for the Union Army. It takes only a few hours after the shelling of Fort Sumter for the famous crusader to volunteer her services to the surgeon general. Throughout the war years she handles the duties under the most difficult of conditions and, at the end of hostilities, resumes her crusade for the humane treatment of institutionalized people.

10 June 1861 The first graduate of the US Military Academy at West Point to be killed in the Civil War is Lt. John T. Greble at the Battle of Big Bethel, Virginia. The battle provides a small measure of encouragement for the South. The Federals have roughly 2,500 men participating, with 18 killed, 53 wounded and 5 missing. The South commits 1,800 men, with 1 killed and 7 wounded.

13 June 1861 A civilian sanitary commission is agreed to by Lincoln (with little enthusiasm) to assist the military medical corps. Ultimately, this organization plays a role in helping the war effort and leads to the formation of the American Red Cross. It is also an acknowledgement of the growing role of serious medical considerations in the conduct of warfare.

18 June 1861 Funded by $250 from the War Department, balloonist Thaddeus S. C. Lowe launches his ship

Below: View of a balloon ascension. It shows Professor Thaddeus S. C. Lowe on the north side of the Chicahoming River, preparing to observe the battle of Seven Pines, (Fair Oaks, Virginia).

"Enterprise" from the Columbian Armory (now the site of the National Air and Space Museum in Washington, D.C.) and has a message sent to Lincoln. His key connects to the White House from a telegraph office in Alexandria, Virginia. The demonstration strengthens his case to be the first aeronaut.

27 June 1861 Commander James H. Ward, the first commandant of midshipmen at the US Naval Academy, becomes the first Navy officer to be killed during the Civil War. He is picked off by a sharpshooting rebel soldier during an engagement at Mathias Point, Virginia, where Confederate batteries had come under attack by Federal gunboats. Union attempts to land at this point were repelled.

7 July 1861 As the Union gunboat *Pawnee* patrols choppy waters near Washington on the Potomac River, a sharpeyed lookout spots a pair of black specks bobbing within 200 yards (185 m) of the ship. The

specks turn out to be mines (torpedoes), the first to be used in the Civil War. No damage is done, but torpedoes will ultimately sink more than 40 Union ships — more than all the ships of the Confederacy.

21 July 1861 Balloonist John Wise completes and delivers the first balloon built to Army order. It features a sheet-iron floor in its basket that serves as protection against gunfire. Sent to be used in the Battle of Manassas (then in progress), it gets snagged in the trees. Repaired, it is sent up in two days, but its tow ropes get cut and it floats free. To prevent its capture, it is shot down.

21 July 1861 The first serious battle in the Civil War occurs at Manassas, Virginia. Also known as the First Battle of Bull Run, it is described by one of the participants as "a square stand-up fight" in open terrain by novices at warfare. Congressmen and other sightseers came out to witness the battle. There are 470 Federals killed and 1,124 wounded; the Confederates lose 387 killed, 1,582 wounded.

1 August 1861 A balloon is launched from the Union armed transport *Fanny* in the Chesapeake Bay to spy out rebel positions in the area. Launched by aerialist John LaMountain, it literally makes the *Fanny* the first aircraft carrier. LaMountain floats other balloons on night flights over the Confederate camps which count tent lights; this triggers orders for the first wartime blackouts.

2 August 1861 Legislation is passed authorizing a national income tax to help finance the war effort by the Union. At the

Flags of the Confederacy, 1860-5

Above is the Confederate National Flag, the Stars and Bars, while to the right is the famous Rebel banner, the Confederate battle flag.

end of the war, this source of revenue produces only 20% of all federal income — with another 23% coming from sales and manufacturing taxes. The cost of war is far greater than the tax base, however, and most of it is covered by loans and issuing paper money.

3 August 1861 A retirement system, limited in scale, is begun for Army officers. An officer can retire after 40 years of service with a pension based on active duty rates. The percentage of pay was not spelled out in the legislation — the thought being that there would be future changes. The principle of recomputation (a pension based on active duty pay scales) has its basis in this legislation.

3 August 1861 Congress authorizes the Surgeon General to employ women as nurses in Army hospitals at a salary of $12 per month plus one ration per day. Other legislation that passes gives the go-ahead to one or more armored ships. The "Great Stone Fleet" also gets its start as the navy orders certain Southern ports blockaded by sinking ships in main channels after they have been loaded with stones.

5 August 1861 Congress abolishes flogging in the Army. The practice of flogging had originally been abolished on 16 May, 1812, but was revived 21 years later on 2 March, 1833. The incident that gave rise to this order — which was negatively noted by many who witnessed it — involved the flogging of a regular who deserted during the First Bull Run campaign of July 1861 at Centreville, Virginia.

11 August 1861 Republican Senator Edward D. Baker of Oregon is drilling his regiment when summoned to oppose a fellow senator who was inveighing against the use of Union troops in the South. Without the time to change to civilian clothing before making his speech, Baker takes off his sword and goes to the floor of the chamber — becoming the first senator in uniform to address that body.

30 August 1861 In Missouri, Union Gen. John Fremont declares martial law throughout the state and frees the slaves. In an unauthorized act, he also announces he will confiscate property — including slaves — of those who take up arms against the United States. Fremont declares he did this because of the "disorganized condition, helplessness of civil authority and total insecurity of life".

13 September 1861 The first naval engagement of the Civil War takes place at Pensacola, Florida. Lieutenant John Henry Russell sails the Union frigate *Colorado* past shore batteries at night; at daybreak, he goes after the Southern privateer *Judah* in the shipyard and takes her in hand-to-hand fighting. The contingent burns her to the waterline and departs with few losses.

24 September 1861 Thaddeus Lowe, Union telegrapher and balloonist, observes the fall of artillery fire from his 25,000-cu ft (707 m³) balloon *Union* and transmits corrections by telegraph. The results are so good that Lowe almost immediately receives orders to provide four more balloons and crews to form the Balloon Corps of the Army of the Potomac — which makes more than 3,000 ascents during the war.

1 October 1861 The Confederate War Department approves the design of what has become the most powerful icon of the Confederacy during the Civil War: the flag designed by Gen. P. T. Beauregard, which was submitted at the request of Gen. Joseph E. Johnston. With a blue St. Andrew's cross edged in white on a red field with a star for each Confederate state. Although it was never officially adopted by the Confederate Congress, the public embraced it wholeheartedly.

1 October 1861 The first American Army Balloon Corps is formed, comprised of 50 men and their commander, Thaddeus Lowe. It is equipped with five balloons and soon adds two more. Lowe, although the title is never made official, signed himself Chief Aeronaut of the Army of the Potomac. He is paid $10 per day for his services, slightly more than the pay of a colonel, but never achieves military status.

1 October 1861 The first Union ship captured in the Civil War, the *Fanny*, is set upon by three rebel steamers and run ashore with very little fight. The *Fanny* was on her way to the camp of the 20th Indiana Regiment at Chicamacomica, North Carolina, when captured. There were 23 men of the Indiana regiment aboard, the captain, the quartermaster of the regiment, the sutler (cook) and a gun crew.

4 October 1861 The Confederate States of America sign treaties with the Cherokee, Shawnee and Seneca Indian tribes, which enables them to use willing Indians in confrontations with Union troops. Each treaty terminates all relations with the US and accepts each Indian nation as a dependent territory of the Confederacy. In return, the Indian nations pledge to raise an army to support the Confederate cause.

12 October 1861 Showing the innovation typical of the Confederate Navy during the Civil War, the *Manassas* is the first ironclad to see action. Catching the Union ship *Richmond* completely off guard, the metalsheathed craft punctures her, forcing her aground. The ironclad's first appearance set off great waves of consternation. The *Richmond* stays on Navy lists to the end of World War I.

2 December 1861 The Bain Code visual signal system is first used by the Army near Fort Defiance, Arizona. Bain Code, best described as Morse Code with some unimportant changes, is a relatively simple set of dots and dashes. Gen. Albert Myer used this as the basis for an efficient flag field communication system that he devised and tested.

5 December 1861 As the end of the first year of the American Civil War draws near, troop strength for Union forces is reported at 20,334 for the regular Army, 640,637 volunteers, and 22,000 sailors and marines. There are 682,971 men in the army and Navy according to the reports of the Secretaries of War and the Navy.

21 December 1861 The Medal of Honor is authorized by Congress. It is not, as commonly thought, all-embracing in its application to the services. It covers enlisted personnel of the Navy and

Marine Corps. and the Army version will not be authorized until 1862. The first Army Medals of Honor will be presented on 25 March. 1863 and the first Navy medals a few days later (3 April).

30 January 1862 The *Monitor*. the first turreted warship. is launched at Greenpoint. Long Island. It was designed by John Ericson. whose design the Union accepted four hours after it was submitted. Its displacement is 987 tons. length 172 ft (52.43 m). beam 41.5 ft (12.65 m) and draft 10.5 ft (3.20 m). Two 11-in (279 mm) smoothbore guns firing 180 pound (81kg) shot are mounted in the ship's revolving armored turret which is 20ft (6m) in diameter.

Above: Deck scene aboard the *Monitor*, which was taken by photographer James Gibson some six months after the famous "clash between the ironclads". In December 1862 the *Monitor* foundered and sank in a storm.

1 February 1862 The "Battle Hymn of the Republic". a poem by Julia Ward Howe. is published in the *Atlantic Monthly*. People read the words and begin to sing them: the song grows in popularity and becomes one of the most renowned in the nation. Howe had heard Union troops singing "John Brown's Body" the previous December and promptly wrote some more dignified words to go with the music. The "Battle Hymn" is the result of her work.

4 February 1862 The president is authorized by the Congress to take possession of all railroads. Within a week. an experienced railway executive. Daniel C. McCallum. is given the rank of brigadier general and empowered to take possession of and use all railroads that might be required for the transport of troops.

arms. ammunition and military supplies and a military railway service is established.

7 February 1862 Flag Officer Andrew Foote and four ironclads followed by three wooden gunboats move up the Tennessee River and shell Fort Henry. It was not defended since Brig. Gen. Lloyd Tilghman had sent everybody but those on his hospital boat (the *Essex*) and artillerists to Fort Donelson. The fort and boat are taken in the first victory of the war for the Union navy.

25 February 1862 Nashville. Tennessee. becomes the only city in the US over which the original "Old Glory" will float as an emblem of war. The flag. which had received its nickname from Capt. William Driver and had gone around the world with him twice. was hoisted when Union troops occupied the city. The 6th Ohio Volunteers at first hoisted a US flag. but it was taken down and replaced by "Old Glory".

8 March 1862 The Confederate ironclad *Merrimack*. which became the *Virginia* by the time the battle of the ironclads revolutionized naval

Above: The *Cumberland* is sunk off Newport News, Virginia, and Chaplain John Lenhart becomes the first naval chaplain killed in the war. At least 66 chaplains died in Federal service during the conflict.

warfare. becomes involved in another first. During her clash with the Union frigate *Cumberland* off Hampton Roads. Virginia. she rams her prow through the *Cumberland* and John L. Lenhart is killed. He is the first naval chaplain to be killed in action.

9 March 1862 The Union *Monitor* and Confederate *Virginia* fight the first engagement between ironclads. Lieutenant S. Dana Greene. 22 and just three years out of Annapolis. fires the first shot from the *Monitor*. He writes later: "I triced up the port run the gun out & fired the first gun and thus commenced the great battle". The battle at Hampton Roads. Virginia. changes naval warfare.

Below: The battle of the *Monitor* and the *Merrimack* at Hampton Roads, Virginia. The two ironclads fought "mercilessly and ineffectively" for four hours, but despite this the the the impact on naval warfare was profound.

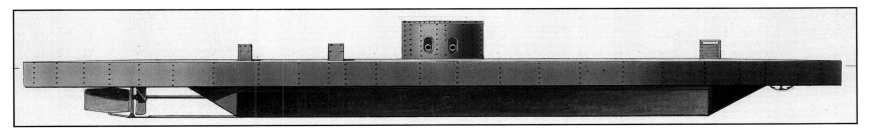

Casualties in Major Battles of the Civil War 1862

Shiloh April 6-7, 1862

	UNION	CONFEDERATE
Dead	1,754	1,723
Wounded	8,408	8,012
Missing	2,885	959
Total	13,047	10,694
Grand Total: 23,741. Duration, Two Days		

The Seven Days June 25 — July 1, 1862

	UNION	CONFEDERATE
Dead	1,734	3,478
Wounded	8,062	16,261
Missing	6,075	875
Total	15,849	20,614
Grand Total: 36,463. Duration, Seven Days		

Second Manassas/Bull Run Aug. 29-30, 1862

	UNION	CONFEDERATE
Dead	1,724	1,481
Wounded	8,372	7,627
Missing	5,958	89
Total	16,054	9,197
Grand Total: 25,251. Duration, Two Days		

Sharpsburg/Antietam Sept. 17, 1862

	UNION	CONFEDERATE
Dead	2,108	2,700
Wounded	9,549	9,024
Missing	753	2,000
Total	12,410	13,724
Grand Total: 26,134. Duration, One Day		

First Battle of Fredericksburg Dec. 13, 1862

	UNION	CONFEDERATE
Dead	1,284	595
Wounded	9,600	4,061
Missing	1,769	653
Total	12,653	5,309
Grand Total: 17,962. Duration, One Day		

Below: Union engineers construct telegraph lines. Efforts like this frequently took place close to the front and telegraph operators suffered casualties of about 10 percent — the same rate as frontline combat troops.

6 April 1862 The first Army field hospital is set up at Shiloh, Tennessee, by medical inspector Bernard D. Irwin of the 4th Division, Army of the Ohio. Using the tents of a recaptured camp of a division of troops who had been made prisoners the preceding day, he sets up accommodation for 300 patients. Large field hospitals of this type were used to support Union armies in later campaigns.

21 April 1862 A naval academy is authorized by the Confederate Congress. Its superintendent will be Lieutenant William H. Parker, former head of the Department of Seamanship at the US Naval Academy. Classes at the academy start in October 1863 aboard the ship *Patrick Henry* at Drewry's Bluff, Virginia, below Richmond. There are 52 of the Confederacy's 106 midshipmen in attendance at the first class.

3 May 1862 Land mines are used for the first time by the Confederates at Yorktown, Virginia, when they are left behind as Southern forces withdraw from the site. Called "infernal machines" (they are live artillery shells with fuses buried just beneath the surface) by blue and gray alike. Confederate Brig. Gen. Gabriel J. Rains is lambasted by his superiors for using them.

9 May 1862 Union forces launch a successful invasion in the area of Norfolk and Portsmouth, Virginia, which is evacuated by Confederate troops. Lincoln, in an unusual move for a chief executive, had been at nearby Hampton roads and toured the area looking for a place for Union soldiers to land.

13 May 1862 The steamship *Planter* is seized by Robert Smalls and a crew of blacks after martial law is declared in South Carolina. The first ship seized during the war, the incident takes place in Charleston Harbor.

Flying the Confederate flag, they take the ship northward and salute forts along the way. They run up a flag of truce only when out of gunshot range.

13 May 1862 Jefferson Davis's wife Varina flees the capital of the Confederacy — Richmond, Virginia — which is being threatened by Gen. George C. McClellan and his troops. The danger to the city will not be over until late in the summer, and then only after the Confederates have mounted what will become known as the Seven Day Campaign to relieve the pressure.

15 May 1862 Corporal John Mackie becomes the first Marine to receive the Medal of Honor. He was on duty aboard the *Galena* during an attack on Fort Darling at Drewry's Bluff, Virginia. As fire raked the deck of the ship, the corporal kept up return fire against the rifle pits along the shoreline and filled vacancies at guns left by fallen comrades "with skill and courage".

24 May 1862 During the Peninsular campaign of the Civil War, a wire several miles long is strung from the headquarters of McClellan near Williamsport, Virginia, to an advance guard at Mechanicsville in the same state. It is used by the army as a field telegraph, the first such use in warfare.

7 June 1862 Union Maj. Gen. Benjamin F. Butler, military governor of New Orleans, Louisiana, has William B. Mumford hanged for tearing down a US flag from the city's mint. During his tenure, the general also issues his infamous Order 28, which warns that any disrespect or contempt shown his men by a female will be taken as evidence of moral disrepute and treated accordingly.

2 July 1862 The Morrill Act grants public lands to establish colleges and requires military tactics be taught in them. Rationale: "... it must not be understood that our youth are intended to be so severely drilled, nor is it to render them ready for warfare alone that the training will be introduced ... the health-giving exercises will be equally beneficial to them in every walk of life."

8 July 1862 A revolving battery tower invented by Theodore Ruggles Timby receives approval of the US patent office. His idea, which is really not officially accepted until 20 years after he first advances it, was used in the construction of the revolving armored turret on the ironclad *Monitor*. Timby not only advocated this concept, but was a firm believer in the use of iron in the construction of ships.

12 July 1862 The Medal of Honor is authorized for the Army's enlisted men. Eight months earlier, Lincoln had signed legislation approving the medal — which was and still is the highest US award for valor — for enlisted men of the Navy and Marine Corps. Officers were included in later legislation. When first approved, it was the only medal awarded by the US to its armed forces.

16 July 1862 Congress creates the rank of rear admiral and promotes David Farragut to it in recognition of his victory over Confederate forces at New Orleans. He is the first person to hold this rank in the Navy. For the next two years, he will be engaged in blockading the Gulf coast and controlling traffic in the lower Mississippi. This results in Union forces gaining control of the entire river.

17 July 1862 An act is passed by Congress granting pensions to every "officer, seaman, or marine disabled in the line of duty". Several other measures become law on the same day. One permitted the president to tender pardon and amnesty to those to whom he saw fit to grant the privilege. Yet another provided for the use of postage stamps as money — a wartime measure designed to help alleviate the serious shortage of metal coins in circulation within the Union.

17 July 1862 A law is signed by Lincoln that empowers him to accept "persons of African descent for the purpose of constructing intrenchments or performing camp competent". Eventually, almost 200,000 blacks serve in the Union army and navy. They fight in 449 engagements in every theater of war and suffer 35% greater losses than the white troops. They also serve as spies and scouts.

17 July 1862 Congressional legislation authorizes national cemeteries "for the soldiers who shall die in the service of the country". Carrying out the provisions of this law proves to be extremely difficult; however, nearly 300,000 remains are reinterred in national cemeteries in five years following an effort to recover and identify the Civil War dead from hundreds of battlefields.

30 July 1862 A Cincinnati paper coins the term "Copperhead" to denote Southern sympathizers. Leaders of this movement include Horatio Seymour, New York's governor during the Civil War, and Clement L. Vallandigham, member of Congress from Ohio, who is arrested for treason during the war. Copperheads (or Peace Democrats) urge an end to the war and a reunion of North and South through negotiation.

25 August 1862 Orders go out from the Union Secretary of War Edwin Stanton that provide for the enlistment of black soldiers "up to five thousand in number and to train them as guards for plantations and settlements". Before the war is over, a total of 178,892 blacks will officially serve in the Union army, of whom 134,111 are from slave states and 93,346 are from seceded states.

Above: Company E, 4th US Colored Infantry. Eventually, about 200,000 black troops served in the Union army and navy; by 1865, they provided two-thirds of the Federal troops operating in the Mississippi Valley.

31 August 1862 The Navy abolishes the rum issue for enlisted men and compensates the "dry" seamen at the rate of five cents per day. The grog ration — actually one and one half pints (0.71 litre) per week — fell victim to the rising temperance consciousness in the US. That was only good in the US Navy; the Confederates served the ration throughout the Civil War.

15 September 1862 Gen. Thomas J. "Stonewall" Jackson captures Harper's Ferry, Virginia (now West Virginia), site of the famous incident involving the radical abolitionist John Brown. The 12,000-man Federal garrison falls to Jackson, and with it the Confederacy gains much needed supplies and equipment. Moreover, the way has now been opened for Gen. Robert E. Lee to advance to Hagerstown, Maryland.

Below: "Bloody Lane" at Antietam. This farm lane in the center of of the battle became the focus of the Battle at Antietam for three hours. Bodies were piled several men deep, the carnage earning the road its grisly name.

17 September 1862

17 September 1862 In what turns out to be the bloodiest single day of the Civil War, the North and South meet at Antietam. Casualties for the North are: 2,108 killed, 9,549 wounded and 753 missing. For the South, estimates are 2,700 killed, 9,024 wounded and about 2,000 missing. It is a tactical win for the South, and a strategic win for the North. Lee's invasion of the North is stopped.

17 September 1962 The brothers George and Godfrey Gleasman are killed at the Battle of Antietam by a Confederate sharpshooter. Members of the 97th Regiment, New York Volunteers, they signed up the year before — both of them swearing to officials that they were "just below" the maximum enlistment age of 44. The "twins" were hardly that: Godfrey was 56 when killed — and George was 62!

22 September 1862 Lincoln issues what many have described as the most important document of his Presidency — the preliminary Emancipation Proclamation. It promises that the slaves in Confederate states will be declared free on 1 January, 1863. The North is now seen as fighting slavery; since Europeans will not support slavery, the South's hope of receiving aid from that direction is gone.

Above and right: It is 19 November, and a little over 5 months after the Confederate invasion of Pennsylvania and the bloody struggle at Gettysburg, thousands assemble to watch the official dedication of the Gettysburg National Cemetery for those who had fallen. It is here that President Lincoln makes his famous address to the American people.

Casualties in Major Battles of the Civil War 1863

Stone's River/Murfreesboro Dec. 31, 1862 — Jan. 2, 1863
	UNION	CONFEDERATE
Dead	1,677	1,294
Wounded	7,543	7,945
Missing	3,686	2,476
Total	12,906	11,795

Grand Total: 24,701. Duration, Three Days

Chancellorsville May 1-4, 1863
	UNION	CONFEDERATE
Dead	1,575	1,665
Wounded	9,594	9,081
Missing	5,676	2,018
Total	16,792	12,764

Grand Total: 29,556. Duration, Four Days

Gettysburg July 1 — July 3, 1863
	UNION	CONFEDERATE
Dead	3,155	3,903
Wounded	14,529	18,735
Missing	5,365	5,425
Total	23,049	28,063

Grand Total: 51,112. Duration, Three Days

Chickamauga Sept. 19-20, 1863
	UNION	CONFEDERATE
Dead	1,657	2,312
Wounded	9,756	14,674
Missing	4,757	1,468
Total	16,170	18,484

Grand Total: 34,654. Duration, Two Days

29 October 1862 The Union's 79th US Colored Troops — or the 1st Kansas Colored Volunteers — earns the distinction of being the first black regiment of volunteers to fight in combat in the Civil War when they engaged at Island Mount, Missouri. The 79th spent the entire war west of the Mississippi River and fought in 12 engagements and a host of minor actions. It was mustered out on 1 October, 1865.

4 November 1862 Dr Richard J. Gatling of Indianapolis, Indiana, is issued patent number 36,836 for the gun whose staccato sound would become famous and change the face of warfare. The "father of the machine gun" had bundled together six barrels which could be fired in sequence. Tests showed that the gun could maintain the astonishing rate of fire of 200 shots per minute for hours at a time.

12 December 1862 The *Cairo*, one of the seven Union ironclad river gunboats called "Pook Turtles" after designer Samuel M. Pook, sails up the Yazoo River and is struck by two torpedoes (mines). Within a matter of 12 minutes she sinks to the bottom with no loss of life. *Cairo* is the first Union warship of the Civil War to be sunk by torpedoes. The first Confederate loss will occur two years later.

1 January 1863 Confederate "cotton-clads" make their appearance. Texas temporarily breaks the Union blockade that has been strangling them at Galveston by equipping two steamers (the *Bayou City* and the *Neptune*) with artillery and sharpshooters placed behind bales of cotton. They force one ship to surrender and drive another down river. Yet another is run aground — and the blockade is temporarily broken.

31 January 1863 The first black regiment in the Civil War — the 1st South Carolina Colored Volunteers — is mustered into the regular Federal service. The unit was started up by Maj. Gen. David Hunter, but had been undermined by his rude treatment of blacks and his radical abolitionism. It was first tested in battle — successfully — during raids along the coast of Georgia and Florida in November 1862.

1 February 1863 At the approximate mid-point of the Civil War, inflation has ravaged Confederate currency so seriously that it is estimated to be worth about 20 cents on the dollar. Later in the month, a simple half loaf of bread will cost the typical Southerner $2.50. Southerners repeated the saying often: "You take your money to market in a basket and bring home what you buy in your pocket book".

2 February 1863 The Negro Regiment Bill is passed by the US House of Representatives. Among other things, the bill calls for enlistment of any number of Negroes, not to exceed 300,000; pay of $10 per month for these recruits; and arms and equipment of the same kind as "other soldiers", with white men as officers.

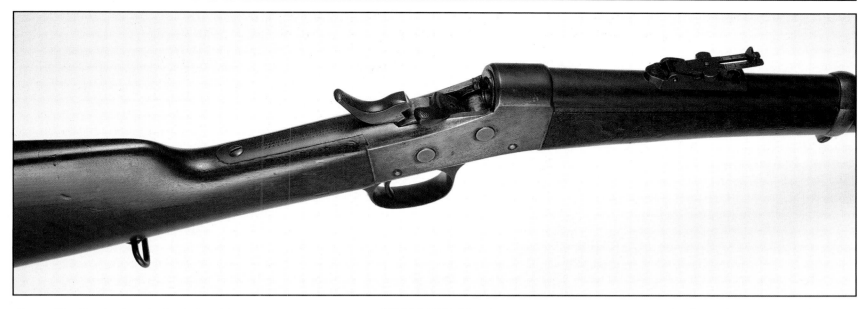

Above: The Remington single-shot carbine. Carbines were used by the cavalry because of their inherent lightness; but even the best of them would not permit the cavalry to stand up to the infantry on equal terms.

25 February 1863 The Confederates, who saw their ironclad *Indianola* grounded the previous day, burn her to the water-line when they spot a large Union "gunboat" coming down the Mississippi River near Warrenton. The "gunboat" is a ruse thought up by Rear Admiral David Porter. It is actually a barge that has been rigged with a superstructure and guns that achieve the intended result.

1 April 1863 The Draft Act of 1863 goes into effect. It is the Union's first compulsory recruitment of manpower in wartime and applies to all males between the ages of 20 and 45. There are two legal draft-evading practices allowed: substitution, under which the draftee hires another to serve for him; and commutation, under which a flat $300 is paid by the draftee to be released from service.

16 April 1863 President Davis of the Confederacy signs a bill that will allow persons below the age of majority to hold military commissions. The age is lowered to 18 and, as Davis' proclamation states, allows every man capable of bearing arms to drive back the invaders "now within the limits of the Confederacy". In reality, the law is a reflection of the South's concern over manpower shortages.

17 April 1863 General Ulysses S. Grant announces there will be no more prisoner exchanges with the South unless they are balanced equally. The move is designed to put pressure on the dwindling supply of manpower for the Confederate army. Grant strongly feels exchanges work to the North's disadvantage. During the war, Union forces captured

215,000-220,000 prisoners, not including those at war's end.

21 May 1863 The siege of Port Hudson, Louisiana, the longest battle of the Civil War (it will end 48 days later on 8 July) begins. More than 30,000 Union troops attack the site, which is defended by 6,500 Confederate soldiers behind earthen embankments. An estimated 5,000 Union soldiers lost their lives in the battle; Confederate casualties were lower.

1 June 1863 The Balloon Service is abandoned by the Army. A total of nine "aeronauts" (the term describing them) were on hand, but only seven seemed to have been used in the field at any one time. They made a variety of signal and observation tests, but from the time of disestablishment until 1890 there are no military balloon operations in the US.

1 July 1863 The three-day Battle of Gettysburg, Pennsylvania, begins. After bloody battle, it ends with the Confederates in retreat and attempting to regroup. Union casualties are: 3,155 killed and 14,529 wounded, with 5,365 missing. The South: 3,903 killed; 18,735 wounded and 5,425 missing. It is widely acknowledged that Gettysburg represented the high water mark of the Confederacy in the war.

13 July 1863 Union troops are called into New York City to quell riots that start out over the draft act, but increasingly become directed toward blacks. More than 1,000 are killed and wounded in what history will note as one of the darkest homefront episodes of the war and the worst race riot in US history. Only the return of Union troops from Gettysburg ended the riots on 16 July.

18 July 1863 At the head of Union dash into the battle at Battery Wagner in

Charleston (South Carolina) Harbor is the 54th Massachusetts Colored Infantry. The battle is furious: 246 Federals die and another 880 are wounded. Among those who fight in the battle are Charles and Lewis Douglass, sons of Frederick Douglass, the abolitionist who escaped slavery in 1838.

15 September 1863 Lincoln issues an order that suspends the legal right to habeas corpus. This dramatic action comes as a result of the existing "state of rebellion", says the order, and the suspension will apply throughout the US in cases where military or civil authorities hold persons under their command or in their custody.

16 September 1863 Twelve-year old drummer boy Willie Johnston of Company D, 3rd Vermont Infantry, becomes the youngest recipient of the Medal of Honor. Even though the War Department does not record the date and place of the act, it has been established that the citation was for coolness under fire during the Peninsular Campaign in the Civil War.

19 November 1863 A crowd of more than 15,000 gathers for the dedication of the National Soldiers' Cemetery on the battlefield at Gettysburg, Pennsylvania. The speaker is Lincoln, who thinks his "little speech" is a failure because of the unethusiastic reception it gets. Only a handful in the audience recognize it as one of the most eloquent speeches ever given.

23 December 1863 The single-shot Remington carbine is patented. It features a rolling-block breech that rises to accept a round of fixed ammunition, and fires a .56-.50 rimfire cartridge. The Union War Department bought 15,000 of these weapons from the Remington Arms Co. Less expensive than the multishot Spencer repeating carbine, it accepts that carbine's ammunition.

9 February 1864

9 February 1864 Lincoln sits for a series of several photographs at the White House. One of these photographs is eventually used as the basis for the portrait of Lincoln that appears on the $5 bill.

9 February 1864 109 Union prisoners dig their way out of Libby Prison, Richmond, Virginia, in the largest and most daring escape of the Civil War. Of the escapees 48 are recaptured, two drown and 59 reach Federal lines. The men, all of whom are officers, had dug a tunnel under the streets 50 ft (15.2 m) long and crawled to freedom. The famous Confederate prison will be dismantled and rebuilt as a museum in Chicago in 1889.

17 February 1864 The Confederate submarine *H. L. Hunley* sinks the *Housatonic*, a Union sloop-of-war, in what was the first successful submarine attack in the history of naval warfare. The original plan of attack was to dive under the target while towing a mine (torpedo) on a line that would explode on the hull of the *Housatonic*. Instead, the mine was mounted on a long spar and rammed into the victim ship. A far more efficient method.

29 February 1864 The grade of lieutenant general is revived when Lincoln approves Congressional legislation. It is obvious that Maj. Gen. Ulysses S. Grant is in line for promotion to the now-highest rank in the army for his service in the Union's behalf. The grade had previously been held by Winfield Scott, but by brevet only.

11 March 1864 The Army Ambulance Corps is established by action of the Congress. The Corps becomes a regular Army unit and the Medical Department receives the right to train and examine men for this service — and to reject those who are unfit. By the same law, a prohibition is written against soldiers in combat leaving the field to help their stricken comrades; it is now to be the responsibility of trained personnel.

Above: Libby Prison, Richmond, Virginia, the most famous Confederate prison outside of Andersonville. It housed captured Federal officers, who did not dare show themselves at the windows for fear of being shot.

Above: Lt. Gen. Ulysses S. Grant at the time of Cold Harbor. The Second Battle of Cold Harbor, Virginia, was the final engagement of the Overland Campaign and resulted in nearly 7,000 Federal casualties.

12 March 1864 General Order Number 98 is published, which assigns Lt. Gen. Ulysses S. Grant to the command of the armies of the US — even though it is somewhat after the event. Grant had actually been provided with official authority to take over command of the armies on March 10, but he was not in the nation's capital to receive the order at the time.

13 April 1864 President Davis of the Confederacy signs into law a bill that calls for the arming of blacks so they can fight in Confederate armies. It is left to the individual states whether the black soldiers should be freed, but it appears they will be. It is approved grudgingly and only after the public intervention of Gen. Robert E. Lee, who sees no other way to stall advances by Union forces.

10 May 1864 George Armstrong Custer — the famed cavalry general of the storied "last stand" at Little Big Horn — recaptures 378 Union prisoners taken at the Battle of the Wilderness. Custer's Civil War record was outstanding. Within three days of graduating from West Point, he had fought at the First Battle of Bull Run. At war's end, he had taken part in scores of major engagements.

13 May 1864 Arlington National Cemetery opens at Arlington, Virginia. Pvt. William Christman, a farmer from Pennsylvania and a member of Company G of the 67th Pennsylvania Infantry, becomes the first soldier to be buried there. Today, his grave remains among other Civil War dead in Section 27 near the northern boundary of the national cemetery.

14 June 1864 The James River Bridge, the longest (2,200 ft / 671 m) pontoon bridge ever used in war, is constructed in eight hours by 450 Union engineers. Extending from Windmill Point to Fort Powhatan in Virginia, the structure enabled Grant's forces to cross the James River and move on to Petersburg, a vital communications center south of the Confederate capital of Richmond.

18 June 1864 During the Petersburg (Virginia) Campaign, a Union regiment sustains the highest casualty rate of any regiment in a single battle during the Civil War. The regiment loses 632 of its 900 men. Despite the costly losses, Petersburg is not taken by the Union forces and the only recourse left to Grant at this point is to lay siege to the city.

19 June 1864 Under Captain John Winslow, the Federal warship *Kearsarge* sinks the *Alabama*, which was probably the most famous Confederate Civil War commerce raider. The hour-long battle takes place in international waters off Cherbourg, France, and is witnessed by cheering crowds on the French cliffs. The legendary *Alabama* had taken 65 Federal merchant vessels and caused close to $6 million in damages to Union shipping during the war, boosting Southern morale in the process.

11 July 1864 For the first time since the War of 1812, and the last time since, the nation's capital finds itself under attack by an enemy army. The Confederate forces of Gen. Jubal (Jubilee) Early attack its environs. More than 20,000 are organized for defense of the city (even office personnel are put under arms), and Lincoln is at the parapet to witness the unsuccessful assault at nearby Fort Stevens.

22 July 1864 Maj. Gen. James Birdseye McPherson becomes the sole Union army commander to be slain in action during the Civil War. During the battle for Atlanta before the beginning of Sherman's "March to the Sea", the 36-year old general and another 3,721 Union soliders are killed, captured or wounded. The Confederate losses were at twice the level, yet the strategic situation remained essentially unchanged.

5 August 1864 Admiral David G. Farragut leads his fleet through the narrow entrance to Mobile Bay before dawn, past powerful bombardment. The decks of the ship slippery with blood, he climbs into the rigging to command the action and sees the bay is studded with mines (torpedoes). "Damn the torpedoes! Full speed ahead"! he cries, and battles the Ironclad *Tennessee*. He takes her ... and Mobile Bay.

12 August 1864 Captain Thomas M. Dungan dies of a bullet wound and becomes, as far as can be determined from official Civil War Records, the only man in the Revenue Cutter service (later US Coast Guard) killed in action during the war between the states. On an errand of mercy on the cutter *Reliance*, he was forced to confront hostile crowds on the shoreline in eastern Maryland and was struck down.

16 September 1864 Confederate "cowboys" pull off one of the greatest cattle rustling operations in American history. Brig. Gen. Thomas L. Rosser's Laurel Brigade tears into the camp of the Union army's 1st D.C. Cavalry at Coggins Point, Virginia. They regroup and attack the detail guarding the cattle, which they reckon will help with their food supply problem. 2,486 cattle are taken back to Confederate lines.

19 September 1864 With information supplied by Confederate army Capt. Charles Cole — an escapee from a prison camp on Johnson's Island in upper Ohio — Confederate navy Captain John Y. Beall leads a daring and unsuccessful attempt to free 1,000 prisioners. They are almost all officers, including seven generals. Captured, Beall is tried in a military court and hanged in New York as a spy.

19 October 1864 In the northernmost land engagement of the Civil War, a small group of Confederate raiders crosses from Canada and raids the Vermont town of St Albans. Led by Lt. Bennet H. Young and made up mainly of escaped prisoners, the raiders rob local banks of more than $200,000. Eleven raiders make it back to Canada, where they are first arrested, but then released for lack of jurisdiction.

Above: Maj. Gen. William Tecumseh Sherman, commander of the Union forces in the Military Division of the Mississippi during the later stages of the war. After the war, he became general-in-chief of the Army.

16 November 1864 Union Gen. William Tecumseh Sherman begins his "March to the Sea" with about 60,000 troops of the Army of the Tennessee. With the XIV Corps, he leaves Atlanta behind, a smoldering city, its economy in ruins, its people desolate and bitter. As Sherman advances, the Georgia legislature will pass a levy en masse for troops and then flee. He reaches the sea on 13 December after the capture of Fort McAllister, Georgia.

25 November 1864 The notorious outlaw, Jesse James, in a Civil War encounter, kills Chaplain U.P. Gardner of the 13th Kansas after telling him to turn so he won't be shot in the back (the chaplain would not). James was part of a guerrilla force that had bested Unionists earlier in a sharp clash near Cane Hill in the Cherokee Nation. The incident occurred as the guerrillas hit out after the Union force.

13 January 1865 Unionists under Admiral David Porter, with tremendous firepower — 627 guns in 59 vessels — begin to bombard Fort Fisher, at the mouth of the Cape Fear River in North Carolina. Troops under Gen. Alfred Terry, meanwhile, are put ashore and begin the only successful full-scale amphibious assault of the Civil War. Union dead number 691 men and Confederate losses are 700.

15 January 1865 The last Confederate port still open is slammed shut as Federal forces, after a two-pronged assault, capture Fort Fisher, North Carolina. The two top Confederate officers in the fort are injured and overall losses are 500; Federal losses are 266 killed, 1,018 wounded and 57 missing. The city of Wilmington is successfully cut off as a blockade-running port.

1 February 1865 Gen. Robert E. Lee is unanimously confirmed by the Confederate Senate as Commander-in-Chief of all the armies of the South. Editorializes the Richmond (Virginia) *Sentinel*: "Let our whole people and our Government, in all its departments, rally to the support of Gen. Lee in the position to which he has been appointed with all the zeal and energy at our command". It is too late for the action to have any effect on the war, and Lee will continue to serve primarily as commander of the Army of Northern Virginia.

13 March 1865 Slaves are made subject to military service in the Confederate army under the provisions of bill signed by Davis. Less than one month earlier, the Confederate House of Representatives had passed a bill authorizing the use of slaves as regular soldiers.

3 April 1865 The Union cavalry dashes into Richmond, Virginia, capital of the Confederacy. The Confederates surrender at City Hall at 8:15 in the morning. Maj. Atherton H. Stevens, Jr., of Massachusetts, raises the first Federal flag — a GUIDON — over the State House as the symbol of the Confederacy lies in smoldering ruins, the result of a firestorm.

Below: Gen. Robert E. Lee. It is not well known that Lee, through President Abraham Lincoln's personal emissary, had been offered field command of the Federal armies after the attack on Fort Sumter. Lee declined.

Above: Wilmer McLean's home at Appomattox, Virginia, where Generals Grant and Lee met on Palm Sunday to discuss the terms of the latter's surrender. The actual surrender did not occur until three days later.

9 April 1865 Lee surrenders the Army of Northern Virginia to Grant at Appomattox Court House, thus effectively ending the Civil War. Grant writes out the terms of surrender in his own hand and, at Lee's request, lets men who claim to own a horse or mule take them home "to work their little farms". Despite legend, Lee did not surrender his sword.

10 April 1865 During a speech to 3,000 people gathered at the White House to celebrate Lee's surrender, Lincoln asks the brass band to play him a rendition of "Dixie". Lincoln claims that the song has always been a personal favorite of his even though, he adds, the South had claimed it as its own.

28 April 1865 The worst ship disaster in US history takes the lives of 1,700 persons when the steamer *Sultana* explodes on the Mississippi River. Of 2,300 persons on board, 2,134 were Union soldiers returning from Confederate prison camps at Cahawbe and Andersonville, Georgia. The explosion took place at 2:00 in the morning about 7 miles (11.25 km) up the river.

10 May 1865 Early in the morning, Union troops surprise the encampment of Jefferson Davis near Irwinville, Georgia, and he is taken into custody. This date will become Confederate Memorial Day in North and South Carolina — and is still widely observed throughout the South on varying dates.

13 May 1865 At Palmito Ranch in Texas, Union soldiers under Lt. Col. Theodore H. Barrett are hit by the 12-pounders of Confederate troops under Texas Ranger John S. Ford. Barrett retreats. But, anticipating the arrival of reinforcements, Ford breaks off the action. Union forces suffer 30 casualties, the Confederate Cavalry of the West 5, in the last engagement of the Civil War.

23 May 1865 For two days, the Grand Armies of the Republic review for the last time. A host of soldiers of the Union armies march in triumph down Pennsylvania Avenue, pass dignitaries including President Andrew Johnson. On 24 May it is the turn of Gen. Sherman's veterans of the West, who arrive in Washington complete with their mules and spoils of foraging.

26 May 1865 Second Lt. Thomas W. Custer receives his second Medal of Honor, thereby becoming the first person to be so recognized. His first came for action at Namozine Church, Virginia, on May 10, 1863. The second results when he vaults over the enemy's works on his horse and captures their colors — even as his horse is shot from under him at Sailor Creek, Virginia. Custer was severely wounded.

26 May 1865 The last Confederate troops surrender, thus ending the Civil War. A terse statement issued by Edwin M. Stanton, Secretary of War, says, "A dispatch from Gen. Canby, dated at New Orleans, yesterday, the 26th inst., states that arrangements for the surrender of Confederate forces in the Trans-Mississippi have been concluded. They include the men and material of the army and navy".

23 June 1865 In the Oklahoma Territory, Brig. Gen. Stand Watie, a leader of the Cherokee nation who had allied with the Confederacy, surrenders his sword at Doaksville in the Choctaw nation. He becomes the last Confederate to surrender. In 1861, he had used his influence to associate with the South and organized the 1st Cherokee Mounted Rifles. He had been elevated to brigadier general in 1864.

28 June 1865 Using the time-honored technique of a shot across the bow, the Confederate cruiser *Shenandoah* halts and burns 10 Union whaling ships in the Bering Sea. They are considered the last shots fired in the Civil War (the war is over, but the commander of the *Shenandoah* is not aware of it). He learns otherwise from the British, feels his acts will be seen as those of a pirate, and sails for England.

5 November 1865 Lieutenant James I. Waddell brings the Confederate cruiser *Shenandoah* into Liverpool.

Below: The Grand Review in Washington, D.C., of the Union's main northern armies as seen from the dome of the Capitol. More than 80,000 veterans marched down Pennsylvania Avenue during the course of the review.

England, after completing a voyage of 122 days completely out of the sight of land. The following day, Waddell hauls down the "Stars and Bars" the *Shenandoah* is flying; it was the last official flag of the Confederate States of America flying anywhere in the world.

10 November 1865 Capt. Henry Wirz, one-armed commandant of the notorious Confederate prisoner of war camp at Andersonville, Georgia (the prison's actual name was Camp Sumter), is executed. He had been tried for allowing mistreatment of Union soldiers during the war and even conspiring to kill prisoners. Wirz became the only individual executed after the war for any crime committed during its course.

24 January 1866 Dr Mary E. Walker becomes the first woman to be awarded the Medal of Honor. She abandoned her practice as a physician in Cincinnati, Ohio, and spent three years working as a nurse for the Union army. In 1864, an Ohio regiment hired her as a contract surgeon. She became an active spy and spent four months in a Confederate prison camp in the latter stages of the war.

21 March 1866 An act of Congress authorizes national soldiers' homes under legislation which is "an act to incorporate a national military and naval asylum for the relief of the totally disabled officers and men of the volunteer forces of the United States". The first two homes opened under this legislation (in 1867) are located at Dayton, Ohio, and Togus, Maine.

6 April 1866 The first post of the Grand Army of the Republic, an organization whose membership is limited to persons who served in the Union forces during the Civil War, is organized. Dr B.F. Stephenson and Rev W.J. Rudolph, the surgeon and chaplain of the 14th Illinois Infantry, organize the post at Decatur, Illinois. Peak membership of GAR will be 409,489.

25 July 1866 Ulysses S. Grant is voted the rank of full general and becomes the first officer since Washington to hold the rank. Congress reactivated the rank to honor him, and he will serve as the interim Secretary of War for five months in 1867-1868. He goes on to become the US president and in March 1885 the Congress creates for him the rank of general of the army on the retired list.

28 July 1866 President Andrew Johnson signs an "Act to increase and fix the Military Peace Establishment of the United States". For the first time, the army is radically expanded after a war — the artillery remained constant, but the infantry mushroomed from 19 to 45 regiments and the six regiments of US Cavalry were joined by four more. The army is also allowed to raise 1,000 Indian scouts.

20 August 1866 Johnson proclaims the Civil War over and declares the insurrection at an end in Texas. That state had been omitted from an earlier declaration (2 April) that had declared the war over in the other states of secession — but only because it was still forming a government. Thus ended a war that began 5 years and 4 months earlier and left indelible scars on America.

21 December 1866 Capt. William J. Fetterman and 82 soldiers are ambushed and killed near Fort Phil Kearny by Sioux.

Below: Delegates from Massachusetts Regiments, Grand Army of the Republic, at Gettysburg, October 1883. Virtually every Northern state had GAR posts, as did those in the South with many Federal veterans.

US Army Campaign Streamers Civil War

Sumter	Apr 12-13, 1861
Bull Run*	Jul 16-22, 1861
Henry and Donelson	Feb 6-16, 1862
Mississippi River	Feb 6, 1862 — Jul 9, 1863
Peninsula	Mar 17 — Aug 3, 1862
Shiloh	Apr 6-7, 1862
Valley	May 15 — June 17, 1862
Manassas*	Aug 7 — Sep 2 1862
Antietam*	Sep 3-17, 1862
Fredericksburg	Nov 9 — Dec 15, 1862
Murfreesborough	Dec 26, 1862 — Jan 4, 1863
Chancellorsville	Apr 27 — May 6, 1863
Gettysburg	Jun 29 — July 3, 1863
Vicksburg	Mar 29 — Jul 4, 1863
Chickamauga	Aug 16 — Sep 22, 1863
Chattanooga	Nov 23-27, 1863
Wilderness	May 4-7, 1864
Atlanta	May 7 — Sep 2, 1864
Spotsylvania	May 8-21, 1864
Cold Harbor	May 22 — June 3, 1864
Petersburg	Jun 4, 1864 — Apr 2, 1865
Shenandoah	Aug 7 — Nov 28, 1864
Franklin	Nov 17-30, 1864
Nashville	Dec 1-16, 1864
Appomattox	Apr 3-9, 1865

*For Confederate service, campaign honors to indicate Bull Run, Manassas and Antietam, use First Manassas, Second Manassas and Sharpsburg, respectively.

Cheyenne and Arapaho warriors led by Chief Red Cloud. The massacre will have long-range effects as the Congress within months passes a bill to establish "peace with certain Indian tribes now at war with the United States".

29 October 1867 US troops occupied Alaska and established the first US military post in that territory at Sitka. A battalion of troops under the command of Maj. Charles O. Wood of the 9th Infantry drew up in front of the governor's mansion in the newly-born Sitka to receive the transfer of territory from Russia.

28 December 1867 The US claims Midway, a Central Pacific island over which Captain William Reynolds of the screw sloop *Lackawanna* raised the United States flag on August 28. The island is the first territory the US annexes outside its continental limits.

30 May 1868 Memorial Day is first celebrated as Gen. John A. Logan calls on soldiers and veterans to decorate military graves with flowers. Logan had an excellent combat record in the Civil War and served in the US House and Senate. Instrumental in founding the Grand Army of the Republic (GAR), he was its commander and in that capacity started observance of Decoration (later Memorial) Day.

27 July 1868 Congress passes legislation that permits Japanese nationals to attend the Naval Academy at Annapolis as long as their government pays the cost. Jiunzo Matsumura becomes the first Japanese midshipman to take advantage of this and graduates with the class of 1873; he eventually rises to the rank of vice admiral in the Imperial Japanese Navy. Overall, 16 Japanese midshipmen attend the academy between the years 1869 and 1906.

13 November 1868 The present Marine Corps emblem, the eagle, globe, and anchor, is recommended for adoption by a board of officers appointed by Colonel Commandant Jacob Zeilin. Within a week, the design is approved by the Secretary of the Navy.

25 December 1868 Unqualified amnesty is granted to those who had participated in the "insurrection or rebellion" against the US in the Civil War. President Johnson issues the order, which has the effect of pardoning all but some 300 Confederate leaders. The Congress, however, take another view and will proceed to enact laws that will have the effect of nullifying much of the effect of this executive clemency.

6 February 1869 The first caricature of "Uncle Sam" with a chin and whiskers appears in *Harper's Weekly* magazine. Cartoonists had been using the caricature, but without the whiskers, for years. The person Uncle Sam was based on — Sam Wilson — was actually a meat packer who stamped "US" on meat intended for use in the War of 1812. Workers joked and said it stood for "Uncle Sam", and the character grew from there.

5 April 1869 Daniel F. Blakeman, the last surviving veteran of the American Revolution, dies at the age of 109. The number of persons who fought in the war on the Congress side is generally thought to be about 200,000 men (although record-keeping was poor and multiple enlistments confused the issue). Nearly 10 percent of those serving died — in equal parts from battle, disease and the hardships of primitive military prisons.

11 July 1869 The 5th Cavalry attacks the summer encampment of Tall Bull and his Cheyenne "Dog Soldiers" at Summit Springs in the northeast Colorado Territory. Tall Bull and 52 of his warriors are killed in the ensuing battle which successfully frees Kansas and the surrounding country from the danger of future Indian attacks. "Buffalo Bill" Cody plays a key role in the operation by scouting out the village's location for the cavalry.

The Growth of the United States to 1869

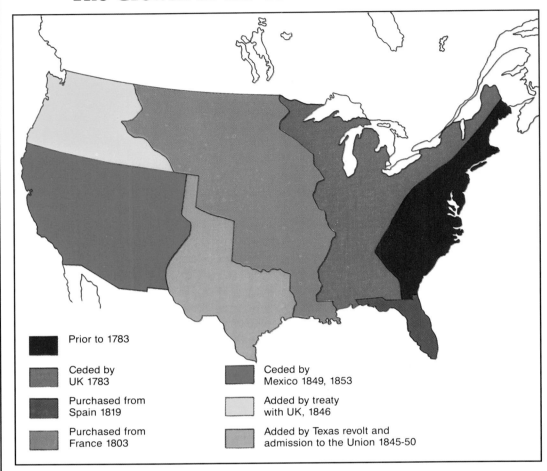

Prior to 1783 · Ceded by UK 1783 · Purchased from Spain 1819 · Purchased from France 1803 · Ceded by Mexico 1849, 1853 · Added by treaty with UK, 1846 · Added by Texas revolt and admission to the Union 1845-50

After the Civil War had run its bloody course and the future of the Union was secure, ambitions and hopes once again turned West. Ranchers, miners, prospectors, farmers, even religious visionaries drove beyond the safe confines of the settled states to create new territories out of the old wilderness. By 1900 over 11 million people lived in these wide open spaces which included Alaska which had been purchased from Russia in 1868. For the native Indians, however, the progress of the white man would mean only their own destruction.

28 September 1869 Fort Sill becomes the site at which the first post office in the Oklahoma Territory is established. John S. Evans became its first postmaster. From 1869 to 1890, its postmark read "Fort Sill, Indian Territory" and from 1890 to 1907 it read "Fort Sill, Oklahoma Territory", which when constructed was originally known as Camp Wichita, had personally been laid out by Gen. Philip Sheridan.

1 November 1870 Observer-sergeants with the Army Signal service report from across the nation the simultaneous weather conditions in 22 US cities. The first networked reporting of its kind, the observations these men make are telegraphed at 7:35 a.m. to Washington from locations such as Wyoming; Key West, Florida; Duluth, Minnesota; and Boston, Massachusetts.

13 January 1871 Marines from the Marine Barracks in the Brooklyn Navy Yard occupy all illegal distilleries seized by revenue officers in "Irishtown", Brooklyn, New York. The marines main tasks in the operation are protecting the revenue agents and guarding all materials seized.

9 February 1867 The US Weather Service is established as a unit of the Army. President Ulysses S. Grant signs a joint resolution of the Congress directing such a formation for "meteorological observation and for giving notice of the approach and force of storms". The first observations were made by 22 observer-sergeants of the Army Signal Corps.

11 June 1867 Lieutenant Hugh W. McKee is speared on the parapet of the Citadel, Kanghoa Island, Korea and dies of his wounds the same day. The lieutenant is with a five-ship expedition to the "Hermit Kingdom" that carries a US minister who is to negotiate a treaty of peace with Korea. The ships are fired upon and respond, taking two forts and storming the Citadel. The expedition completes a withdrawal on 3 July.

21 September 1872 James Henry Conyers is the first black midshipman to enter the US Naval Academy. According to contemporary accounts, his appointment hits the Academy like a "bombshell". Midshipmen, faculty and the public debate the issue of his attendance. Conyers handles his problems well, however, but resigns from the academy in 1873 because of a deficiency in mathematics and French.

11 April 1873 During a peace council with the Modoc Indians, who have been holed up in the lava beds of northern California, Brig. Gen. E. R. S. Canby is shot full in the face by Kintpuash (Captain Jack) and then stabbed repeatedly until he dies. Following the treacherous act, the Modoc escapes — only to be caught and hanged later.

24 November 1873 Barbed wire, which will have significance in future wars, is patented. Its applications had been foreshadowed during the Civil War, when Union soldiers had stretched wires between stumps and trees which served to stall troops. The initial use of these entanglements — which usually consisted of telegraph wire — occurred 29 November, 1863 during the Knoxville, Tennessee campaign.

2 June 1875 The first telegraph line into Indian Territory is completed; it stretches from Fort Richardson, Texas to Fort Sill in Oklahoma territory. The line had been built by the 4th Infantry under the direction of Lt. Adolphus W. Greely, who will later become a full general, a polar explorer of some accomplishment and the Army's chief signal officer.

2 March 1876 The US House of Representatives recommends the impeachment of Secretary of War William W. Belknap of five charges, one of which is that he took a $1,500 bribe to permit John S. Evans to maintain a trading establishment at Fort Sill, Oklahoma. The articles of impeachment are sent to the Senate, which tries Belknap, even though he had resigned from office. He is found not guilty.

25 June 1876 At 12:07 p.m., the 7th Calvary of General George Armstrong Custer enters the valley of the Little Big Horn in Montana, where it is faced with thousands of Sioux and Cheyenne Indians. The battle lasts about and hour: "Long Hair"

Custer and the 210 men under his immediate command are wiped out, the only survivor of the massacre being a troop horse called Comanche. The 7th has a whole loses 263 killed and 59 wounded in what will be the Indians' greatest victory over the Army.

24 April 1877 Under the orders of President Rutherford B. Hayes, Federal troops are withdrawn from their quarters in New Orleans, Louisiana. This state is the last of the former Confederate states which is governed from the North; the withdrawal means that the Reconstruction Period is over.

6 May 1877 A procession of more than 1,000 Indians and 2,500 ponies approaches Fort Robinson in Nebraska and surrenders — throwing their rifles to the ground. In the van is Sioux Chief Crazy Horse, the object of pursuit by the Army since the Battle of the Little Big Horn. Bayoneted under a set of unexplained circumstances later, Crazy Horse's death ends an era in the Indian Wars.

14 June 1877 2nd Lt. Henry O. Flipper becomes the first black man to graduate from the US Military Academy at West Point. Flipper finished 50th in his class. He will go on to serve with the all-black 10th Cavalry in the West, and will be accused of making false statements and of

Above: Gen. George Custer's Crow scouts. Only a few months prior to this time, President Andrew Johnson had signed legislation reorganizing the Army and authorizing the hiring of Indian scouts on the Western frontier.

Above: Gen. George Armstrong Custer. During the Battle of the Little Big Horn, Custer and his 7th Cavalry were outnumbered three to one by Chiefs Sitting Bull and Crazy Horse with their well-armed, well-led Indians.

Below: The Winchester lever-action repeating rifle. Developed by Oliver F. Winchester, the 1873 model contained 40 grains of powder and could fire rapidly. It became popularly known as "the gun that won the West".

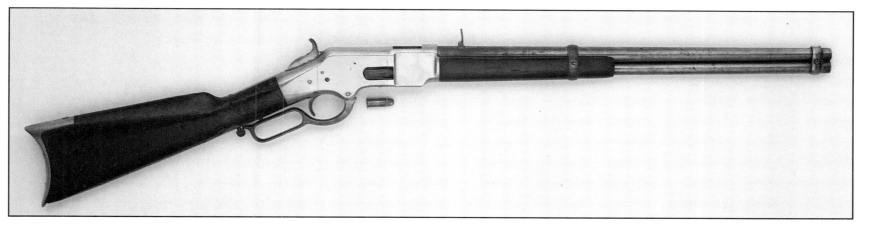

US Army Campaign Streamers Indian Wars

Miami	Jan 1790 — Aug 1795
Tippecanoe	Sep 21 — Nov 18, 1811
Creeks	Jul 27, 1813 — Aug 9, 1814;
	Feb 1836 — Jul 1837
Seminoles	Nov 20, 1817 — Oct 31, 1818;
	Dec 28, 1835 — Aug 14, 1842;
	Dec 15, 1855 — May 1858
Black Hawk	Apr 26 — Sep 30, 1832
Comanches	1867-1875
Modocs	1872-1873
Apaches	1873 and 1885-1886
Little Big Horn	1876-1877
Nez Perces	1877
Bannocks	1878
Cheyennes	1878-1879
Utes	Sep 1879 — Nov 1880
Pine Ridge	Nov 1890 — Jan 1891

embezzlement. Dismissed from the army in 1882, efforts to clear his record will be sucessful, but not until 1977.

5 October 1877 Weary of fighting, Chief Joseph of the Nez Perce Indians surrenders his tribe in the Bear Paw Mountains in northern Montana Territory. It takes place only 30 miles (48 km) from the sanctuary of the Canadian border and after a 1,300 mile (2,090 km) flight from four different army columns. The chief declares, "My heart is sick and sad. From where the sun now stands, I will fight no more forever".

17 January 1878 A commercial treaty with Samoa is signed and the harbor at Pago Pago is reserved as a coaling station for US naval vessels. The Samoan government, says the treaty, "will hereafter neither exercise nor authorize any jurisdiction within this port adverse to such rights of the United States or in restriction thereof".

18 June 1878 The US Life-Saving Service is established by an Act of the Congress. A $4,000 sum had been appropriated earlier in the century to equip lighthouses and places where ships might be driven ashore — but it remained unspent. In 1915, the Life-Saving Service will be combined with the Revenue Cutter Service; the resulting organization will be the United States Coast Guard.

28 June 1879 The first shipboard electric lighting system is installed aboard the *Jeannette* at Mare Island Navy Yard, San Francisco, California. It is among the latest equipment that is being put into the former Royal Navy gunboat, as it is being fitted out for a polar expedition. On that expedition, she gets caught in an ice pack and is crushed and sunk

under its pressures in a matter of months.

30 June 1879 One of the results of Gen. Custer's "Last Stand" at Little Big Horn is increased army attention to the theory and practice of marksmanship. One visible result of this is Gen. E.O.C. Ord's general order to the Department of California (he is commander), directing weekly target practice and reports that detail the number of shots per man, etc. The best shot is excused from a tour of guard.

18 April 1880 Capt. Henry Carroll, together with elements of the 9th US Cavalry, is surprised on Eyebrow Trail, Dog Canyon (in New Mexico) by warring Apache Indians. As a result, several soldiers are trapped and killed by falling boulders.

1 October 1880 John Philip Sousa accepts leadership of the Marine Band and becomes its 14th leader. He will be paid $94 a month to pull the band out of its doldrums, which he does with a flair. Before his tenure is over 12 years later, he is dubbed the "March King" and his and the band's reputation will have grown to great heights. Sousa dies on 6 March, 1932 at Reading, Pennsylvania.

9 November 1880 The *Ticonderoga* becomes the Navy's first steam-powered ship to circle the globe when she arrives back at Hampton Roads, Virginia after a two-year cruise. She had departed on 7 December, 1878. During her voyage she stopped at more than 40 ports and covered more than 36,000 miles (57,935 km). The

Below: Clara Harlowe Barton. Much involved with caring for the sick and wounded during the Civil War, she performed most of the services during that time that would later be associated with the American Red Cross.

Ticonderoga's mission was to expand existing trade relations and establish new ones.

9 February 1881 Maj. Gen. George Miller Sternberg, the army surgeon general, discovers the pneumococcus germ as a result of long research. Sternberg, often called the father of American bacteriology, was a great scientific investigator; he made the first photomicrograph of the tubercle bacillus and did research on cholera, yellow fever and septicemia. He founded the Army Medical School in 1893.

25 April 1881 A statue cast by the government of Admiral David G. Farragut is accepted by President Garfield. Farragut was more than 60 years old when he became a Civil War hero and uttered the famous words, "Damn the torpedoes, full speed ahead", during the Battle of Mobile Bay in 1864. The ranks of vice admiral and admiral were created for him by the Congress.

21 May 1881 The American Red Cross is founded by Clara Barton and a few friends. Known as "The Angel of the Battlefield" for her work with the wounded during the Civil War, she learned of the International Committee of the Red Cross during the Franco-Prussian War. Under Barton's leadership, the Red Cross introduced the idea of taking supplies to soldiers — as in Cuba in the Spanish-American War.

3 November 1881 Four surfmen are hired by Station No. 10 of the Ninth Life Saving District at Louisville, Kentucky near the Ohio River. The station is commanded by Capt. William M. Devan, who has the honor of being the first commander of the first inland station of the US Coast Guard. Within four days, the unit makes its first rescue when it floats a stranded steamer (with 26 people on board) off the rocks.

16 May 1882 Samuel Powhatan Carter is made a rear admiral in the Navy, thus becoming the only American to ever attain the ranks of both rear admiral and major general of the army. A graduate of the Naval Academy, he stayed loyal to the Union and was brevetted as a major general in March 1865. Following the Civil War, he returned to the Navy and served until his retirement in 1882.

26 July 1882 The US accepts the terms of the Geneva Convention of 1864 for the care of the wounded, which had originally been signed by representatives of 16 European countries. It provides that sick and wounded should be cared for, that medical personnel and buildings be spared in war, and that a distinctive emblem such as the Red Cross be used as a symbol of identification.

3 March 1883 Steel vessels are authorized for the first time in the Navy. Generally regarded as the first truly modern ships to enter the Navy since the end of the Civil War, the four steel warships become known as the White Squadron. Protected by armored decks, the four ships are the cruisers *Atlanta*, *Boston* and *Chicago*, and the dispatch-vessel *Dolphin*.

6 October 1884 The Naval War College, a first for the US or any nation, is established at Newport, Rhode Island. Rear Admiral Stephen Bleecker Luce is named its first president. Luce organizes the college as a "place of original research on all questions relating to war and the statesmanship connected with war, or the prevention of war". It is the oldest continuing institution of its kind.

21 February 1885 The Army Corps of Engineers finishes construction of one of the best-known landmarks in the US (the Washington Monument in the nation's capitol), which is dedicated on this date. Almost 100 years went into the planning and execution of a fitting memorial to George Washington and it was finally turned over to the Army to be completed in 1876. The monument made of granite and faced with marble, is nearly 600 ft (183 m) high and weighs over 90,000 tons.

7 July 1885 A patent is received by G. Moore Peters of Xenia, Ohio, for a round table loading machine that will later be installed at his factory, the Peters Cartridge Factory, Xenia, Ohio. Patent number 321,848 is for machinery with which to load cartridges.

16 May 1886 An Act of Congress of this date provides that graduates of the US Military Academy will be commissioned 2nd lieutenants.

6 August 1886 Congress authorizes construction of the *Maine*, originally designated an armored cruiser, and the *Texas*, which in contrast is referred to as an "armored battleship" from the beginning. The immediate impetus to the appropriation is Brazil's acquisition of the British-built armored cruiser *Riachuelo*. The *Texas* and the *Maine* are considered the first American battleships.

Right: Chiricahua Apache prisoners seated on an embankment outside a railroad car in Arizona. The prisoners include (first row, third from right) Geronimo, who, along with his followers, was exiled to Florida.

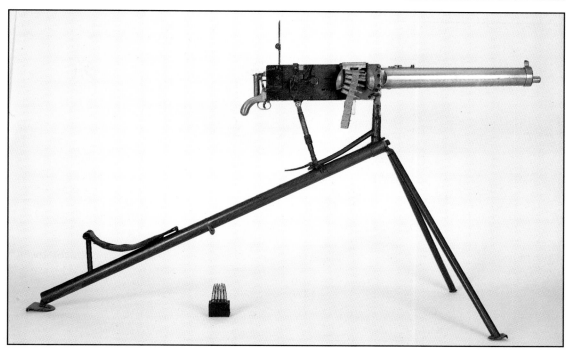

4 September 1886 Geronimo, the Apache Indian leader who unleashed a reign of terror throughout the Southwest US, is captured in Arizona by a force under Brig. Gen. Nelson A. Miles, after a chase of over 1,600 miles (2,500 km). The Army detachment that captures the Apache's band — by then reduced to 35 warriors — is led by Capt. Henry W. Lawton. Geronimo and his followers are sent to Florida, Alabama and finally to Fort Sill, Oklahoma, where they will remain. Geronimo dies in 1908.

1 March 1887 The Army Hospital Corps is formally organized under a General Order. The Hospital Corps when fully established is made up of hospital stewards, acting hospital stewards and privates.

Above: An early prototype of Hiram Maxim's machine gun, made in his London workshop. Its cycle of fire was fully automatic and self perpetuating. Each round was fired and ejected by the explosive force of the previous round.

17 May 1888 Massachusetts becomes the first state to organize a naval militia. Others follow, and eventually these units become part of the Naval Reserve.

21 June 1889 The Maxim gun, a forerunner of the machine gun, is successfully tested at Annapolis, Maryland. One of the guns fires 750 shots in a minute and the other 350. Hiram Maxim's brother witnesses the momentous event. Maxim had been demonstrating these weapons in England since 1884.

7 January 1890

Right: The cruiser *Baltimore* (C-3). Though ultimately to become the first minelayer in the Navy, as a cruiser she had role in helping to capture a garrison on Corregidor in Manila Bay during the Spanish-American War.

7 January 1890 The ship *Baltimore* (Cruiser Number 3), with Captain W. S. Schley in command, is commissioned. She will become the first minelayer in the Navy when converted to that specialist role at the Charleston Navy Yard in South Carolina. Following her extensive conversion, she was recommissioned on March 8, 1915, and during the next two years carried out a series of mining experiments along the Atlantic coast.

23 January 1890 The first torpedo boat in the navy, the *Cushing* (TB-1), is launched at Bristol, Rhode Island. She is attached to the aptly-named Squadron of Evolution and equipped for experimental work with torpedoes. In her only combat experience, she will capture four small vessels during the Spanish-American War and help with the capture and burning of a 20-ton schooner.

8 August 1890 Swedish inventor Captain John Ericson dies in New York City on this day. Among other contributions to the Navy, Ericson developed the ironclad *Monitor* at a cost of $275,000. A monumental sendoff for the inventor is in store. On 23 August, a host of Navy ships, each flying the colors at half mast, joins with numerous tugs and ferries to send him off in the *Baltimore*, which takes his body home.

15 December 1890 Sitting Bull, Sioux Indian chief, is shot and killed by soldiers in South Dakota. He had been ordered arrested because it was felt he had incited religious agitation among the Sioux. Widely known, Sitting Bull was involved in his first

Above: The *Cushing* (TB 1), the first purpose-built torpedo boat to serve in the Navy. She was 140ft (42.67m) long and a narrow 15ft 1in (4.60m) abeam. The boat carried a crew of 22 men and featured a top speed of 23 kt.

conflict with the Army in 1863 after the Minnesota uprising. At Little Big Horn, he took no part in fighting Gen. Custer, but instead "made medicine".

29 December 1890 The last major battle between US troops and Indians — the Sioux — occurs at Wounded Knee Creek, South Dakota. As 500 7th Cavalry troopers move in to disarm Sioux

warriors of Winchester rifles, the Indians shoot at them at point-blank range. The soldiers return the fire and kill 150 Sioux and wound another 50; some 25 bluecoats are killed and 50 hurt.

9 March 1891 The Adjutant General of the Army's Office issues General Order 28, which authorizes the formation of eight troops of Indian cavalry and 19 companies of Indian infantry. By June of the following year, 837 braves — some of them former allies, like the Crow Indians, and many of them former enemies — have joined the ranks of the Army.

12 May 1896 The acting engineer's office of the Department of the Dakotas authorizes the formation of the 25th Infantry Bicycle Corps at Fort Missoula, Montana. The corps is designed to provide soldiers with simple, fast and reliable transportation. Second Lt. James A. Moss is named commander and becomes the first man to command a cycle corps as well as the only white man in the all-black outfit.

8 February 1898 The Army establishes a safety zone in Alaska so life and property may

Left: The victors of Battle of Wounded Knee Creek. One of the sparks that set off the battle: Sioux scouts — not cavalrymen — were sent into disarm the Indians. This aggravated an already hostile situation.

be protected during the Gold Rush. Four companies of the 14th Infantry will be sent to Dyea and Skaguay to preserve law and order. The government acts on information that the rush to the gold fields had attracted hundreds of lawless characters and that the troops were absolutely necessary to prevent trouble.

15 February 1898 The American battleship *Maine* is blown up in Cuba, killing 260 of the 358 aboard. She had been sent there to "protect life and property" after riots in Havana earlier in the year endangered American lives on the island. Technical experts conclude the *Maine* was sunk by partial explosions in her magazines, but could not say what or who caused it. Despite assurances by the Spanish, the loss of the *Maine* becomes the proximate cause of the Spanish-American War.

17 March 1898 The *Holland* (SS-1) is launched. The first submarine in the Navy, it is commissioned into the service on 12 October, 1900 and towed to Annapolis where she is used to train cadets of the Naval Academy as well as the officers and enlisted men from the fleet ordered there to prepare for operations with other submarines. Lieutenant H.H. Caldwell is named the first commanding officer of the *Holland*.

25 March 1898 Assistant Secretary of the Navy Theodore Roosevelt recommends to his superior that he appoint two officers "of scientific attainments and practical ability" who, with representatives from the War Department, will be able to examine Professor Samuel P. Langley's "flying machine". They are to report upon its potential for use in the conduct of war.

21 April 1898 The Spanish-American War officially begins. It is over in a few months — ended by the treaty of Paris of 10 December, 1898 — and the US gains control of Cuba, Guam, and the Philippines. It is not much of a war as the 19th century goes. The Navy loses 18 men killed and 67 wounded; the Army suffers 4,000 casualties, but more than half of these are from fever. There are 1,500 wounded.

22 April 1898 The first shot of the Spanish-American War is fired by the gunboat *Nashville* (PG 7) across the bow of the Spanish steamship *Buena Ventura* off Key West, Florida. The *Nashville* goes on to capture four Spanish vessels within the next three months and helps cut off the undersea telegraph near Cienfuegos.

24 April 1898 Spain declares war on the US after rejecting America's ultimatum to withdraw from Cuba. The sinking of the battleship *Maine* (BB 10) in Havana Harbor, Cuba, was the immediate cause of this war, even though the cause of the explosion was never positively established.

1 May 1898 Commodore George Dewey gives his famous command, "You may fire when you are ready, Gridley", as American ships prepare to destroy the Spanish fleet at Manila Bay in the Philippines. His words are spoken to Captain Charles V. Gridley at 5:30 am aboard the flagship *Olympia*. Rapid, accurate fire sinks all 10 ships of the Spanish fleet before noon with little or no damage to American vessels.

11 May 1898 Ensign Worth Bagley is the first naval officer to be killed in action in the Spanish-American War. The action occurred in Cardenas Harbor between Spanish gunboats and shore batteries and the blockading vessels of the US fleet — including the torpedo boat *Winslow* — aboard which Bagley served. Fireman first class George B. Meek is also killed, the first enlisted casualty of the war.

Above: John Philip Holland poses for photographs in the conning tower of his submarine *Holland*. Built by the Crescent Shipyard, Elizabeth, New Jersey, she had a six man crew and was capable of 2 kt submerged.

Below: The battleship *Maine*, which was blown up in Havana Harbor. The slogan "To hell with Spain, remember the Maine" became a popular cry throughout America. War was declared on Spain two months later.

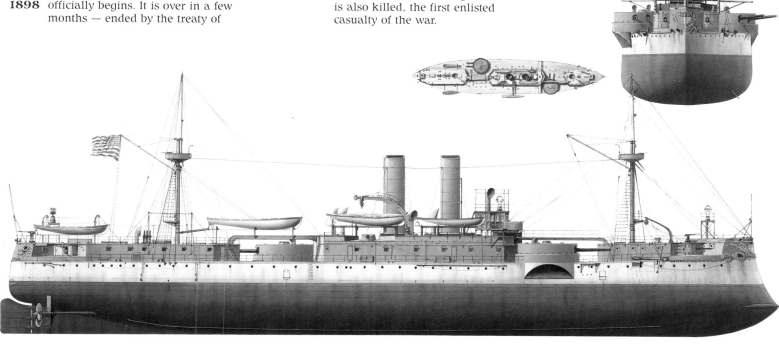

Spanish-American War (April — August, 1898)

The Spanish-American War has been the shortest and least costly war in US history. However, it marked the country's emergence as a world power with major interests in the Caribbean and Pacific areas.

Its immediate cause was the explosion of the battleship *Maine* in Havana on 15 February, 1898, although the American people were already highly excited over Spanish cruelty in suppressing a recent Cuban revolt. The mysterious explosion — Americans claimed it was sabotage, the Spanish called it an accident — killed 260 American sailors in all.

The actual cause of the explosion was never determined. However, American public opinion was inflamed over the incident and "Remember the Maine" became the battle cry of the Spanish-American war.

The Navy found itself in excellent shape for the conflict, largely due to a modernization program it had undertaken a decade earlier. It could count on 69 warships of all types — including four first-class battleships — at the outbreak of hostilities. They were also well-positioned to undertake operations around the world; the Pacific squadron was in Hong Kong and the Atlantic force was based in Florida.

The Army numbered around 28,000 men. They were considered well prepared, even though they had never trained for combat in units higher than the regimental level; however, they were not considered prepared as a land force to fight a major war overseas. The National Guard in its turn numbered about 100,000 men, but their equipment was generally scarce or obsolete.

Regulars were equipped with Krag-Jorgensen rifles that used smokeless powder; National Guard regiments were still using Springfield rifles with black powder ammunition. Manpower was quickly increased in the regular Army to 65,000 and the call went out for 125,000 volunteers. This number was soon raised to 267,000.

The peak active duty strength of the Army was 209,714 in June 1898. The total number of persons serving in the war in all the services was 306,760 (Army 280,564, Navy 22,875 and Marines 3,321).

Probably the most serious problems for the Army in what could almost be called a "come as you are" war were the lack of any mobilization plan, a unified higher staff, and experience in carrying out joint operations with the Navy.

Ranged against the US forces were 155,302 Spanish regulars and 41,518 Cuban irregulars. The Naval balance favored the US, as Spain had a total of 49 warships of all classes. Moreover, many of its ships were old and improperly equipped.

Unlike previous American wars, the Spanish-American War was one in which the Navy played a dominant role. In fact, the Army conducted only three campaigns, only one of which — Santiago — involved serious fighting with any great numbers.

The Navy won the truly decisive battles of the war. On 1 May, the Pacific Squadron under Commodore George Dewey sailed into Manila Bay in the Philippines and routed the Spanish fleet. At a cost of seven wounded, Dewey's squadron took out three ships, killed 167 Spanish sailors and wounded 214.

This essentially ended Spanish resistance in the Philippines since the loss of the fleet meant the troops ashore could not be resupplied. Dewey stayed moored in Manila Bay until the first American troops arrived on 30 June, 1898.

Sea power also played a major role in the Santiago campaign. The campaign got under way on 22 June, 1898 when an expeditionary force under the command of Maj. Gen. William R. Shafter landed at Daiquiri with 17,000 men. They were

Above: Theodore (Teddy) Roosevelt and his Rough Riders. Just prior to the famous ride up San Juan Hill, Roosevelt and Lt. John J. Pershing with two black cavalry regiments had successfully driven the Spanish off Kettle Hill.

Above: After the Rough Riders had taken San Juan Hill, the task began of securing the position against counter attack. Trenches and gun emplacements were created, this particular position featuring the oddly named dynamite gun.

bolstered by about 5,000 Cuban rebels.

The primary land battle of the war — the charge up San Juan Hill — took place during this campaign around the city of Santiago de Cuba. It was during this particular engagement that future president Lt. Col. Theodore Roosevelt and his Rough Riders distinguished themselves.

Conditions in Santiago itself deteriorated and the Spanish fleet — blockaded in the harbor by American ships since 19 May — moved to escape on 3 July. The blockading American squadron gave chase; all of the Spanish ships were sunk, driven ashore or completely disabled. On 16 July, the Spanish surrendered.

Service and Casualties in the Spanish-American War (1898)

	Army	Navy	Marines	Total
Number Serving	280,564	22,875	3,321	306,760
Battle Deaths	369	10	6	385
Other Deaths	2,061	—	—	2,061
Wounds not Mortal	1,594	47	21	1,662

Another operation was taking place at the same time and involved the conquest of Puerto Rico. More than 3,000 soldiers under the command of Gen. Nelson Miles landed on the island on 25 July. They were soon reinforced by another 10,000 soldiers.

A few skirmishes occurred, resulting in a total of 3 casualties and 40 wounded for the US forces. Fighting ended on 13 August when the news of the signing of the peace protocol finally reached the island.

Tropical diseases such as yellow fever claimed many times the death toll of battle. Parenthetically, at the beginning of the war, the Army had been seeking 10,000 men "possessing immunity for diseases incident to tropical climates" — for a unit called the "Immunes". A total of 385 men died in battle during the war (369 Army, 10 Navy and 6 Marines), but

another 2,061 died as a result of disease and accidents. There were 1,662 men wounded in action.

Hostilities in the war — which cost about $250 million — ended on 12 August, 1898 under terms of a protocol. The peace treaty (the Treaty of Paris, signed 10 December 1898) formally ending the conflict was approved by the Senate on 6 February, 1899.

The US established a temporary military administration in liberated Cuba that was to last until 1902, but the most important outcome of the conflict was that the US began to acquire possessions away from its shores in key areas of the world. It would now play a much more important role in the Caribbean and the Far East through Puerto Rico, Guam and the Philippines, which came under US control under terms of the peace treaty.

An interesting footnote: the UK stood almost alone among European nations during the conflict, sympathy to the American cause. This symbolized a rebirth of solid relations between America and the mother country foreshadowed a 20th century with cordial relations and alliances that carried through several major crises and two world wars.

Key Battles: Spanish American War (1898)

Manila Bay	May
Santiago de Cuba I	June
Las Guasimas	June
El Caney	June
San Juan Hill	July
Manila Hill	July

Above: During the final days of the Spanish-American War, men of the Signal Corps under the guidance of their officer, extend telegraph lines from the trenches during the American force's advance on Manila.

3 July 1898 The Navy defeats the Spanish fleet in the harbor at Santiago, Cuba, as it tries to run a blockade during the Spanish-American War. The concentrated fire from American ships is withering; within four hours of the beginning of the attempt, every fleeing ship is either sunk or forced ashore in flames. The Spanish lose 323 killed, while and the Americans lose one — a sailor aboard the *Brooklyn*.

12 August 1898 The Spanish-American war ends as Spain signs the US peace protocol. "Remember the Maine" had been the rallying cry for this war, whipped up by what is called the "yellow press".

3 June 1898 The Congress authorizes the award of the Dewey Medal to the officers and men who participated in the Battle of Manila Bay, which makes it the first official American campaign medal.

1 July 1898 During the Spanish-American War, Col. Theodore Roosevelt and his "Rough Riders" wage a victorious assault up San Juan Hill in Cuba — one of the two decisive land battles in the war in that theater. Supported by Gatling guns, the heavily-defended hill was ultimately secured but at great cost. American soldiers suffered 1,500 casualties; the Spanish 605.

1 July 1898 An American Expeditionary Force lands at Manila, Philippines during the Spanish-American War. It consisted of 115 officers, 2,386 enlisted men and was under the command of Gen. Wesley Merritt. The force had sailed for the Philippines from San Francisco in three ships on 25 May. When it arrives, Merritt and Commodore Dewey demand that Manila surrender, which it does after a bombardment on 13 August.

Above: Marines fighting insurgents in the Philippines in 1899. The US sent 70,000 men to deal with the insurrection. Organized resistance against the US continued until 1899, with guerrilla warfare continuing through to 1902.

10 December 1898 The Treaty of Peace is signed at 8:45 pm in Paris, ending the Spanish-American War. The Philippines are ceded to the US for $20,000,000, which prompts President McKinley to say they are "not to exploit but to develop, to educate, to train in the science of government". Puerto Rico and Guam are also turned over to the US and Spain agrees to give up any claims she may have to Cuba.

4 February 1899 The Philippine Insurrection begins when US troops are attacked by Filipinos along the San Juan River. Sparked by the demand for independence and led by Emilio Aguinaldo, the Insurrection is a continuation of the Filipino's struggle against their Spanish masters that had been going on since 1892. It will become a morass and last for several more years. The cost of the action to the US is 4,000 dead; to the Filipinos, 20,000. Its financial cost is put at $170 million.

Below: The Marine detachment from the *Brooklyn*, which distinguished herself at Santiago. The Spanish lost their entire fleet, with 323 dead and 151 wounded. The US suffered 1 dead, 1 seriously wounded.

Left: Allied troops on parade at a victory parade in Peking after the successful suppression of the Boxer Rebellion. The US used its portion of the indemnity money paid by China to educate Chinese students in the US.

Above: Commanders of the International Force, China, 1900-1903. Russian, British, French, Japanese and US detachments were part of the Expeditionary Force that was formed to go to the relief of the foreign legations in Peking.

26 May 1900 War Department General Order No. 155 implements legislation passed by the Congress establishing an Army War College for regularly commissioned officers. A sum of $20,000 had been authorized to start the college. Its first class of officers will convene four years later and complete the school's courses on May 1, 1905. Its first president was Maj. Gen. Samuel B. M. Young.

13 July 1900 The walled city of Tientsin, China, is stormed by Allied troops during the Boxer Rebellion, with the American contingent consisting of 1,021 men of the 1st Marines and 9th Infantry. The overall effort is

Above: Marines in Peking in 1900 during the height of the Boxer Rebellion. They were part of the First Relief Expedition, a small allied force of some 2,000 marines and sailors, which included 112 Americans.

the Navy. Capable of remaining submerged for nearly two hours, she is 53 ft 11 in (16.43 m) long and 10 ft 3 in (3.12 m) in beam. She was built by the John P. Holland Torpedo Boat Company of New York at a cost of $150,000.

Below: The shape of things to come? Old and new meet in October 1901 as the submarine *Holland* berths at the New York Navy Yard. Facing her is the battleship *Retvisan*, of the Imperial Russian Navy.

2 March 1899 Congress authorizes the position of Admiral of the Navy in legislation that will result in Dewey becoming the highest ranking member of the US armed forces and the first to occupy this position. Voted in recognition of his service to the country, the legislation authorizes pay of $13,000 per year and a 17-gun salute. It also waives mandatory retirement age.

4 January 1900 Beginning date of Cavite Campaign (second phase) in the Philippine Insurrection. The campaign ends on 9 February, 1900. A legacy of the Spanish-American War, the Philippines had been riddled by insurgency since the departure of the defeated Spaniards. More than 100,000 American troops take part in handling some phase of the Insurrection, which was formally declared ended on 4 July, 1902.

11 April 1900 The *Holland* (SS-1) becomes the first submarine to be accepted by

US Army Campaign Streamers Philippine Insurrection

Manila	Feb 4 — Mar 17, 1899
Illoilo	Feb 8-12, 1899
Malolos	Mar 24 — Aug 16, 1899
Laguna de Bay	Apr 8-17, 1899
San Isidro	Apr 21 — May 30, 1899;
	Oct 15, — Nov 19, 1899
Zapote River	Jun 13, 1899
Cavite	Oct 7-13, 1899;
	Jan 4 — Feb 9, 1899
Tarlac	Nov 5-20, 1899
San Fabian	Nov 6-19, 1899
Mindanao	Jul 4, 1902 — Dec 31, 1904;
	Oct 22, 1905
Jolo	May 1-24, 1905;
	Mar 6-8, 1906; Jun 11-15, 1913

under the command of British Brigadier General A.R.F. Dorward, DSO. It is the first time since the Revolution that Americans joined with other powers in an allied military operation.

2 February 1901 The Army Nurse Corps is established, with some 202 charter members who will form the first component of women in the armed forces. Nurse appointments are for three years, the pay is $40 a month, with chief nurses earning more. The uniform consists of a waist and skirt of suitable white, adjustable white cuffs, Bishop collar, white apron and cap. Two-year tours are established for overseas duty.

2 February 1901 The Philippine Scouts are established. Congress authorizes the president to enlist Filipinos for service and to organize them as scouts in military units under US Army officers. By 1921, there will be 7,000 Philippine Scouts and by the early days of World War II, they represent a third of the army contingent on that island and the core of its mobile defense forces.

2 February 1901 The Congress passes the Army Reorganization Act, which increases the 25 regular infantry regiments to 30 and the 10 regiments of cavalry to 15. The artillery regiments are dissolved to make way for an artillery corps of 30 batteries of field and 126 companies of coast artillery. With three battalions of engineers, the authorized strength of the new regular Army is 88,619.

1 January 1902 The traditional blue uniforms of the Army are discarded in favor of olive drab. The Spanish-American War experience had taught that blue was too deadly a target. Blue had been the official color of army uniforms since 1784 — although gray and brown were used by US soldiers during the War of 1812. The move to the olive drab represented a codification of existing policy.

20 May 1902 The US ends its occupation of Cuba. Maj. Gen. Leonard Wood had served as military governor of the island and had been responsible for modernizing the school system, and for establishing a new constitution and body of laws. Wood turns over his executive power to the popularly-elected new president of Cuba, Tomas Estrada Palma, as 15,000 visitors stream through Havana.

24 November 1902 The torpedo boat destroyer *Bainbridge* is commissioned. Of 420 tons displacement, she is 250 ft (76.2 m) in length, carries a crew of 75, and has a speed of 29 kt. She is considered the first US destroyer — and, in fact, carries the designation Destroyer No. 1. The *Bainbridge* served on patrol and convoy duty in World War I (until July 1918), when she returned to the US.

22 January 1903 The Hay-Herran Treaty is signed, which provides rights to the Panama Canal from Colombia. A 100-year lease is included on a 10-mile (16 km) wide strip in the Panamanian province in Colombia. The price is $10,000,000 and the annual rental is $250,000. When the Hay-Buneau-Varilla treaty is signed later in the year, permanent rights are obtained. "I took the Canal", boasts President T. Roosevelt.

21 February 1901 Roosevelt is among dignitiaries present as the cornerstone is laid for the US Army War College at the Washington Barracks. There are about 1,000 troops present for the ceremony. Says Secretary of War Elihu Root: "Not to promote war, but to preserve peace by intelligent and adequate preparation to repel aggression, this institution is founded".

23 February 1903 Roosevelt signs a lease with Cuba for Guantanamo Bay, which establishes US control over the present naval base at that location. The site is selected because of its magnificent harbor — almost the entire US fleet can lie at anchor there — and because it is well sheltered, easily accessible to large ships and commands the Windward Passage.

23 June 1903 The Springfield rifle — which became the first semiautomatic American rifle — is adopted for use by the Army. Probably influenced by the experience of the Spanish-American War and the lessons of the Anglo-Boer War, the Army felt the time had come for a short universal rifle for the troops. It proved a durable weapon, and was even used with success as a sniping rifle in World War II.

17 December 1903 Orville Wright makes the world's first powered, manned, heavier-than-air flight. A coin toss on Kill Devil Hill, determines that he, not brother Wilbur, will make the flight in the Wright Flyer, which lasts 12 seconds and 102 ft (31 m) at 22-27 mph (35-43 kmh). There were actually four flights made that day, but first is the one that goes down in the history books.

7 October 1904 The *Nebraska* (BB 14) is launched at Seattle, Washington, the first

Above: The Springfield rifle. An adaptation of the German Mauser, it became in time the first American semiautomatic rifle. The design of such a rifle had been proposed by the Army Chief of Ordnance in 1900.

Right: The Springfield first became popular as a sniping rifle in World War I. Being shown off to the camera by its owner in May 1918, this particular weapon boasts a fitted telescopic sight and full camouflage.

battleship to be built on the West Coast of the US. She joined the "Great White Fleet" in its famous round-the-world display of naval muscle at San Francisco, California, and arrived with it at Hampton Roads, Virginia, when it returned. She served as a principal escort ship and troop transport during World War I.

18 January 1905 The Wright brothers offer priority in negotiations to the US government should it have an interest in buying their flying machine. Representatives from the UK had already approached the Wrights and asked the price of the airplane. Maj. Gen. G. L. Gillespie responds to the brothers with a form letter stating that the government does not grant financial assistance to inventors.

13 May 1905 The last surviving veteran of the War of 1812, Hiram Cronk, dies at the age of 105. Cronk had enlisted in the Army at the age of 15 and served with the New York Volunteers at the defense of Sackett's Harbor with great valor. Cronk defied all the accepted rules for a long life: he drank at least a gallon (3.79 litres) of wine twice a month and was constantly chewing tobacco.

9 November 1906 The first foreign trip by a US president is made by Roosevelt on a Navy ship. He travels aboard the battleship *Louisiana* to visit the Isthmus of Panama to inspect the canal and will return to the US on November 26.

22 November 1906 SOS is adopted on this day as an international distress signal. A radio call for help, it is easy to send and receive and consists of three dots, three dashes and three dots. Although still in use today, in most cases it has largely been supplanted by the call "Mayday", a phonetic rendering of the m'aider (French for "help me") which is widely used by ships and aircraft in distress.

8 January 1907 Roosevelt orders all ships in the navy to be called "United States Ship" (USS). There was no official consistent terminology in use prior to this date. Nor was there consistent use of symbols for the ships themselves, although battleships were referred to as BB and submarines as SS. It won't be until July 17, 1920 that those designations will be officially authorized.

1 July 1907 The Aeronautical Division is established by the Army Signal Corps to take "charge of all matters pertaining to military ballooning, air machines and all kindred subjects". At the time, there were

US Monthly Pay Chart Army Enlisted Personnel: 1907

Sergeant Major and Quartermaster Sergeant Engineer Corps	$36
Ordnance Sergeant, Sergeant of Ordnance and of Engineer Corps	$34
Hospital Stewards (First Class)	$30
Sergeant Major and Quartermaster Sergeant of Cavalry, Artillery and Infantry	$23
Chief Trumpeter, Principal Musician, Saddler Sergeant, Hospital Steward (Second Class), First Sergeant (Cavalry, Infantry, Artillery)	$22
Hospital Steward (Third Class), Corporals of Ordnance and Engineer Corps	$20
Sergeants of Cavalry, Artillery, and Infantry; First Class Privates of Engineer and Ordnance Corps	$17
Corporals of Cavalry, Artillery and Infantry; Saddler; Farrier	$15
Trumpeter, Musician, Second Class Privates of Engineer and Ordnance; Privates of Infantry, Cavalry, Artillery	$13

very few aeronautical "subjects" of which to take charge. Between the end of the Civil War and 1907, the Signal Corps had acquired only eight balloons. Two more were purchased in 1907.

16 December 1907 The Great White Fleet departs from Hampton Roads, Virginia on its famous round-the-world voyage, a symbol of the emergence of the US as a major world naval power. Roosevelt is on hand aboard the

Below: The Great White Fleet. Before the fleet left on its 46,000-mile (74,000-km) voyage, it had been freely predicted that it would prove technologically impossible. The fleet did not suffer a single serious breakdown.

presidential yacht *Mayflower* to receive the salute of 16 battleships when the fleet departs; it will return to Hampton Roads one year and 60 days later.

23 December 1907 Brig. Gen. James Allen, the Army's chief signal officer, issues Specification No. 486 for a military airplane. It required that each bid be accompanied by a certified check for 10% of the price of the aircraft, which was $25,000. Interestingly, the War Department came under editorial attack for expecting so much from an airplane.

10 February 1908 A conditional first contract for an Army airplane is issued to the Wright brothers and two other sources. They are expected to deliver a plane at a cost of $30,000 to the Army Signal Corps on 2 August, 1909. Among requirements for the plane were that it be capable of a speed of 40 mph (64 kmh); be able to carry two people; have fuel to cover 125 miles (200 km); fly for one hour; and be controllable in any direction.

Below: The brothers Orville (left) and Wilbur Wright make repairs to one of their earlier aircraft. In 1909 they deliver the first military aircraft to the Army — and by doing so ensure that warfare will never be the same again.

Left: Lt. Frank Lahm (left) and Orville Wright — both in foreground — stand in front of one of the Wright-designed planes at Fort Myer, Virginia in 1909. Lahm was one of the original 24 military aviators created by the Army.

and Secretary of War William Howard Taft could not effect a compromise. The US then governed Cuba until the 1909 elections when Jose Miguel Gomez became president.

21 February 1909 The Great White Fleet completes its around-the-world voyage. Taking its name from the white hulls of its ships, the fleet undertakes the voyage to demonstrate the newly-established naval power of America. No cruise like it had ever been attempted by steam-powered battleships (there are 16 in the fleet), which departs and arrives from Hampton Roads.

6 April 1909 Commander Robert E. Peary reaches the North Pole, where he raises the US flag and claims it for the United States. Accompanied by Matthew Henson, Peary had started

8 March 1908 Three bids for nation's first military aircraft are approved by the Secretary of War. The Wright brothers bid $25,000 and promise to produce a plane within 200 days; A. M. Herring of New York City bids $20,000 and asks for 180 days; and J. F. Scott of Chicago bids $1,000 and asks for 185 days to deliver. After the other bids fall through, the Wrights build and deliver their plane.

23 April 1908 The Army Reserve is established. Its mission, as directed by the Congress, is to "provide trained units and qualified persons available for active duty in the armed forces in time of war or emergency and at such other times as the national security requires".

25 April 1908 The first turbine-propelled ship of the Navy — the *Chester* — is commissioned. She performs diplomatic duties during her career, including carrying a Congressional committee on a tour of North Africa (1909); guarding American citizens during the revolution in Mexico (1913); and carrying Allied Armistice Commissioners on inspection tours of German ports following World War I.

13 May 1908 "The Sacred Twenty", as the first nurses to report for duty in the newly-established Nurse Corps in the Navy are known, assume duties at the Naval Hospital, Washington, D.C. The only women in the Navy, they are officially considered neither officers nor enlisted personnel, but have military status and are subject to naval discipline. During World War I, some 1,835 Navy nurses see active duty.

9 September 1908 Lt. Frank P. Lahm becomes the first military airplane passenger during a 6.5 minute flight with aviation pioneer Orville Wright at Fort Myer, Virginia. The honor of being the first passenger in an airplane belonged to Charles Furnas, an employee of the Wright Brothers, who had gone up in the Wrights' plane at Kitty Hawk when the

plane was being readied for delivery to the government.

17 September 1908 Lt. Thomas Selfridge, Army Signal Corps, becomes the first military airplane casualty. He is riding as a passenger in a Wright Flyer with Orville Wright when one of its propellers fails in flight, damaging the airframe and causing the machine to plunge 75 feet to the ground out of control. Selfridge suffers a fractured skull and dies at 8:10 pm without recovering consciousness.

28 January 1909 The withdrawal of US troops from Cuba after the Spanish-American War is completed. For the second time an independent Cuban republic is established following occupation. Disorders had occurred after the US withdrawal in 1902

Right: Lt. Thomas E. Selfridge (left), first Army officer to lose his life in an airplane crash, with Orville Wright. This photograph was taken just prior to take-off on that fatal flight at Fort Myer, Va. *Below:* The wreck of the Wright plane. Orville Wright has already been pulled from the wreck. The plane is being lifted to get Lt. Selfridge out; he never regained consciousness.

Above: Commander Peary with his dogs during a polar expedition. His claim to have been the first to reach the North Pole was quickly disputed by Dr Frederick H. Cook, but leading authorities reject Cook's claim.

Above: The first military airplane, which was delivered to the Army by the Wright brothers in 1909. It is shown here at the Air Service's hangar at Fort Sam Houston, Texas, site of much pioneering work.

the expedition 36 days earlier. At the outset, the expedition had 17 Eskimos, 19 sledges and 133 dogs. When Peary and Henson arrive at the Pole, they are accompanied by only four Eskimos and 40 dogs.

2 August 1909 The Wright Flyer is formally accepted as the first Army airplane. A series of official acceptance trials for the Flyer were held between June 27 and July 30. Its first flight more than satisfied the contract's requirements for endurance (one hour) and lasts one hour, 12 minutes and 40 seconds. The brothers earned a $5,000 bonus with an average speed of 42.5 mph (68.4 kmh) — 2.5 mph (4 kmh) over the contract speed.

16 August 1909 A Navy Bureau of Equipment request for authority to advertise for construction of "two heavier than air flying machines" is disapproved by the Secretary of the Navy with this comment: "The Department does not consider that the development of an aeroplane has progressed sufficiently at this time for use in the Navy".

3 November 1909 Lieutenant George C. Sweet is taken up by Lt. Frank P. Lahm as a passenger in the first Wright army plane at College Park, Maryland. Sweet is credited with having been the first Navy officer to fly in an airplane. He had acted as official observer for the Navy when official acceptance trials for the Wright plane began.

2 March 1910 First Lt. Benjamin D. Foulois makes a solo flight over Fort Sam Houston, Texas, thus becoming the first Army aviator to make a military flight west of the Mississippi. It lasts 7.5 minutes in total. Foulois had earlier been directed by his superiors to take the army's only airplane and teach himself how to fly.

30 June 1910 Glenn Curtiss carries out the first experiment in aerial bombing at Keuka Lake, New York, when he drops dummy bombs (which are in fact 8-in/0.203-m pieces of lead pipe) into a ring of buoyed flags the shape of a battleship. Military witnesses see 15 of 17 hits go on target. One admiral is unconvinced. He says such attacks should not cause the "slightest uneasiness to the commanding officer of a well-ordered ship".

11 July 1910 The first US military submarine accident occurs off Provincetown, Massachusetts. The *Bonita*, later renamed the *C-4*, rams the gunboat *Castine*, forcing her to beach to prevent her from sinking. Under the command of Ensign Sloan Danenhower and with a crew of 15 men, the *Bonita* had risen from beneath the *Castine* and scraped her whole length across the bottom of the gunboat. There are no injuries from the incident.

20 August 1910 The first military firearm to be discharged from a United States' military airplane is a rifle used by Lt. Jacob Earl Fickel. He is in a two-seater Curtiss biplane at Sheepshead Bay near New York City when he fires a Springfield (Model 1903 caliber .30-06) at an altitude of about 100 ft (30 m) over a 3 x 5 ft (0.91 x 1.52 m) fixed target. Fickel fires on each of four passes over the target and actually scores two hits.

14 November 1910 Eugene Ely becomes the first pilot to fly an aircraft off a ship at Hampton Roads, Virginia. The 24-year old Ely nurses his Curtiss pusher biplane into the air from a

wooden platform that has been erected over the bow of the light cruiser *Birmingham* (CL 2). Ely will also make the first landing of an aircraft aboard a ship, landing on the *Pennsylvania* (CA 4) in January 1911.

23 December 1910 Lieutenant Theodore G. Ellyson receives orders to go to the Curtiss Aviation Camp at North Island, San Diego, California, and becomes the first naval officer to undergo flight training. Ellyson will pilot the first Navy aircraft, the A-1 Triad, in six months, as well as go on to make the first night flight by a naval aviator and do much other pioneering work in the growing field of military aviation.

Below: At the simple controls of his Curtiss Pusher biplane, sometime in 1911, the Navy's first aviator Lieutenant T.G. Ellyson undergoes his initial flight training at Curtiss Aviation Camp, San Diego, California.

Above: William Howard Taft, who served under President Roosevelt as his Secretary of War. On his advice, 5,000 troops (the Army of Cuban Pacification) were sent to Havana in 1906, where they stayed until 1909.

Above: Pilot Eugene Ely flies a Curtiss biplane off the stern of the armored cruiser *Pennsylvania* to great cheers from the crew. The person who made the first landing on a ship with an airplane also was the first to take off from one.

11 January 1911 President William Howard Taft asks the Congress to appropriate $5,000,000 to begin fortifying the Panama Canal. It is part of an overall amount of $12,475,328 that will be used, as the legislation states, for "sites, emplacements, guns, carriages, ammunition, power plants, searchlights" and other equipment to form a garrison on the Isthmus of Panama.

15 January 1911 At the San Francisco Air Meet (Tanforan Race Track), Lt. Myron Sidney Crissy, flying with Philip O. Parmalee in a Wright biplane, drops a heavily charged piece of shrapnel — a live bomb — on a target in a distant part of the field. The first experiment with live bombs from an airplane in flight, it proves a weight of up to 36 lb (16.33 kg) can be dropped within a 20-ft (6.1-m) area from 1,500 ft (455 m).

18 January 1911 At 11:01 a.m. pilot Eugene Ely, flying a Curtiss pusher biplane, lands on a specially-built platform on the stern of the *Pennsylvania*. The length of the platform upon which he lands is 119 ft (36.2 m). The commanding officer of the *Pennsylvania*, Captain C. F. (Frog) Pond witnesses the successful landing and says, "This is the most important landing of a bird since the dove flew back to the ark".

21 January 1911 The first radio-telegraphic transmission from an airplane is made. Using a transmitter of his own design, Lt. Paul W. Beck accomplishes the feat by sending the transmission from a Wright plane at an altitude of 100 ft (30 m) over Selfridge Field, Michigan, to a receiver that is 1.5 miles (2.4 km) away.

14 February 1911 US pistol (Cal. 45) M1911 is patented by John Browning, easily the most famous of the US firearm designers. The "Colt 45" is perhaps the most reliable self-loading pistol ever made, and will be used without change for the first 10 years it is in production. Modified in 1921, it was used in World War II, Korea and Vietnam — and remains in service even today.

17 February 1911 The seaplane is first demonstrated to the Navy by Glenn Curtiss. In the early days of aviation for that branch of the service, official judgments are still being made about the suitability of the airplane for a variety of naval roles. Curtiss taxies his plane alongside the *Pennsylvania* in San Diego Harbor, is hoisted aboard and then off again by the ship's crane. He then returns to base.

3 March 1911 The first aviation appropriation is authorized for the Army in the amount of $125,000. With that goes the authority to pay 51 personnel in the Aviation Section. Direct appropriations for the aviation field, with a slight lull in

1913, will climb. In 1915, for example, the figure will almost double to $200,000. On the eve of US entry into World War I, the amount will be $18 million.

11 April 1911 The Army establishes the first permanent flying school at College Park, Maryland, just outside the nation's capital, with a request that four hangars be constructed. It will begin operations in June of the year, with the aviators moving to

Below: The Army's Colt .45-caliber automatic pistol. The need for the weapon grew from the experience in the Philippines where a sidearm of this kind was needed to stop bolo-throwing fanatics in their tracks.

Augusta, Georgia during the winter months. After a second unpleasant winter at that site, Army pilots will be trained in San Diego, California.

12 April 1911 Lieutenant T. Gordon Ellyson, upon the recommendation of Glenn Curtiss and completion of his training at the Curtiss Aviation Center, North Island, San Diego, California, becomes the Navy's first pilot. He subsequently makes the first night flight by a naval aviator and registers a number of other firsts during his distinguished career.

8 May 1911 Requisitions are prepared by Captain W. I. Chambers for two Curtiss biplanes. Even though the Chief of the Bureau of Navigation did not sign the requisitions — thus making them official — the Navy considers this the birthday of naval aviation. It is the date which the A-I (also known as the "Triad" because it embraced the elements of land, sea and air) was ordered.

1 July 1911 Glenn Curtiss makes the first flight of the Navy A-1 at 6:50 p.m. The first aircraft built for the Navy is taken up for a flight of five minutes and achieves an altitude of 25 ft (7.6 m). There are three other flights made that same evening, one of which is by Curtiss with Ellyson as a passenger, and two by Ellyson alone.

14 December 1911 The *California* (CA 6), flagship of the Pacific Fleet, becomes the first major ship of the Navy to pass through the channel at Pearl Harbor. In order to accommodate naval ships, the Hawaiian Dredging Company had widened the channel in the harbor to 600 ft (183 m) at the ocean's entrance, a minimum of 500 ft (152 m) on the harbor's side, and to a depth of 35 ft (10.7 m). Work started in 1909.

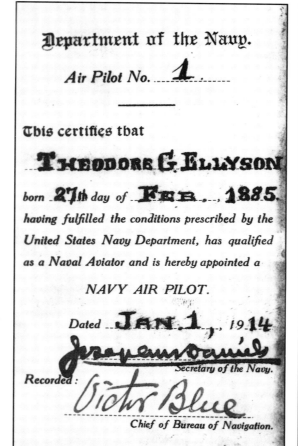

Department of the Navy.

Air Pilot No. **1**

This certifies that

THEODORE G ELLYSON

born **27**th day of **FEB.**, **1885**, having fulfilled the conditions prescribed by the United States Navy Department, has qualified as a Naval Aviator and is hereby appointed a

NAVY AIR PILOT.

Dated **JAN. 1**, 19**14**

Josephus Daniels
Secretary of the Navy.

Recorded: Victor Blue
Chief of Bureau of Navigation.

14 February 1912 The *Skipjack* (SS 24), later renamed *E-1*, is commissioned into the Navy. The first US submarine with diesel engines, her captain is Lieutenant (later Fleet Admiral) Chester W. Nimitz. The *Skipjack* is to become a pioneer underwater test boat, experimenting in such innovative developments as submerged radio transmission and the gyrocompass. She will also be the first US submarine to cross the Atlantic Ocean under her own power.

17 February 1912 Pilot physical examination requirements are first published by the army. It is a start. The medical officers of the time did not understand the unique medical aspects of aviation. In effect, if the

[SEAL.]

Received February 1, 1915.
T. G. Ellyson
(Rank) Lieutenant U. S. Navy.

Above: Aero Club of America Certificate No. 28, which it awarded to the first naval aviator, Lieutenant T. Gordon Ellyson. He tested the Navy's first flying boat, the C-1, at Lake Keuka in Hammondsport, N.Y., in 1912.

pilot seemed healthy, had no obvious defects of coordination, balance or vision, it was assumed he could fly as readily as he could drive a car.

23 February 1912 War Department Bulletin 2 recognizes a new rating of "Military Aviator". The test for the rating required that the candidates, among other things, attain an altitude of at least 2,500 ft (760 m), fly in a 15-mph (24 kmh) wind, take a passenger to at least 500 ft (150 m) and immediately make a dead-stick landing to within 150 ft (45 m) of a spot that had been previously designated.

1 March 1912 The first parachute descent from an aeroplane is recorded by Capt. Albert Berry, who jumps from a Benoist aircraft flown by Anthony Jannus over Jefferson Barracks, Missouri. Berry leaves his seat at 1,000 ft (300 m), slips under the aeroplane and climbs to a trapeze bar attached to the parachute. He jerks the rope, cuts it loose with a knife and begins his drop. The 'chute opens at 500 ft (150 m).

Left: Aviation pioneer Glenn Curtiss at the controls of a Curtiss Pusher. Curtiss's later achievements included the first US flight over a kilometre distance and the development of amphibious aircraft.

Left: The hospital ship *Solace*. One of the most up-to-date of its type in the years immediately prior to World War I, the introduction into its complement of a dentist in 1913 was a pioneering step in naval health care.

12 November 1912 Lieutenant Ellyson succeeds in getting his Curtiss A-1 hydroaeroplane into the air as part of the first successful catapult launch in the service's history. The catapult launch takes place from a specially converted barge securely anchored in the Anacostia River near the Washington Navy Yard.

27 November 1912 A Curtiss F two-seat biplane (No. 15) becomes the Army Signal Corps' first flying-boat. The Army eventually purchases three and others are built for the Navy and for private pilots. The C-1, as it is designated by the Navy, is tested three days later at Hammondsport, New York, by Lt. Ellyson.

11 May 1912 Rear Admiral Bradley A. Fiske becomes the first officer of flag rank to be taken off and returned to his ship by a hydroaeroplane — a converted Wright B-1 landplane. Some 2,000 sailors from the battleships *Georgia* (BB 15) and *Rhode Island* (BB 17) cheer as the admiral leaves his flagship for the 10-minute flight at Salem, Massachusetts. Fiske is a strong advocate of the use of planes for scouting and other work.

19 May 1912 An outgrowth of the tragedy that befell the White Star liner *Titanic*, which struck an iceberg the previous month and sank with a loss of about 1,500 lives, is the first ice patrol. The cruiser *Birmingham* (CL 2) begins the patrol in the North Atlantic; out of this grows the International Ice Patrol (1914), responsibility for which will be ultimately shouldered by the Coast Guard.

22 May 1912 First Lieutenant Alfred A. Cunningham becomes the first Marine Corps officer assigned to flight instruction. Later designated Naval Aviator No. 5, he reports to the superintendent of the Naval Academy for "duty in connection with aviation" and is subsequently ordered to the Burgess Company, Marblehead, Massachusetts for flight instruction. This is the birthday of Marine Corps aviation.

5 June 1912 Lt. Col. Charles B. Winder of the Ohio National Guard becomes the Guard's first pilot. His unit had received the approval of the War Department for the training, for which he arrives on 12 March at Augusta, Georgia. Winder returned to College Park, Maryland, to complete his instruction and was issued FAI aviation certificate No. 130 for his accomplishments.

7 June 1912 Capt. Charles DeF. Chandler and Lt. T. D. Milling complete the first US firing of a machine gun from an airplane in flight. The gun is a ground type light weapon designed by Col. Isaac N. Lewis and the airplane a Wright B model. Flying at 250 ft (76 m), Chandler scores five hits and several near misses on the target — a piece of cheesecloth 6 x 7 ft (1.83 x 2.13 m) in size. The next day, he fires at a cloth target, scoring 14 of 44 shots.

5 July 1912 Capt. Charles DeForrest Chandler and Lts. Thomas DeW. Milling and Henry H. Arnold become the first fliers to qualify as "Military Aviators". They are presented certificates which consist of a few typewritten lines, signed by an officer in the Adjutant General's office, which states that a notation has been made in the officer's record that he is qualified for Military Aviator.

12 August 1912 Signal Corps airplanes fly during Army maneuvers for the first time at Bridgeport, Connecticut. This gives the War Department its first chance to test how effectively airplanes can work with ground troops. Three planes are used in the maneuvers, with radio tests and reconnaissance efforts used to report the location, composition and strength of the "enemy".

26 October 1912 First trials in America to determine the ability to spot submarines from the air begin under the direction of Lieutenant John H. Towers. The tests will not be completed until 18 December. Towers' conclusions: the best altitude for observation is about 800 ft (245 m) and, while submarines can be detected a few feet below the surface of the muddy Chesapeake Bay water, further tests are needed.

6 January 1913 Aircraft are used on fleet maneuvers by the Navy for the first time. An aviation camp is set up at Guantanamo Bay, Cuba, on Fisherman's Point. The entire aviation element of the Navy becomes involved in the exercises, which are designed to demonstrate the capabilities of the aircraft and to stimulate interest in aviation among fleet personnel during the eight-week event.

2 March 1913 Flying pay is first authorized at 35% over base pay for Army officers detailed to aviation duties. It goes to a maximum of 30 officers who were "actual fliers of heavier-than-air craft". This is interesting in comparison to the present system in operation, with its sliding-scale of up to $400 per month over base pay, an amount that goes up through the sixth year and then declines.

5 March 1913 As the result of a crisis on the Mexican border, Army aviation is alerted for possible action. The 1st Provisional Aero Squadron is formed with five pilots, 21 enlisted men and seven Wright pusher aircraft. They are shipped — by train — to Texas City, Texas, from Georgia, where they were training. The immediate crisis passes, but the unit joins the Pershing expedition against Pancho Villa four months later.

5 March 1913 Dr Harry E. Harvey becomes the first dentist to serve aboard a ship of the Navy when he is assigned to the *Solace*, a hospital ship. He will serve aboard her until October 1915.

26 March 1913 Floods in Ohio and Indiana lead to the Army Corps of Engineers being assigned responsibility for flood

Right: Construction work on the Panama Canal. This view of the acitivity was photographed in August 1910 and shows the west bank looking towards the north. The two lock-bypass tunnels can be clearly seen.

control — permanently. The flooding in Ohio, primarily in Dayton, prompts the governor to ask for 50,000 tents and 100,000 rations through the National Guard. Across the border, meanwhile, West Indianapolis is put under martial law; state troops are ordered to protect life and property.

7 April 1913 The first electrically propelled ship in the navy, the *Jupiter* (AC 3), is commissioned. She goes on to become the first naval vessel to cross the Panama Canal; to transport the first naval aviation unit (First Aeronautical Detachment) to France in 1917; and is ultimately converted to the first aircraft carrier, the *Langley* (CV 1), commissioned on March 20, 1922.

20 June 1913 Piloting the B-2 at 1,600 ft (490 m) over the water near Annapolis, Maryland, Ensign W. D. Billingsley is thrown from the aircraft and falls to his death — becoming the first fatality in naval aviation. A passenger riding in the plane with Billingsley, Lieutenant J. H. Towers, is also thrown from his seat, but manages to cling to the plane and fall with it into the water. He receives serious injuries.

5 October 1913 Under the supervision of Holden C. Richardson, the first trials of the Navy's first amphibian flying boat are conducted at Hammondsport, New York. The aircraft — called the OWL, for Over Water Land type and subsequently redesignated the E-1 — was an A-2 hydroaeroplane. The pontoon was replaced with a flying boat hull which contained a three-wheel landing gear.

7 October 1913 An Aeronautic Board is appointed by the Secretary of the Navy. Among other things, it

recommends establishing an aeronautic center at Pensacola, Florida; establishing an aviation office under the Secretary of the Navy; assigning a ship for training in operations at sea — as well as to test equipment; and the assignment of one aircraft to every major combatant ship.

30 December 1913 A communication milestone is marked when the Navy station at Arlington, Virginia, picks up the time flashed from the Eiffel Tower in France. The "time" was received at the Arlington Station at 6:40 a.m. The demonstration convinces the experts that news and information can be flashed around the world at any time by wireless.

25 April 1914 Lt. (jg) P.N.L. Bellinger, Naval Aviator No. 8, flies the Curtiss AB-3 flying boat from the *Mississippi* (BB 23) over the city of Vera Cruz, Mexico, to observe the site and conduct a preliminary search for mines in the harbor. It represents the first time an airplane has been flown into a combat zone by the Navy.

1 July 1914 The Office of Naval Aeronautics is officially formed to oversee the development of air operations in the Navy. It is the first formal recognition accorded aviation by that service. Within months, the title "Director of Aeronautics" also arrives and will be used to designate the Navy's officer in charge of naval aviation. Captain Mark L. Bristol will be the first man picked for the job.

11 July 1914 The first battleship to use fuel oil exclusively, the *Nevada* (BB 36) is launched at Quincy, Massachusetts. The arrangement of its main battery of 10 14-in (356 mm) guns is different from that on any other battleship, which is expected to provide more firepower. In Washington on the same day, it is announced two new battleships will be built, including the *Arizona* (BB 39), later a symbol of Pearl Harbor.

18 July 1914 The Aviation Section is created within the Army Signal Corps. A predecessor organization to the Air Force, it has six airplanes, 67 officers and 260 enlisted personnel. Its mission is to supervise "all military (US Army) aircraft, including balloons and aeroplanes, all appliances to said craft, and signalling apparatus of any kind when installed on said craft".

3 August 1914 Work on the Panama Canal is completed by the Army Engineers under Col. George W Goethals, a project made possible by the work

Left: The *Nevada* in April 1945 participating in the pre-invasion bombardment of Okinawa. She was one of 10 battleships in the task force, which also included 10 cruisers and 32 destroyers and destroyer escorts.

of Col. William Gorgas when he eliminated malaria and yellow fever from the Canal Zone. On this date, the steamship *Cristobal*, with full cargo and a large number of passengers, makes the first trip through the waterway.

6 August 1914 Under the command of Captain Benton Clark Decker, the cruiser *Tennessee* (CA 10) departs anchorage in New York with $5,867,000 in gold to aid Americans who are stranded in Europe by the outbreak of war. Plans call for the *Tennessee* to link up with the cruiser *North Carolina* (CA 12) and proceed to Europe. The ships will then split up and provide funds to Americans in England, France and the Mediterranean.

6 August 1914 Denis Patrick Dowd, Jr, sails to Europe to enlist his services in World War I, thus becoming the first American to sign up for the war. Dowd fought with the French Foreign Legion, found himself transferred to a line regiment, was wounded and then joined the Lafayette Escadrille. He was killed in 1916 when his plane crashed in a nose dive at Buc, near Paris.

12 October 1914 The *Jupiter* (AC 3) becomes the first naval vessel to transit the Panama Canal on her way from the West Coast, where she had bolstered Navy strength during the tense days of the Vera Cruz crisis, to Philadelphia, Pennsylvania.

1 January 1915 The Panama Canal, which had been built by the Army Corps of Engineers, opens. A French syndicate had tried to build the canal over the 10-mile (16 km) strip of land in the 1880s, but had not succeeded. When the US was approached to do the job, the Congress appropriated the money and President Theodore Roosevelt turned the job over to the Army. Col. George W. Goethals oversaw the eight-year effort.

7 January 1915 Mexican Pancho Villa and Gen. Hugh Scott begin negotiations in El Paso, Texas, to end fighting on the US-Mexican border. Scott, the Army chief of staff, was skilled at diplomacy and had previously recovered property confiscated by Pancho Villa.

28 January 1915 The US Coast Guard Service is created and the US Revenue Cutter Service ceases to exist. The missions of the newly-created unit remain unchanged. Of particular significance: the Coast Guard will no longer be under the control of the Treasury Department in times of war, but will be directly under control of the Navy.

Above: The *Lusitania* heads homeward on her last trip. This was probably the last photograph ever taken of her before she was sunk by a German submarine with the loss of 1,195 lives, a major factor in US entry into the war.

7 May 1915 The British passenger ship *Lusitania* is sunk by the Germans without warning and 128 American lives are lost. Munitions were being carried aboard according to the Germans, which the British deny. Secretary Franklin D. Roosevelt brands the action "murder on the high seas". The sinking alienates American opinion, which prior to the incident was one of strict neutrality.

5 November 1915 An AB-2 is launched from the cruiser *North Carolina* (CA 12) in the first shipboard catapulting of an airplane. Announcement of the successful effort is made by Franklin D. Roosevelt, at the time Assistant Secretary of the Navy. Lieutenant Commander H. C.

Left: This cartoon from the *New York Herald*, 1917 reflects the move of American opinion towards war. The Kaiser and the German Ambassador gloat beneath a monument to atrocities against Americans.

Below: A group photograph of the first graduating class of aviators at the Pensacola Naval Air Station. In early 1914, the Secretary of the Navy had announced that aerial navigation "must form a large part of our naval force . . ."

Mustin serves as pilot for the flight, which takes off from the stern of the *North Carolina* at Pensacola Bay, Florida.

19 November 1915 The first squadron cross-country flight in the Air Service begins at Fort Sill, Oklahoma; it will end 429 miles (706.5 km) later at Fort Sam Houston, Texas, on 26 November. Pilots for the flight were Lts. Thomas S. Bowen, Joseph E. Carberry, Carlton E. Chapman, Ira A. Rader and Thomas DeW. Milling, and Capt. Benjamin D. Foulois.

1 December 1915 The first Navy flying school opens at Pensacola, Florida, with a commanding officer, three instructors and 12 mechanics. They had moved there to the old Navy Yard in the Florida panhandle from the established training camp at Annapolis, Maryland, where much of early naval aviation history had been made. Meanwhile, Congress had voted its largest naval aviation appropriation ever — $1,000,000.

4 December 1915 The first admiral to receive the Medal of Honor is Frank Friday Fletcher. He receives the award for his distinguished performance under fire in engagements in Vera Cruz, Mexico. The senior officer present there, "he was at times on shore and under fire" during the operations, as stated in the citation. The battles took place on 21-22 April, 1914.

6 January 1916 Instruction starts for the first group of Navy enlisted men to receive flight training at the new school at Pensacola, Florida. By the end of the year, the station has a complement of "58 officers ... 431 enlisted men ... 33 seaplanes, one kite balloon, one free balloon, and one dirigible (and) was equipped to handle 32 student aviators, 32 student airmen and 64 mechanicians every six months".

17 January 1916 The strength of the Signal Corps Aviation Section as the US begins to approach hostilities in World War I consists merely of 49 personnel and 25 aircraft. That changes soon ... and radically. In the period from April 1917 to November 1918, the US Air Service will accept 11,754 American- and Canadian-built airplanes. In all, US defense forces will receive 19,068 aircraft for the war effort.

15 March 1916 The Punitive Expedition under Gen. John J. (Blackjack) Pershing crosses the Mexican border in pursuit of Pancho Villa and his forces. The expedition is mounted in response to a raid by Villistas on Columbus, New Mexico, where 18 Americans were murdered and eight wounded. President Woodrow Wilson orders the Army to take up pursuit to capture Villa and prevent further such raids into American territory.

16 March 1916 According to orders from the War Department, the 1st Aero Squadron prepares to support the Punitive Expedition to Mexico from its headquarters at Columbus, New Mexico. From here, according to its commander, the squadron "started immediately to assemble aeroplane equipment". Capts. Townsend F. Dodd and Benjamin Foulois will make the first reconnaissance flight into Mexico on this date.

15 April 1916 Based on highly satisfactory results from tests carried out this date, the Navy orders 3,500 Lewis machine guns, which become standard equipment for the Marine Corps. The army shortly orders 18,400 more. Designed by Col. Isaac N. Lewis, who turns over royalites estimated at $1 million to the government, the air-cooled weapon could fire between 300 and 700 shots a minute.

20 April 1916 The Escadrille Américaine is established as an American

Above: The commander of the Expeditionary Force sent by Washington to seek out and destroy guerrilla leader Pancho Villa, John J. Pershing leads his men across a Mexican river during the 1916 campaign.

volunteer unit flying with the French Aéronautique Militaire on the Western Front. It later becomes the famed Lafayette Escadrille. Many of the original pilots had first seen service with the French Foreign Legion. More than 200 Americans were trained through the *escadrille* by the French.

3 June 1916 President Wilson signs a bill that provides for a commissioned Veterinary Corps. A ratio is set up in the legislation that provides for one officer and 16 enlisted men for each 400 animals in the service. The law provides (in proper proportion) for 5 sergeants first class, 10 sergeants, 10 corporals, 40 farriers, 2 horseshoers, 1 saddler, 3 cooks and 129 privates.

Below: The Lewis machine gun, of the kind involved in the first firing of such a gun from an aircraft in the US. Lewis offered the gun to the US after the successful test but was unfortunately rebuffed in his effort.

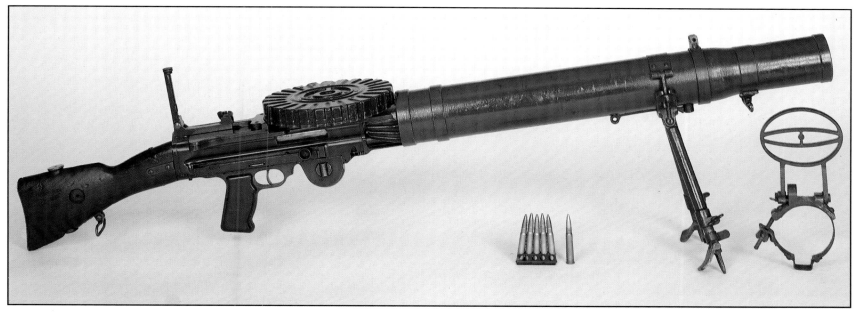

12 September 1916 Lieutenant T. W. Wilkinson, Jr., makes a test flight with the son of gyroscope inventor Elmer Sperry. Under automatic control and flying a set distance before diving, the test gives the lieutenant some insight into what an aerial torpedo (or missile) will do. "They are practically indestructible", he writes, "unless a well-aimed shot disables the engine or control devices".

6 January 1917 A Board of Army and Navy officers recommends the design and construction of the first US rigid airship to the Secretaries of War and the Department of the Navy. Funding for the Zeppelin-type aircraft is to be provided by the Navy and Army in equal amounts and a board of officers is set up to ensure that the most effective cooperation between the services is achieved.

3 June 1916 Under the authority of the National Defense Act of this year — an "act for making further and more effectual provision for the national defense and for other purposes" — the Reserve Officers Training Corps for the Army is established. Men were accepted for training in times of peace so they could take the place of other officers in the time of war.

18 June 1916 H. Clyde Balsley becomes the first American flyer to be shot down during World War I. A member of the Lafayette Escadrille, his fight over Verdun against terrific odds inspires the French air commandant to fly to the front to personally award Balsley a Military Medal with a War Cross. His wound is more serious than it first appeared, appeared, splinters of an explosive bullet had penetrated his body.

23 June 1916 Victor Emmanuel Chapman, flying with the famous volunteer fighter group Lafayette Escadrille, is the first American pilot to be killed in action when he is shot down near Verdun. Noted for his bravery, Chapman went to the rescue of a fellow pilot engaged with five Germans and was killed in mid air. In six weeks, Chapman had seven planes shot from under him and recorded four kills.

30 July 1916 German saboteurs blow up munitions on Black Tom Island near New York City, spreading panic and destruction throughout the city and its suburbs. Fourteen barges laden with high explosives go up. Thousands of people swarmed into the streets in all parts of the city, with the force of the explosion so great that plate glass windows as far away as Times Square were shattered.

29 August 1916 The Marine Corps Reserve is authorized. Within two days, Navy

Above: A shell from a German submarine hits a steamship in the Atlantic. The unrestricted submarine warfare policy carried out by Germany was one of the major reasons leading to US entry into World War I.

Department General Order No. 231 is issued, which informs "all persons belonging to the Navy" that such a reserve force is hereby established. It consists of five types of personnel: Fleet Marine Corps Reserve; the Marine Corps Reserve A; the Marine Corps Reserve B; the Volunteer Marine Reserve; the Marine Corps Flying Corps.

29 August 1916 The first Coast Guard Aviation Division is authorized, but no appropriation is provided until 1926. Although the Coast Guard did not obtain any planes until then, its interest in aviation began 10 years earlier when two of its pioneer aviators convinced the service of their use for search and rescue work. Its aviators served with the Navy during World War I.

29 August 1916 Composed of 150 officers and 350 enlisted men in addition to those already provided for by law in other branches of the navy, the Naval Flying Corps is founded. The legislation setting up the corps also establishes a Naval Reserve Force of six classes, including a Naval Reserve Flying Corps, surplus graduates of aeonautics schools and those Reserve Force members with aviation experience.

2 September 1916 The capability to transmit messages by radio from plane to plane is demonstrated by Lt. W. A. Roberts and Cpl. A. D. Smith, who send radio telegraph messages to Lt. H. A. Dargue and Capt. C. C. Culver. The planes were 2 miles (3.2 km) apart and over North Island, San Diego, California, at the time. The transmitter set was an SCR-51, which could send signals for several hundred miles.

9 January 1917 Germany declares a policy of unrestricted submarine warfare. Losses to German submarines (designated U-boats) will crest this year, with the Allies losing more than 2,600 ships — U-55 alone accounts for 226 ships for a total of 500,000 gross tons. An effective convoy system and entry of the US into the war (which gives the Allies bases on both sides of the Atlantic) help turn the tide.

30 January 1917 The Punitive Expedition under Pershing begins to withdraw from Mexico. Pershing has about 11,500 soldiers in the expedition, with approximately 10,000 in the area around Colonia Dublan. Some 170 empty trucks had been dispatched from Columbus, New Mexico, earlier in the month to support the withdrawal with orders to return any excess supplies along the communications lines.

3 February 1917 The US breaks diplomatic relations with Germany after its announcement of a policy of unrestricted submarine warfare. Germany's policy had been to sink the maximum number of British ships and to frighten neutral countries — particularly the US — from trading with the UK. But a system of convoys and new antisubmarine tactics and equipment combined to neutralize the threat.

17 March 1917 The Navy gets authorization to enlist women to perform yeoman's duties who become known, not surprisingly, as "yeomanettes". Besides serving in clerical and administrative tasks, they also perform as draftsmen, translators, munitions workers, camouflage designers and recruiters. In all, 11,275 yeomanettes serve their country during the course of World War I.

2 April 1917 Saying, "The world must be made safe for democracy", Wilson asks the Congress to declare war against Germany. World War I became the bloodiest, most widespread war the world had known to date and resulted in more than 30 million casualties, destroyed the old European order, and revolutionized modern warfare, particularly in the areas of tanks, machine guns and armed aircraft.

6 April 1917 The US enters World War I on the side of the Allies — including France, the UK, Italy, Russia and others. The opposition consists of the Central Powers — Germany, Austria-Hungary, the Ottoman Empire and others. The war sets great social and economic changes in motion and is essentially responsible for helping pave the way for World War II.

13 April 1917 The first warship propelled by a turbine electric drive, the battleship *New Mexico* (BB 40), is launched at New York City. She is commissioned one year later. The battleship will serve as escort for the home transport *George Washington* when it brings Wilson back from the Versailles Peace Conference in February 1919.

18 April 1917 The first encounter with a German U-boat takes place in the Atlantic. *Mongolia*, a steamer with a Navy armed guard aboard, is attacked by the submarine. *Mongolia* fires on

the attacker, wrecking her periscope and conning tower. She serves as a transport during World War I and makes 15 voyages to France.

19 April 1917 Three companies of Marines garrison the Virgin Islands, which the US has only recently purchased from Denmark. Coastal batteries will be manned by the Marines during World War I to guard against any German attempt to use the harbor facilities. The garrison will be withdrawn in 1931 when President Herbert Hoover turns the island over to civilian control.

24 April 1917 The Congress passes the "Liberty Loan Act" authorizing the Treasury to issue a public subscription for

Above: The *New Mexico* (BB 40) enters the locks of the Panama Canal. She had just served as escort for the ship bringing President Wilson home from Versailles and was on her way to become flagship of the Pacific Fleet.

$2 billion in bonds for World War I. Secretary of the Treasury McAdoo handles the subscription for 3.5% convertible gold bonds.

24 April 1917 William "Billy" Mitchell becomes the first American officer to fly over enemy lines. This Army officer and

Below: Brig. Gen. William (Billy) Mitchell, air power advocate. Although the war ended before he could carry them out, Mitchell's plans included strategic bombing of Germany and massive parachute invasions.

Below: A German painting showing the first U-boat war in the Atlantic. Though small and unsophisticated, these boats posed a terrible threat. In April 1917 alone, 430 Allied and neutral ships were sunk.

World War I (1917 — 1918)

The participation of the US in World War I marked America's emergence as a world power.

When war first broke out in August 1914 between the Allied and Central Powers, the US declared neutrality. Throughout 1915 and 1916, the country struggled to maintain that neutrality and President Woodrow Wilson offered to mediate a settlement to the conflict.

But the growing German submarine menace and worldwide publicity surrounding German atrocities in Belgium and northern France gradually pushed American sentiment toward the Allies. The sinking of the British liner *Lusitania* by a German U-boat with the loss of 1,198 lives — including 124 Americans — brought stiff protests from the American government.

The German submarine campaign was highly effective. In 1915, 600 ships were sunk. By the end of 1916, the toll rose to 1,100 and by 1917 escalated to more than 2,600.

In January 1917, the Germans had declared unrestricted submarine warfare. The US broke diplomatic relations with Germany in January and started arming its merchantmen in February. War was declared on 6 April.

The US Navy was the third largest in the world at the time. Its ships were modern and manned by professionals. They quickly proved themselves up to the task of convoying the American Expeditionary Force to France.

The US Army numbered 210,000 men, which included 127,000 regulars, 5,000 Philippine Scouts and 80,000 National Guardsmen. Throughout 1917, the Army continued to grow. A draft was instituted and 2.8 million men were eventually inducted into service.

On 26 June, 1917, the first contingent of US troops reached St Nazaire, France, vanguard of the more than 2 million men who would be sent to France before the war ended.

They were welcomed by the Allies since the revolution in Russia and the subsequent Treaty of Brest-Litovsk had freed millions of German troops for action on the Western Front. In the French and British view, only the arrival and piecemeal use of American battalions could stem this tide.

The commander of the American Expeditionary Force, General John J. (Blackjack) Pershing fought against this piecemeal use of American troops. In face of pressure from the Allies, he held that American troops would themselves form an army and fight under American commanders and American orders. And fight they did, after receiving proper training.

American military leaders acknowledged from the beginning that training was seriously deficient for the kind of warfare to be faced on the Western Front, and thus devised an intensive program to deal with the problem. In consequence it was not until October 1917 that parts of the US 1st Division saw action on the line; nor would it be until early in 1918 that US troops were deemed ready enough to move into a quiet sector of the trenches.

The last German offensives of the war were to end in July 1918, but not before failing in their primary mission of winning the war before American reinforcements could be trained and brought to bear at full strength.

Allied counter-offensives followed. American soldiers formed the bulk of the troops reducing the Marine and St Mihiel salients. In the offensives that led to the end of the war, Americans fought through the Argonne Forest to the Meuse River. Meuse-Argonne was the greatest battle yet fought by the Army. Almost 1.25 million troops participated in the offensive and casualties were high — 125,000 of all types — but the victory was without question.

It was successes like this on the field of battle, combined with growing disquiet within Germany, that led to an armistice, which effectively stopped the fighting on 11 November, 1918 at 11 a.m.

From the American perspective, the

Above: Lt. Col. George S. Patton Jr., at the 1st Tank Center at Langres, France. The tank was then a new weapon. Patton commanded the 304th Tank Brigade at St Mihiel and in the Meuse-Argonne offensive.

I WANT YOU FOR U.S. ARMY
NEAREST RECRUITING STATION

Above: One of the most famous recruiting posters in military history, originally drawn by James Montgomery Flagg. "Uncle Sam" as a national symbol was a figure whose origins went back to the War of 1812.

dimensions of war were staggering. The Army had been forced to maintain its efficiency even as it expanded at unprecedented rates. The Navy, along with the British, helped move more than 2 million men over 3,000 miles (4,825 km) of sea — one of the most incredible logistics accomplishments of this or any other war. Air power was coming into its own and this had to be dealt with.

In the short period between the time the US entered World War I to the armistice, more than 4.73 million persons served in the armed forces of the US. By branch of service this was: Army 4.05 million, Navy 599,000 and Marines 78,800.

There were more than 53,400 battle deaths. As might be expected the Army bore the brunt of them (50,510); there were 431 Navy deaths and 2,461 Marine deaths. Non-battle deaths — as was the case in previous wars — exceeded those due to battle: 63,100 (Army 55,868, Navy 6,856 and Marines 390).

A total of 204,002 servicemen were wounded in action, with the Army at 193,663, Navy at 819 and Marines at 9,520. Of the 2 million servicemen who reached France, officials estimate that 1.39 million saw active service at the front.

The airplane developed into an instrument of warfare. Strategic bombing was employed, the term ''aces'' came into use for the first time, and aircraft were used in tactical support of front line troops. While airpower did not play a decisive role in the war, its potential was there for all to see.

When America entered the war, there were 55 flyable aircraft in the Army Signal Corps and 54 in the Navy. By November 11, 1918, there were 45 American squadrons with approximately 800 pilots. The Air Service lost 289 airplanes and 48 balloons against confirmed kills of 781 enemy aircraft and 73 balloons. The Navy ended the war with 2,156 aircraft, 15 dirigibles and 215 observation balloons.

American participation in the war, it has been said, is often exaggerated by Americans and minimized by Europeans. The British and the French supplied the vast majority of American artillery pieces, tanks and aircraft.

However, there is no quarrel with this: America provided a military force that helped rejuvenate the fortunes of the Allies at a particularly critical time. Moreover, it was a contribution that provided sufficient advantage to assure victory for the Allies.

Right: The first American contingent to arrive in England. As the war proceeded, American strength grew to 4,057,101 men at its peak. This included some 62 divisions, 43 of which were sent overseas.

aviator, who commanded the aviaton branches of several Army units during World War I, was the foremost champion of air power in the 1920s. He was ultimately court martialed for his outspoken views, but in 1946 the Congress voted him a special Medal of Honor.

2 May 1917 Liberty Loan subscriptions are taken, the first of four that will be used to finance World War I. Other drives will take place in October and again in April/October 1918. Bonds were sold in denominations of $50 to $100,000 and the five drives (there was also a Victory Drive in 1919) raised a total of $21 billion. Not surprisingly, the drives featured appeals to patriotism.

11 May 1917 A petition is received by Wilson from the Central Committee of the Negro College Men, which asks for an officers' training camp for black men. Desegregaton of the Army — the group's goal — will come in another era. In the meantime, says the petition: "Our young men are so anxious to serve their country in this crisis that they are willing to accept a separate camp."

17 May 1917 The Senate debates and passes the Army Draft Bill by a wide margin. Machinery to register and draft the first half million men has already been established by the War Department, with more than 10,000,000 Americans eligible for registration. One of the more interesting provisions of the bill is its ban on the sale of liquor at or near Army training camps.

29 May 1917 Gen. John J. Pershing, the newly designated commander of the American Expeditionary Forces, sets sail from New York to England with his staff. He arrives in June ahead of his troops and sets about planning their training, supply and deployment. Pershing assumes the rank of general later in the year.

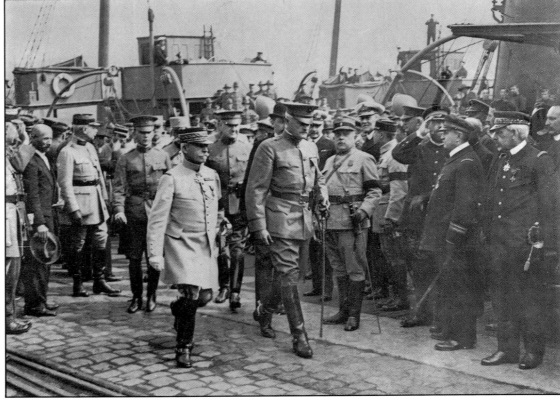

Above: Gen. Pershing receives an official welcome upon arrival at Boulogne harbor, France, in 1917. The commander of American Expeditionary Forces, he arrived ahead of the troops to set up training, supply and deployment.

Service and Casualties in World War I

(April 6, 1917 — November 11, 1918)

	Number Serving	Battle Deaths	Other Deaths	Wounds
Army	4,057,101	50,510	55,868	193,663
Navy	22,875	431	6,856	819
Marines	3,321	2,461	390	9,520
Total	4,734,991	53,402	63,114	204,002

1 June 1917 It is agreed by the Supreme War Council of the Allies that shipping should be concentrated for the task of transporting US troops across the Atlantic Ocean. By the end of the month, more than a quarter of a million troops under the command of Gen. Pershing have arrived in Europe, even though in many cases they are not prepared or trained for the trench war on the Western Front.

5 June 1917 More than 10 million sign up on World War I Draft Registration Day. The law requiring men between the ages of 21 and 30 to register for sevice in the Army was signed by

Wilson on May 18. Known as the Selective Draft Act, it goes into effect over the objections of a minority, who argue that all military recruiting should be done on a completely voluntary basis.

5 June 1917 The 1st Aeronautical Detachment, under the command of Lieutenant Kenneth Whiting, arrives at Bordeaux and St Nazaire, France.

aboard the colliers *Jupiter* (AC 3) and *Neptune* (AC 8). It is the first naval aviation unit to reach the European continent in World War I. The naval effort will grow to 16,000 officers and men, 500 naval aircraft, plus balloons and dirigibles before the war ends.

8 June 1917 The first American troops to land in England in World War I arrive aboard the British liner *Baltic* at 9:00 am. They consist of Pershing and his personal staff; the officers of the General Staff (53 in all); approximately 70 enlisted men and a clerical force of about the same number. The *Baltic* had been escorted through the danger zone by American destroyers.

14 June 1917 Pershing and his headquarters staff arrive in Paris. A top priority on his agenda is training for the 1st Division and the others who follow before the end of the year — including the 2nd, 26th and 42nd (Rainbow) Divisions. Pershing felt that training was seriously inadequate and therefore did not commit troops to battle until October.

14 June 1917 With Col. Charles A. Doyen in command, the first marine regiment that will land in Europe in World War I sails from New York on board three ships, the *Henderson, De Kalb* and *Hancock*. The entire regiment lands at St Nazaire, France, within a month. The 5th Marine Regiment had been attached to the Army by Wilson for service in France.

26 June 1917 The first American troops to arrive in Europe set up in St Nazaire, France, under the command of Maj. Gen. William L. Sibert. A second contingent quickly came ashore and set up not far from where Sibert was established. The doughboys had crossed the Atlantic swiftly; despite U-boats and mines, not a single man was lost.

14 July 1917 While he is serving with the Medical Corps of the British Army at Arras, France, 1st Lt. Louis J. Genelba becomes the first American casualty of World War I, when he is wounded by a shell splinter.

20 July 1917 The draft lottery of World War I officially goes into operation. Blindfolded Army officers draw 10,500 capsules from glass jars to determine the order in which the 9 million plus men who had

Right: American infantry in the front lines, Toul section, 1918. They were not sent to the front lines until January 1918 because Gen. Pershing felt that a number of training problems had to be overcome.

Army and Navy Military Aircraft Production

1914	15	1917	2,013
1915	26	1918	13,991
1916	142	1919	682

registered for the draft on 5 June will be called up for active duty. The drawing takes place in Room 226 of the Senate Office building opposite the Capitol.

24 July 1917 The first large air appropriation for the Army Aviation Section is made: $640 million. Growth in this area has been substantial since 1912, when 16 aircraft were purchased and a total of 51 personnel were involved at a cost of $125,000. By the end of World War I, there are 19,023 personnel in the Aviation Section, and aircraft purchased had shot up to 13,991.

14 August 1917 The first of the National Guard divisions that is to be sent to France in World War I is organized. Known as the 42nd Division, it consists of approximately 19,000 and will be commanded by Maj. Gen. William A. Mann, who graduated from West Point in 1875 and has a reputation as an old Indian fighter. The composite division will be made up of guard commands from throughout the US.

14 August 1917 Lieutenant Edward O. McDonnell launches a torpedo from an aircraft in an experiment carried out at Huntington Bay, New York. The test, and the idea, are something that Rear Admiral Bradley A. Fiske had been trying to get the Navy interested in since 1912. The dummy torpedo was launched from a seaplane, but struck the water at an unfavorable angle and ricocheted, almost hitting and downing the plane.

19 August 1917 The going price for outfitting the American doughboy for the front in World War I is $156.30, according to the War Department. Each soldier will receive 107 pieces of fighting equipment (this includes 100 rifle cartridges), 50 articles of clothing and 11 cooking implements. The rifle is the most costly of the items at $19.50. The trench tool is 50 cents and the bedsack 98 cents.

15 October 1917 The first commissions to black officers are given at the training camp at Des Moines, Iowa. More than 400,000 blacks served in uniform in World War I — approximately 10% of them in combat units. There were more than 1,300 commissioned black officers, most of them lieutenants. Three other black officers made field rank; two in the 370th Infantry and one in the 9th Cavalry.

16 October 1917 Gunner's Mate Osmond Kelly Ingram is killed when the German submarine *U-61* attacks the destroyer *Cassin* (DD 43) just south of Mind Head, Ireland. Ingram is the first Navy enlisted man to be killed in World War I. Nine other members of the crew were wounded in the torpedo attack, which resulted in the *Cassin's* rudder being blown off and her stern being extensively damaged.

21 October 1917 The first American division to hit the trenches in World War I and the first to get a taste of the action is the 1st Division. It enters the line in the Lunéville sector near Nancy, France; each unit was attached to a corresponding French unit.

23 October 1917 The first American artillery shell is fired in World War I by Battery C, 6th Field Artillery. Sgt. Alex Arch fires the shell, which lands in a crowded German trench near the

staff, Colonel Douglas MacArthur. The 42nd joins the swelling ranks of the American Expeditionary Forces, which began arriving in June and is mostly billeted in small towns on the outskirts of Paris.

2 January 1918 On this day the Army authorizes a new insignia, the wound chevron. With a pattern identical to that given for service, it will be worn on the lower half of the right sleeve of all uniform coats, fatigues excepted. It will be awarded to men who are wounded in action and must be treated by a medical doctor. A wound chevron is also approved for the wear of those soldiers who are gassed and get treatment.

8 January 1918 President Wilson's annual message to the Congress sets forth his famous "Fourteen Points" for American war aims. Hundreds of thousands of copies of the "Fourteen Points" will be airdropped in Germany during the war as part of the Allied propaganda effort, and the American president's view of an equitable solution to World War I will become his position at the Paris Peace Conference.

26 January 1918 The US Army Tank Corps is created, with Brig. Gen. Samuel D. Rockenbach in command. The tank as an instrument of warfare is just coming into its own. The Tank

Swiss border. The shot leads to retaliation and the American forces sustain their first casualties of the war on November 3 when James B. Gresham, Thomas F. Enright and Merle D. Hay are killed in action.

Above: American artillery in action during World War I firing French 75-mm rounds. Of the 2,250 American artillery pieces used by American forces in France during the war, only 100 were of American manufacture.

2 — 3 November 1917 Cpl. James B. Gresham and Pvts. Thomas F. Enright and Merle D. Hay become the first American troops to be killed in combat in World War I. Members of Company F, 16th Infantry, 1st Division, they are killed when Germans raid their trenches near Bathelemont, France during the night. The French Army's General Bordeaux commends their heroism and sacrifice.

power. First called the *Skipjack* (SS 24), *E-1* left for the Azores where she patrolled between Ponta Delgada and Horta, protecting the islands from attack by Germans and their use as a haven for their submarines.

7 December 1917 The 42nd Division, nicknamed the Rainbow Division because it is composed of units from the National Guards of many states, arrives in France with its chief of

17 November 1917 *U-58* becomes the first U-boat to be sunk by American naval ships in World War I. Based at Queenstown (Cobh), Ireland, the two destroyers involved in the operation — the *Fanning* (DD 37) and *Nicholson* (DD 52) — bombarded the underwater boat with depth charges. The commander brings his stricken submarine to the surface, which permits the crew to be rescued before her final plunge.

Below: American troops are shown at Southampton, England, prior to embarking for France. The British provided transport for 10 divisions of Americans as the buildup of troops on the continent gained momentum.

21 November 1917 The Navy's robot bomber — actually a flying bomb — is demonstrated to Army, Navy and civilian experts at Amityville, New York. Also called an aerial torpedo, it is designed for automatic operation while carrying 1,000 lb (454 kg) of explosives for 50 miles at a top speed of 90 mph (145 kmh). A close cousin to the guided missile, it was manufactured for the Navy by the Curtiss Company.

4 December 1917 *E-1* leaves Newport, Rhode Island, on a voyage that will see her become the first submarine to cross the Atlantic Ocean under her own

Right: On 26 September 1918 French-built Renault FT-17 light tanks of the 326th battalion 311th Tank Center rumble into action near Boureilles, Meuse, during the battle for the St Mihiel salient.

Corps will enter its first engagement on 12 September in the reduction of the St Mihiel salient. By the end of the war, tanks will have been used by the Allies in 91 separate engagements.

1 February 1918 The first operation squadrons of the American Expeditionary Forces are formed in France. The US Air Service — actually still the Aviation Section, but commonly called the Air Service — was able to put pursuit and observation squadrons into action by April. At the end of the war, there would be 45 American squadrons in action with 740 airplanes, about 800 pilots and 500 observers.

5 February 1918 First Lt. Stephen W. Thompson shoots an Albatros pursuit plane out of the skies over Saarbrucken, Germany. A member of the 1st Aero Squadron, Thompson is credited with being the first Army pilot to record a victory over an enemy airplane.

6 February 1918 The War Department announces that the *Tuscania*, with 2,179 American soldiers aboard, has been torpedoed and sunk. It is the first American troopship of World War I to be torpedoed by a German submarine. Many of the soldiers aboard the stricken ship — 267 are killed — were from small units, but most were from Michigan and Wisconsin National Guard organizations.

8 February 1918 Pershing authorizes publication of the *Stars and Stripes*, a weekly newspaper for American soldiers. Seventy-one issues will be published before the end of the war in November. Other papers were published under the *Stars and Stripes* name during the Civil War, it will be found out later, but there was no official link between them and Washington.

12 February 1918 An assigned service number is first authorized for Army personnel under American Expeditionary Forces General Order 27 of this date. Master Sgt. Arthur B. Crean will receive Army Service Number ASN-1 on 28 February; Pershing will receive No. O-1 when officers are brought into the system in 1921. The system ends in the 1970s when Social Security numbers are used.

16 February 1918 The 2nd Balloon Company moves into position on the front at Royamieux in the Toul sector in France. The Balloon Section makes a total of 5,866 ascents in France during the war and spends a total of 6,832 hours in the air. American balloon observers will be forced to make 116 parachute jumps under enemy fire; spot 12,018 enemy shell bursts; and report 11,856 enemy airplanes and 2,649 enemy balloons.

18 February 1918 The first American fighter squadron to arrive in France proper is the 95th Aero (Pursuit) Squadron, followed by the 94th Aero Squadron on 4 March. It will be on March 15 that American pursuit pilots, American trained and from squadrons organized with American enlisted personnel, will make their first patrol of the front at Villeneuve-les-Vertus, Marne, south of Epernay.

26 February 1918 At 1:20 a.m., a German gas attack which uses asphyxiating phosgene and chloropicrin is launched against American troops on the Western front, their baptism of fire in this type of warfare. A total lack of gas discipline on the part of the Americans, who had never been exposed to chemical warfare and did not take it as seriously as they should have, led to a 95% casualty rate.

6 March 1918 The War Department announces that President Wilson has authorized four new decorations for bravery, service or wounds. They are the Distinguished Service Cross; the Distinguished Service Medal; war

---

Chemical Warfare Stocks on Hand American Expeditionary Forces 1918

Box respirators	1,850,000
Protective gloves (pairs)	184,794
M-2 masks	75,623
Canisters	903,345
Sag paste (tubes)	2,228,092
Chloride of lime (tons)	1,396
Livens projectors	4,095
Livens drums, filled	36,468
Stokes mortar bombs, smoke	5,022
Stokes mortar bombs, filled	39,105

Below: Modishly attired women giving flowers to US troops as they parade down New York City's Fifth Avenue. It is 1917 — and these troops are preparing to embark for Europe where they will join their comrades at the front.

Right: US 11th Bombardment Squadron at Maulan, France. It was part of the 1st Day Bombardment Group, which participated heavily in the St Mihiel offensive and acquitted itself well in difficult circumstances.

service chevrons; and wound chevrons. Both medals are bronze — with the former awarded for extraordinary heroism and the latter for exceptionally meritorious service.

11 March 1918 The first Distinguished Service Cross awarded to a person in the Army Air Service goes to Lt. Paul Baer for his action on this date. He goes after seven German pursuit

Leading Aces of World War I

Rickenbacker, Capt, Edward V. (AEF)	26	Rose, Capt. Oren J. (RFC)	16
Lambert, Capt, William C. (RFC)	22	Warman, Lt. C.T. (RFC)	15
Gillette, Capt. Frederick W. (RFC)	20	Libby, Capt. Frederick (RFC)	14
Malone, Capt. John J. (RN)	20	Vaughan, 1st Lt. George A. (AEF)	13
Wilkinson, Maj. Alan M. (RFC)	19	Baylies, Lt. Frank L. (FFC/LE)	12
Hale, Capt. Frank L. (RFC)	18	Bennett, 1st. Lt. Louis B. (RFC)	12
Iaccaci, Capt. Paul T. (RFC)	18	Kindley, Capt. Field E. (AEF)	12
Luke, 2nd Lt. Frank, Jr. (AEF)	18	Putnam, 1st Lt. David E. (LE/AEF)	12
Lufbery, Maj. Raoul G. (FFC/LE)	17	Springs, Capt. Elliott W. (AEF)	12
Kullberg, Lt. Harold A. (RFC)	16	Iaccaci, Lt. Thayer A. (RFC)	11

AEF-American Expeditionary Force
FFC-French Flying Corps
LE-Lafayette Escadrille
RFC-Royal Flying Corps (British)
RN-Royal Navy (British)

Captain E. V. Rickenbacker

planes, one of which he destroys. Baer, from Fort Wayne, Indiana, had come to France in February 1917 as a member of the Franco-American Flying Corps.

19 March 1918 Naval Aviator Number 130, Ensign Stephen Potter, destroys a German seaplane near the island of Heligoland in the North Sea while on a long-range patrol with the Royal Flying Corps. Potter becomes the first Navy pilot to shoot down an enemy aircraft in "the Great War". One month later, he is killed in an air battle with seven German aircraft over England.

8 April 1918 The 1st Aero Squadron, which is to handle observation duties, becomes the first air squadron of the Army to be assigned to the front-line in World War I. The first combat action, however, will not take place until four days later when the squadron is attacked while on a reconnaissance mission.

14 April 1918 1st Lt. Douglas Campbell and 2nd Lt. Alan F. Winslow of the 94th Squadron, 1st Pursuit Group, become the first American-trained pilots to shoot down enemy aircraft in World War I. The action comes over Toul airdrome, France, and it will be Winslow who receives credit for the first kill.

29 April 1918 Captain Edward V. Rickenbacker, who will become America's top ace of World War I, shoots down the first of his 26 victims, an Albatros scout, over Toul, France. Later in the same year, he attacks seven enemy aircraft in a single day near Billy, France, an exploit for which he later receives the Medal of Honor.

18 May 1918 The first bomber squadron of the American Expeditionary Forces is formed as the 96th Aero Squadron at Amanty airdrome, France. The US Army Air Service in France will constitute 10% of all Allied forces, drop 139 tons of bombs and reach as far as 160 miles (257.5

km) behind German lines. Before the war is over, 237 American airmen will be killed in battle.

20 May 1918 The *New Mexico* (BB 40) is commissioned at the New York Navy Yard. The Navy's first warship to be propelled by electricity, she quickly becomes the flagship of the newly organized Pacific Fleet. She was 624 ft (190.2 m) in length, displaced 32,000 tons, and was armed with 12 14-in (356 mm) and 14 5-in (127 mm) guns. The *New Mexico* earned six battle stars for service in World War II.

28 May 1918 The 1st Division opens an assault to capture the village of Cantigny, marking the first time in World War I that an American unit takes part in an offensive operation. The village, a fortified German observation point, was taken and then held against German counter-attacks. Even though it was a local operation, the victory against veteran troops boosted morale.

6 June 1918 The 91st Squadron starts active operation in the Toul sector of France, the first Army observation

Below: An after-the-war demonstration at Langley Field, Virginia, of how aerial photographs were taken. Photo interpreters formed composites of the resulting prints and modeled them to train aerial observers.

unit to do so in World War I. Its mission is to keep the command informed by photographic and visual means of the general situation within and behind enemy lines. In addition, special missions will be flown that will be particularly helpful in making proper artillery adjustments.

12 June 1918 The first bombs are dropped by a bomb unit of the American Expeditionary Forces. Some eight Breguet 14s of the 96th Aero Squadron, led by Maj. Harry M. Brown, drop the bombs on the Dommary-Baroncourt railyards in France in the first day bombing done by the AEF. This type of bombing put to work the ideas of the major practical theorists of air warfare, among them ''Billy'' Mitchell.

29 June 1918 During the convulsions in Russia brought about by the revolution, Marines are landed at Vladivostok by the cruiser *Brooklyn* (CA 3), the flagship of the Asiatic Fleet. The mission of the Marines is to safeguard the American consulate in Vladivostok, which they carry out — remaining ashore until relieved by an infantry brigade from the Philippines.

4 July 1918 Pershing announces that a million Americans had arrived in France and more are on the way. Nine of the American divisions, he says, have had some combat experience, mainly in the quiet sectors; two others have completed their training; and eight more have recently arrived. The total was 19, each one double the size of an Allied or German division.

21 July 1918 *U-156* fires shots at the tugboat *Perth Amboy* and four barges loaded with stone off Nauset Bluffs, Massachusetts. She fires between

Above: A railway artillery gun fires in support of the Argonne advance in France during World War I. The battle cost the Germans 100,000 casualties; American losses were at 117,000 in the lengthy engagement.

70 and 80 shots, all of them from a distance of about 3 miles (4.8 km) offshore. A few of them land at Meeting House Pond, Massachusetts, the first enemy ordnance to land on the US in World War I.

15 August 1918 Two army regiments land at Vladivostok, Russia, and take control of the Trans-Siberian Railway. They are there to aid the evacuation of anti-Bolshevik Czech prisoners of war, marching eastward at the time. The action also prevented the Japanese domination of the Russian Maritime Provinces.

6 September 1918 Using a railway battery of five 14-in (356 mm) guns, a naval unit begins long-range bombardment of German forces near Soissons, France. The unit is under the command of Rear Admiral Charles P. Plunkett and represents the first use of major-caliber naval guns in a land offensive. The unit is known as the Woozlefinches.

12 September 1918 The St Mihiel campaign opens, which witnesses the largest aggregation of air support in World War I. Under Col. Billy Mitchell

could be found 1,476 aircraft, 20 balloons and 30,000 airmen and support personnel from the British, French and Italian air forces, including nearly 600 American airplanes and crews. On the ground were 400,000 men waiting to advance.

12 September 1918 Under the command of Lt. Col. George S. Patton, Jr, the 304th Tank Brigade, manning French Renault light tanks, pushes forward in the St Mihiel offensive. The first time the tank was used by the American military in warfare, the advance begins before first light. Unfortunately most of the tanks fall victim to mud or mechanical failure. Fortunately, German resistance during the battle is moderate.

Below: American Intelligence officers search a German prisoner for letters and any orders of military value. The search takes place at the 2nd Division Headquarters, St Mihiel Salient, St Jacques, France.

Below: Tanks on the move. A procession of tanks from the 326 Battalion, 311th Tank Center, goes forward in action in the Argonne near Boureuilles, Meuse. More than 1.2 million Americans took part in the 47-day campaign.

24 September 1918 Lieutenant David S. Ingalls, 19, becomes one of the very few navy aces of World War I. While flying his Sopwith Camel on temporary duty with No. 213 Squadron of the Royal Air Force, he scores his fifth aerial victory in six weeks to record the achievement. With his victory, Ingalls also lays claim to the distinction of becoming the US Navy's first ace.

25 September 1918 First Lt. Eddie V. Rickenbacker of the 94th Aero Pursuit Squadron, while patrolling over enemy lines, sets out after seven German aircraft — five Fokkers and two Halberstadts — near Billy, France. He dives at a Fokker and shoots it down; turning his attention to a Halberstadt, he knocks it out of the sky as well. His feat earns America's "Ace of Aces" a well-deserved Medal of Honor.

29 September 1918 Second Lieutenant Frank Luke, American Expeditionary Forces, becomes the first aviator to receive the Medal of Honor, which is awarded posthumously for action on this date. Luke had scored 18 kills in 18 days, with another 10 kills highly probable, according to observers. Eddie Rickenbacker, American "Ace of Aces", says Luke was the "greatest fighting pilot of the war".

8 October 1918 Sgt. Alvin Cullum York — then a private first class — captures 132 Germans after leading a 17-man patrol in an attack against an enemy machine gun nest. The conscientious objector, whose petition to remain exempt from the draft was officially denied twice, ultimately received the Medal of Honor for his work. When asked how he performed the legendary deed, he replied: "I surrounded 'em."

14 October 1918 Marine Corps aviation makes an auspicious debut in World War I. Members of the 1st Marine Force set out on a strike mission against German-occupied railyards in Belgium. It is the first mission flown by the Corps on its own; and it yields the first two Medals of Honor for marines in aerial combat. They are earned by 2nd Lt. Ralph Talbot and Cpl. Robert G. Robinson.

18 October 1918 A shoulder sleeve insignia — or "shoulder patch" — is authorized for the American Expeditionary Forces, then fighting in France. This practice will be adopted Army-wide in May 1920. Unit identity and morale are big factors in permitting the adoption of a "wildcat" on the sleeves of the 81st Division, who were wearing them anyway. Another factor: bringing some style to the "doughboy" uniform that made everybody look alike.

US Army Campaign Streamers World War I

Cambrai	Nov 20-Dec 4, 1917
Somme Defensive	Mar 21-Apr 6, 1918
Lys	Apr 9-27, 1918
Aisne	May 27-Jun 5, 1918
Montdidier-Noyon	Jun 9-13, 1918
Champagne-Marne	Jul 15-18, 1918
Aisne-Marne	Jul 18-Aug 6, 1918
Somme Offensive	Aug 8-Nov 11, 1918
Oise-Aisne	Aug 18-Nov 11, 1918
Ypres-Lys	Aug 19-Nov 11, 1918
St Mihiel	Sep 12-16, 1918
Meuse-Argonne	Sep 26-Nov 11, 1918
Vittorio Veneto	Oct 24-Nov 4, 1918

11 November 1918 Armistice Day — which is now celebrated in the US as Veterans Day and honors the dead of all wars — ends hostilities in World War I. Signed at Compiegne, France, it goes into effect on the 11th hour of the 11th day of the 11th month. The terms, later changed at the peace conference in Versailles, call for (among other things) German evacuation of all occupied territories, the return of prisoners and reparations.

1 December 1918 The first US troops to arrive back from Europe following the signing of the armistice ending World War I arrive in New York City aboard the British transport *Mauretania* at Pier 54. Some 4,467 soldiers are in the contingent, which takes three hours to disembark. They then head for Long Island on two large ferryboats; the sick and wounded on board the ship are put in a hospital at Ellis Island.

1 December 1918 The newly-activated 3rd Army moves into Germany to occupy a segment of territory between Luxembourg and the Rhine River around Coblenz. As many as nine divisions participated in the occupation during the spring of 1919. In a similar manner, an army regiment sent to Italy before the end participated in four months of occupation duty in Austria.

4 December 1918 The first coast-to-coast flight by army pilots across the US is started in four Curtiss JN-4 Jennies under the command of Maj. Albert D. Smith. The flight originates in San Diego, California and ends in Jacksonville, Florida, which was reached on 22 December.

American forces, November 1918

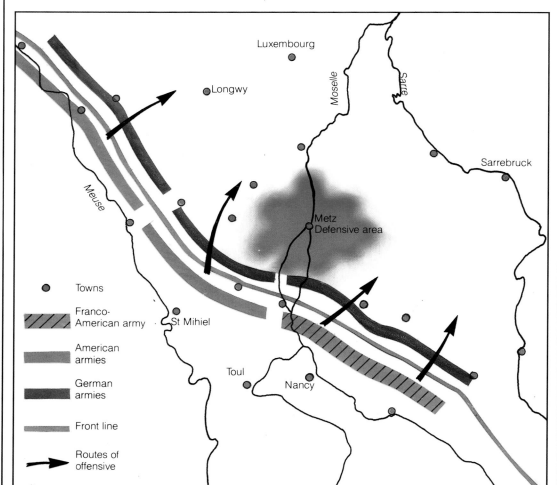

Above: The approximate positions of American forces in the St Mihiel sector on Armistice Day. The successful offensive against the St Mihiel salient had left Metz as Pershing's next objective. The American 1st and 2nd Armies (25 divisions) were to strike towards Luxembourg, while a joint force of French and Americans under Gen. Mangin (25 divisions) were to push towards Sarrebruck and the Sarre river.

Above: Company A, 353rd Infantry, waits by the church in Stenay, Meuse, at 10:58 a.m. on Armistice Day. In two minutes, the armistice ending World War I will go into effect, ending the "war to end all wars".

Above: Cheering American troops arrive at Hoboken, New Jersey at the conclusion of the war. Joining thousands of other doughboys who were back home to stay, they had just returned from France aboard the *Agamen.*

16 January 1919   Presidential Executive Order 11,488 establishes the Meritorious Service Medal. A noncombat award, the new medal ranks between the Legion of Merit and the Service Commendation Medal. It is only outclassed by the Distinguished Service Medal.

4 February 1919   The Distinguished Service Medal is approved by an act of the Congress. Awarded for either combat or non-combat service, it is given to the person who distinguishes himself by meritorious service to the government in a duty of great responsibility. Paul Manship is the designer of the gilded bronze medal.

21 February 1919   The prototype of the first US-designed fighter to enter large-scale production (the Thomas Morse MB-3) makes its maiden flight. During World War I, the US relied almost exclusively on European aircraft, but in the early 1920s will place an order for 200 Boeing-built MB-3As. It will be the largest single order placed for US military aircraft for the next 17 years.

28 February 1919   The *Osmond Ingram* (DD 255), first navy ship named for an enlisted man, is launched. Gunner's Class Osmond K. Ingram was aboard the *Cassin* (DD 43) when she was attacked by a German submarine. He spotted its torpedo when it was launched and rushed to jettison the ammunition as the torpedo headed for it, thus saving ship and crew. He was the first enlisted man killed in action in World War I.

12 March 1919   Lieutenant Harry Sadenwater demonstrates that voice radio and telephone relay are perfectly feasible for air-to-ground communications when he carries on a lengthy conversation with the Secretary of the Navy, who is seated at his desk some 65 miles (105 km) away. Sadenwater is airborne in a flying boat at the time.

15 March 1919   The American Legion, an organization of war veterans, is formed. Its first caucus was held at the Cirque de Paris two days later. The Legion idea originated with Theodore Roosevelt, Jr. at a meeting held at the Allied Officers Club in Paris in early 1919 when he suggested an organization for American veterans of the World War. The Legion is formally incorporated by the Congress in September.

17 May 1919   The War Department orders the use of national star insignia on all military aircraft. In fact, the star painted on the bottom surface of the lower wings of airplanes had been used in the US. But in Europe the circle insignia used on American airplanes at the front was confusing and many failures on the part of infantry to respond to them were laid to this.

19 May 1919   Master Sgt. Ralph W. Bottriell makes the first jump by a military man with a free backpack type parachute from USD-9 two-place biplane at McCook Field, Ohio. He uses a US airplane, Type 'A' parachute, which is the granddaddy of all parachutes that will come into use in the Army. All the components are pulled together for the first time for the jump, including an on-the-body ripcord.

21 May 1919   Marine Gunnery Sergeant Ernest A. Janson receives the first Medal of Honor awarded as the result of action in World War I. Attached to the 49th Company, 5th Regiment, 2nd Marine Division, Janson had spotted 12 enemy soldiers near Château-Thierry, France, with light machine guns. He bayoneted two of them and forced the others to abandon their guns and flee.

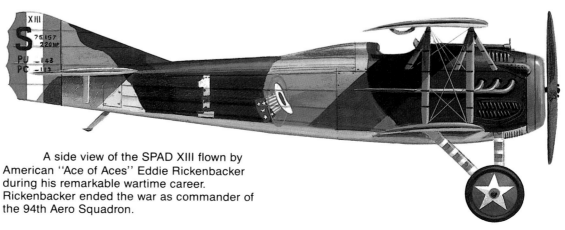

A side view of the SPAD XIII flown by American "Ace of Aces" Eddie Rickenbacker during his remarkable wartime career. Rickenbacker ended the war as commander of the 94th Aero Squadron.

Above: The Navy-Curtiss Boat (NC-4) lands gently in Lisbon harbor, Portugal. It arrived there after achieving the first transatlantic crossing by air. Waiting for its arrival in Lisbon (left) were a congratulatory party including Lieutenant Ralph Talbot, Ensign Rodd, Lieutenant Hinton, Lieutenant Commander Read and Secretary of the Navy Josephus Daniels.

27 May 1919 At 8:01 p.m., the first transatlantic crossing is achieved by air when a Navy NC-4 flying boat lands gracefully in the harbor at Lisbon, Portugal. Under the command of Lieutenant Commander Albert C. Read, the aircraft and its crew had left the Naval Air Station, Rockaway, New York on the first leg of the flight which took it to Nova Scotia, Newfoundland, the Azores and Lisbon.

28 June 1919 The Treaty of Versailles is signed ending World War I. Delegates sign the treaty in Galerie des Glaces, in the Palace of Versailles near Paris. Ushering in what has been termed an era of "borrowed peace", the treaty forces Germany to admit guilt for the war and strips her of Alsace-Lorraine, the Saar Basin and overseas colonies. It also sets up a League of Nations.

9 August 1919 The Secretary of the Navy authorizes construction of the Navy's first rigid airship, the ZR-1 *Shenandoah*. The giant ship — it was 682 ft (207.88 m) long, or the equivalent of three city blocks — had 20 gas bags and its design was almost identical to that of the German Zeppelin *L-49*. The major difference was that US engineers were able to use helium, an inert and thus non-flammable gas, as the lifting agent.

Right: Boeing GA-IX, the first armored plane. The armor was inspired by Gen. Bill Mitchell. Ten GA-Is were built before production was discontinued in favor of an aircraft that could provide greater maneuverability.

3 September 1919 President Wilson signs a bill providing for the permanent rank of general. The legislation is known throughout the country as "The Pershing Bill", since it will make Pershing ranking army general officer as long as he chooses to stay on active duty. Unanimous support for enacting the bill (it was passed without discussion) was seen as the "graceful and proper thing" to do after Pershing's war efforts.

6 October 1919 The *Nautilus* (SS 29), which is later renamed the *H-2*, becomes one of the first submarines to send a wireless message while submerged. She is on the Hudson River in New York at the time and operating from her home base at New London, Connecticut. She operated often in Long Island sound with student officers from the submarine school aboard.

20 November 1919 The first capital ship constructed on the west coast of the US, the battleship *California* (BB 44), is launched at Mare Island Navy Shipyard, California. The behemoth gets off to less than an auspicious start as she crosses the channel upon launching and, while out of control, smashes a ferry pier. She makes up for it later, though, by earning seven battle stars in World War II.

23 December 1919 The *Relief* (AH 1), the first ship of the Navy to be built from the keel up as a hospital ship, is launched at the Philadelphia, Pennsylvania, Navy Shipyard. With bed capacity of 500 patients, she is one of the world's best equipped and most modern hospital ships. *Relief* serves with great distinction in World War II, at one point serving some 200,000 men of the Fifth Fleet.

6 July 1920 A radio compass is tested for the first time in an airplane as an aid to navigation. A Navy Curtiss seaplane flies a round trip from Hampton Roads, Virginia, to the *Ohio* (BB 12) 94 miles (151 km) at sea. It is guided only by the radio compass as an aid to navigation. Without landing, the F-5L returns to Hampton Roads, this time navigating by signals from Norfolk.

17 July 1920 Letter symbols are established by the navy to identify ships — "BB" for battleship; "DD" for destroyer; "AO" for oiler, and so on. Standard nomenclature is also adopted by the Secretary of the Navy for aircraft as well. Lighter-than-air craft become identified as type "Z"; and heavier-than-air as type "V". Within the V type are other designations such as P for patrol aircraft.

21 February 1920 The first solo transcontinental flight within 24 hours is made by Lt. W. D. Coney in a DH-4B from San Diego to Jacksonville in 22 hours, 27 minutes. One month later, Coney tries to reverse his route in the plane in which he flew eastward — it has been thoroughly overhauled and a new propeller installed. But engine trouble develops and he crashes in Louisiana and breaks his back.

1 May 1920 The army's first production armored airplane flies for the first time as the Boeing GA-1 triplane.

Carrying eight 0.3-in (7.62 mm) machine guns and a 37-mm Baldwin cannon, plus 10 25-lb (11.3 kg) fragmentation bombs, in addition to very heavy armor plating, the aircraft manages only 105 mph (169 kmh).

21 July 1920 The possibilities of concentrated bombing are shown in a test directed by Gen. Billy Mitchell. The former German battleship *Ostfriesland* is sunk off the Virginia capes. Tests against the ship began the previous day when Army, Navy and Marine aircraft dropped 52 bombs and ended on 21 July when the Army delivered 11 1,000-lb (454 kg) and 2,000-lb (907 kg) bombs on the hapless ship.

23 July 1921 Operations Plan 712, "Advanced Base Operations in Micronesia", is approved by the Commandant of the Marine Corps. Prepared by Lt. Col. Earl H. (Pete) Ellis, the remarkable document details what the Corps can expect to contribute in the event of a war with Japan. It calls for developing the amphibious capability used by the corps in the war and forecasts the general course of the campaigns.

10 August 1921 The first major battleship to be built on the west coast of the United States, the *California* (BB 44), is commissioned and reports to the Pacific Fleet as its flagship. She serves as the flagship for 20 years and is one of the victims of the onslaught by Japanese forces at Pearl Harbor in 1941, where she loses 98 of her crew in the aerial attack. The battlewagon is refloated, however, and reenters the war in 1944.

25 August 1921 The US signs a peace treaty with Germany in Berlin which officially ends World War I. It stipulates that none of the provisions of the Treaty of Versailles will be removed by the treaty, nor will the joint Resolution of the US Congress of 2 July, which claims all rights, reparations, or indemnities awarded to the country under the Treaty of Versailles.

3 October 1921 The *Olympia* (C 6) sails to Le Havre, France, from Philadelphia, Pennsylvania, to bring back the remains of the Unknown Soldier from the battlefields of France, for interment in Arlington National Cemetery. The cruiser will sail for the US on 25 October, escorted by French destroyers for the first leg of the passage home. She will arrive in Washington on 9 November.

8 October 1921 The Bureau of Aeronautics is established under a Navy General Order. Its duties comprise "all that relates to designing, building, fitting out, and repairing Naval and Marine Corps aircraft..." Aeronautic training and assignments to the aviation field became its responsibility, and provisions were made to furnish information on to the Chief of Naval Operations.

7 November 1921 President Warren G. Harding details 53 Marine Corps officers and 2,200 men to guard the US

Above: The *Ostfriesland* was not the only captured German ship sunk by the Army to test the effects of air power. Also sunk were the cruiser *Frankfurt* here), a German submarine (*U-117*) and a German destroyer (*G-102*).

mail. Unable to cope with an increasing number of attacks on the mail by organized crime, Harding directs them to be detailed as guards for the mails in sufficient numbers "to protect the mails from depradations by robbers and bandits". The Marines will be withdrawn from this duty in 1927.

Above: Grim-visaged National Air Transport employees supervise mail being loaded onto a plane at Hadley Airport, Brunswick, N.J., in 1927. Marines were called in to help guard the mail from attacks by organized crime.

Below: The *California* as she would have appeared in the mid-1920s. Her refit after Pearl Harbor left her with a single funnel and a much augmented secondary armament.

11 November 1921

Above: The first non-stop coast-to-coast flight across North America in this Fokker T-2 monoplane took 26 hours, 50 minutes, 3 seconds. Planes were getting faster, forcing record flights to be measured in seconds.

Above: The *Langley* with Vought VE-7 aircraft on deck. This photograph was labeled ''Harbinger'' to show how the first carrier was first in a line of ships that would drive the battleship into the background.

11 November 1921 The monument to the Unknown soldier is dedicated at the National Cemetery in Arlington, Virginia. Nearly 100,000 people gather together at the amphitheater at Arlington to pay silent homage to a soldier who had fallen unknown on the fields of Europe. His body is placed in a marble sarcophagus, his namelessness is intended to symbolize the 50,000 comrades who died on the field of battle in World War I.

12 November 1921 With implications for the military application of air power, the first ''air-to-air'' refueling takes place. Wesley May, a 5-gal (18.9-litre) can of gasoline on his back, transfers from his plane (a Lincoln Standard) to the wing skid of a JN-4, climbs to the engine, and pours the gasoline into the tank.

19 November 1921 The *West Virginia* is launched as BB 48 at Newport News, Virginia. Her armor protection is superior to anything that has been built up to the time; she will also be the last battleship of the Navy to be launched before the Washington Naval Treaty restricts naval armaments. *West Virginia* will be heavily damaged at Pearl Harbor, but will still earn five battle stars in World War II.

25 January 1922 The US Army Band is established. Pershing issues the order — ''You will organize and equip the Army Band'' — to Capt. Parry W. Lewis at Fort Hunt, Virginia. ''Pershing's Own'' is the name that attaches to the unit; direct descendants of the American Expeditionary Force Band formed by Pershing at Chaumont, France, during World War I.

6 February 1922 The Washington Naval Treaty is signed, which is designed to limit naval armament through the device of ratios. Representatives of the US, France, Italy, Japan and the UK sign the treaty. It establishes tonnage ratios for capital ships, a 10-year moratorium on the laying down of new capital ships and permits the Japanese to increase defenses of the Home Islands.

20 March 1922 The *Langley* (CV 1), the Navy's first aircraft carrier, is commissioned. More than just another ship, she is a rich piece of American history. She had started as a collier (1912), became an aircraft carrier (called the ''Covered Wagon'') on this date and was redesignated a seaplane tender in 1937. She will be sunk in World War II after being attacked by nine twin-engine Japanese bombers.

4 September 1922 The first transcontinental flight in a single day is made by Lt. James H. Doolittle in a modified DH-4B Liberty 400. He flies the aircraft from Pablo Beach, Florida, to Rockwell Field at San Diego, California. Interestingly, Doolittle makes the flight at his own expense because he wants to demonstrate to those in authority, the feasibility of moving air cargo over long distances quickly in emergencies.

17 October 1922 Lieutenant Commander Virgil C. Griffin, at the controls of a Vought VE-7 fighter, achieves the first takeoff of an aircraft from the deck of a carrier when he leaves the *Langley* (CV 1). At the time, the carrier was at anchor in the York River.

26 October 1922 The first carrier landing by an airplane while a ship is underway is achieved. Lieutenant Commander Godfrey DeC. (Chevy) Chevalier becomes the first pilot to accomplish that feat when he puts his Aeromarine 39B on the deck of the *Langley* (CV 1) while she is underway off Cape Henry, Virginia. This Navy ''first'' comes nine days after an airplane takes off from a carrier for the first time.

20 January 1923 The US occupation of Germany after World War I ends when the Stars and Stripes are lowered from Fortress Ehrenbrietstein, Coblenz. Command of the occupation zone was turned over to the French.

2 May 1923 Lts. Oakley Kelly and John Macready start on the first non-stop flight across the US: it will take 26 hours and 50 minutes. Flying a Fokker T-2 monoplane with a 400-hp (298 kW) Liberty engine, they cover 2,650 miles (4,265 km) from Roosevelt Field, Hempstead, Long Island, to Rockwell Field in San Diego, California. A crowd of more than 100,000 people greets them upon their arrival.

27 June 1923 The first complete midair pipeline refueling takes place between two

Below: A Barling NBL-1 Army bomber in flight. The world's largest airplane, it was designed by Walter Henry Barling and piloted by H.R. Harris on its first flight. Its powerplant consists of six 400 hp (298-kW) Liberty engines.

airplanes. Lts. Lowell H. Smith and John P. Richter stay up in their DH-4 for four days, with Lt. Frank Seifert commanding the fuel plane. The pipe line is dropped by rope control, and 25 gal (94.6 litres) flow into the ship below. Flying 40 ft (12.2 m) apart while transferring the fuel, the process is repeated eight times.

22 August 1923 The first six-engined American aircraft, the Barling XNBL-1 triplane bomber, is flown for the first time at Wilbur Wright Field, Ohio. It flies for 28 minutes, travels 25 miles (40 km) and reaches 93 mph (150 kmh). The world's largest airplane up to that time, it had a wing span of 120 ft (36.58 m), an overall length of 65 ft (19.81 m), a height of 38 ft (11.58 m) and a maximum weight of 42,569 lb (19,309 kg).

5 November 1923 At Hampton Roads Naval Base, Virginia, the Navy completes a series of experiments to show that a reconnaisance seaplane can be stowed aboard, assembled and launched from a submarine on the open sea. The submarine *S-1* is used during the tests, crewed by officers and men of the *Langley* (CV 1); the aircraft employed is the Martin MS-1.

21 March 1924 The Bureau of Aeronautics directs that all Navy personnel use parachutes on all flights. Navy men had begun training in the care and packing of parachutes two years prior to this direction. Ten chief petty officers had reported for two months of instruction at the Army school at Chanute Field in Rantoul, Illinois.

22 July 1924 Mitchell predicts that the Japanese will attack on Pearl Harbor after returning from his second tour of the Pacific. In a classified report that was dubbed at the time by the

Above: A Martin MS-1 scouting floatplane on the deck of the *S-1*, probably at Norfolk, Va. In October 1923. It was involved in tests demonstrating quick assembly and disassembly of aircraft for storage aboard submarines.

Chief of the Air Service as likely to be "of extreme value some ten or fifteen years hence", Mitchell pins down the day of the week on which the Japanese attack occurred and only missed the actual time by 25 minutes!

28 September 1924 Army pilots complete the first successful flight around the world. Four Douglas World Cruisers had departed Seattle, Washington, on 6 April. One crashed and the crew returned; another gave up. The *Chicago* — Maj. Frederick Martin, pilot, and Sgt. Alva L. Harvey, mechanic; and the *New Orleans* — with three aboard — completed the flight in 365 flying hours and covered 27,553 miles (44,341 km).

11 November 1924 Lieutenant Dixie Kiefer makes the first catapult launch from the *California*, which is at anchor in San Diego Harbor. The launch is made in the late evening and aided only by the searchlights trained about 1,000 yards (915 m) ahead. Kiefer advances through the ranks to commodore and will be killed in an airplane crash in 1945, exactly 21 years to the day after his historic launch.

17 November 1924 Ending more than two years in experimental status, the *Langley*

reports for duty and becomes the first operational flagship of Aircraft Squadrons, Battle Fleet. With this action, she also becomes the first operational aircraft carrier in the Navy.

4 March 1925 The Navy Band is recognized by the Congress with a special act that makes it a permanent organization whose leader has the rank of lieutenant, senior grade. In the fall of the year, the band began the first of what becomes annual concert tours that took it into more than 300 cities and villages in the US.

4 March 1925 A Naval Reserve Officers Training Corps is authorized. The first programs began at George Washington University and at St John's College, Annapolis, Maryland. There were 1,000 men soon enrolled and the program expanded to colleges in the rest of the nation. By 1927, 5,500 officers were enrolled — the maximum number allowed under the law.

29 May 1925 The Navy modifies the standard color of its aircraft: hulls and floats to navy grey; wings, fuselage, landing gear, etc., to aluminum color; and top surface of upper wings, stabilizers and elevators to orange yellow.

29 September 1925 Billy Mitchell, outspoken advocate of air power, testifies before the Congress; he proposes creation of an independent military branch for aviation and brands the existing

Below: The Douglas "World Cruisers" — *Seattle, Boston, Chicago, New Orleans* — before take-off on their epic first aerial circumnavigation of the globe.They are shown lined up here at San Diego, California.

military command as incompetent. Later court martialed for his outspokenness, it will not be until 1942 that Mitchell is rehabilitated posthumously and promoted to the rank of major general.

28 October 1925 The court martial of Mitchell begins on charges of "conduct prejudicial to good order and military discipline". The proceedings last until 17 December, with the court voting five to one (the lone dissenter was Gen. Douglas MacArthur) to convict him. Mitchell responded to the conviction — even though it was mitigated on review — by resigning.

20 November 1925 The President's Aircraft Board, better known as the Morrow Board, submits its report to President Calvin Coolidge, and provides the basis for the Air Commerce Act of 1926. This results in the appropriation of funds for the long-range development of army and naval aviation.

27 January 1926 Mitchell, assistant chief of the Army Air Service, officially tenders his resignation from the Army. It will take effect on 1 February. Mitchell later states: "The military bureaucracy, resisting all innovations, has become such that it is impossible to secure any needed changes in the system. The reasons they give us are veiled in mystery and secrecy, so as to confuse the public".

16 March 1926 Robert H. Goddard launches the first liquid-fuel rocket on a farm in Auburn, Massachusetts, at 2:30 p.m. The gasoline and liquid oxygen-powered rocket rises 41 ft (12.5 m) in 2.5 seconds (a rate of 60 mph/96.6 kmh) and lands 184 ft (56 m) from the launch site. Many consider the launch of the first "missile" in the same category as the first heavier-than-air flight by the Wright brothers.

Above: This unprepossessing collection of tubes, spars and tanks is in fact the test rig for one of R.H. Goddard's liquid-fueled rocket experiments. This particular prototype example was test-fired on 20 April, 1927.

9 May 1926 The very first airplane flight over the North Pole is accomplished by aviators Lieutenant Commander Richard E. Byrd and Chief Aviation Pilot Floyd Bennett. The roundtrip flight from Spitzbergen across the frozen wastes covers a distance of 1,600 miles (2,575 km) and lasts 15.5 hours. They reach the Pole at 9:03 Greenwich Central Time in their trimotor Fokker, which is named *Josephine*.

24 June 1926 The Congress authorizes the buildup of naval aircraft to a force of 1,000 within five years. This same legislation also provided that command of aviation stations, schools and tactical flight units be assigned to naval aviators; that command of aircraft carriers and tenders be assigned to naval aviators or naval aviation observers; and that an office be created to foster naval aeronautics.

2 July 1926 The Congress establishes a new medal (Distinguished Flying Cross) for anyone who, "while serving in the armed services, distinguished himself by heroism or extraordinary achievement while participating in aerial flight". Charles A. Lindbergh, a member of the Air Corps Reserve, will become the first person to receive the medal on 11 June, 1927.

2 July 1926 The Army Air Corps is created by an act of the Congress. Passed as a result of recommendations by the Morrow Board, the act provides for an Assistant Secretary of War for Air and a five-year expansion program for the Air Corps.

28 July 1926 Submarine *S-1* surfaces and launches a Cox-Kelmin XS-2 seaplane piloted by Lieutenant D. C. Allen. It later recovers the aircraft and submerges, thereby completing the first cycle of operations testing the feasibility of basing aircraft on submarines. The test effort took place on the Thames River at New London, Connecticut, culminating a series of such tests that started in late 1923.

1 November 1926 The Coast Guard Air Service is inaugurated with the arrival of three Loening amphibians at Coast Guard stations at Ten Pound Island, Gloucester, Maine, which receives two, and Cape May, New Jersey, which receives the other. The machines will be used to go after

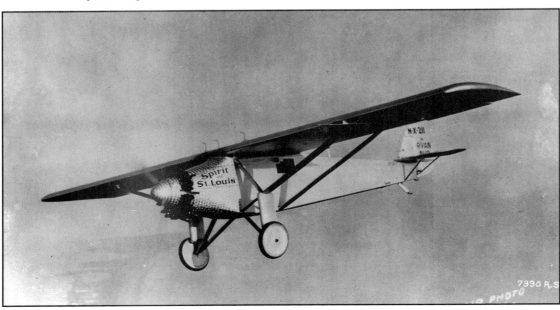

Below: The *Spirit of St Louis* in flight. The tiny, silver airplane in which Charles A. Lindbergh flew from New York City to Paris on his historic flight can now be found at the National Air and Space Museum in Washington.

Below: Charles Lindbergh in his Lockheed Sirius aircraft shortly after his famous flight. During a stop in Greenland, his Sirius was christened "Tingmissartoq" (man who flies like a big bird) by an Eskimo boy.

smugglers and rum-runners. They have larger radio outfits than ordinary planes and are armed with Lewis machine guns.

5 January 1927 A commission to the rank of commander, signed by President Calvin Coolidge, is given to Lieutenant Commander Richard E. Byrd (retired) for his historic flight over the North Pole. Byrd receives the Medal of Honor by the same act of Congress that permitted the commission. Navy machinist Floyd Bennett, the aviation pilot who accompanied Byrd over the Pole, is also awarded a Medal of Honor in the same act.

21 May 1927 Charles Lindbergh makes first solo crossing of the Atlantic in 33 hours, 29 minutes, 30 seconds. The world-famous feat is accomplished in his Ryan monoplane named *The Spirit of St Louis*. For "Lucky Lindy", the honors are fast and furious, including a Medal of Honor from the Congress and a promotion to the rank of colonel in the Air Service reserve.

24 May 1927 Lt. James H. Doolittle performs the first known successful outside loop of an aircraft. "Lucky Jimmy", as he is called, takes his Curtis P-18 up to 8,000 ft (2,440 m), points the nose down, and pulls a circle 2,000 ft (610 m) in diameter. It is estimated by observers that he hits 280 mph (451 kmh) at the bottom of the circle. With bloodshot eyes and fatigue etched on his face, Doolittle lands after his triumph.

27 May 1927 Dive bombing comes under official study as the Chief of Naval Operations orders the Commander in Chief, Battle Fleet, to conduct tests that will evaluate its effectiveness against moving targets.

11 June 1927 The *Memphis* (CL 13) moors at the Washington Navy Yard after returning from France in record time. She had embarked Captain Charles Lindbergh and his plane, the *Spirit of St Louis*, on 3 June at Southampton, England, after his record nonstop flight from New York to Paris. After stopping at Cherbourg, France, she headed straight to the US with her famous passenger.

29 June 1927 The first nonstop flight from the United States to Hawaii is made by Lts. Albert F. Hegenberger and Lester J. Maitland in a Fokker C-2 monoplane named the *Bird of Paradise*. They take off from Oakland, California, and touch down at Wheeler Field, Honolulu, flying the 2,407 miles (3,874 km) in 25 hours and 50 minutes using directional beams at two locations for navigation.

6 January 1928 Making repeated landings at Quilali, Nicaragua, while evacuating Marines, 1st Lt. Christian F. Schilt performs the first air evacuation of the wounded. Schilt makes 10 flights in an aircraft with no brakes, in the rough, rolling street of a burning village — all under the enemies' withering hostile fire. He saves a total of 18 wounded officers and men during three days of flights, and earns a Medal of Honor.

23 January 1928 The aircraft carriers *Lexington* (CV 2) and *Saratoga* (CV 3) appear in fleet exercises for the first time. The *Saratoga*, which carries 69 aircraft, takes part in a mock attack against the Panama Canal. It is the demonstration of this capability that makes a profound impression on the Navy's tacticians.

27 February 1928 Commander Theodore G. Ellyson, the first Navy aviator, is killed — ironically, it is his birthday — on a flight from Hampton Roads, Virginia, to Annapolis, Maryland. Two other airmen are with him on the flight — Lieutenant Commander Hugo Schmidt and Lieutenant

Above: A Fokker tri-motor transport plane comes in low to make a drop to Marine ground forces operating in Nicaragua. The 2nd Battalion, 5th Marines had been in the country since early 1927 to preserve order there.

Rogers S. Ransenhousen. Ellyson was one of the real pioneers of Naval aviation, and had many "firsts" to his credit.

28 September 1928 An official demonstration is held at Brooks Field, Texas, in what might be considered the first jump by paratroops. The demonstration included two formations of nine de Havillands and three Douglas transports. Circling the field at 2,000 ft (610 m), the De Havillands drop 18 men while the transports drop three padded containers of logistical supplies from 3,000 ft (915 m) — proving the practicality of tactical paratrooper deployment in warfare.

Below: The *Saratoga* with a 02U Corsair plane overhead. The 02Us were equipped with a Pratt & Whitney Wasp engine and were later involved in experimental work with blind flights and a float device for seaplanes.

Above: The *Ranger* enters Hunter's Point Drydock, San Francisco. The .50 caliber antiaircraft machine guns are uncovered along the flight deck, forward; the 5-in 6127-mm) guns are shown (covered) at the bow.

16 January 1929 By official order all heavier-than-air naval aviators of both the Navy and Marine Corps must now have experience in night flying. Qualified pilots must have 10 hours of such flying and it must involve at least 20 landings. Student aviators must also meet those same requirements during their first fleet duty assignment.

13 February 1929 Congress authorizes construction of the *Ranger* (CV 4), the first Navy ship designed and built from the keel up as an aircraft carrier. she conducts her first air operations off Cape Henry, Virginia in August 1934 and goes on to become a distinguished performer in World War II, serving as the only large carrier with the Atlantic Fleet. She will earn two battle stars for her service.

23 February 1929 Successful development of special goggles, heated gloves and a device for warming oxygen before use is announced at Wright Field, Ohio. Announcements of this kind were fairly common at the time and reflected more in the way of successful experimentation rather than achievement. For example, the heated gloves were not developed to where they could be used until the 1940s.

14 April 1929 The first electro-mechanical flight simulator, the Link Trainer, is patented. Its significance is that Edwin A. Link has effectively launched the military flight training industry. At the onset of World War II, the need for pilots is critical; more than half a million American and Allied personnel will ultimately go through the 10,000 "blue boxes" for training.

10 May 1929 Lieutenant Charles B. Momsen and Chief Gunner Clarence L. Tibbals receive Distinguished Service Medals and Frank R Hobson, a Navy civilian engineer, receives a year's pay, for work in developing the Navy's submarine "lung". The device had been adopted as standard equipment for all submarines; a bag filled with oxygen and air, it is used by crews to escape to the surface from sunken boats.

3 September 1929 Owen Thomas Edgar, the last surviving veteran of the Mexican War (1846-1848), dies at the age of 98. Edgar had enlisted in the navy as a second-class apprentice on February 10, 1846 and served aboard the frigates *Experience, Potomac, Pennsylvania* and *Allegheny* until his discharge on August 8, 1849. The former printer was a native of Philadelphia, but settled in Washington after the war.

24 September 1929 The first blind-flight takeoff, level flight and landing is accomplished by Doolittle at Mitchell Field, Long Island, New York. Doolittle receives directional guidance from a radio range course aligned with the airport by means of radio markers; a sensitive altimeter helps to control airplane altitude; a gyro and artificial horizon in the covered cockpit guide altitude.

29 November 1929 Richard E. Byrd makes the first flight over the South Pole from Little America in Antarctica in a Ford trimotor named the *Floyd Bennett*. The plane actually took off on November 28 and reached the Pole at 8:55 a.m. on this date. The time for the round trip to base camp, which includes a fuel stop on the return flight, is almost 19 hours.

5 December 1929 Marine Reserve Capt. Alton U. Parker becomes the first pilot to fly over the Antarctic continent as a member of the Byrd expedition to the South Pole. "All of this country over which we will fly", Byrd writes, "will be mapped with the aid of aerial cameras ... From these photographs maps will be drawn which for the first time will give nearly accurate details of the country".

18 December 1929 When a severe drought causes a serious water shortage in the Puget Sound area of Washington state, hydroelectric power no longer available for use. The Navy, in the first instance of its kind, uses the facilities of a steamship — the *Lexington* — to furnish complete electrical power to a US city, Tacoma, Washington. The carrier furnishes more than 4 million kilowatt hours to the city during an amazing 30 day period.

14 February 1930 The first monoplane designed for operations from an aircraft carrier arrives at Naval Air Station, Anacostia, D.C. A Boeing Model 205 fighter, which will later be designated the XF5B-1, is delivered for tests. They result in adverse comments on its landing, takeoff

Above: Bust of Rear Adm. Richard E. Byrd. His expedition reached the Bay of Whales in Antartica in 1929 and established its base, "Little America". It was from there he made the first flight over the South Pole.

and high-altitude characteristics, but further development is encouraged so biplanes and monoplanes can be effectively compared.

20 July 1930 The Veterans Administration is created, combining all federal agencies dealing with relief of ex-servicemen under a single department. An executive order consolidates the Bureau of Pensions, the United States Veterans Bureau and the National Home for Disabled Volunteer Soldiers. The new organization now becomes an independent agency of the government.

16 November 1930 Maj. Gen. James E. Fechet, Chief of the Army Air Corps, makes public his annual report in which he set the enlisted strength of the corps at 12,032, a figure which includes 378 flying cadets. There are 1,266 commissioned officers. Less than one generation has passed since the entire military air arm of the US had consisted of a single airplane.

22 January 1931 The Navy purchases its first autogyro, the XOP-1, from Pitcairn Aircraft, Willow Grove, Pennsylvania for $29,500. Known as the "Flying Windmill", it will undergo testing at the Naval Air Station at Hampton Roads, Virginia, for use in the patrol and observation missions. It has a

357-hp (266 kw) engine that can pull it to an altitude of 6,100 ft (1,860 m) within 10 minutes.

3 March 1931 President Herbert Hoover signs legislation to make the "Star Spangled Banner" the national anthem. It reads: "Be it enacted by the Senate and House of Representatives of the United States of America in Congress assembled, that the composition consisting of the words and music known as 'The Star-Spangled Banner' is designated the national anthem of the United States of America".

2 April 1931 Grumman receives a Navy contract which leads to the development of the two-seat FF-1 fighter. It will

Below: The *Akron* (ZRS 4), the Navy's 6.5 million-cu ft (184,060-m³) rigid airship, during the early 1930s. She was based at Lakehurst, New Jersey, during her brief life; the *Akron* crashed in a severe storm in April 1933.

become the first Navy fighter aircraft — only 27 are built — with a retractable undercarriage. Later modified as the F2F "Flying Barrel", it is the first of its type to have an enclosed cockpit and serves aboard carriers in the fleet from 1935 to 1940.

23 September 1931 The Navy tests the suitability of autogyros in the first such tests of the kind at sea. The tests are conducted aboard the carrier *Langley* (CV 1) by the Navy's experimental division. Lieutenant A. M. Pride is at the controls of the Navy's first rotary-wing aircraft (an XOP-1) and makes four takeoffs and landings during the tests, each time with a different passenger.

23 September 1931 The world's first fighter-carrying airship which the Navy intends to put into operational service (the *Akron*) makes her maiden flight. The 125-mile (200 km) flight lasts almost four hours over the northeastern part of Ohio. There are 113 naval men and civilians aboard the huge ship, which is 785 ft (239.3m) long and has 6,500,000 cu ft (184,060 m³) of lifting gas capacity.

1 November 1931 Randolph Field, called the army's "West Point of the Air", starts to train its first cadet class. About half the 198 students come from West Point, the rest are enlisted men and civilian candidates. Instead of a straight line of hangars like other fields, notes one observer, Randolph Field is a city surrounded by hangars. Everything is within a hexagon, the hangars forming a "city wall".

2 November 1931 Two Marine aviaton squadrons, VS-14M and VS-15M, deploy on board the *Saratoga* and the *Lexington*, which marks the first time that Marine squadrons have served on carriers. They will stay carrier-based until 1941 and then other Marine squadrons will maintain some carrier proficiency with the conduct of periodical operations afloat.

9 April 1932 The Tomb of the Unknown Soldier is opened to the public at Arlington, Virginia. It was sculpted by Thomas Hudson Jones and built at a cost of $48,000 by architect Lorimer Rich; it honors the nation's war dead. Its 48-ton main segment, called the die, was cut from Colorado Yule marble and is the largest single piece of marble ever quarried in the US.

9 May 1932 On this day the first blind solo flight made entirely on instruments and with no check pilot on board is made at Patterson Field, Ohio, by Capt. Alfred F. Hegenberger. One of a series of nine complete blind flights (this is the seventh and only one he will make alone), Hegenberger flies the craft up to an altitude of 1,000 ft (305 m), makes two 180-degree turns and sets the plane safely back on the ground in 5 minutes.

28 July 1932 Federal troops disperse the Bonus Army of World War I veterans who had gathered in Washington to demand money they were scheduled to receive. President Herbert Hoover orders the 2,000 veterans removed from government property they have been occupying. Army Chief of Staff Gen. Douglas MacArthur leads the troops against the veterans.

30 January 1933 Adolf Hitler, leader of the National Socialist party, is appointed Chancellor of Germany. A news account cabled to the US at the time states, ''The composition of the Cabinet leaves Herr Hitler no scope for gratification of any dictatorial ambition''. History proves otherwise. Less than a

Above: The ''Flying Barrel'' (Grumman F3F) which first flew in 1935. The national insignia near the nose of this particular aircraft was worn by the ''Neutrality Patrol'' in 1940. This VF-7 airplane flew from the *Wasp. Right:* The F2F/F3F saw service with the Navy and Marine Corps from 1935 to 1940 and equipped the aircraft carriers *Ranger, Yorktown, Lexington* and *Wasp.*

Service-Connected Veterans Benefits All Wars

	(In millions)
American Revolution	28
War of 1812	20
Mexican War	26
Civil War (Union)	3,289
Civil War (Confederate)	***
Spanish-American War	2,111
World War I	19,091
World War II	83,156
Korea	15,861
Vietnam	23,332

Below: The army of the Third Reich at a massive Nazi rally. After Hitler took office, Germany's traditional nationalism was roused to fever pitch through the effective and continuing use of propaganda techniques such as this.

decade later, the Allies are fighting shoulder-to-shoulder to eliminate the tyranny of Hitler.

25 February 1933 The first aircraft carrier to be built from the keel up as an aircraft carrier, the *Ranger* (CV 4), is launched at Newport News, Va. In her last official act as First Lady, Mrs Herbert Hoover christens the vessel, which has more than an acre of hangar space and can carry more than 140 aircraft in its winged complement. The enormous vessel displaces 15,575 tons.

16 June 1933 Roosevelt agrees to an allotment of slightly more than $9 million to the Navy for 290 aircraft and two aircraft carriers, which, however, are not to exceed 25,000 tons each. At the same time, the Navy recommends taking $5.9 million out of public works funds for new fighters. Each of the carriers will carry a complement of about 90 airplanes.

29 August 1933 Rocket pioneer Robert H. Goddard is informed by the Navy's Acting Secretary Admiral W. H. Standley that adaptation of his rockets to depth-charge projectors, projectiles, bombs and anti-aircraft torpedoes would be impractical. He adds that the practical application of the rocket principle for propulsion of aircraft would require extensive work, ''with success probably very remote''.

20 November 1933 The first Americans ever to accomplish a free balloon flight into the stratosphere, Lieutenant Commander Thomas G. W. Settle and Maj. Chester L. Fordney of the Marine Corps, land their balloon at Bridgeton, New Jersey, after having climbed to a height of 61,237 ft

(18,665 m). They had departed in the 600,000 cu ft (16,990 m³) free balloon from Akron, Ohio.

9 February 1934 Roosevelt orders that all existing domestic air mail contracts be cancelled and that the army fly the mail in emergency created by his action. The order takes effect on 20 February and was prompted by what the president believes are grounds of collusion or fraud among the domestic carriers. Twenty-six routes flown by 12 companies are affected.

1 March 1935 General Headquarters Air Force, a new formation within the US Army Air Corps, is established, with Brig. Gen. Frank M. Andrews in command. This is seen by the proponents of air power as the first move toward an autonomous US Air Force. It is also the first time the term ''Air Force'' is used to describe any US military organization.

22 March 1935 First flight of the Grumman XF3F-1, last biplane fighter in the Navy. A variant of the F2F ''Flying Barrel'' plane, called this because it was the first of its type with a fully-enclosed cockpit, it has a longer fuselage and wings for better maneuverability. It will be the Navy's standard fighter until the late 1930s when it is replaced with the Grumman F4F.

15 April 1935 The first American naval aircraft to feature hydraulically-operated folding wings, which will also be the first carrier-based monoplane torpedo-bomber to enter production (as the Douglas TDB Devastator), is flown in prototype form. The aircraft will remain in operational use through June 1942.

22 May 1935 Roosevelt goes before the Congress to explain his veto of the Patman Greenback Bonus Bill, which would have paid veterans of World War I the remainder of their 1924 bonuses. He tells the Congress it is a measure that will be the opening wedge for spending and inflation, something which with they obviously disagree as they vote to override the veto by 322 to 98.

12 June 1935 An exercise called Fleet Problem XVI — a large-scale Navy air and sea maneuver involving 520 naval aircraft, four aircraft carriers as well as battleships and cruisers — begins. The exercise in the Pacific will last until 10 July and cover 5 million sq miles (12.95 million km²). One of its problems to solve: to determine whether naval and air forces based in Hawaii can fend off an enemy attack on the mainland of the US.

30 July 1935 The first blind carrier landing is made by Lieutenant Frank Akers aboard the *Langley* (CV 1) in a Berliner-Joyce OJ-2 aircraft. Akers had taken off from the Naval Air Station, San Diego, located the *Langley* underway, and completed the landing in his hooded cockpit when he caught the number four arresting wire. He receives the Distinguished Flying Cross for his achievement.

9 January 1936 The M1 rifle is standardized for the Army. This .30 caliber rifle, commonly known as the Garand, is the first self-loader adopted by any Army as a standard weapon. It proves to be a good weapon and was used by the Army throughout

Above: A Consolidated P2Y-2, of the kind in which the first military squadron flight was made. During the 1930s, some civilian planes were exceeding military aircraft in the category of speed, but not in engineering.

World War II. An astonishing total of 5.5 million Garands will be produced by the 1950s when the rifle will go out of production.

13 October 1936 Lt. John W. Sessums visits rocket expert Robert D. Goddard at Roswell, New Mexico. He is to officially assess the military value of the rocket pioneer's work. Sessums reports there is little such value, but that the liquid-fuel rockets appear useful for driving turbines and propelling gliders for use in towing targets.

1 March 1937 General Headquarters of the Army Air Corps at Langley Field, Virginia, receives an operational B-17 ''Flying Fortress''. It is the first four-engined bomber to enter the Air Corps and also the first plane to fulfill Mitchell's concept of an effective all-weather, long-range bomber.

2 July 1937 By Roosevelt's direct order an aircraft carrier, a battleship, four destroyers and a minesweeper begin to scour 250,000 miles (400,000) of the Pacific for downed aviatrix Amelia Earhart. Her last message: ''We are on the line of

Below: Profile of what became commonly known as the Garand rifle (M1), the first self-loader ever to be adopted by any army as a standard weapon. A series of similar rifles were tested before the M1 was accepted for service.

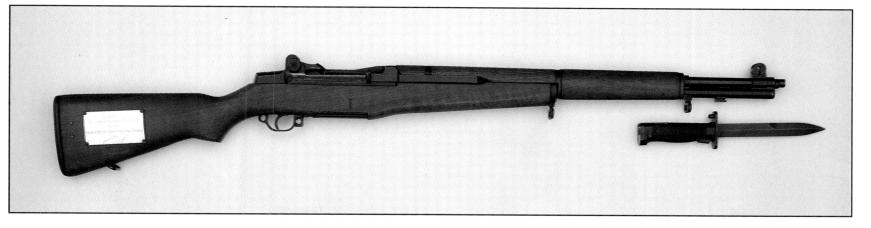

Left: The Bell P-39, especially in the early part of the war, also operated as a fighter-bomber. It could carry a 500-lb (227-kg) bomb under the fuselage. The P-39 was used by the Army Air Force, Britain, and the Soviet Union.

competition for a service song that would express some of the hell-bent-for-leather traditions of aerial flight.

position 157 dash 337. Will repeat this message on 6210 kilocycles. Wait. Listening on 6210. We are running north and south".

23 August 1937 The first wholly automatic landings in history are made at Wright Field, Ohio. A large transport aircraft makes the landings repeatedly under very difficult wind conditions. Even though further experiments will be made with the landing device, says the War Department: "This (makes) it possible to land a plane in absolute darkness or under other adverse conditions."

12 December 1937 The gunboat *Panay* (PR 5) is sunk in Chinese waters by low-flying Japanese planes. The planes hit the ship, despite her prominently displayed American markings, near Nanking. Two crewmen are killed in the incident and another 43 are wounded. Japan says she regrets the attack "most deeply", calls it an unfortunate error and pays a large indemnity.

7 January 1938 The Army first mentions publicly that it will discontinue the use of spiral khaki leggings in a letter, but it will not be until it issues Circular No. 59 on 31 December, 1940 that it becomes official. Trousers and canvas leggings are to replace breeches and wrap leggings (known as puttees) for all the armed services. The only exceptions to the new order will be the mounted services.

6 April 1938 The first US fighter plane to carry a cannon — the P-39 Airacobra — is tested at Wright Field, Dayton, Ohio. The 37-mm cannon is located on the fuselage center line, and the barrel projects through the reduction gear box and propeller hub. It will be tested by pilot Jimmy Taylor within two days. The aircraft was built by Bell Aircraft at Niagara Falls, New York.

1 May 1938 Maneuvers are held on the east coast — involving blackouts for the first time — to determine if an air

Above: German-born theoretical physicist Albert Einstein, who persuaded President Franklin D. Roosevelt an atomic bomb was feasible. He was forced to leave Germany in 1933 after Hitler came into power.

force can repel an attack against the eastern seaboard without help from the fleet. Some 220 planes and 3,000 officers and men participate in the three-day exercise. The maneuvers go well, but doubt remains a force could assemble in time and in the right places during the "real thing".

23 May 1939 The submarine *Squalus* sinks during a practice dive in 240 ft (73m) of water off the New Hampshire coast. There are 26 deaths including one officer, 23 enlisted men and two civilian observers. Cause of the accident was an air valve that was left open during a routine dive. She is refloated, renamed the *Sailfish* and serves with distinction in World War II.

15 July 1939 The US Army Air Corps acquires the performance rights to a stirring song that, two days before, had existed only in the head of composer Robert Crawford. "Off we go into the wild blue yonder . . ." thus enters the nation's historical inventory, the result of a

2 August 1939 Urged on by his fellow scientists, Albert Einstein writes a letter to President Franklin D. Roosevelt informing him that some sort of atomic weapon is feasible. To indicate the power of such a device, he adds that if such a bomb were to explode in port, it "might blow up the entire port together with the surrounding territory". The letter leads to the Manhattan Project.

23 January 1940 The first American test of the practicality of moving complete troop units by air is completed. An entire battalion of the 65th Coast Artillery is transported 500 miles (805 km) by 38 bombers of the 7th Bombardment Group, Hamilton Field, California.

22 March 1940 Development of guided missiles is initiated at the Naval Aircraft Factory with the establishment of a project for adapting radio controls to the torpedo-carrying TG-2 airplane.

20 April 1940 The first seaplane tender designed and built for the US Navy — the *Curtiss* (AV 4) — is launched at Camden, New Jersey. She enjoyed a distinguished career: during World

Above: Russian-born designer Igor Sikorsky at the controls of his VS-300 prototype helicopter. It would be developed into the world's first practical single-rotor helicopter and awaken military interest in its potential.

Right: Martin Mars long-range patrol flying boats of the Navy in flight. The Mars originally was ordered in 1938 by the Navy for this mission, but it served principally as a cargo transport in its lifetime.

War II, she was ripped open during a kamikaze attack that killed 35, but survived; was the base for technicians during atomic tests at Eniwetok; and supported Antarctic operations during "Deep Freeze II".

21 April 1940 Capt. Robert M. Losey, an Air Corps Weather Service Commander, is killed in Norway by Germans during a raid. An official military observer, he nevertheless could be classified as the first American military officer killed in hostile action during World War II.

13 May 1940 Igor Sikorsky completes the first flight of the Sikorsky VS-300 helicopter, the first successful free flight by a single-rotor helicopter. Based on patents he had filed as early as 1931, the VS-300 will ultimately change design more than 18 times, but will prove capable for carrying one man. The VS-300 finally convinces the Army of the feasibility of a practical rotary-wing aircraft.

16 May 1940 The Congress is asked by President Franklin Delano Roosevelt to authorize production of 50,000 military planes per year and for $900 million in extraordinary credit to finance this operation. By the middle of 1945, with World War II in its latter stages, the US will have produced about 300,000 military airplanes.

Above: The *McLanahan* (DD 264), a four-stack flush deck destroyer on the Hudson River, New York. She was transferred to the Royal Navy under the lend-lease agreement of the period and became the *Bradford.*

5 July 1940 Roosevelt invokes the Export Control Act against Japan by prohibiting the export, without license, of strategic minerals and chemicals, aircraft engines and parts and equipment. Within three weeks, he invokes the same authority to deny aviation gasoline and certain classes of iron and steel scrap to the Japanese as well. This halts their flow to that country.

10 July 1940 The Armored Force which combines elements of the cavalry, infantry and the artillery is established by the Army. Originally, the force consists of 242 officers, 7,015 enlisted personnel and 393 light tanks. First Chief of the new organization is Brig. Gen. Adna R. Chaffee, the "father of the Armored Force", long time advocate of an armored striking force centered around the tank.

1 August 1940 The training of the Army's first parachute troops starts at Hightstown, New Jersey. The training at this point is purely in the experimental stage, consisting of a parachute platoon of 48 men and two officers in what is known as the Safe Parachute Company. It forms a nucleus that is expanded to much larger units later when the War Department gives the go-ahead.

17 August 1940 The first regular-serving US pilot to die in action in World War II is Pilot Officer William M. L. Fiske III, who is serving with the RAF in England. He dies of wounds suffered in aerial combat the previous day over Tangmere, Sussex, during the Battle of Britain. Believed to be the first "Yank in the RAF", before the war Fiske had been one of the greatest bobsled aces in America and won medals in the 1928 and 1932 Olympics.

22 August 1940 The keel is laid for the first of the Navy's flying boats at the Martin factory in Baltimore, Maryland. The enormous PB2M Mars is the first aircraft to be accorded keel-laying and launching ceremonies. She will carry 13,000lb (5,897kg) of cargo on her first mission from Maryland to Natal, Brazil. The nonstop flight of 4,375 miles (7,041 km) takes 28 hours and 25 minutes.

3 September 1940 Some 50 drydock US destroyers are transferred to the UK on a 99-year lease. As a result of the transfer, the US gets the rights to bases in Antigua, the Bahamas, Bermuda,

Above: A new sight for the US Army It could not have been done nine months earlier since the US had just begun training a parachute force. Here, Capt. J.W. Coutts inspects newly-packed parachutes of jumpers.

British Guiana, Jamaica, Newfoundland, St Lucia and Trinidad. The first eight destroyers under the "destroyers for bases" agreement are transferred within three days of the announcement of the agreement.

9 September 1940 In the largest naval procurement order in history, the Navy awards contracts for the construction of 210 ships, to include 12 aircraft carriers and 7 battleships. The Navy Department announces the signing of the contracts two hours after Roosevelt approves a supplemental defense appropriation bill for $5 billion. Cost of the Navy's contracts is estimated at $3 billion.

16 September 1940 Roosevelt signs America's first peacetime draft, the Selective Service Act. The legislation provides that 900,000 selectees are to be taken annually. Men between the ages of 20 and 36 are required to register for tours of duty one year in length, a requirement that is extended to 18 months in August 1941.

25 September 1940 US intelligence is able to decode a Japanese message in its entirety for the first time, even though it is sent in Purple supersecret diplomatic code. It means that most messages of extreme sensitivity can now be read by Washington. Along with the breaking of the German code Enigma, it is considered one of the intelligence coups of World War II.

10 November 1940 The first organized transatlantic ferry flights of aircraft built in the US for service with the Allied nations involved in World War II begins.

18 November 1940 The Chief of Naval Operations authorizes use of the abbreviation "RADAR" (Radio Detection and Ranging Equipment) in unclassified correspondence and conversation.

2 January 1941 A program is announced by Roosevelt to produce 200 7,500-ton freighters, which will be produced to standardized designs. Later, they

Above: Gen. Henry H. (Hap) Arnold, chief of the Army Air Forces, with Jack Northrop, president of the Northrop Corp. In 1949 Arnold will be made General of the Air Force, the first such commission ever made.

will become known as "Liberty Ships". The first batch of 14 slip down the way at various construction yards in the US on September 27. By this time, there are now 312 ships on order, with a total tonnage of 2,200,000 tons.

4 February 1941 The United Services Organization is established as several groups band together to coordinate and finance a national program with the aim of giving religious, recreational and welfare services to American troops. The USO, as it becomes known later, says in its charter statement that its efforts are vital for the maintenance of military morale and the future of American youth as citizens in peacetime.

11 March 1941 The Lend-Lease Bill becomes law. Its aim is to give the US greater authority to lend military supplies to countries fighting the Axis powers in World War II. Within five minutes of signing the bill, the president approves the transfer of war materials to the British and the Greeks.

9 April 1941 An agreement is signed with Denmark under which the US takes control of Greenland and agrees to ensure it remains a Danish colony. It establishes the right of America to develop air bases and other military facilities in the strategic area. The accord — signed on the anniversary of the day the Nazis invaded Denmark — envisages the use of Greenland as a base for delivery of war supplies.

Below: The "Liberty" ship *Robert E. Peary* is about the be launched in November 1942 folliwing her building in four days, 15 hours and 29 minutes. She is named after the famous naval officer and Arctic explorer.

Draftees: Armed Forces Civil War through Korea

(In Thousands)

Charac-teristics	Civil War (Union Forces)	World War I	World War II	Korea
Classified	777	24,234	36,677	9,123
Examined	522	3,764	17,955	3,685
Rejected	160	803	6,420	1,189
Inducted	46	2,820	10,022	1,560

29 May 1941 The US agrees to train British pilots who will fly American planes exported under a lend-lease arrangement. Among the types of aircraft supplied to British under the agreement were 2,552 P-40s (Tomahawks and Kittyhawks) as well as the entire production run of the Baltimore Martin A-30, an American-built bomber that was never actually used by American forces.

6 June 1941 The *Terror* (CM 5), the Navy's only ship built specifically for the minelaying mission, is launched at Philadelphia, Pennsylvania. It will not be until November 1942 that she begins laying a minefield in a battle area — a 7-mile (11.25 km) barrier at the channel entrance to Casablanca. The minefield is designed to protect the Allied ships in the harbor.

20 June 1941 The Army Air Forces are established under Maj. Gen. Henry H. (Hap) Arnold. The first major organizational step toward autonomy for the yet-to-come US Air Force, since General Headquarters Air Force was formed in 1935, Army Regulation 95-5 stipulate that it "shall consist of the Headquarters Army Air Forces, the Air Force Combat Command, the Air Corps, and all other air units".

1 August 1941 The US bans the export of aviation fuel, except to the UK and those unoccupied nations resisting the Nazis. The decision comes as a severe blow to the Japanese, who are engaged in a continuing war with China, and hastens its decision to join with Axis partners in a war against the Allies.

18 August 1941 The US announces that Pan American Airways is ferrying combat planes from the Middle East by way of Brazil and West Africa. The measure is one way to speed up the delivery of aircraft to the hard-pressed British.

Above: A Martin Baltimore taxies on an airfield at Accra (Gold Coast), another aircraft safely delivered to its destination. These aircraft served with light bomber squadrons during the North African campaigns.

---

11 September 1941 Roosevelt issues an attack-on-sight order, which applies to German or Italian vessels found by American ships or planes to be operating in US defensive waters. The order became necessary after a number of US vessels had been sunk or fired on by submarines.

17 September 1941 Navy ships escort their first troop convoy of World War II. Under Rear Adm. A. B. Cook, the convoy sailed from Halifax, Nova Scotia escorting 20,000 British troops. The Navy had been given the responsibility for trans-Atlantic convoys on September 1, and Roosevelt had announced he was ordering the Navy to attack any vessel threatening ships under US escort.

26 September 1941 The Secretary of War establishes a permanent Military Police Corps in the Army, which is to consist of three battalions and four separate companies. Approximately 2,000 men in all, the corps is to grow during the course of World War II to a strength of more than 200,000 enlisted men and 9,250 officers.

27 September 1941 The first US Liberty Ship, the *Patrick Henry*, is launched at Baltimore. (A total of 2,742 of these vessels will be delivered by 1945). They are dubbed "ugly ducklings" by the president, but the ships were the backbone of the merchant fleet. They were built at a cost of $1.5 million each, with bonuses awarded for earlier-than-scheduled deliveries.

14 October 1941 The first authenticated Nazi war operatives to be captured by American armed forces are brought to Boston, Massachusetts, under escort of the Coast Guard cutter

Bear. A Marine force had seized the operatives off Greenland aboard the freighter *Busko,* which flew a Norwegian flag. A powerful radio transmitter was also seized. There were 18 sailors, a boy and a Gestapo agent on the ship.

17 October 1941 The destroyer *Kearny* (DD 432) is torpedoed and damaged south west of Iceland while on escort duty. She immediately begins dropping depth charges and continues the barrage throughout the night. Some 11 bluejackets are killed and another 22 injured; they are considered the first American casualties of World War II.

31 October 1941 The destroyer *Reuben James* (DD 245) is torpedoed and sunk while on patrol off Iceland, the first loss of a Navy ship to enemy action in World War II. She had sailed from Argentia, Newfoundland eight days earlier with four other destroyers on convoy escort duty. Torpedoed by the German submarine *U-562* at 5:25 a.m., she sank with the loss of 115 lives after a magazine explosion.

5 November 1941 Secret instructions (Combined Fleet Ultrasecret Operations Order I) are issued to the Japanese Navy for the attack on Pearl Harbor. Talks with the US were to continue, according to the Imperial agreement, but the decision was to go to war if they failed to produce a settlement. The military was ordered to prepare for the worst.

29 November 1941 The Commander in Chief, Asiatic Fleet, is directed by the president to charter three small vessels, establish their identities as US men-of-war and to station them in the West China Sea and the Gulf of Siam. Behind Roosevelt's order: if the Japanese had fired on any of these craft, it would have constituted an overt act of war. As it was, Japan's plans would ensure that war came within days.

World War II (1941 — 1945)

There is simply no effective way for the mind to comprehend the cataclysmic event history records as World War II. It was the greatest and most destructive war ever waged on the face of the Earth. The pain, death and suffering it visited on the planet and its people were immeasurable.

The armies of those nations who fought it numbered in the millions. Its costs were in the trillions. And its consequences will be with us for as far as the mind can see.

The conflict involved all of the great powers and many of the lesser nations as well. Ranged on one side were the Axis powers — led by Nazi Germany, Italy and Japan; on the other were the Allies — led by the UK, the USA, France and the USSR.

When the planes of the Japanese Navy attacked Pearl Harbor and other military installations in Hawaii on 7 December, 1941, killing more than 2,000 Americans and gutting the US Pacific fleet, America declared war on Japan. Neither Germany nor Italy was bound to support their Axis partner, but both did so on 11 December, 1941.

This involved the US in a truly global war. At its outset, the Navy had 284,427 seamen and 347 warships; there were 17 battleships, six aircraft carriers and 32 cruisers, split evenly between the Atlantic and Pacific fleets. The Army numbered 1,644,000 men, including the Army Air Forces.

Before the war was over, the US would have 15,144,306 personnel in uniform, led by the Army and Army Air Forces with 10,420,000 men and women; the Navy with 3,883,520; the Marine Corps with 599,693; and the Coast Guard — part of the Navy during wartime — with 241,093.

The major theater for the Army was Europe, where more than 3 million soldiers served. US naval forces had massive involvement worldwide in all theaters; the Marine Corps played its greatest role in the Pacific. From the first amphibious operation on Guadalcanal in 1942 to the invasion of Okinawa in April 1945, the Marines lost 19,733 men. Air power realized its potential. By the end of the war, the Army Air Forces had dropped 2.7 million tons of bombs on Germany alone.

Some 292,131 Americans lost their lives in World War II. There were an additional 115,187 non-battle deaths — the first time in the history of American warfare that battle deaths outnumbered those due to accident or disease. In addition, 671,801 Americans were wounded in action.

After Pearl Harbor, Japan had hoped to capitalize on the advantages provided by its attack on the US fleet. But by 1942, the tide was slowly but inexorably turning in favour of the US and its allies. In June, Japanese naval air power was decimated by the Navy in the Battle of the Midway. As the war production capabilities of America began to take hold, the initiative began to swing with it.

In July-August 1943, the Allies invaded and captured Sicily, soon forcing Italy out of the war. Less than one year later, the greatest amphibious assault ever mounted in the history of warfare took place on the Normandy coast in France. It pressed the Germans to the fullest, prompting them to launch a counterattack (the "Battle of the Bulge") that ultimately failed.

Assailed on all sides by the Allies, their major cities absolutely devastated by aerial bombardment, Nazi Germany surrendered on 7 May, 1945.

In the Pacific theater, meanwhile, a persistent two-pronged offensive across the Central Pacific and along the Solomon Islands pushed the Japanese back and the Philippines were reclaimed in early 1945. Then it was Okinawa, accompanied by a general deterioration of the Japanese position throughout Asia, followed by the dropping of atomic bombs on Hiroshima and Nagasaki. Japan capitulated on 14 August and formally surrendered on 2 September.

During the war, the US produced 296,429 warplanes, 102,351 tanks, 372,431 artillery pieces, 2.5 million trucks, 87,620 ships, 5,425 cargo ships, 5.8 million tons of bombs, more than 20 million small arms and more than 44 billion rounds of small arms ammunition.

The US also produced the atomic

Below: Sunday morning 7 December, 1941, and ships of the US Pacific Fleet lie within Pearl Harbor all but defenseless against the bombs and torpedoes of the attacking Japanese aircraft. The surprise is total and defeat almost complete.

bomb, an innovation of the war that has been a shadow on the world's stage since 1945, with the potential to determine future world strategy and diplomacy — or to become a more powerful addition to the world's military arsenals.

It was not, of course, the only change in military technology wrought by the war. Tanks and warplanes were improved considerably by advances made in internal combustion engines; the ubiquitous, hand-held bazooka and the deadly German V-2 rocket meant that rocket weapons had reappeared on the battlefield; electronics, particularly in the form of radar and radio communications, burgeoned.

Air power emerged as a combat force every bit the equal of land power and sea power. A doctrine of mobile warfare was made possible by improved ordnance and faster vehicles. Weapons and equipment were devised — landing craft, for example — that would get troops to the edge of the beach and let them offload rapidly.

The aircraft carrier reigned supreme as the capital ship of the American fleet — providing, as it did, the capability to extend fire power to destroy enemy surface forces. Naval fire power was used in support of landing operations. And the final effectiveness of an air offensive was improved when long-range fighters able to accompany and protect bombers came on the scene.

Even as the war was coming to a close, technology were still moving forward. Nazi Germany succeeded in building a number of warplanes with a jet aircraft engine that was faster and much more powerful than its propeller-driven counterpart. Fortunately for the Allies, the development came too late to affect the final outcome of the war.

"There is an understandable fascination — which is neither macabre nor militaristic — about World War II", offers one observer. "Any event approaching its ghastly dimensions would command infinite attention. The experience is still near enough in time to provide retrospective interest for those who lived through it and to spark intellectual curiosity among those unborn at the time."

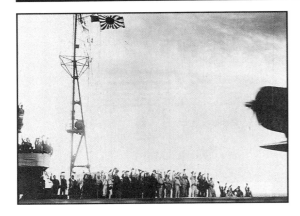

Above: The morning of 7 December. From Japanese carriers, aircraft and their pilots are given a rousing farewell from those on deck. The first wave of attacking planes will appear over Pearl Harbor at approximately 7.55 a.m.

Above: Ground installations and airfields are amongst those targets first hit by the leading squadrons of bombers and fighters, leaving the way open for the primary objective: the Pacific Fleet.

Above: Battleship Row seconds before the attack. Within 40 minutes of the opening of the first Japanese strike on the lines of ships safely at berth, four battleships had been sunk and another two had been critically damaged.

7 December 1941 The Japanese attack Pearl Harbor. In an episode described by Roosevelt as a "day that will live in infamy", Admiral Nagumo's carriers launch an attack that sparks US entry into World War II. The effectiveness of the surprise attack is reflected in the figures: 19 US ships lost, 188 planes destroyed and more than 2,400 killed or wounded. The Japanese lost 28 aircraft and fewer than 100 men.

7 December 1941 Aircraft from the *Enterprise* (CV 6) engage enemy aircraft in the first aerial combat by the Navy in World War II. The *Enterprise* was about 200 miles (320 km) from Pearl Harbor when the Japanese made their attack and was returning from Wake Island after delivering a Marine fighter squadron there. The *Enterprise*'s VS-6 squadron arrives during the attack and successfully engages the Japanese.

7 December 1941 The destroyer *Ward* (DD 139) fires the first shot of the Pacific war at 6.45 a.m., with the shot falling harmlessly beyond the small conning tower of a Japanese submarine. The next round went through the conning tower and, as the midget submarine started to sink, the *Ward* dropped four depth charges on her. The first Japanese submarine had been sunk.

7 December 1941 The highest ranking US naval officer killed during World War II loses his life on the first day of the war. Rear Admiral Isaac C. Kidd was aboard the *Arizona* (BB 39), his flagship, when the Japanese attacked. Kidd manned a machine gun and was last seen firing at the attacking aircraft. His body is entombed in its hull, which is now a memorial to the 1,103 sailors who went down with her.

7 December 1941 Credit for destruction of the first Japanese Zeros of by the Army Air Corps is shared by four pilots, each of whom registers kills near Oahu, Hawaii. Three belonged to the 46th Fighter Squadron: 1st Lt. Lewis M. Sanders and 2nd Lts. Philip M. Rasmussen and Gordon H. Sterling, Jr. 2nd Lt. George S. Welch bagged his Zero between Wahiawa and Haleiwa; he belonged to the 47th Fighter Squadron.

8 December 1941 The US declares war on Japan. The majority of Latin America joined with the US in declaring war. The number of belligerents rose to 38, only 10 of whom were in the Axis camp. The operational area extended from Ethiopia to the Aleutians and from the Arctic Circle to the Tropic of Capricorn. An interesting historical footnote: the UK actually was the first to declare war against the Japanese following Pearl Harbor — not the US!

9 December 1941 B-17s bomb shipping in the Philippines in the first American bombing mission of World War II. In concert with P-40s and P-35s, the heavy bombers attack a convoy landing troops and equipment at Vigan and at Aparri in North Luzon. The strike includes the widely-publicized attack of Capt. Colin P. Kelly on a warship. He is killed when his B-17 is shot down returning to Clark Field.

10 December 1941 Aircraft from the *Enterprise* (CV 6) attack and sink the Japanese submarine I-70 in waters north of the Hawaiian Islands. This was one of the submarines used to scout the Hawaiian area in connection with the Pearl Harbor attack and the first Japanese combatant ship sunk by US aircraft during World War II.

11 December 1941 The Axis powers — Germany and Italy — declare war on the US.

11 December 1941 *Haruna*, a 29,330 ton battleship, is sunk off north Luzon, Philippine Islands, by American forces and becomes the first Japanese battleship to be sunk in World War II. She went down after being set afire by aerial bombardment from Navy aircraft. At the time, *Haruna* was supporting an attack in which the Japanese had completed a landing at Aparri on the Philippine northern coast.

Above: After such an attack only one response was conceivable. On 8 December Roosevelt like Woodrow Wilson before him addresses the Congress on the necessity for war. His call is met with almost total unanimity.

Above: President Roosevelt, surrounded by Congressional leaders ends two years of neutrality by signing the bill which declares war on Japan. Three days later Germany and Italy declare war on the US and global war has begun.

16 December 1941 Lt. Boyd D. "Buzz" Wagner becomes the first American ace of World War II when he bags his fifth enemy plane in succession. Flying a Curtiss P-40 Warhawk, as he always did, Wagner was one of the handful of pilots who remained in the Philippines after the Japanese attacked Pearl Harbor. Within four months of the time he becomes the

Below: A groundcrew prepares the P-40 that belongs to Gen. Claire Chennault's famous volunteer unit, the "Flying Tigers". Easily the most colorful air unit of the war, their warplanes sported a distinctive decoration.

first ace of the war, he will be promoted and make lieutenant colonel.

20 December 1941 Col. Claire Chennault's American Volunteer Group (The Flying Tigers) enters combat against Japanese at Kunming, China. Composed entirely of Army Air Force fliers who resigned in order to defend the Burma Road, the Flying Tigers meet 10 Japanese planes and shoot down four of them — without losing any of their own — in this first encounter.

22 December 1941 The first American troops arrive in Australia. US troops aboard an Allied convoy proceeding from Hawaii toward the Far East under close escort of the cruiser *Pensacola* (CA 24) had been organized as Task Force South Pacific under the command of Brig. Gen. Julian F. Barnes. It will formally become Task Force South Pacific upon the arrival of the troops in Brisbane.

24 December 1941 The 26th Cavalry, which was the only American outfit to fight on horseback during World War II, repulses an attack on Binalonan in the Philippines, checks a drive by Japanese infantry and launches a blistering counterattack. This crack regiment of 55 officers and 787 enlisted men was effectively reduced to 450 men, but they will hold on to Binalonan until dusk.

26 December 1941 Since any building in the nation's capital is considered in danger during World War II, the most famous document in US history — the Declaration of Independence — is moved under escort to Fort Knox, Kentucky. It was packed in a special bronze container for the move; it would not be until late in

Below: Gen. Chennault's "Flying Tiger" pilots scramble to their Curtiss P-40 fighters in China. The "Flying Tigers" shot down 299 Japanese planes during seven months of combat and lost only 32 of their own.

Above: An early version (the Y1B-17) of Boeing's "Flying Fortress", seen over Washington D.C. in 1937. Deliveries of the B-17 were first made to US forces in June 1939, and continued without pause until April 1945.

the war (1944) that the document would be returned to the Library of Congress.

3 January 1942 In a joint statement, the Army and Navy disclose every American airplane type will have a name of its own, not just a number designation. It is a clear and acknowledged emulation of British practice and includes names the British have already adopted for American planes. Names such as the 'Flying Fortress,' 'Avenger,' 'Corsair' and 'Mustang' will soon become familiar to the world.

14 January 1942 The Army Air Corps awards a contract to Sikorsky Aircraft for a fixed-rotor machine, the XR-4, which made its first flight on this date. It is the first helicopter that will be designed and built for US military service. The machine has about twice the size and twice the power (a 175hp/130kW Warner R-500-3 engine) of the earlier non-military VS-300 helicopter.

26 January 1942 The first contingents of American troops land in Northern Ireland, the first US force to arrive in Europe during World War II. The 18 officers and 18 enlisted personnel were the advance party

Above: American troops march past on their arrival in Belfast. They were the first group of United States' troops to arrive in Europe during World War II. In time over 1½ million other servicemen would follow.

of the first contingent. By the time of the Normandy landing in 1944, the number of American troops in the UK will swell to a total of 1,562,000.

26 January 1942 Just seven weeks after the terrible event, the Board of Inquiry officially constituted to investigate the Pearl Harbor disaster publishes its findings. The former commander in chief of the Pacific Fleet (Admiral Husband E. Kimmel) and the then-commander of the Hawaiian Department (Gen. Walter C. Short) are both judged guilty of dereliction of duty. Both officers had already been dismissed from their positions, and no court martial was ever held.

27 January 1942 The *Gudgeon* (SS 211) becomes the first US submarine to sink an enemy warship in World War II. The victim is Japanese submarine *I-173*, which has just returned back

from a patrol in American waters off the California and Washington coasts. The *Gudgeon* sank 71,047 tons of enemy shipping and accounted for a confirmed total of 12 kills during the war.

1 February 1942 Task Forces 8 and 17 carry out the first US carrier offensive of World War II. The *Enterprise* (CV 6) and *Yorktown* (CV 5) are at the core of the task forces. It is their aircraft which attack a number of military installations on Wotje, Makin, Kwajalein, Jaluit and Mili on the Marshall and Gilbert Islands.

19 February 1942 Roosevelt signs an executive order that makes wartime detention of Japanese-Americans possible. It uses the simple expedient of giving the Secretary of War the authority to bar from specified areas anybody who presents a security risk. Within weeks, 112,000 Japanese are moved to secure

Below: The *Enterprise* (CV 6) enters Pearl Harbor in May 1942, six months after the surprise attack at the base by the Japanese Imperial Navy had virtually wiped out the US Pacific Fleet. Thankfully she had not been there that day.

internment camps, where they will remain until 17 December, 1944.

21 February 1942 Lieutenant Edward ("Butch") O'Hare shoots down five Japanese bombers in five minutes. The first Navy ace of the war, he left the deck of the carrier *Lexington* (CV 2) to intercept bombers that had been sent to the Bismark Archipelago area. O'Hare eventually records 11 victories in the war, but is shot down accidentally as he conducts the first night fighter operation from a carrier.

23 February 1942 The first American air headquarters of World War II is established in England as Brig. Gen. Eaker assumes command of the newly-established VIII Bomber Command. On 17 August, 1942, he will lead the first heavy bomber attack on the European continent. His unit will be redesignated the 8th Air Force and carry out a sustained campaign against targets across Europe.

23 February 1942 Japanese submarine *I-17* shells the Elwood oil refinery near Santa Barbara, California, in the early evening. About 25 shells are fired by the boat, most of which explode close but harmlessly among the derricks and storage facilities. One rig is hit, causing $500 in damages. The Japanese commander of *I-17*, who ordered the shelling, had been embarrassed during a pre-war incident at the site.

25 February 1942 The US Coast Guard assumes responsibility for the security of American ports. The Coast Guard began the war with approximately 25,000 men, a number that goes up dramatically until it hits a peak in June 1944 at 175,000 regulars and reservists. Thirty-two Coast Guard-manned vessels were lost to enemy action during World War II as were 1,917 men.

5 March 1942 The personnel of the newly-established Navy construction battalions are officially designated "Seabees". It derives from the abbreviation CB, for construction battalion. This date is the official birthday of the Seabees and the date on which the famous "fighting bee" emblem receives approval.

Comparative Submarine Strengths Start of World War II

US Navy	73
Japanese Navy	60
German Navy	59.2*

*Average on duty in the Atlantic area.

Above: Gen. Douglas MacArthur, supreme commander of the Allied forces in the Southwest Pacific, during inspection tour in Australia. He had been ordered there after the fall of the Philippines in early 1942.

11 March 1942 Gen. Douglas MacArthur, with his personal staff and members of his family, plus Rear Admiral F. W. Rockwell together with members of the General Staff, depart from the beseiged Philippines on four torpedo boats bound for Mindanao and safety. Although the Japanese invaders have forced this retreat, it gives rise to MacArthur's famous promise: "I shall return." The general redeems the pledge on 20 October, 1944.

17 March 1942 MacArthur and his staff arrive in Australia in two Army planes that have flown from the Philippines over Japanese fronts in the Pacific. It is officially disclosed that MacArthur, with the "most enthusiastic" support of the host government, will become the supreme commander of all Allied forces in the Southwest Pacific theater.

23 March 1942 The US begins moving Japanese-Americans from their west coast homes to detention centers. Some three months after the attack on Pearl Harbor, the Army rounded up 112,000 men, women and children of Japanese ancestry — two-thirds of them native born citizens — and shipped them to remote locations. With limited exceptions, they remained there until 1945.

9 April 1942 The Bataan "Death March", during which 5,200 Americans lose their lives, begins. Overall, 76,000 men (including 12,000 Americans) started on the march, which lasted for six days. Thousands died of dysentery, starvation and exposure and only 54,000 survived. General Masaharu Homma, who commanded the march of American and Philippine troops, will be hanged in 1946 as a war criminal.

29 April 1942 The Pentagon is first occupied. Proposed for construction just before the US enters World War II. Remarkably, the time to build it covers a period of just over 16 months. Built to accommodate some 40,000 military and civilian personnel from all the services, the Pentagon is built on what was originally a swampy wasteland used as a dump. The former airport for Washington (Hoover) was located at its north end.

Left: A birdseye view of the Pentagon headquarters nearing the end of its construction. The specially built access roads are much in evidence, as is the building's unique design, which covers a total of 34 acres (14 hectares).

Above: Under the watchful gaze of their Japanese captors, American servicemen prepare to march through Bataan to captivity. Through deliberate mistreatment and starvation, as many as 22,000 are reckoned to have died.

30 April 1942 The Army on this day signs production contracts with General Motors for the first prototypes of an amphibious landing vehicle (the DUKW) which becomes the most widely used transport vehicle of its type during the war. It is basically a floating truck and can move on either land or water with no special preparation. More than 37,000 are built and some 800 modifications were made to it during its working lifetime.

6 May 1942 After a full day of negotiations, Gen. Jonathan Wainwright surrenders Corregidor and his 3,500 men to the Japanese under

Below: A DUKW in its characteristic role, Sicily 1943. Built because of the realization that amphibious operations were going to be a major characteristic of this war, this unique vehicle proved perfect to the task.

Above: The Japanese carrier *Shokaku* under dive-bomber and torpedo attack during the Battle of the Coral Sea. The Japanese aim in this operation was to secure the Solomon Islands and isolate Australia.

Right: During the Coral Sea, planes line-up aboard the *Lexington*. Between 7-8 May the fleets of both sides exchanged approximately 6 air strikes between them, destroying one carrier from either side and a number of smaller craft.

Above: Torpedo strikes hit the Japanese carrier *Shoho* during the Battle of the Coral Sea. This was the first time that carrier had battle with carrier, and the result was a strategic victory for the US.

Below: The American carrier sunk during the battle was the *Lexington*. Hit many times by Japanese air strikes from enemy carriers, her crew gallantly kept her afloat until it was obvious that the only thing to do was abandon her, she sank soon afterwards.

Gen. Yamashita. Under orders that he is forced to broadcast the next day, he implicitly invites commanders elsewhere in the Philippines to surrender, which they do one by one. By June 9, the American command in the Philippines ceases to exist.

7 May 1942 The Battle of the Coral Sea, the first naval battle in history to be fought without opposing ships making visual contact, begins. The US carrier forces stop a Japanese attempt to land at Port Moresby, New Guinea, by turning back the covering carrier force. It represented a major strategic victory in the Pacific, with each side losing about 30 aircraft.

8 May 1942 The 41,000-ton *Lexington* (CV 2) is sunk after the Battle of the Coral Sea and becomes the first US aircraft carrier lost to enemy action in World War II. She had taken

three hits from enemy dive bombers, righted herself and then exploded. She left a lasting legacy: the pioneering role she had played in developing naval aviators and the techniques for fighting the war in the Pacific.

14 May 1942 Congress creates the Women's Army Auxiliary Corps (WAAC). Women between the ages of 21 and 50 are eligible to join and within the first year five WAAC (later WAC — for Women's Army Corps) units are activated, an all-black one at

Below: One of the US casualties of Midway was the *Yorktown*. Crippled by air strikes from the *Hiryu* she became uncontrollable and was abandoned. Taken into tow, she was later torpedoed by a submarine.

Right: The Japanese carrier *Hiryu* maneuvers successfully to avoid a bombing strike by land-based B-17s, flying at around 20,000 ft (6,100 m). Notice the bomb patterns on either side falling well-short of the ship.

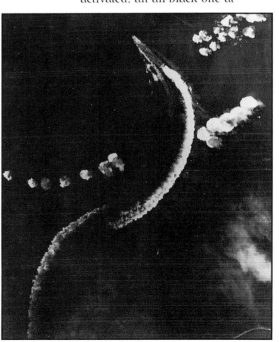

Fort Des Moines, Iowa, and four others at training centers in the states of Georgia, Florida, Massachusetts and Louisiana. Pay is $21 per month.

1 June 1942 Machinery which had been put in motion 10 days earlier results in the start of an effort to recruit blacks for combat service with the Navy and the Marine Corps. The Navy's effort is directed at absorbing 1,000 men a month and training them in almost all the skills that will fit them for duty ashore and on the high seas. The Marines will recruit a complete battalion of 900 men.

4 June 1942 The Battle of Midway takes place as a naval force intercepts a Japanese invasion fleet heading for Midway Island and achieves an overwhelming victory. The battle is considered the turning point of the Pacific War and a confirmation of the lethality of aircraft carrier strike forces.

6 June 1942 The official birth date of Army aviation. It marks the beginning of light aviation as a major part of the Army Field Artillery fire direction center. Each artillery battalion was usually authorized two airplanes (of the light, Piper Cub type), two pilots and a maintenance mechanic. The Army used the light airplanes as observation posts, to evacuate the wounded and for other missions.

7 June 1942 While gallantly fighting against the enemy Maj. Gen. Clarence L. Tinker is officially declared missing in action during the Battle of the Midway. He will be declared dead one year later and is posthumously awarded a Distinguished Service Medal on 10 November, 1942. Tinker was the first general to be killed in action in the history of the US Army Air Forces.

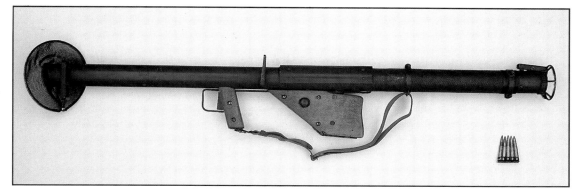

Above: Profile of the famous "bazooka", an anti-tank weapon that came off General Electric's production lines in great quantities during World War II. Nearly 5,000 were completed within the first month of production.

Right: GIs in Italy demonstrate use of the bazooka. The anti-tank weapon gave good service throughout the war. Its name is derived from a comic wind instrument played by a well-known American entertainer.

7 June 1942 Japan invades and occupies the Aleutian Islands with a force of 1,800 men. It is the only time an Axis power will occupy any US territory in North America during World War II. The Navy makes an announcement of the event the following week. It will not be until May 1945 that the islands will be retaken by American military forces.

11 June 1942 The USA and USSR sign a lend-lease agreement that will assist the Soviet war effort. It contains three essential points of agreement: the need to open a second front in Europe; measures to step up the shipment of planes, tanks and other kinds of war materials; and that fundamental problems of cooperation will be addressed in the post-war world.

13 June 1942 Six Nazi saboteurs are electrocuted in a District of Columbia jail. They had been sentenced to die by a military commission of seven general officers for their covert efforts at Long Island, New York, and Ponte Vedra Beach, Florida. Landing from enemy submarines in two groups, they were captured with explosives, incendiaries, fuses, timing devices and acids.

14 June 1942 Known in typical Army jargon as "Launcher, Rocket AT, M-1", the bazooka of World War II fame comes off the General Electric assembly line at Bridgeport, Connecticut. Weighing 12lb (5.4 kg) and operated by a two-man team, it is a steel tube about 50in (1.97 m) long that sets off a rocket-propelled charge when the trigger is squeezed.

17 June 1942 The first issue of *Yank*, a weekly magazine that is published for American servicemen in World War II, is distributed. Says Roosevelt in the first issue: "In *Yank* you have established a publication which cannot be understood by your enemies. It is inconceivable to them that a soldier should be allowed to express his own thoughts . . ." *Yank* is "discharged" in December 1945.

Below: A Japanese Mikuma-class cruiser is left wrecked and burning, after having been on the receiving end of some of the US Navy's carrier-borne air strikes during the Battle of Midway. It is only a short time before she sinks.

Below: The carrier *Hiryu* burns after an American attack. Essentially Midway was won in five minutes when aircraft from *Enterprise* and *Yorktown* destroyed 3 Japanese carriers, *Kaga*, *Akagi* and *Soryu* in a single strike.

18 June 1942 Bernard Robinson is commissioned an ensign in the US Naval Reserve, the first black man to become an officer in the Navy. It was not until 1942 that the Navy accepted black volunteers for general service — and, even then, they were not allowed to go to sea. Much later in the war, a destroyer and submarine chaser had all-black crews. Almost 150,000 blacks served in the Navy during the war.

4 July 1942 Date of the first American bombing mission over enemy-occupied territory in Europe. Six American-manned A-20 Boston bombers accompany six British-manned Bostons on a daylight attack on German airfields at Alkmaar, Hammstede and Valkenburg in the Netherlands. Only two of the American planes reach their targets; the others are shot down or damaged.

20 July 1942 The first detachment of the WAAC begins basic training at Fort Des Moines, Iowa. Col. Don C. Faith is commandant for the nearly 100 officer candidates, who are enthusiastic about serving their country. Sgt. Earl Walterbach is reputed to have given the WAACs their first military command, a "Turn left!" on their way to the mess hall.

20 July 1942 The Legion of Merit Medal is officially authorized. Capt. Ralph B. Praeger is the first to earn the award — which is presented posthumously for his service in the Philippine Islands in the early years of the war. The Legion of Merit is one of three decorations that stem from the first US military decoration, the Badge of Military Merit, established by George Washington in 1782.

22 July 1942 Gasoline rationing begins in the US. The rationale behind this move and others in the market place was that by using it to limit consumption, the government in effect made the purchase without monetary value. No amount of money (theoretically, at least) would give citizens more than the allotted share of such items as gasoline, tires, sugar and so on.

7 August 1942 US forces take the offensive in the Pacific for the first time with the invasion of Tulagi and Guadalcanal in the Solomon Islands. Naval and air support aid the 1st Marine Division which puts ashore on Guadalcanal and four other islands. Benefitting from the bad weather, the invasion force of 11,000 Marines lands without initial opposition; however, that changes and the operation lasts six months. Air support for the operation is provided by three aircraft carriers and airplanes operating from bases on New Caledonia and in the New Hebrides. The carriers will withdraw two days later, but will continue to provide support.

16 August 1942 One of the nation's most famous military units is formed when the 82nd Airborne ("All American")

Above: The Douglas A-20 bomber, which was later named the Havoc. It was a reliable and potent fighting machine and saw widespread service with both US Army Air Forces and Soviet squadrons after 1942.

Division is activated in Louisiana. After a period of intense training and less than a year after it came into existence, the 82nd was the first unit of its type to go overseas and the first airborne division in combat. It racked up a total of 422 days in combat in World War II. The original 82nd was an infantry division and was activated in 1917.

Right: At last US ground forces take the offensive in the Pacific war. In the Solomon Islands, dead soldiers from the defending Japanese 17th Army litter the beach at Tenura River on Guadacanal, August 1942.

Above: The return from the disastrous amphibious assault on Dieppe. The weapons and uniforms of the two closest soldiers on this launch indicate that they may well be part of the US Ranger unit involved.

Above: The XP-59A Airacomet jet-powered fighter in flight. The "X" designation indicates it is an experimental aircraft, the "P" that it is a pursuit type. Its first flight was in California. Only 66 of these aircraft saw service.

Below: The Boeing XB-29. A technologically advanced bomber with a novel gun system, the B-29 was plagued with problems. But it was effective and will be remembered for its role at Hiroshima and Nagasaki.

17 August 1942 While helping conduct the first all-US bombing operation over Rouen, France, 2nd Lt. Sam F. Junkin becomes the first American pilot to down a German fighter — a Focke-Wulf Fw 190. The American B-17 Flying Fortress making the raid over the railroad yards had the protection of escorting wings of Royal Air Force, Canadian and Allied fighters.

19 August 1942 Four American Rangers, attached to the British Commandos, become the first US troops to fight on French soil in World War II. Their assignment is to knock out a six-gun battery in the gunpits around Dieppe during the amphibious assault on that coastal town. The four are SSgt. Kenneth Stemson, Sgt. Alex Szima and Cpls. William Brady and Franklin Koon. "It looked like a suicide mission," says one of them, "but damned if we didn't make it."

31 August 1942 The National Naval Medical Center is dedicated at Bethesda, Maryland. The site for what has now become a world-renowned medical institution was personally chosen by Roosevelt, whose initial sketches are used as the architectural guide for its design. The inspiration for the sketches by the president was the existing State Capitol Building at Lincoln, Nebraska. During the war years, its capacity is expanded to 2,000 beds.

9 September 1942 A Yokosuka E14Y1 light submarine-borne reconnaissance floatplane, which is launched from the Japanese submarine *I-25* offshore, makes two overflights of the wooded Oregon coast while dropping four incendiary bombs. It is the first and only time Japanese fixed-wing aircraft raid the mainland US during World War II. No damage is done.

21 September 1942 First flight of the Boeing XB-29 Superfortress. The heaviest combat aircraft of the war with a 141,000-lb (63,957 kg) maximum take-off weight, it will enter service in the early summer of 1944. First conceived as a strategic bomber for use against Germany, it will in fact operate only against the Japanese. A B-29, the *Enola Gay*, dropped the atomic bomb at Hiroshima.

1 October 1942 The maiden flight of XP-59A Airacomet, America's first jet aircraft is made. It is rated at 400 mph (644 kmh) with a ceiling in excess of 40,000 ft (12,190 m). The aircraft is powered by two kerosene-fueled turbojet engines. It was originally intended to be a fighter in its own right, but mediocre performance led to it being used instead for the instruction of pilots destined to fly the far more advanced P-80 Shooting Star.

3 October 1942 Verne Haugland, a war correspondent for the Associated Press, receives the first Silver Star awarded to a civilian by the Army. General MacArthur did the honors in New Guinea in recognition of Haugland's heroic efforts to fight his way out of the New Guinea jungles after being lost for 45 days when forced to bail out of a crippled Army plane.

8 November 1942 During Operation "Torch", the 509th Parachute Battalion, dropping from C-47 transports, makes the first American combat jumps in North Africa. The objective is to assist in the capture of the La Senia and Tafaroui airports on the outskirts of Oran, in what is now Algeria. They encounter resistance from the Vichy French forces stationed there, which leads to a break in diplomatic relations with the Vichy government in France.

12 November 1942 The draft age in World War II is lowered from 20 to 18 under terms of legislation enacted by the Congress. Coming just one month after Roosevelt asked for the legislation, the bill grants deferments only to those who need to complete a half-finished academic year in high schools or similar institutions. New deferments for college students are banned.

2 December 1942 The first nuclear chain reaction (achieved through the fission of uranium isotope U-235) is achieved on this date at an abandoned football stadium on the campus of the University of Chicago. Under the direction of physicists Enrico Fermi, an antifascist Italian, and American Arthur Compton, the US had produced the much needed scientific breakthrough that would lead to the creation of a practical atomic bomb.

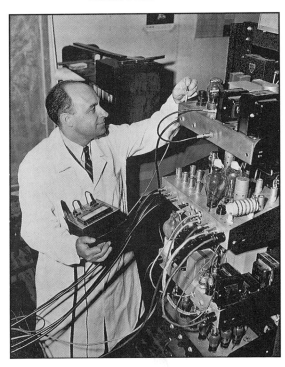

Above: Scientist Enrico Fermi at work in his laboratory at the University of Chicago. A fervent antifascist, Fermi guided the research efforts that resulted in the breakthroughs in nuclear fission that led to the atomic bomb.

Statistical Tidbits About the Pentagon

Number of Stairways	150
Elevators	13
Restrooms	280
Fixtures	4,900
Drinking Fountains	685
Electric Clocks	4,200
Light Fixtures	65,000
Daily Lamp Replacements	1,000
Windows	7,748
Glass Area	309,276 sq. ft. (28,731 m²)
Equals	7.1 acres (2.8 hectares)
Parking Space	64 acres (25 hectares)
Capacity	10,000 vehicles
Office Space	3,705,793 sq. ft. (344,268 m²)

15 January 1943 The Pentagon is completed. The five-story five-sided structure is finished in just 16 months from the laying of its foundations. It consolidates War Department offices that have been spread among 17 different buildings. With round-the-clock shifts, more than 40,000 people work on the completion of the structure. Total cost of the effort, which included extensive landfill and 30 miles (48 km) of access roads, came to $85 million.

20 January 1943 The first destroyer escort, the *Brennan* (DE 13), is commissioned at Mare Island Navy Yard. During its comparatively short life as a naval vessel — less than four years from start to finish — the *Brennan* will operate as a training ship for prospective officers and the crews of destroyer escorts that were then under construction. She was scrapped on 12 July, 1946.

27 January 1943 The first mission is flown by US forces against the German homeland during World War II. Flying from the UK, 8th Air Force Bombers — 55 B-17s and B-24s of the 1st and 2nd Bomb Wings — attack warehouses and industrial plant at Wilhelmshaven. Three bombers are shot down and the Germans lose 22 planes during the engagement.

27 January 1943 The 149th Post Headquarters Company, dubbed the "first American women's expeditionary force in history", arrives ready for duty in North Africa for assignment to signal and postal duties at Allied Forces Headquarters, Algiers. These are the first women of the Women's Army Auxiliary Corps to see active duty overseas; the 1st Separate WAAC Battalion will be the next unit, landing in Scotland on 16 July, 1943.

Above: Dejected Japanese fill a prisoner of war compound on Guadalcanal early in 1943. In a fiercely fought battle that raged from August 1942 through February 1943, nine marines won the Medal of Honor for their valor.

9 February 1943 The first US offensive action of World War II is completed when organized Japanese resistance on Guadalcanal ends. Swift Japanese destroyers take out the remaining 12,000 ground troops from Cape Esperance at the north west tip of the island. Left behind are 14,000 killed or missing, 9,000 dead of disease and 1,000 captured. Japan's grip on this group of Pacific islands is broken.

12 February 1943 The Marine Corps Women's Reserve is organized. Women from 20 to 50 are welcome to join, but the enabling directive states that no member will be able to go "outside the continental United States" and, among other jobs, they can serve as clerks, stenographers, parachute riggers, laundry workers, or electricians. Major is the highest rank in which women can be commissioned.

2 – 3 March 1943 The feasibility of "skip bombing" is demonstrated during the Battle of the Bismarck Sea. American and Australian bombers under Lt. Gen. George C. Kenney fly low-level attacks under cloud cover and destroy 7 Japanese transports and 4 destroyers. The bombers flew just a few feet above the waves and "skipped" the bombs to the target, which had the effect of neutralizing Japanese aerial support. The Allies lose 2 bombers and 3 fighters. More than 3,000 Japanese drown. As a result of this victorious battle for the Allies, the Japanese cease further efforts to send merchant ship convoys to New Guinea. It will now be done by fast destroyer transport.

26 March 1943 The first Air Medal awarded to a woman is given to 2nd Lt. Elsie S. Ott, a 29-year old Army nurse. She receives it for gallantly flying over more than 10,000 miles (16,090 km) of jungle and ocean with five patients on a trip from India to Walter Reed Army Hospital in Washington. The high altitudes encountered forced Ott to use innovative procedures in treating the patients during her first flight on an airplane.

29 April 1943 The US Civil Air Patrol (CAP) is transferred to the War Department. This organization was first formed in 1941 to enlist volunteer civilian airmen to perform wartime tasks. Another transfer in 1948 established CAP as a civilian auxiliary to the Air Force. It handles the operation of 4,700 light aircraft, 4,000 vehicles, and an almost 17,000-station radio network.

7 May 1943 Trials conclude aboard the merchant tanker *Bunker Hill*, which persuade the Navy of the value of the helicopter in operating from ships at sea. The pilot, Col. Frank Gregory, makes about 15 flights in the XR-4 in Long Island Sound. Little difficulty is found in landing on the ship when she steams at speeds of up to 7.5 kt; above that speed, the problems increase.

13 June 1943 The OSS — or Office of Strategic Services — is activated under Gen. "Wild Bill" Donovan. Donovan had been an unofficial observer for the Secretary of the Navy in the UK in 1940 and was sent on several subsequent missions throughout the world to observe resistance movements. The OSS, forerunner of the CIA, reportedly had about 13,000 people for its wartime clandestine operations.

21 June 1943 Edith Greenwood receives the first Soldier's Medal ever awarded to a woman, for her heroism in saving the lives of her patients in a fire in a station hospital near Yuma, Arizona. The medal is usually "awarded to any member of the Armed Forces who, while serving in any capacity with the Army, distinguishes himself by heroism not involving actual conflict with an enemy".

22 June 1943 For the first time in history, Army and Navy decorations are awarded to Soviet soldiers and sailors. Ambassador William H. Standley makes the presentation at a

Right: The successful landings on Sicily in 1943 saw further developments the growing sophistication of amphibious warfare. Here a landing ship tank (LST) has been beached and is unloading supply lorries.

ceremony in the Kremlin. Given for combat service, they are, in Standley's words, intended to "pay tribute to all the armed forces and the civilian population of the Soviet Union".

1 July 1943 The Women's Army Auxiliary Corps becomes the Women's Army Corps, which means it is now a component of the Army, rather than an auxiliary. Its members now have full military status. WACs were assigned to the Army Ground Forces, Army Service Forces and Army Air Forces — and worked in nearly 300 different types of jobs. Some worked on the ultra-secret Manhattan Project.

8 July 1943 Col. Malcolm G. Grow, surgeon of the 8th Air Force, receives the

Above: The first trials of a helicopter on a ship at sea. A Sikorsky XR-4 touches down gently on the converted deck of a tanker. These successful operations would guarantee Navy acceptance of ship-borne helicopters.

Legion of Merit for his work in developing the flak jacket. Grow had done a study of combat wounds which showed that about 70 percent of combat wounds are caused by fragments of comparatively low velocity. This resulted in the flak vest and steel helmet, which saved the lives of thousands in combat.

10 July 1943 In one of the largest amphibious operations of the war, Allied forces invade Sicily. Gens. George Patton and Bernard Montgomery land their troops in the southern part of

Left: Using bicycles and mule carts for transportation, American troops move up toward newly-established front lines through the town of Vittoria, four days after the invasion of Sicily began.

Below left: A crew of WASPS having just successfully delivered another B-17. Despite their invaluable contribution to the war effort, these women flyers were never considered members of the military.

the island. Three new vehicles are unveiled during the assault which will play major roles in similar future amphibious landings: the landing ship tank (LST) the landing craft tank (LCT) and the landing craft infantry (LCI).

19 July 1943   For the first time in World War II, the Allies bomb Rome. Some 700 American bombers drop 800 tons of explosives on the Littorio and Ciampino airports and the railway junction that crosses the San Lorenzo district. Carried out in two phases, one in the morning and one in the afternoon, the attack kills about 2,000 people, causes immense damage and severely damages Italian morale.

22 July 1943   American forces enter Palermo, Sicily, with the effect of cutting off 50,000 Italian troops on the west end of the island. But mobile forces, which include most of the Germans, are managing to escape to the north east corner. Stronger resistance will develop there and reinforcements will be brought in from North Africa, including the 9th Division.

5 August 1943   The Women's Air Force Service Pilots (WASPs) are organized for the purpose of ferrying planes from the factories to the fields, and thus relieving more male pilots for combat duty. They are known under their new designation as of October 20 when the War Department officially announces the name. They serve in civilian status during the war, and are not considered members of the armed forces.

15 August 1943   US and Canadian forces, 34,000 strong, land at Quisling Cove on the west coast of Kiska in the Aleutian Island chain, which had been assaulted by the Japanese on June 6, 1942. What the Allies did not know is that the Japanese had already withdrawn from the site.

17 August 1943   Allied forces gain complete control of Sicily when the 7th Army's 3rd

Left: An aerial view of the Allied assault on the Aleutians. Well prepared to take on stiff Japanese resistance, the force was unaware that the defenders, mindful of what was happening elsewhere, had already left.

Division enters Messina at 10:00 a.m. They are joined shortly thereafter by British forces who arrive from Ali.

31 October 1943 Lt. H. D. O'Neil accomplishes the first successful kill by a radar-equipped night fighter of the Pacific Fleet. Flying an F4U Corsair from Munda, New Georgia in the Solomon Islands, he destroys a Mitsubishi G4M during an attack off Vella Lavella. The ground-based direction for the flight is provided by Marine Maj. T. E. Hicks and Tech. Sgt. Gleason from VMF(N)-531.

16 November 1943 The Army combat boot is approved. Essentially the service shoe with a cuff added at the top, the concept of a boot evolved from problems of a very practical nature.

20 November 1943 Marines make a costly landing on Tarawa atoll in the Gilbert Islands. By noon on 23 November, when the engagement is over, the Japanese garrison of 4,500 men with 50 artillery weapons and seven light tanks has been annihilated.

2 December 1943 About 30 German aircraft attack Bari, Italy. Bombs blow up two ammunition ships in the harbor and 17 other ships are lost. The port's capacity is curtailed for three weeks. The ships were actually carrying supplies of mustard gas, something discovered by many Air Corps personnel when the ships went up.

1 January 1944 Gen. Thomas Holcomb is appointed the first four-star general in the history of the Marine Corps. Likewise the first to achieve three-star rank in that service (as commandant in 1942).

5 January 1944 The headquarters for the Strategic Air Force in Europe moves to England. Gen. Carl (Tooey) Spaatz is appointed commander in chief of the 8th and 15th Air Forces there, which have the responsibility for

Above: The F4U Corsair first flew into combat from carriers, but began land-based operations with the Marines in the Solomons in early 1943. This particular version, the F4U-4C displays post-war insignia.

Below: The Marines go into Tarawa atoll. The troops are being ferried onto the beachhead by specialized amphibious tanks or LTVs. These vehicles had first seen service at Guadacanal in 1942. This was their first tactical use.

Above: A marine brings up a belt of ammunition through heavy enemy fire. Nearly 5,000 Japanese were securely dug in on this, the largest atoll in the northern Gilberts. They would take 3 days to clear after bitter fighting.

Above: The advance along Tarawa's Red Beach 3 towards Burns Phillips Pier. Fighting for what was essentially an elongated reef 22 miles (35 km) long the distinction between beachhead and atoll was a fine one when under fire.

8 January 1944

Above: The Lockheed P-80 Shooting Star. This turbo-jet fighter had a maximum speed of 600 mph (960 km/h) and a ceiling of 50,000 ft (1,524 m). A very small number served in Europe before the end of the war.

Left: The TBF Avenger, one of Navy's excellent carrier-borne torpedo bombers. It was well-armed with up to five machine-guns and could fight its way through enemy defenses to make an attack with a variety of torpedoes, bombs or rockets.

all deep bombing missions against the German homeland. Spaatz ultimately becomes the first chief of staff of the separate US Air Force in September 1947.

8 January 1944 The prototype of the Lockheed P-80 (later F-80) Shooting Star is flown for the first time at Muroc Dry Lake (Edwards Air Force Base), California. In late 1945, it becomes the first operational turbojet-powered fighter/bomber in the Army Air Forces. Unfortunately, the jet aircraft arrives too late to be used by the American military in the war.

11 January 1944 The first US attack with forward-firing rockets is made against a German U-boat by two TBF-ICs of Composite Squadron 58 from the escort carrier *Block Island* (CVE 21). The TBF Avenger was one of the most successful torpedo bombers of the war, with a power-operated gun turret and the capacity to carry a 22-in (559 mm) torpedo internally. Its range was 1,000 miles (1,609 km) with a full load.

16 January 1944 Gen. Dwight D. Eisenhower takes command of the Allied invasion force in London. By spring, some 2,000,000 tons of war materials, and 50,000 vehicles supported by detailed planning are in place. In early May this mass of men and materiels moves to points of debarkation, ready for the cross-channel invasion of France on D-Day in the largest amphibious assault in the history of warfare.

22 January 1944 Allied forces begin landing at Anzio, Italy, in an attempt to divert German forces from the Cassino area, where the advance on Rome

Above: After Allied forces have successfully cleared the landing areas during Operation Shingle, and the fighting has moved on inland, logistical support vehicles disembark from landing ships onto Anzio harbor.

Top: Eisenhower with a group of paratroopers at a training camp in England sometime before D-Day. Prior to being Supreme Commander of the Allied forces in the West, Eisenhower had directed the invasions of North Africa and Italy.

had been halted. Known as Operation "Shingle", the effort quickly results in Anzio and Nettuno harbors being taken. Within 24 hours, more than 36,000 men have landed, even as Allied aircraft drop leaflets on Rome announcing the arrival of liberation forces.

12 February 1944 Eisenhower assumes command as the Supreme Allied Commander, Allied Expeditionary Force, which will invade the European continent and destroy enemy armed forces.

The tentative date set for the operation, which will become known to history as Operation "Overlord" and come off on 6 June, is tentatively targeted for some time in May 1944.

24 February 1944 The first detection of a submerged enemy submarine with magnetic airborne detection (MAD) equipment is made off the Strait of Gibraltar. Catalina aircraft of Squadron VP-63 detect the submarine, *U-761*. They attack the boat and with the assistance of two

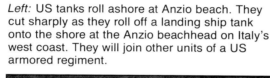

Left: US tanks roll ashore at Anzio beach. They cut sharply as they roll off a landing ship tank onto the shore at the Anzio beachhead on Italy's west coast. They will join other units of a US armored regiment.

Above: "Ducks" of the 5th Army come ashore at Anzio. Landing ship tank (LST) vessels in the background continue to unload troops and equipment on the beach, which is located in an area almost due west of Rome.

Above: Eisenhower and his immediate staff at Allied Headquarters, London, early 1944. It was these men who were to direct the planning and execution of "Overlord", the largest amphibious assault in history.

Above: The ruins of the Abbey at Monte Cassino, the result of massive preliminary bombardment. The Italian hill town defended by crack German units was attacked four times by Allied troops and finally fell to Polish troops in May.

approximately 1,400 tons of bombs and 190,000 shells are rained down on the bitterly-resisting German forces. Despite the massive firepower brought to bear, mounting tolls to the allies will force frontal attacks against Cassino to be called off while the combatants wait for better weather.

ships and aircraft from two other squadrons, send the German ship to the bottom.

6 March 1944 Some 600 heavy bombers drop 1,600 tons of bombs in the first large-scale aerial attack on Berlin by US air forces. As might be expected there is heavy resistance. Between 800 and 900 fighters take to the air and somewhere between 160 to 170 are shot down. Vigorous anti-aircraft fire is encountered at first, but it slows down and then stops altogether.

14 March 1944 It is announced that the *Corvina* (SS 225) with her crew of 82 has been lost. It is probably the only Navy submarine to have been sunk by the Japanese in World War II. She was patrolling close to the stronghold of Truk on assignment in 1943 and was never heard from again. Japanese war records indicate *I-176* fired three torpedoes at an enemy submarine in the Truk area, which exploded.

15 March 1944 The Italian town of Cassino is utterly devastated by the Allies as

31 March 1944 Navy F6F Hellcat fighters finish sweeping the Japanese from the skies over the Palau Islands. The aerial mining of Palau Harbor by Torpedo Squadrons 2, 8 and 16 is the first such mission by carrier aircraft and the first large-scale, daylight mining operation in the Pacific war. The operation has the intended effect as the enemy is denied the use of the harbor for six weeks.

3 April 1944 Budapest and other Hungarian cities come under aerial attack by Army Air Force and Royal Air Force bombers. This successfully marks the end of an August 1943 agreement for each country to refrain from such attacks in exchange for full and safe access over Hungary. Germans and not Hungarian forces are now manning the anti-aircraft batteries.

23 April 1944 Four men stranded behind enemy lines are rescued by a YR-4, described by an official report as "the first use of the helicopters in evacuation — certainly behind enemy lines". The YR-4 belonged to the US 1st Air Commando Group and was used to pick up four British special operations troops who had been forced down by engine failure not far behind enemy lines in the jungles of north Burma.

28 April 1944 Exercise "Tiger" turns into a nightmare for the troops engaged in a mock rehearsal for the D-Day invasion at Normandy. Some 749 Americans are killed, off southwest England's Devon coast when a mock assault by 30,000 American troops becomes real as nine German E-boats torpedo the landing craft. Hundreds were trapped and killed; details were not made public until long after the war os over.

29 May 1944 The only carrier lost in the Atlantic during World War II, the *Block Island* (CVE 21), is torpedoed and sunk by a U-boat while engaged in operations in the Azores area. She was torpedoed by *U-549*, which had slipped undetected through her screen. The German submarine put several torpedoes into the carrier before being sunk by two US destroyer escorts.

Above: Fascinated by the arrival of this strange, ungainly looking aircraft, Army Air Force personnel crowd round to look over the first R-4 helicopter to land in the fighter command area on Iwo Jima, March 1945.

Left: The Sikorsky R-4B as she looked in flight before delivery to either Army or Navy — note the lack of insignia. This photograph was probably taken at the manufacturers at Bridgeport, Connecticut.

2 June 1944 Americans fly their first shuttle bombing mission of World War II (Operation "Frantic") to bases in the USSR. Some 130 bombers and 70 US fighters based in Italy, fly north and attack rail targets in Debrecen, Hungary. They continue east to three new American bases in the USSR — Poltava, Morgorod and Piryatin.

4 June 1944 Units of the 88th Division enter Rome late in the evening, arriving at Piazza Venezia at 7:15 p.m. The Eternal City is liberated six months after the landings at Anzio beach-head by the VI Corps. With this action over, Italy now becomes a secondary theater. The impending invasion of Normandy takes precedence since it will open yet another front for the Germans to defend.

6 June 1944 Operation "Overlord" (D-Day) begins. Supported by a strong air offensive and under the command of Eisenhower, Allied naval forces begin landing 155,000 troops at Normandy on the coast of France. It is the largest amphibious assault in

Below: D-Day. A protective screen is formed by 13 Liberty ships for vessels unloading on the beach. These ships were scuttled deliberately off the beaches at Normandy to provide makeshift breakwaters.

Below: American troops enter Rome as the Germans quickly fall back to prepared positions to the north. This permits the Allies to move quickly up the peninsula, but opposition stiffens when German reinforcements begin to arrive.

Left: B-25 bombers on the deck of the *Hornet* just prior to the famous "Doolittle raid" over the Japanese homeland. Lt. Col. Jimmy Doolittle was promoted to brigadier general on the day after the attack.

Above: The first raid on Japan by B-29 bombers did not take place until June 1944. From November of that year until August 1945, up to 20 bombardment groups flew regularly over Japanese cities in day and night operations.

history and includes paratroops and glider-borne infantry. "Fortress Europe" has been cracked and the war will end in less than a year.

6 June 1944 Brig. Gen. Theodore Rooosevelt, Jr., son of the former US president, is the only general officer who storms ashore during the assault on Normandy on D-Day. Serving as assistant commander of the 4th Infantry Division, Roosevelt leads groups repeatedly from the beach over the sea wall and establishes them inland. His coolness and leadership under fire earn him a Medal of Honor.

7 June 1944 The Army Air Forces begin helicopter training. An announcement had been made the previous September that the school would open at Freeman Field, Indiana. Its commanding officer, Col. E. T. Rundquist, said personnel of the new helicopter section were officer-instructors rated as pilots and field mechanics, who were enlisted men.

12 June 1944 In the first deployment of a guided missile unit into a combat theater, elements of Special Task Air Group 1 arrive in the Russell Islands in the South Pacific.

15 June 1944 Forty-seven B-29s, operating out of Chengtu, bomb Japan. They hit the Imperial Iron and Steel Works at Yawata. With the exception of the 11th Air Force's raids on the Kuriles, this is the first air attack against Japan since the famed raid by 16 B-25s under the command of Lt. Col. Jimmy Doolittle from the *Hornet* about 650 miles (1,045 km) off the Japanese coastline.

22 June 1944 The Serviceman's Readjustment Act, which is known more popularly as the "GI Bill of Rights", is signed into law by Roosevelt 16 days after D-Day. Public Law 78-346 provides broad benefits for the nation's returning veterans and includes a generous educational program. It goes on to change the concept of

adult education in the US and starts a home construction boom.

27 June 1944 The first American general to be captured by the Germans in World War II, Brig. Gen. Arthur W. Vanaman, is reported missing. The native of Millville, New Jersey, is acting as an observer during an aerial bombing mission over Germany when his plane is shot from under him. Vanaman will ultimately be assigned to Stalag Luft III, a prison camp for Allied airmen southeast of Berlin.

5 July 1944 Featuring a prone cockpit in which the pilot had to lie flat in order to withstand the pull, an MX-324 rocket airplane is flown at Hawthorne, California by Northrop pilot Harry Crosby. The first military rocket airplane, it was known as the 'Rocket Ram" and featured an Aerojet XCAL-200 rocket motor with monethylanine fuel. It had originally been tested as a glider.

29 July 1944 A battle-damaged B-29 of Bomber Command lands near Vladivostok and is quickly seized by the Soviets. This B-29 is followed by another three on August 20, November 11 and November 21, 1944. The aircraft are dismantled, examined and serve as patterns for

the Tupolev Tu-4, the first modern Soviet heavy long-range bomber.

29 July 1944 Marine Sgt. Lee Powell, who may have been the only actor-combatant killed in World War II, is reported killed in action. Powell portrayed the "Lone Ranger" in 15 serial episodes beginning in 1938 and was the first filmed "masked man". He served 22 months in the Pacific where he fought at Tarawa in 1943 and at Saipan in 1944. The press reported him killed in action at Tinian that year.

25 August 1944 Allied forces liberate Paris, ending four years of German occupation. The surrender of the city by Gen. von Choltitz — who defied Hitler's order to level Paris rather than give it up — set off wild celebrations in the streets. The reception was tumultuous, with cheers and tears greeting Gen. Charles de Gaulle as he marched down the Champs Elysées.

12 September 1944 In the first American engagement on German soil, the 1st Army

Below: American troops of the 23rd Infantry Division march down the Champs Elysées in Paris, 1944, in a victory parade. The German commander surrendered the city rather than resist and cause needless damage.

Above: American troops unload supplies from landing ship tank (LST) vessels in Leyte Gulf, the Philippines, two days after Gen. Douglas MacArthur is able to redeem his famous pledge to return to the Philippines.

Above: Landing operations on Tolosa, Leyte, the Philippine Islands. Landing parties were equipped with detailed invasion maps, and infantry units proceeded inland along routes previously plotted on those maps.

pushes 5 miles (8 km) into west central Germany. Tanks and infantry smash over the frontier north of Trier and bring the war, for the first time, into territory where the population is hostile. The effort puts the Allies in contact with central positions of the Siegfried Line.

20 October 1944 American troops return to the Philippine Islands. There are landings on the east coast of Leyte as the 5th Air Force provides support. The landing ships and bombardment and escort groups are from the 7th Fleet; the troops are from the 6th Army. There is little fighting on the beaches as the Japanese retreat inland and await reinforcements. By nightfall, 132,000 men are ashore. MacArthur leads US troops in their return to the Philippines. "I have returned", he declares. "Rally to me!" Accompanied by his chief of staff and Sergio Osmena, the president of the Philippines, he disembarks a few hours after the start of operations on Leyte Island. Using a small radio transmitter, MacArthur solemnly tells the Filipinos he has redeemed his pledge to return.

21 October 1944 The 1st Infantry Division (Big Red One) and the 30th Infantry Division of the VII Corps, 1st Army, capture Aachen, after fierce fighting. This battle costs the Germans heavily in terms of badly needed reserve strength. Col. Thomas Lancer of the 1st Infantry Division becomes the first military governor of the city.

26 October 1944 The first organized suicide missions of the war (kamikaze attacks) are flown by Japanese pilots in the Philippines. A kamikaze plane crashes into the escort carrier *St Lo* (CVE 63) and damages it so badly she must be sunk. Four other escort carriers are also hit in the attack. Kamikaze attacks will ultimately prove to be the most effective anti-ship weapon of the war.

24 November 1944 Land-based aircraft bomb the Japanese capital of Tokyo. Led by the commanding general of the 73rd Bombardment Wing, Gen.

Above: While sailing off the islands of the Philippines, the *White Plains* (CVE 66) is attacked in a suicide run by a Japanese "Zeke" (Zero) fighter; its pilot flying up beneath the ship's waiting anti-aircraft guns.

Below: The assault on the German city of Aachen. An American tank destroyer fires in infantry support on an enemy position, as the city is taken in bitter street fighting. Much of the city was destroyed in the process.

Below: Pilots of the kamikaze (the word means "divine wind" in Japanese), in full regalia. This suicidal method of attack was first used in large numbers during the Battle of Leyte Gulf, and had succeeded in sinking 40 ships by 1945.

Bombers Procured by Army Air Forces (1940-1945)

Type and Model

Very heavy bombers	(Total)	3,899
B-19		11
B-29 Superfortress		3,888
Heavy bombers	(Total)	31,000
B-17 Flying Fortress		12,692
B-24 Liberator		18,190
B-32 Dominator		118
Medium bombers	(Total)	16,070
B-25 Mitchell		9,816
B-26 Marauder		5,157
B-42		1
Other models		1,096
Light bombers	(Total)	18,133
A-20 Havoc		7,385
A-24 Dauntless		615
A-25 Helldiver		900
A-26 Invader		2,450
A-28 A-29, Hudson		2,189
A-30 Baltimore		1,575
A-31, A-35 Vengeance		1,951
A-36 (P-51 type), Mustang		500
Other models		568

O'Donnell, 111 B-29s head for the mainland. The Musashino aircraft plant is the primary target and is attacked by 35 bombers; 50 B-29s hit secondary targets; 17 abort en route; and the remainder are unable to bomb due to mechanical difficulties. One B-29 crashes.

15 December 1944 Maj. Glenn Miller, director of the Army Air Forces Band, and one of the nation's leading band leaders before he entered the Army as a captain in 1942, disappears on a flight between England and Paris. A trombonist who achieved first place in national popularity polls many times, he had last led his band in a broadcast three days before the plane went down.

15 December 1944 The rank of five-star general is created by the Senate under terms of legislation authorizing the new rank. Four generals are promoted to the new rank immediately: George C. Marshall, Chief of Staff of the Army; Douglas MacArthur, commander in the Southwest Pacific; Dwight D. Eisenhower, Supreme Allied Commander in Europe; and Henry H. Arnold, Commanding General of the Army Air Force.

17 December 1944 Maj. Richard Ira Bong, the most successful US ace of World War II, scores his 40th and final victory. It

Right: Two suicide boats found on the west shore of the Motobu peninsula a scant five months after the Japanese first used them in warfare. They were laden with explosives and then rammed into American ships.

comes over Mindoro in the Philippines five days after General Douglas MacArthur presents him with the Medal of Honor. The "Ace of Aces" will be brought home on "safe" duty later in the war to test aircraft . . . and will die in the flaming wreckage of a P-80 while performing that duty.

17 December 1944 German SS troops massacre approximately 90 US soldiers at Malmedy, Belgium, during the Battle of the Bulge. Following the war, an American war tribunal in Dachau orders 43 Germans who participated in the massacre to be executed, including the commanding officer SS Col. Joachim Peiper. According to the evidence, the SS was under orders to "act without pity".

27 December 1944 The 3rd Army raises the siege of Bastogne, thus ending the "Battle of the Bulge". It began with German forces breaking through Allied defenses at the Ardennes on 16 December. Bad weather neutralized Allied air superiority and supply efforts during the siege.

27 December 1944 American B-24 Liberators score direct hits on a railway bridge in Burma with "Azon" bombs, the first use of guided bombs in warfare. The Azon is a 1,000 lb (454 kg) general purpose bomb with a radio receiver in its tail that enables the bombardier to control it by radio. Its name is derived from the fact it can be guided only to the right or left, or in azimuth only.

9 January 1945 American soldiers invade Luzon, the Philippines, as Operation "Mike I" begins. Gen. Yamashita,

the Japanese commander, has a formidable force of 250,000 ground troops at his disposal as fighting gets under way. Before it is over, the Japanese have lost 24 of their troops (more than 192,000 in all) for every American killed — a glaring exception to the rule of higher losses for attackers.

9 January 1945 For the first time in the war, the Japanese make use of explosive boats piloted by the equivalent of kamikaze. During the first stages of the battle at the Gulf of Lingayen on the western coast of Luzon, in the Philippines the Imperial Japanese Navy launches one of these boats against an American transport ship and succeeds in sinking her.

25 January 1945 Some 70 plus B-29 bombers drop 366 mines in the six approaches to Singapore harbor and in the waters off Saigon, Cam Ranh Bay, the Pakchan River as well Penang harbor, Koh Si Chang Channel and Phan Rang Bay. The 20th Air Force mission, which is completed on January 26, is the largest single mining operation that will be conducted during World War II.

31 January 1945 Pvt. Eddie D. Slovik is shot by a firing squad, the first soldier since the Civil War to be executed for desertion. Eisenhower approves the execution as a deterrent to other desertions. Slovik, who had twice deserted his unit, was buried in France with 94 others soldiers who had been hanged for rape and murder. His body is exhumed and returned to the US in 1987.

14 February 1945 At midday, 311 B-17 Flying Fortresses drop 771 metric tonnes

19 February 1945

Above: A B-17 Flying Fortress of the kind that dropped hundreds of tons of bombs on Dresden, Germany. Nearly 8,700 of these aircraft were built and used over Germany as well as in operations in the Far East and Pacific.

of bombs on the burning city of Dresden, Germany. On the next day, 210 B-17s drop 461 more tonnes into the inferno. In easily the most controversial and deadly raid of the war (RAF bombers had started bombing the historic city a day earlier), approximately 130,000 people — most of them civilians — are killed in the firebombing.

19 February 1945 The amphibious assault on Iwo Jima begins. Under Maj. Gen. Harry Schmidt, the 3rd, 4th and 5th Marine Divisions land and cut the island in two. Organized Japanese resistance will not end until 16 March, but the operation will prove to be the hardest and costliest in the history of the Corps. Some 19,938 casualties are sustained, with 5,931 killed or missing.

20 February 1945 The Secretary of War approves a plan for a rocket firing installation at the White Sands Proving Grounds, New Mexico. It follows on

Below: Landing craft from the 6th Fleet loaded up with marines, head towards shore during the initial attacks on Iwo Jima. The first objective was to secure the beachhead and to land as many men as possible.

The Invasion of Iwo Jima

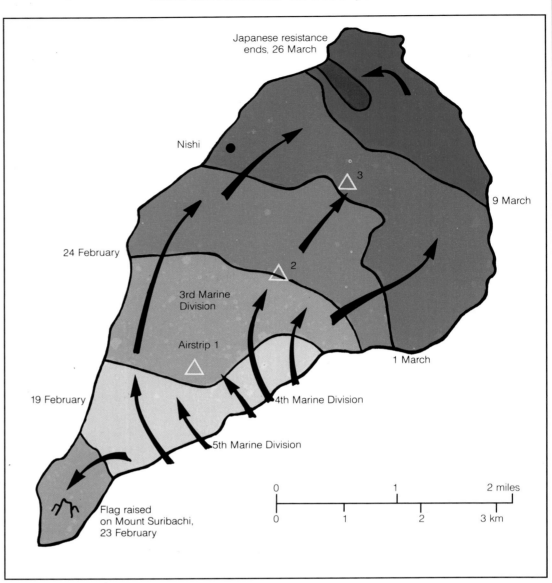

Japanese resistance ends, 26 March

Nishi

24 February

3rd Marine Division

Airstrip 1

19 February

9 March

1 March

4th Marine Division

5th Marine Division

Flag raised on Mount Suribachi, 23 February

0 1 2 miles
0 1 2 3 km

The main stages in the capture of Iwo Jima. Although the Japanese defenses were divided in two very early on in the assault, resistance remained extremely stiff in the north of the island until they very end. The positions of airfields built during the invasion can also be seen.

the heels of warnings by key officials that the USSR was likely to win the race to develop an intermediate range ballistic missile. Earlier in the month, the Army had activated the Army Ballistic Missile Agency at Huntsville, Alabama.

23 February 1945 Despite continuing enemy fire, a platoon of Marines reaches the top of Mount Suribachi on southern Iwo Jima and raises the American flag in fitting triumph after the bitter battle below. Photographer Joseph Rosenthal captures the event

Above: Men of the 5th Marine Division wait in readiness as their landing craft approaches the shores of Iwo Jima. The heights of Mount Suribachi can be seen rising menacingly in the background.

Above: The US Marines raise the American flag on the summit of Mount Suribachi, Iwo Jima. The battle for the island, however, will rage another month before all Japanese resistance is successfully wiped out.

on film in what will be among the most easily recognized wartime photos ever taken. The men belonged to the 28th Regiment of the 5th Marine Division.

24 February 1945 American soldiers liberate the Philippine capital of Manila from Japanese control. The liberation is complete after three weeks of bitter fighting that results in the complete

Above: The landing craft has finally arrived with a jolt and the marines hit the beach at a run. Facing these men was a garrison of over 20,000 Japanese who were dug-in and well-prepared to die to the last man.

Above: Men and equipment of the 1st Army pour across the Remagen Bridge. It was damaged but still standing, prompting Hitler to sack Field Marshal Rundstedt from command since he had been ordered to destroy it.

Above: Douglas AD Skyraider, a single-seat carrier-based aircraft was developed too late for use in World War II. However, the Douglas SBD Dauntless had fewer casualties per mission than any other Navy type.

destruction of the Japanese garrison there. More than 12,000 enemy dead are counted, with the worst fighting having occurred at a walled section of the old town known as the Intramuros.

7 March 1945 Troops of the 1st Army seize the Bridge at Remagen thus establishing a firm bridgehead over the Rhine River. It is accomplished

Above: Holding their first beach position and keeping their heads down, marines move forward under enemy fire. Every inch of Iwo Jima's 8 square miles (20 km²) would have to be taken in this dreadful way.

despite Hitler's order that not a single bridge is to be captured intact.

14 March 1945 American bombers based in Italy cooperate with the Red Army and attack targets that have been selected by the Soviets. The targets are located in Austria, Hungary and Yugoslavia. Some 90 P-38 Lightning aircraft of the 15th Air Force hit bridges at Ptuj and strafe rail traffic. 21 P-51s also strafe rail traffic in Austria.

18 March 1945 The Navy's first single-seat, carrier-based dive bomber, the Douglas A-1 Skyraider, is flown for the first time. It was probably the most effective close support aircraft used in Korea, and remained in production until 1957 — mainly because it was so difficult to find something better to replace it.

27 March 1945 The last German V-2 rocket lands on southeast of London. More than 2,700 civilians were killed by the 1,115 rockets launched against the UK. A further 2,050 V-2 rockets were launched at Antwerp, Brussels and Liège in Belgium. Unfired V-2s and those who worked on them will be captured at the end of the war and put to work on the US missile program.

Below: The liftoff of an A4 (V2) rocket from test launch pad 7 at Peenemünde, Germany in 1943. Originally designed as transportable artillery support weapons, these rockets first came into service in October 1944.

Above: Close air support comes in as American troops consolidate the beachhead on Okinawa. Resistance by the Japanese defenders, though light in this initial phase of the operation became fanatical later on.

Below: Armor moves off from the beaches of Okinawa into the interior. It would take over 3 months to subdue the Japanese here. In the process 12,000 Americans would die together with 100,000 defenders.

30 March 1945 The Allies get their first close-up look at the German Me 262A-1 jet fighter when a defecting pilot delivers one to Americans. During the war, there were approximately 1,430 Me 262s produced, with the first entering service in 1944. Roughly 100 of these flew in combat operations. They were faster than the fighters of the Allies, but a number were destroyed because of the greater maneuverability of Allied planes.

1 April 1945 The invasion of Okinawa ("Operation Iceberg") begins in what is to become the last and bloodiest major amphibious operation in the entire Pacific Theater of Operations. Admiral Turner's Task Force 51 provides the 1,200 transport and landing ships and embarks 450,000 Marine Corps and Army personnel. A solid beachhead 3 miles (4.8 km) deep is established on the first day.

7 April 1945 The first fighter-escorted missions by B-29 bombers are flown against Japan. Some 91 P-51s escort the bombers and claim 21 kills as 101 bombers blast the Nakajima aircraft engine plant in Tokyo and another 150-plus hit the Mitsubishi aircraft plant at Nagoya. Nearly 30 other bombers hit other targets of last resort.

9 April 1945 B-29s firebomb Tokyo and other Japanese cities in one of the most destructive air attacks in the history of mankind — outstripping even the death tolls of the first atomic bombs. Some 84,000 are killed in the Tokyo raids, compared to estimates of 70,000 killed at Hiroshima and 20,000 at Nagasaki. The 279 bombers drop a total of 1,665 tons of incendiary bombs during the attack.

10 April 1945 American soldiers liberate the notorious Nazi concentration camp Buchenwald near Weimar, in what is now East Germany. It was one of the first Nazi concentration camps and served as a "model" for many later camps. In all, more than 50,000 people died in the Buchenwald complex (there were satellite camps) during the war.

23 April 1945 Navy PB4Ys of Patrol Bombing Squadron 109 launch three Bat missiles against enemy shipping in Balikpapan harbor, Borneo, in the first combat use of automatic homing missiles in World War II. The radar-controlled missiles (ASM-N-2 is their designation) sink or damage two small freighters, and destroy a storage tank. Erratic devices, they leave the main target (a transport) untouched.

25 April 1945 The 69th Division and the Soviet 59th Guards Division link up patrol forces for the first time in World War II, near Torgau, Germany, on the Elbe River. Allied forces had been ordered by Eisenhower not to advance beyond the Elbe and Mulde Rivers.

24 April 1945 The 8th Air Force makes its last attack on an industrial target. Some 274 escorted heavy bombers drop 500 tons of ordnance on the Skoda works at Pilsen, Czechoslovakia. The raid smashes 40 percent of the buildings and 70 percent of the manufacturing capacity of Skoda's 126 factories.

29 April 1945 The concentration camp at Dachau is liberated by troops from Gen. George S. Patton's 3rd Army. There are about 30,000 surviving prisoners. Located 11 miles (17.7 km) northwest of Munich at an abandoned factory site, it was run by the SS and became a research center for some of the most horrible medical experiments carried out by the Nazis. Over 30,000 are reckoned to have perished there.

2 May 1945 Berlin falls to the Soviets and the 341-sq mile (883 km²) city thus becomes the largest city ever to be taken in battle. The seat of Adolf Hitler's "Thousand Year Reich" — an empire that died in less than six years of war — cost the Nazis 343,000 killed or captured and had been wrecked by American and British bombers.

Above: An early version of the Bat, an automatic homing missile used against Japanese shipping in the later stages of World War II. The Bat is the precursor of "smart" missiles that will be developed for use in later wars.

Above: Scientists for the Manhattan Project, which guided efforts to create the atomic bomb. They are shown after the war on the steps of Eckhart Hall at the University of Chicago, where much of the work took place.

Below: The George McDonald Ranch House, 2 miles (3.2 km) from where the first atomic explosion occurred. It was here that the plutonium core for the world's first atom bomb was assembled by scientists.

Above: The first atomic explosion at Trinity in Alamagordo, New Mexico. The bomb used was based on plutonium and had a yield of 15 to 20 kilotons. The explosion can be seen and heard up to 180 miles (290 km) away.

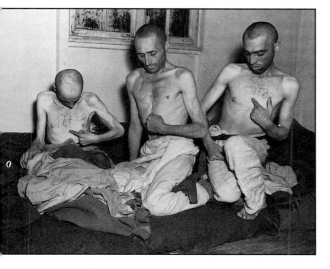

Above: Survivors of a Nazi concentration camp. Millions were exterminated by the Third Reich. At the Nuremberg trials, the camp commandant at Auschwitz confessed to the murder of 2 million people.

7 May 1945 Germany submits to the inevitable and signs an unconditional surrender at Eisenhower's headquarters in Rheims, France. This takes effect the very next day and ends the European conflict of World War II. The document is signed in the small schoolhouse by German representatives including Col. Gen. Alfred Jodl. Present at the signing are delegations from the US, USSR, UK and France. All military action on all fronts by both sides stops at midnight 8 May.

5 June 1945 Postwar occupation zones in Germany are set up by the victorious Allies of World War II. A joint statement by the US, USSR, UK and France is issued, article one of which says, "Germany, within her frontiers as they were on Dec. 31, 1937, will, for the purposes of occupation, be divided into four zones . . ." Berlin would be occupied by the four Allies and be governed jointly. The country has remained that way to the present.

14 July 1945 The first major shore bombardment of the Japanese homeland is carried out by the Navy against the Japan Iron Company plant at Kamaishi, Honshu. The plant is put out of action by shells raining in from

three battleships — *Indiana* (BB 58), *Massachusetts* (BB 59) and *South Dakota* (BB 57) — two heavy cruisers, *Chicago* (Ca 136) and *Quincy* (Ca 71) — and nine destroyers

16 July 1945 The first atomic bomb explosion occurs at Trinity site in Alamagodo, New Mexico, ushering in the nuclear age at 5.30 a.m. The plutonium device (the equivalent of 15,000 tons of TNT) released energy equivalent to the energy produced and consumed in all of the US in half a minute. For miles around the explosion the surface of the desert is fused to glass. The ball of fire formed by the explosion reaches 35,000 ft (10,670 m).

Below: The battleship *Indiana* (BB 58) in a camouflage scheme appropriate to operations among the Pacific Islands. She participated in the first major shore bombardment of the Japanese homeland in 1945.

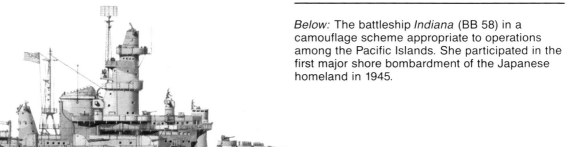

25 July 1945

Above: The remains of the city of Hiroshima. Over 4 square miles (11 km²) were devastated and over 70,000 people killed; another 70,000 inhabitants were seriously injured by blast, radiation and burns. *Right:* The commander of that atomic bomb mission, Col. T. W. Tibbets (center) with the other members of his crew in front of their converted B-29, *Enola Gay*.

25 July 1945 In a law promulgated by the US Military Government in Germany, all military training for Germans is banned. On the list of expressly forbidden acts are: wearing or using military or Nazi uniforms, badges, banners, military or party salutes; the singing or the playing of military or Nazi music; making or selling dummy/miniature arms for training purposes; or holding unauthorized parades.

2 August 1945 The top secret operational orders for the world's first atom bomb attack are signed. Hiroshima, on the southern end of Honshu is named as the primary target, with Kokura or Nagasaki as alternates.

6 August 1945 The first atomic bomb mission. A B-29 bomber with the 509th Composite Group, the *Enola Gay* (it has been named for the mother of its pilot, Col. Paul W. Tibbets, Jr.) leaves Trinian and levels the city of Hiroshima. Sixty percent of the city is destroyed by the blast and firestorm; 80,000 Japanese are killed; thousands more are burned or develop radiation poisoning. Warfare is changed forever.

9 August 1945 The second atomic bomb used in warfare is dropped on Nagasaki from a B-29 bomber called *Bock's Car* and commanded by Maj. Charles W. Sweeney. Even though

the bomb is of the more technologically advanced plutonium type, the attack itself is less devastating than the earlier one at Hiroshima. Within days, the Japanese have agreed to an unconditional surrender.

14 August 1945 Victory over Japan — or V-J Day. Japan surrenders unconditionally. Emperor Hirohito assembles the Imperial Council to announce his

Above: Bocks Car, the B-29 that dropped the bomb on Nagasaki. This was due to fall on the city of Kokura, but due to sighting difficulties, a secondary target was chosen. Fifty per cent of the city was destroyed.

acceptance of unconditional surrender will be broadcast to the people by radio. But more than 1,000 soldiers storm the Imperial Palace, trying to prevent the message from being sent. They fail. The Allies receive it and prepare to occupy Japan.

21 August 1945 President Harry S. Truman ends the Lend-Lease program that had shipped some $50 billion in aid to US allies during World War II. In so doing, he is carrying out the intent of the Congress, which had directed the extension of the Lend-Lease program earlier in the year with the proviso that it not be used for "postwar relief, rehabilitation or reconstruction".

28 August 1945 The first American units — actually technicians of the Army Air Forces — arrive in Japan. Their arrival has been delayed for 48 hours because of the forecast of a typhoon.

30 August 1945 MacArthur arrives in Japan and sets up Allied Occupation Headquarters. Airborne troops had raised the stars and stripes over the soil of Japan the previous day at Atsugi airfield, southwest of Tokyo, as part of preparations for greeting the general upon his arrival with thousands of troops in air transports from Okinawa.

2 September 1945 The formal Japanese surrender ending World War II occurs aboard the *Missouri* (BB 63) in Tokyo Bay. Documents are signed by the Japanese at 9:03 a.m., followed by MacArthur's signature at 9:07 a.m. MacArthur says: "It is my earnest hope and indeed the hope of all mankind that from this solemn occasion a better world shall emerge out of the blood and carnage of the past."

2 September 1945 With American officers from the Office for Strategic Services at his side, Ho Chi Minh proclaims the Independent Democratic Republic of Vietnam. He even quotes from

Above: A wave of marines in small boats, framed by the American flag, arrives on the Japanese mainland. The landing was made just nine days after the Japanese had signed the official surrender documents.

Above: Gen. Douglas MacArthur countersigns the Japanese surrender document aboard the *Missouri*. The brief ceremony took 23 minutes, with the sun bursting through the clouds just as the ceremony ended at 9:30 a.m.

Above: Mamoru Shigemitsu, Japanese Foreign Minister, signs surrender document on behalf of his government during the official ceremonies held aboard the *Missouri* in Tokyo Bay. It was the long-awaited V-J Day.

20 November 1945 The International War Crimes Tribunal trials begin at Nuremberg, Germany. It is an ironic setting for the trials since the city has been the site for numerous Nazi party congresses and rallies. The trial of leading Nazi war criminals results in 18 convictions and three acquittals. Eleven of the convicted were sentenced to hang; only Hermann Goering cheated this sentence by swallowing poison.

3 December 1945 The P-80 Shooting Star becomes the first combat-ready jet fighter aircraft of the Army Air Forces. Fitted with a General Electric J-35 turbojet of 4,000-lb (1814 kg) thrust, it had maximum speed of 558 mph (898 kmh). Its "stretched" two-place version is the T-33 trainer — still in service. P-80s, by then called F-80s, saw combat in Korea.

the American Declaration of Independence and says he has high hopes of US support for an independent state of Vietnam. Within five years he proclaims independence, and the country is promptly recognized by China, Yugoslavia and USSR.

2 September 1945 On V-J Day the Navy reaches the greatest strength in its history. As Japanese officials sign the surrender the Navy has 1,300 combatant ships and auxiliaries and 11,000 vessels overall (excluding small landing craft). The number of personnel is 3,066,758 enlisted and 325,074 officers.

5 September 1945 Iva Toguri D'Aguino, a Japanese-American suspected of being radio broadcaster Tokyo Rose, is arrested in Yokohama. An American citizen with Japanese parents, she had been visiting with relatives in Japan when war broke out and chose to join the Japanese Broadcasting Company. Her propaganda broadcasts during the war were an attempt to demoralize Allied troops in the East.

7 September 1945 Hoisting the same flag up the pole that had flown over the US capitol

on the day Pearl Harbor was attacked, Gen. MacArthur enters the defeated Japanese capital of Tokyo as the Supreme Commander for the Allied Powers in Japan. The flag goes up at the American Embassy. During the occupation, MacArthur's power is almost uncontested and has wide-ranging effects on the lives of the Japanese.

1 November 1945 Pfc. Desmond T. Doss becomes the first conscientious objector to be awarded the Medal of Honor. He earns the award for his action as a member of the Medical Detachment, 307th Infantry, 77th Infantry Division on Okinawa. Doss saved the lives of many of his comrades through his efforts to treat their wounds and ensure their safe evacuation.

6 November 1945 The first American aircraft to land under jet power on a ship is a Ryan FR-1 fighter, which is fitted with a conventionally-mounted Wright R-1820-72W radial piston-engine as well as a General Electric I-16 turbojet installed in the rear fuselage. The jet being used for take-offs. Ensign Jake West pilots the aircraft to the successful landing aboard the aircraft carrier *Wake Island* (CVE 65).

17 December 1945 The Army Air Forces' 509th Composite Bomb Group (Very Heavy), assembled to carry out atomic bomb operations for the US, is established. The 509th dropped the bombs on Hiroshima and Nagasaki, but the Army Air Forces had peripheral involvement in bomb development. It modifies the aircraft to carry bombs and trains personnel, but fewer than 20 of its officers have basic knowledge of the bomb.

26 January 1946 The Army announces the 1st Experimental Guided Missiles Group has been set up. The War Department announcement says the unit was created to perfect tactics and techniques for robot bombs and other guided missiles of future aerial warfare. It is headquartered at Eglin Field, Florida, and has two immediate projects: a bomb that is attracted to heat and a standard bomb equipped with television.

Below: The Ryan FR-1, which had a conventional reciprocating engine for use in normal operations and a turbojet for use as a booster during take-off and combat. Numerous bugs with the FR-1 prevented the plane from entering combat.

Above: "Tokyo Rose" and her husband. Her soft patter about home had little influence on GI morale in the Pacific. She went to Japan to "visit a sick aunt" in 1941 and was recruited by Tokyo radio for propaganda purposes.

Above: The A4 (V-2) rocket. Thousands were produced in Germany during the war, and the Army captured many of them intact. They were shipped to the US, assembled and became in integral part of the nation's rocket program.

5 March 1946 Former British Prime Minister Winston Churchill, during a speech at Westminster College at Fulton, Missouri, introduces a phrase (the "iron curtain") that will characterize a significant part of the post-World War II era. "From Stettin in the Baltic to Trieste in the Adriatic," he proclaims, "an iron curtain has descended across the continent."

16 April 1946 The first test flight of an American-assembled V-2 rocket, is launched by the Army at the White Sands Proving Ground, New Mexico. It is part of a 64-rocket launch program that provides the US with valuable experience in the assembly, pre-flight testing, handling, fueling, launching and tracking of large missiles.

25 June 1946 An XB-35 aircraft takes off from Hawthorne, California, and makes a successful flight of 85 miles (1,308 km) to the Army Air Force Base at Muroc, California. The first bomber with a flying wing design, it weighs 209,000 lb (94,802 kg), has a span of 172 ft (52.43 m) and an overall length of 53 ft (16.15 m). Its operational range is about 10,000 miles (16,100 km) and the aircraft can carry 28 tons of bombs.

2 July 1946 Some 500 members of the "Nisei" combat unit are treated to a rousing reception in New York City. The Japanese-American 442nd Regimental Combat Team had performed with distinction during three years in Italy and France.

They had received more citations and decorations than any Army unit of comparable size.

21 July 1946 The first all-jet airplane to land on a carrier, the FD-1 Phantom, sets down on the carrier *Franklin D. Roosevelt* (CVB 42) at Camp Henry, Virginia. Lieutenant Commander James Davidson, the pilot, is testing the adaptability of jet aircraft to shipboard operations. A production line of 100 FD-1s began 7 March, 1945, but only 60 aircraft had been delivered when Japan surrendered and the war ended.

25 July 1946 The US detonates an atomic bomb at Bikini atoll in the Pacific, which is the second atomic bomb to be exploded in peacetime and the first detonated under water. The battleship *Arkansas* (BB 33), a concrete oil barge and a tank landing ship are among ships in the target fleet sunk by the test blast. The mushroom cloud achieves its greatest height at 150 seconds after blast at 8,400 ft (2,560 m).

30 July 1946 At the White Sands Proving Ground New Mexico, a captured V-2 German rocket is the first to reach a height of 100 miles (161 km). Hitler's "brain child" of World War II, the V-2 is the grandfather of the American family of large intercontinental missiles. Captured V-2 parts, components, scientists and specialists were transplanted to New Mexico in 1946.

17 August 1946 A manned test of an ejection seat is made by Sgt. Lawrence Lambert of the Army Air Forces while flying over Wright Field, Dayton, Ohio, in a P-61 Black Widow. At the time he ejects, the plane is flying at 302 mph (486 kmh) and at an altitude of 7,800 ft (2377 m). The name given to his test gear, not surprisingly, is "jack-in-the-box".

6 December 1946 An infantryman who fought from North Africa to Germany — former Tech. Sgt. Llewellyn M. Chilson — receives 7 decorations in one day — the largest number of medals ever presented to one man at one time. Truman does the honors at the White House. Chilson earned the medals, in part, for killing 58 Germans and helping capture 243 in front-line action over a five-month period.

12 February 1947 In the first firing of a guided missile from a submarine, a Loon missile is launched from the *Cusk* (SS 348) off Point Mugu, California. The Loon is considered the naval version of the German V-1 rocket and was designated the JB-2 by the Navy. The US eventually built more than 1,000 of these for the Army and Navy, which put the military firmly in the guided missile business.

Below: The McDonnell Douglas' FD-1 Phantom. The plane was later redesignated the FH-1. Sixteen of these aircraft organized together formed Fighter Squadron 17A, the first carrier-qualified jet squadron in the US Navy.

Above: In tests to discover the practicality of arming submarines with guided missiles, a Loon missile is launched from the deck of the *Carbonero* (SS 337), while she lies off Point Mugu, California.

15 March 1947 Ensign John W. Lee becomes the first Negro officer commissioned in the regular Navy. Prior to accepting the commission, Lee had served in the Naval Reserve.

17 March 1947 The Army Air Force's first multi-engined jet reconnaissance bomber, the North American RB-45, flies for the first time. Four RB-45s will be delivered to the 91st Strategic Reconnaissance Wing at Barksdale, Louisiana, in August 1956. An RB-45 from this wing will later make the first nonstop flight across the Pacific from Elmendorf Air Force Base, Alaska, to Yokota Air Base, Japan.

31 March 1947 The wartime draft law expires. Some 10,200,367 men felt the call of the draft during World War II and were inducted into the armed services. At its height, the Selective Service had 27,321 paid employees and 184,325 volunteers. A network of 6,642 local draft boards and 469 appeal boards supported the operation.

27 May 1947 The first American surface-to-surface missile, the Corporal E, is fired at White Sands Proving Ground, New Mexico. The research test vehicle attains a height of 62.5 miles (100.6 km). The all-weather tactical missile system is designed to follow a ballistic trajectory and strike selected targets deep behind enemy lines. The Corporal will go operational in 1954.

18 June 1947 Col. Florence A. Blanchfield is given Serial No. N-1 and Eisenhower presents her the first regular Army commission ever given to a woman. In addition to Blanchfield, 72 others become officers in the Army Nurse Corps.

Right: An aerial view of the heavy launch pads on missile row at Cape Canaveral, Florida, in the early 1960s just as the US space program was gaining momentum. It was established in 1950 as a 5,000-mile (8,050-km) missile test range.

The new Corps will have a strength of 2,558; 700 nurses who were with the regular Army before World War II will automatically be brought into it.

20 June 1947 Cape Canaveral, Florida, is selected as a missile launch site by the Army Air Force and the National Aeronautics and Space Administration. An area that takes in 25 miles (40 km) of largely uninhabited scrubland, it is picked because Florida has a climate that lends itself to year-round operation, it overlooks an almost unlimited overwater flight range, and has excellent physical security.

24 June 1947 A pilot and businessman coins a term that will become an intrical part of the national and military lexicons when he reports seeing nine peculiar aircraft near Mount Rainier in Washington as "saucers skipping over the water". The term "flying saucer" was thus coined by Kenneth Arnold, who reported seeing them moving at 1,700 mph (2,735 kmh). The era of the UFO had begun for the Air Force.

26 July 1947 Truman signs the Armed Forces Unification Act, which places the nation's armed services under the direction of the Secretary of Defense. He nominates James V. Forrestal for the position.

6 September 1947 A V-2 rocket is launched from the flight deck of the *Midway* (CVB 41) in the first firing of a large bombardment rocket from a ship at sea. The rocket explodes prematurely after a six-minute flight, but the launch operation is nevertheless considered a success since it encourages design analysis of fleet ballistic missiles.

17 September 1947 The nation's military services are unified under one structure as the National Security Act goes into effect. It results in the most extensive reorganization of the US military establishment since Washington assumed command of the Continental Army. It provides for unification of the Army, Navy and Air Force under a Secretary of Defense — the newly-sworn-in James V. Forrestal.

18 September 1947 The Department of the Air Force is established as a separate service. W. Stuart Symington is sworn in as

Below: Shield of the Department of Defense. James V. Forrestal was sworn in as the first secretary. It was critical juncture since the peace and prosperity anticipated after World War II was threatening to evaporate.

the first Secretary of the Air Force on this, the effective date of transfer of air activities from the Army to the new department. Authority to begin the independent operations was contained in the National Security Act of 1947. A blue uniform is adopted by the new service.

25 September 1947 Gen. Carl (Tooey) Spaatz is named the first Chief of Staff of the US Air Force. The West Pointer's experience with air warfare covers World War I, in which he shot down three German aircraft during three weeks of combat duty, and as head of the Strategic Air Force in Europe. He directed wartime operations there through the 8th and 15th Air Forces.

1 October 1947 The North American F-86 Sabre, which is to become the Air Force's first sweptwing fighter is flown for the first time as a prototype. It is fitted with a Chevrolet-built J35-C-3 turbojet. Within months, it exceeds Mach 1 in a shallow dive and becomes the first important US fighter to go supersonic. Some 6,553 F-86s will ultimately be produced.

14 October 1947 Capt. Charles Elwood (Chuck) Yeager, in a Bell XS-1 over the Mojava Desert in California, hits Mach 1.06 (700 mph/1,127 kmh) at 43,000 ft (13,105 m) and produces the first recorded sonic boom. The achievement is kept secret by the Air Force for eight months. In 1968, it will earn him an "award" from the Man Will Never Fly Society for "being clumsy enough to break the sound barrier".

21 October 1947 The Northrop YB-49 turbine-powered flying wing makes its first flight. The chevron-shaped eight-engine bomber roars from its pad at Hawthorne, California, runs through a series of Army-devised tests, and lands 34 minutes later. The 44-ton aircraft's flight is accomplished without any problems and the 4,000-lb (1814 kg) engines of the "Flying Wing" work perfectly.

24 October 1947 The first jet fighter squadron in Marine Corps history — VMF-122 — is organized at Cherry Point, North Carolina. Under the command of Maj. Marion E. Carl, the squadron is equipped with McDonnell FH-1 Phantoms, which also served as the Navy's first jet fighter aircraft.

20 February 1948 The first B-50A bomber is delivered to the 43rd Bomb Wing at Davis-Monthan Air Force Base, Arizona. Essentially an improved version of the B-29 Superfortress, it has more powerful engines and a taller fin and rudder. It is also equipped for inflight refueling. Like the B-36,

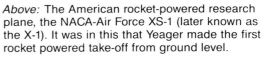

B-47 and B-48, this bomber was never flown in combat.

1 March 1948 The XP-87 aircraft, the first US four-engine jet-propelled fighter, is flight tested at Muroc Air Base, California. The plane flies for 57 minutes. With a span of 60 ft (18.29 m) and a length of 65 ft (19.81 m), it weighs slightly less than a B-17 bomber and is one of the largest fighter aircraft ever built.

6 April 1948 Secretary of Defense Louis A. Johnson orders the Armed Services

Above: The American rocket-powered research plane, the NACA-Air Force XS-1 (later known as the X-1). It was in this that Yeager made the first rocket powered take-off from ground level.

Left: Yeager in the control cabin of the XS-1. One of his many achievements in a career filled with success was the world's first supersonic flight in a manned aircraft in level or climbing flight.

Below: The famous "Flying Wing" aircraft — the Northrop YB-49. In shape and appearance the turbine-powered aircraft bears a close resemblance to the B-2 "Stealth" aircraft, which was unveiled on 22 November 1988. This modern "Flying Wing" proved its air worthiness in its first flight 17 July 1989.

Below: The carrier *Saipan* (CVL 4) with her complement of 16 McDonnell Douglas FH-1 Phantoms, the first carrier-qualified jet squadron in the Navy. The carrier had earlier been used to train student pilots.

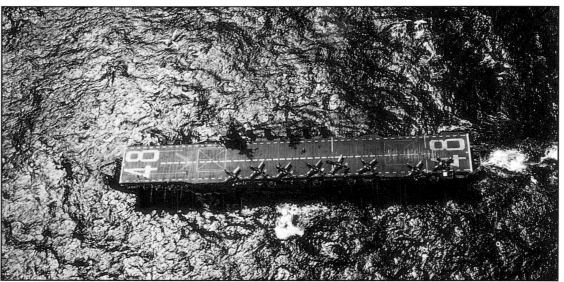

to end racial discrimination. The policy calls for equality of treatment and opportunity within the US armed forces. However, when the Korean War erupted in June 1950, the concept of integration was still more one of policy than of practice.

6 May 1948 Fighter Squadron 17-A receives its first jet aircraft — the McDonnell Douglas FH-1 Phantom — at the Naval Air Station, Quonset Point, Rhode Island. Following three days of operations on the *Saipan* (CVL-48), it becomes the first Navy jet squadron to qualify aboard a carrier.

26 June 1948 Reacting to a Soviet blockade of land routes into Berlin, the Berlin Airlift (Operation "Vittles") begins. By evening, more than 80 tons of food stuffs and medicine will be flown into the beleaguered city. Free World nations continue the operation for 18 months, and will airlift more than 2 million tons of supplies in almost 300,000 flights before the blockade ends on 12 May, 1949.

20 July 1948 In the first west to east transatlantic flight by jet aircraft, 16 F-80s reach Scotland. The actual flight time from Selfridge Field, Michigan, is 9 hours and 20 minutes. The Lockheed Shooting Star aircraft are under the command of Lt. Col. David C. Schilling when they land at Stornoway in the Outer Hebrides. "We had no trouble apart from minor mechanical adjustments," says Schilling.

30 July 1948 The Women's Armed Services Integration Act is passed, which brings women into regular military service. It gives regular and reserve status to women in the Army, Navy/Marine Corps and the fledgling Air Force, but only the WAC is established as an organizational entity. It imposes a two percent ceiling on the number of women in each service's regular establishment.

18 September 1948 Convair test pilot Ellis D. Shannon completes the first flight of the turbojet-propelled Convair XF-92A aircraft. It has a pioneering delta-wing design that leads to the further F-102, F-106, B-58 and F2Y aircraft. The 18-minute flight takes place at Muroc Dry Lake, California, and is powered by a single-jet J33-A-29 engine.

1 October 1948 The Navy places in service the *Norton Sound*, a converted airplane tender that becomes its first guided missile test ship. It will launch a number of missiles, including the pulse-jet powered Loon and the Martin Viking rocket while at sea.

Above: Douglas C-54s are shown being loaded at Wiesbaden Air Base, West Germany, in March 1949 prior to lifting supplies to the beleaguered city of West Berlin as part of the Berlin Airlift (Operation "Vittles").

5 November 1948 The marking "USAF" is approved for use on aircraft wings under Technical Order 07-1-1A issued by the Air Force. The markings will be displayed on the lower surface of the left wing and the upper surface of the right wing. Covered by the order are all Air Force aircraft except those with the Department of the Army, the National Guard and the Military Air Transportation Service.

12 November 1948 Gen. Hikedi Tojo Japan's prime minister and minister of war from 1941-45 — the man instrumental in starting the war in the Pacific and who symbolized the enemy for many Americans — is sentenced to be hanged by the International Military Tribunal for the Far East. Tojo and his generals had whipped Japan into a militaristic fervor and felt the US was soft and lacked the will to fight. Nicknamed "The Razor", he and seven others convicted of war crimes will be hanged on 23 December, 1948.

Below: Japanese premier and war minister Hideki Tojo making his defense during his trial in Tokyo in January 1948. A September 1945 suicide attempt by Tojo was thwarted by American army doctors and he hanged.

5 January 1949 Capt. Chuck Yeager completes the first and only rocket-propelled takeoff made with an American supersonic rocket research aircraft. He will retire in February 1975 with the rank of brigadier general, with a whole string of "firsts" to his credit as a test pilot. His war record on occasion is overlooked: Yeager bagged 13 Germans and was shot down once himself — but escaped.

25 January 1949 The Air Force adopts blue uniforms to stimulate morale and help with recruiting. Seven topflight designers had submitted uniforms in different colors ranging from light gray to green to blue. The switch from the familiar Army olive drab was not an immediate success, however: Air Force enlisted personnel complained of being mistaken by the public for "bus drivers".

24 February 1949 The Army launches a Bumper-WAC sounding rocket, a WAC-Corporal on a V-2 first stage, from the White Sands Missile Range in New Mexico. The rocket reaches an altitude of 244 miles (393 km) and a speed of 5,150 mph (8,290 kmh) while probing the ionosphere above the planet. Since it is the first positively recorded man-made object to enter space, many have said the space age was ushered in on this date in 1949.

2 March 1949 A B-50 bomber, the *Lucky Lady II*, makes the first non-stop round-the-world flight in 94 hours 1 minute. The Superfortress is refueled in the air by tankers four times before touching down at Carswell Air Force Base, Texas. Capt. James Gallagher and his crew of 13 flew a total of 23,452 miles (37,741 km) during the record flight at an average speed of 249 mph (401 kmh).

Below: Launch of a Corporal missile. This missile's origins date to 1944 when the California Institute of Technology, at the request of the Army, started a research and development program on long-range missiles.

11 May 1949 Truman signs a bill creating a 3,000-mile Atlantic guided-missile test range which becomes the Atlantic Missile Range at Cape Canaveral, Florida. $75 million is provided to get the range started, with its ultimate cost expected to be $200 million. The range is needed because present proving grounds of the armed services can only handle 100-mile (160 km) range missiles.

26 March 1949 The first US 10-engine aircraft (a B-36D) makes its first successful test flight. Four turbojets are added to the six piston engines already on the bomber by putting them in paired pods under the wings. This boosts its speed to 435 mph (700 kmh) and its ceiling to more than 45,000 ft (13,715 m), and leads to further production contracts and establishment of the B-36 as a major system of deterrence.

4 April 1949 The North Atlantic Treaty Organization (NATO) is established by the Atlantic nations of Europe and North America to counter the potential threat of the Soviet bloc nations. The 12 original signatories are Belgium, Canada, Denmark, France, the UK, the United States, Italy, Iceland, the Netherlands, Luxembourg, Norway and Portugal. Four other countries join NATO at later dates.

Above: The giant Convair B-36 10-engined bomber. An American legacy of World War II, its requirements were drawn up when it seemed Europe was going to be overrun and strategic missions would have to originate in the US.

16 April 1949 Peak day of the Berlin Airlift. During a 24-hour period, 1,398 sorties are made by an international fleet of aircraft supplying the West Berlin residents with a total of 12,940 tons of essential goods. The airlift had begun nearly a year earlier in response to a blockade of Allied sectors of the city by the Soviets, who refused to allow passage for US and British supplies.

Below: C-47 Dakotas line up at Templehof Airport in Berlin to unload general supplies during the Soviet blockade. American and British aircraft were landing in the city at the rate of one every 61.8 seconds.

3 June 1949 Ensign Wesley A. Brown becomes the first black to graduate from the US Naval Academy. A 22-year old who served in the Army for a year prior to his appointment to the Academy, he is now the 10th black officer on active duty. There had been three blacks at the Academy before, but none graduated. In fact, one resigned in 1937 because he felt so out of place.

1 July 1949 The Air Force Nurse Corps is established. A total of 1,199 Army nurses on active duty — 307 from the regular Army and 892 reserve officers — transfer from that service into the Air Force. They form the nucleus of its Nurse Corps. It is the second Corps formed this date since the Medical Specialist Corps is also organized.

3 July 1949 The B-29 bomber from which the first atomic bomb was dropped on Hiroshima is presented to the Smithsonian Institution's National Air Museum. Col. Paul W. Tibbetts, who piloted the first atomic bomb run, had flown the aircraft from Davis-Monthan Air Force Base in Arizona to the presentation ceremonies, which were held in Chicago, Illinois.

21 July 1949 The US Senate ratifies the North Atlantic Treaty by a vote of 82 to 13. In the aftermath of World War II, the nations of Western Europe recognized a pressing need to seek a means of guaranteeing their freedom and security. This, they felt, could be achieved only by an alliance combining their defensive efforts. The US also recognized this need, and thus joined NATO.

9 August 1949 The first US airman to use an ejection seat for an emergency escape from an aircraft is Lieutenant J. L. Fruin, who ejects from his F2H-1 Banshee aircraft while flying near Walterboro, South Carolina, at a speed of better than 575 mph (925 kmh). At the time, Fruin is attached to VF-171.

10 August 1949 The National Military Establishment is officially redesignated the Department of Defense under terms of an amendment to the National Security Act of 1947. It provides for a limited increase in the authority of the top man in the nation's

defense structure; it further provides that the three military departments — Army, Navy, and Air Force — would continue to be separately administered.

31 August 1949 The Grand Army of the Republic, veterans of the Civil War, holds its 83rd and last encampment. It is attended by six of the 15 surviving veterans at Indianapolis, Indiana. The major goal of the organization had become a Federal pension program, "cash for veterans", which dispensed $156 million annually at a total cost of $4 billion at the death of the last Union veteran of the Civil War.

23 September 1949 Truman announces that the US has evidence that the USSR had set off an atomic explosion, thereby ending the American monopoly. "We have evidence that within recent weeks an atomic explosion occurred within the USSR", he says. Picking his words carefully, the president says Americans should know about atomic developments — but does not say that the USSR has a bomb.

30 September 1949 The Berlin Airlift officially ends, during which the Air Force, through its Military Air Transport Service, airlifted enormous amounts of material to the city. During the 15-month airlift 2 million tons of food, clothing, fuel and medical supplies were flown in. Most of the 277,569 flights to Berlin during these months were made in C-47 and C-54 aircraft.

15 November 1949 Following operational experiments by the Germans with small rocket missiles in air-to-air engagements with Allied aircraft during World War II, the Ryan Aeronautical Company announces development of the Firebird air-to-air liquid propellant rocket, XAAM-A-I, which is the Air Force's first guided air-to-air missile.

31 January 1950 Truman announces that he has instructed the Atomic Energy Commission to produce a hydrogen bomb. This superbomb will be far more destructive than the plutonium bomb dropped on Nagasaki, which killed about 40,000 Japanese, but even then was less devastating than the bomb used on Hiroshima. Truman announces that the code name "Super" has been assigned for the effort.

25 June 1950 Communist forces from North Korea cross the 38th Parallel in a surprise attack on South Korean and American military forces. Under Marshal Choe Yong Gun, seven infantry divisions, a tank brigade and supporting troops, cross the border in four columns, driving on Seoul. According to the North Koreans, it is mounted in the name of "national defense" against an alleged "invasion" by the ROK.

27 June 1950 Truman orders the Air Force and Navy into the Korean conflict, following a call from the United Nations Security Council for member nations to help South Korea repel the invasion from the north. He sends the Air Force and the 7th Fleet; by 5 July, American ground forces are in South Korea fighting under the blue and white flag of the United Nations.

27 June 1950 Lt. William G. Hudson of the 68th Fighter All-Weather Squadron shoots down a North Korean Yakovlev fighter, which is the first enemy aircraft to be downed over Korea. Hudson is at the controls of an F-82G Twin Mustang fighter at the time. Flying with Staff Sgt. Nyle S. Mickey, Hudson is officially credited with the first American air combat victory of the war.

27 June 1950 Truman, not wanting to call the intervention in Korea a war — thus assuming the political burden of leading the nation into one — uses the term "police action" to describe his actions. A precedent is thus set for the chief executive who can now avoid a formal declaration of war by the Congress and still involve the nation's forces in a conflict.

29 June 1950 With Captain Jesse D. Sowell in command, the cruiser *Juneau* (CLSS 119) delivers the first naval gunfire support of the Korean War from Bokuko Ko. She destroys enemy installations on the east coast of Korea at Okkye; the *Juneau* will turn right around and engage in the first naval action of the Korean War on 2 July, sinking three enemy torpedo boats.

3 July 1950 The first naval air strikes of the Korean War are delivered from the carrier *Valley Forge* (CV 45). Corsairs, Panthers and Skyraiders from the carrier are the first Navy jets to enter combat as they attack military installations in the North Korean capital of Pyongyang. These fighters also score the first jet victories when they down two Yak-9 propeller-driven aircraft.

5 July 1950 US troops fight their first engagement of the Korean War. Task Force Smith, which had left Japan five days earlier, watched as North Korean tanks rumbled toward them near Osan. At exactly 8:16 a.m., the first American artillery fire of the war hurtled at the tanks. Four of the 40 tanks were immobilized or destroyed and three others damaged; there were 20 American casualties.

5 July 1950 The first US soldier killed in the Korean War is 20-year old Pvt. Kenneth Shadrick of Wyoming, West Virginia. Shadrick is killed in an attack by North Korean tanks on advance US units south of Suwon. The private was looking down a hill to see the results of his bazooka shot against one of the tanks and was hit in the arm and heart by machine gun bullets from a tank.

Below: The F-82 Twin Mustang was originally developed to provide long-range fighter escort in the Pacific theater during World War II. Though it arrived too late for that, most of those produced saw excellent service in Korea.

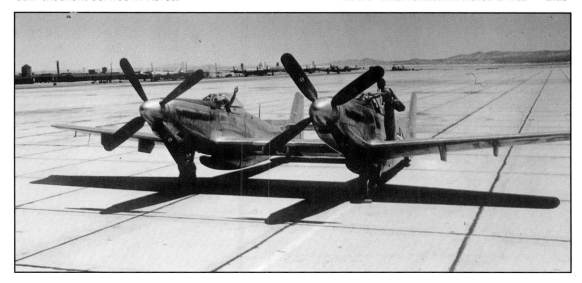

Overseas Service Spanish-American War Through Korea

Characteristic	Percentage of Total who Served Overseas	Average Months Served Overseas*
Spanish American War	29	1.5
World War I	53	5.5
World War II	73	16.2
Korea	56	13.4

*During hostilities only

The Korean War (1950 — 1953)

The Korean War has the distinction of being the first undeclared war the US ever fought. Indeed, it was called a "police action" by President Harry S. Truman when he committed US troops to operations on the Korean Peninsula.

Its seeds were planted in the closing days of World War II, when it was agreed the US would accept the surrender of all Japanese forces south of the 38th degree of latitude (parallel) and the Soviets would accept their surrender north of that line.

Though not intended as a permanent partition of the Korean nation, post-war negotiations never resolved the problem — which was eventually turned over to the United Nations. By 1949, both US and Soviet occupation troops had left the country and North Korean leader Kim Il-sun, seeking a way to consolidate his power, set in motion the events that resulted in the invasion of the south.

North Korea struck across the 38th Parallel on 25 June, 1950 in an attack that routed the ill-prepared South Korean Army, in reality little more than a constabulary force.

American help was quickly sought. On 27 June, Truman ordered US air and naval forces into action; at the same time, the UN Security Council called on its members to help and 21 countries eventually responded.

American ground troops first entered combat on 5 July, but they were unable to stem the North Koreans and their early drive into the south. US Army forces in the Far East had fallen to a low state of readiness, equipment was missing or woefully out of date, and realistic training for the troops had been lacking for some time. Moreover, the first units that went into battle were outnumbered and outgunned.

The advance by North Korean troops down the peninsula was relentless and eventually pushed the besieged American and South Korean troops into a small beach-head covering the approaches to Pusan. Under the direction of General of the Army Douglas MacArthur, American divisions and brigades were thrown into the perimeter, and with air and naval support they were able to stop the North Koreans.

Resistance began to stiffen even as the American buildup continued. Truman federalized National Guard units, Air Force units moved to the Far East, and the Navy's 7th Fleet was augmented.

MacArthur then launched the master stroke of the war — the landing at Inchon just west of Seoul by Marine and Army forces on 15 September under "impossible" conditions. Operation "Chromite", as it was called, was an unqualified success, cutting off the North Koreans, who retreated across the 38th Parallel within days.

UN forces advanced into the North where, on 25 November, massive communist Chinese forces intervened. Having earlier moved across the Yalu river, the two armies of more than 200,000 Chinese soldiers smashed into UN forces and turned the offensive into a full-scale retreat.

Seoul was lost again before the line stabilized. It was recaptured by UN forces in 1951 and the front line pushed to where it had been at the beginning of the war. The idea was to establish a line of defense in the vicinity of the 38th Parallel and then to seek a ceasefire.

MacArthur, however, was urging that the communists be driven from North Korea, a position he took no pains to conceal from anybody, including the Press. At odds with the policies of the Truman administration, he ws relieved of command for insubordination on 11 April, 1951, and replaced by Gen. Matthew B. Ridgway.

Truce negotiations started, then broke off, then restarted. An armistice finally went into effect on 27 July, 1953.

A total of 5,720,000 Americans saw military service during the war. Total US casualties numbered 142,091 — 33,643 battle deaths and 103,284 wounded in action. A further 20,617 died of injuries or disease. A total of 5,178 Americans were listed as captured or missing.

Prisoner of war repatriation following the signing of the armistice resulted in the release of 77,000 prisoners by the UN Command and 12,790 by the North Koreans. Of these 3,597 were Americans. Twenty-one Americans refused repatriation.

Officials estimate that 520,000 North Koreans, 900,000 Chinese and 1.3 million South Koreans were killed or wounded or died of injuries or diseases attributable to the war.

Korea marked the first time the US Air Force participated in a war as a separate service. During the war, the first jet-to-jet aerial combat was fought. Helicopters came into their own. Though developed during World War II, helicopters never really dotted its battlefields. Korea, however, was different — they were used for resupply, the tactical movement of troops and in evacuation efforts.

Another development was the reemergence of body armor in warfare. Flak vests of nylon and fiberglass that

Left: Even in a modern war, cow transport can still come in handy when you've got a lot to carry. Marching through Korea in the first winter of the war, these infantrymen take advantage of a local resident.

weighed about 8.5 lb (3.9 kg) helped prevent chest and abdominal wounds and reduce the severity of wounds received by 25 to 30 percent.

The boundary line between North and South Korea did not change as a result of the war. However, it is a disturbing oversimplification to claim this means a return to the *status quo ante bellum*. South Korea's military capabilities were considerably strengthened during the war, a fact still in evidence today.

And the North Atlantic Treaty Organization was strengthened as well, since Western Europeans would have no reason to doubt the US would move to its defense in the event of an attack by the USSR or its client states. That resolve had been demonstrated in the fierce fighting on the Korean Peninsula. Moreover, the war marked the emergence of China as a major power in the world.

The Korean War left a legacy in terms of its consequences that is unlikely to be forgotten any time soon. In the 36-plus years since peace came to the peninsula, the world has borne witness to that.

Right: Sheltering from the blast of a recoilless rifle. This is perhaps the M20 model, first introduced in 1945. A portable infantry support weapon, it was capable of firing both HE and HEAT rounds.

Left: Air Force B-29 Superfortresses drop bombs over targets during the Korean War. It bridged the gap between the heavy bomber and strategic jet types. Nine B-29 squadrons were in operation during the war.

Left: The 3.5 "super bazooka" was first introduced in Korea. The system was still being used by Marines 22 years later; this training shot on Camp Butler, Okinawa, shows the rocket leaving the launcher.

8 July 1950 MacArthur is named commander-in-chief of UN forces in Korea, capping a series of quick moves. The UN Security Council had passed a resolution urging its members to help South Korea militarily. US forces were ordered in by Truman, and other UN members, indicating they would be sending contingents, ask the US to appoint an overall commander.

8 July 1950 Col. Robert R. Martin becomes the first US officer to be killed in action in the Korean War. The 48-year old colonel, commander of the 34th Infantry Regiment, was engaged in Chonan and found he was the only man present who knew how to fire a rocket launcher. As a convoy of North Korean tanks rumbled into the village, he and an enemy tank fired simultaneously.

10 July 1950 The Army 3rd Battalion uncovers the first known North Korean atrocity against American captives when it discovers the bodies of six members of the Heavy Mortar Company in the Chonui area. The six are found with their hands tied behind their backs and a bullet through the head.

14 July 1950 The first strike by B-29 Superfortresses is carried out against North Korea from Japan. Ten aircraft of the 92nd Bombardment Group take off from Yokota at nine-minute intervals and eight successfully contact control at Taejon and obtain specific targets in the vicinity of Chongjui to hit. They bomb the targets, according to reports, with "fair to good results".

20 July 1950 The 3.5-in (88.9 mm) "super bazooka" is used by the 24th Division against T34 tanks at the battle of Taejon with great success. It is effective, not because of its caliber, but because of its shaped charge that could burn through the armor of any tank then known. The first numbers of the new weapon, which resembled a 5-ft (1.52 m) stovepipe, had arrived in Korea just eight days earlier.

24 July 1950 The Army launches the first rocket from Cape Canaveral, Florida. The vehicle, a V-2 with a WAC-Corporal second stage, is the Bumper-WAC BU-8. The power stays on in the V-2 for only one minute, in which time 10 tons of liquid oxygen and alcohol are consumed. The V-2 achieved speeds up to 2,700 mph (4,345 kmh) and the Corporal goes even faster — as much as 5,000 mph (8,047 kmh).

3 August 1950 The first Marine aviation mission against North Korea is flown from the *Sicily* (CVE 118) by eight Corsairs of VMF-214 in a raid against at Chinju and Sadon-ni.

5 August 1950 After making a shallow dive in his aircraft, near Hanchang, Korea, Maj. Louis J. Sebille draws into point blank range of hidden trucks and fires with six guns. He flies directly into a truck, guns blazing, and deliberately sacrifices his life. He is the first of four Air Force men to be awarded the Medal of Honor (all posthumously) in Korea.

14 August 1950 2nd Lt. Howell G. Thomas is buried at Arlington National Cemetery, the

Below: Leathernecks use scaling ladders to storm ashore during the amphibious invasion at Inch'on, Korea. The perfectly timed invasion witnessed wave after wave of marines landing with great precision.

Below: Marines and soldiers of the Republic of Korea bring communist prisoners out of a sector of Inch'on that is burning furiously. The attack here was so swift that casualties on the allied side were extremely low.

Above: M-4 tanks of the 72nd Tank Battalion, 2nd Infantry Division, provide covering fire to the 1st Battalion, 187th Airborne Regiment during an assault mounted north of Pambol-ni, Korea, on 7 February 1951.

first Korean War hero to be laid to rest in the national cemetery in Virginia. The Army officer had served with Company L of the 21st Regiment. Arlington National Cemetery is a truly national resource. In March 1986, the 200,000th person was interred or inured there. It averages nearly 15 burials per weekday.

4 September 1950 During the Korean War 1st Lt. Paul Van Boven and Corp. John Fuentz, a hospital corpsman, rescue Capt. Robert E. Wayne behind enemy lines. Wayne had been shot down on his 95th mission. It is considered the first helicopter rescue of a pilot behind enemy lines.

15 September 1950 US forces land at Inch'on, in one of the most daring and dramatic

Below: Chinese communist troops cross the Yalu River near the Supung Dam, marking their entry into the Korean War in 1950. They attacked Allied troops just 40 miles (64 km) north of Pyongyang, capital of North Korea.

actions of this or any war. It transforms into a stunning victory a desperate defense that had seemed doomed to complete disaster. The communist effort to grab Korea quickly had been thwarted by US and United Nation's forces, who swept quickly eastward once they were landed and, in coordinated action with the 8th Army, secured the city of Seoul on 26 September.

22 September 1950 Air force Col. David C. Schilling, serving as flight leader, and Lt. Col. William D. Ritchie demonstrate the practicality of operating fighter aircraft over long distances by aerial refueling. Flying their Republic F-84E Thunderjets, they complete the first nonstop jet crossing of the Atlantic. They refuel three times in the air during the course of the flight.

7 October 1950 An American tank crew crosses the 38th Parallel in Korea for the first time in the war. The patrol from the 1st Cavalry Division crosses into the Kaesong area, about 85 miles (137 km) south of Pyongyang. The tank's crew members were Sgt. Homer Lee, Pfc. James Emerich, Sgt. Walter Hill, Cpl. Clarence Johnson and Sgt. Charles Gissendanner. South Korea had been invaded in June 1950.

15 October 1950 The communist Chinese intervene in Korea as major elements of the Chinese Field Army under Lin Piao cross over the Yalu River into North Korea. The movement takes place on foot and at night and is not detected. During the next two weeks, six armies of the communist Chinese forces, 13th Army Group (about 180,000 men in all) will come into North Korea.

20 October 1950 Taking off from Kimpo Airfield, the 187th Airborne Regiment Combat team begins the first parachute assault of the Korean War. The first wave of parachutists blossoms out of C-119s over Sukchon at 2 p.m. and others jump minutes later over Sunchon. Within an hour, 71 C-119s and 40 C-47s will deliver 2,860 paratroopers and 301.2 tons of equipment to the drop zone.

8 November 1950 The world's first jet-vs-jet dogfight takes place over the Yalu River at Sinuiju, on the Chinese-Korean Border. Lt. Russell J. Brown, Jr, USAF, flying an F-80C Shooting Star of the 51st Fighter Interceptor Wing, shoots down a Soviet-built MiG-15 jet fighter of the Air Force of the People's Republic of China. The appearance of the MiG-15 prompts the Air Force to send F-86s to Korea.

27 November 1950 During the two-day battle around the Chosin Reservoir (known as the Battle of the "Frozen Chosin"), members of the 1st Marine Division are under attack by eight Chinese divisions. The Marines hold their ground to the west and south of the Chosin Reservoir, but the Chinese cut the main road between the Marines' main body at Yudam-Ni (headquarters) and other units at Hagaru-Ri.

4 January 1951 North Korean and communist Chinese forces capture the city of

Below: Combat paratroopers pile out of Air Force C-119 cargo planes of the US Far East Air Forces Combat Cargo Command just north of Pyongyang. Troops, equipment and supplies were airlifted during the operation.

Leading Air Service/AAF/USAF Aces of All Wars

Bong, Maj. Richard I.	40	WWII
McGuire, Maj. Thomas B., Jr.	38	WWII
Gabreski, Col. Francis S.	34.50	WWII, Korea
Johnson, Lt. Col. Robert S.	27	WWII
MacDonald, Col. Charles H.	27	WWII
Preddy, Maj. George E.	26.83	WWII
Meyer, Col. John C.	26	WWII, Korea
Rickenbacker, Capt. Edward V.	26	WWI
Mahurin, Col. Walker M.	24.25	WWII, Korea
Schilling, Col. David C.	22.50	WWII
Johnson, Lt. Col. Gerald R.	22	WWII
Kearby, Col. Neel E.	22	WWII
Robbins, Maj. Jay T.	22	WWII
Christensen, Capt. Fred J.	21.50	WWII
Wetmore, Capt. Ray S.	21.25	WWII
Davis, Maj. George A., Jr.	21	WWII, Korea
Voll, Capt. John J.	21	WWII
Whisner, Maj. William T. Jr.	21	WWII, Korea
Eagelston, Col. Glenn T.	20.50	WWII, Korea
Lynch, Lt. Col. Thomas J.	20	WWII
Westbrook, Lt. Col. Robert B.	20	WWII
Gentile, Capt. Donald S.	19.83	WWII

Seoul. The capital city is attacked in waves by communists with automatic weapons and mortar support, but without any artillery or tanks. More than 300 air strikes are called in by UN forces. Remarkably little damage is done to the city, even though 200 fires burn throughout Seoul.

9 January 1951 The UN headquarters opens in New York City. Created at the close of World War II, the intergovernmental organization is designed to maintain international peace and security and to promote economic and social development. A total of 51 nations make up its original members, but its high hopes of peace had already been dashed upon the rocks of reality in Korea.

27 January 1951 An era of atomic testing begins in the Nevada desert as an Air Force plane drops a one-kiloton bomb on Frenchman Flats. The first test by the US since the Soviets had tested its atomic bomb two years earlier, it is one of five tests that will be conducted. The final test on 7 February sets off a flash seen 250 miles (400 km) south of border in Mexico and is felt as far away as Los Angeles.

1 March 1951 Secretary of the Air Force Thomas K. Finletter announces production go-ahead on the Boeing B-52 bomber. In his announcement, Finletter conceded that it was unusual to give the go-ahead for the production of an aircraft before it was tested, as was the case with

Above: One of the first B-52 bombers under construction at the Boeing Airplane Company. This aircraft is still in service nearly 38 years later and has been flown by two generations of Air Force pilots.

the B-52, but he felt there was little risk in the decision. History bears out that judgment — B-52s are still in service today.

14 March 1951 UN forces recapture Seoul, Korea, as South Korean and US units enter the city when the enemy withdraws without a battle. The recapture of the old capital of the Korean Republic marks the fourth time it has changed hands since the Korean War began. The decision to withdraw from Seoul, which has political but little military value, was made under a flanking threat.

11 April 1951 Truman dismisses General of the Army Douglas MacArthur from all his US and Allied commands in the Far East. MacArthur, in public statements, had proposed opening a second front on mainland China. MacArthur has been relieved, says Truman, because he is "unable to give his wholehearted support to the policies of the United States Government."

19 April 1951 MacArthur says farewell to the Congress after being relieved of his command in Korea by Truman. In one of the most famous speeches

Right: Truman and MacArthur at an amicable meeting before their falling-out over Korea. MacArthur's stance over the future of the Korean War became far too public for Truman who dismissed him in April 1951.

ever made by a US military leader, MacArthur tells the congress: "I now close my military career and just fade away, an old soldier who tried to do his duty as God gave him the light to see that duty."

30 June 1951 The army's test program involving captured German V-2 rockets comes to an end. During the five-year program, 67 V-2s — which had been taken apart and reassembled for the effort — had been launched from White Sands, New Mexico, and Cape Canaveral, Florida. The V-2s made several record flights and extensive knowledge was gained about the launch and operation of liquid-propellant rockets.

21 August 1951 A contract for the construction of the nation's first nuclear-powered submarine, the *Nautilus* (SSN 571) is issued to the Electric Boat Company of Groton, Connecticut, for an estimated $29,000,000. Within four years, she will be — in the words made famous by her skipper — "underway on nuclear power" and writing new chapters in the history of technology and the submarine.

24 August 1951 Following successful tests in February of this year in the Nevada desert, Gen. Hoyt S. Vandenberg, Air Force Chief of Staff, reveals that the Air Force is developing small tactical nuclear weapons for battlefield use against enemy ground forces.

25 August 1951 For the first time in aviation history, Navy jet fighters provide escort for an Air Force bombing mission. 12 F2H-2 and 12 F9F fighters escort 30 B-29 bombers on a raid of the marshaling yards at Rashin, Korea. The aircraft were attached to the *Essex* (CV 9); a cruiser and two destroyers serve as navigation and beacon guard ships during the raid.

20 September 1951 The Air Force makes its first successful recovery of animals which have been launched into space by a research rocket. The payload of a monkey and 11 mice is recovered with no apparent ill effects. They rode an Aerobee rocket to 236,000 ft (71,935m) at Holloman Air Force Base, New Mexico. Three earlier attempts to recover animals from rocket flights had failed.

21 September 1951 The first mass transport of troops to the battlefront by helicopter occurs when a company of 228 fully-equipped Marines is lifted in 12 Sikorsky S-55s to the top of a 3,000-ft (915-m) high hilltop in central Korea. It is part of an experimental 10-day mission code-named "Windmill"; the operation

Above: Operation 'Windmill" helped prove the value of the helicopter to the Marines by lifting troops and supplies to the front. One year later the 6th Marines used them regularly in exercises such as this one in Labrador.

Below: Lockheed F-94C Starfire jet interceptor in flight. Its all rocket armament accomodated 48 2.75-in (70-mm) folding-fin aerial rockets — 24 in a ring of firing tubes around the nose and 24 in two cylindrical pods.

took four hours with a helicopter, but it would have taken two days by conventional means.

3 October 1951 The Navy's first anti-submarine warfare helicopter squadron, HS-1, is commissioned at Key West in the Florida Keys. It is under the command of Commander J. T. Watson.

27 November 1951 A Nike missile intercepts an airplane at the White Sands Proving Grounds, New Mexico. The missile was detonated about 25 ft (7.6 m) from the target, which was flying at a range of about 15 miles (24 km), an altitude of 35,000 ft (10,060km) and a speed of 300 mph (483 kmh).

29 November 1951 Development of Air Force's first all-jet heavy bomber, the XB-52, is announced. The aircraft is rolled out of the Seattle, Washington, plant of the Boeing Aircraft Company before dawn. The B-52 eight-jet bomber makes its first flight in April 1952 and is ordered into full-scale production in August of the same year. She will assume a major position in the US strategic bomber force.

23 December 1951 The 3rd Air Squadron begins evacuating 218 Korean War casualties to the ship *Consolation* (AH 15), which is the first hospital

ship fitted out with a helicopter landing pad. She had previously been on station in Korea, but sailed for San Diego on 24 May where she was overhauled and fitted with a helicopter landing platform on her afterdeck. She returned to Korea on 18 December.

28 April 1952 War with Japan officially ends as a treaty that has been signed by the US and 47 other nations takes effect. The US had declared war on Japan on 8 December, 1941.

3 May 1952 An Air Force Douglas C-47 transport aircraft with a ski-and-wheel undercarriage completes the first successful landing by an aircraft at the North Pole. In conditions that require the engines to be started every 15 minutes to keep warm, Lt. Cols. W. Benedict and Joseph Fletcher pull core samples, test seismographs, and find in another test they are 14,140 ft (4,310 m) above the ocean floor.

2 July 1952 Existence of the F-94C jet interceptor, the first Air Force aircraft armed entirely with air-to-air rockets, is announced by the Air Force. With a crew of two and a maximum speed of 646 mph (1,040 kmh), the interceptor carries a total of 48 "Mighty Mouse" aerial rockets which are mounted around the radar nose and in its twin wing pods.

16 July 1952 Public Law 550, formally known as the "Veterans Readjustment Assistance Act of 1952", is signed into law by Truman. Passed by the 82nd Congress, this Korean "GI Bill of Rights" offers similar rights and benefits to eligible veterans of that conflict — their numbers total 5,509,000 — as those given to the veterans of World War II.

29 July 1952 The first turbojet-powered aircraft to complete a non-stop transPacific flight is an RB-45 reconnaissance aircraft. It is flown from Elmendorf Air Force Base, Alaska, to Yokota Air Base, Japan. Commanded by Maj. Louis H. Carrington, who has a two man crew, the flight is made possible by two in-flight refuelings by KB-29 tanker aircraft.

31 July 1952 The first transatlantic crossing by helicopter is completed in H-19s of the Air Force Rescue Service. Capt. Vincent McGovern and Lt. Harold Moore are pilots for the flight, which covers a flying time of 42 hours 25 minutes. They took off from Westover Air Force Base, Massachusetts on July 15 bound for Prestwick, Scotland, by way of Maine, Labrador, Greenland and Iceland.

10 August 1952 Capt. Jesse G. Folmar of VMF-312 becomes the first Marine pilot to shoot down a MiG-15 fighter, an achievement which is all the more notable because he is flying a propeller-drive F4U. Flying from the *Sicily* (CVE 118), Folmar and his wingman, Lt. W. L. Daniels, were jumped by four MiGs, who likely considered the props easy prey. A five-second burst of 20-mm cannon fire does the job.

31 October 1952 Through Operation "Ivy" by Joint Task Force 132, Armed Forces Special Weapons Project, the US explodes its first thermonuclear device.

18 November 1952 Navy pilots of development squadron VX-1 demonstrate the feasibility of the helicopter for mine sweeping in a series of tests off Panama City, Florida. A specially equipped HRP-1 "Flying Banana" helicopter is used in the tests. Later, the Navy will use Sikorsky helicopters to clear mines from the Suez Canal and North Vietnamese waters as part of the truce accords.

26 November 1952 An N-25 Snark turbojet-powered subsonic long-range missile is launched for the first time from zero length. The swept-wing missile would have a proposed 5,000-mile (8,050-km) range with a nuclear warhead. The N-25 will later evolve into the actual prototype of the SM-62 Snark, which sees brief service with the Strategic Air Command.

Above: The MiG-15. This plane and the US F-86 Sabre tangled many times over Korean skies in what has been called a "more sophisticated repeat of the Spitfire-versus-BF 109 dogfights of the Battle of Britain".

Below: Aerial view of the *Antietam* (CVA 36) underway in the Virginia Capes area of the Atlantic Ocean. It is here testing the suitability of canted flight decks as the primary means of operating carrier aircraft.

7 January 1953 Truman reveals in his State of the Union address that the US has developed a thermonuclear, or hydrogen bomb. The tests on the device, which were conducted the previous November at Eniwetok atoll in the Pacific, had proved successful. Truman warns Soviet Premier Josef Stalin that, in the hydrogen era, a war provoked by the USSR would mean a ruined homeland.

12 January 1953 The Navy's first angled-deck aircraft carrier, the *Antietam* (CVA 36) begins operational tests with Navy aircraft. Captain S. G. Mitchell, the ship's commanding officer, makes the first landing in his SNJ aircraft. Over the next four days, six aircraft models make landings, touch-and-go landings, night landings, and takeoffs under varying conditions.

Service and Casualties in the Korean Conflict

	Number Serving	Battle Deaths	Other Deaths	Wounds Not Mortal
Army	2,834,000	27,709	9,429	77,596
Navy	1,177,000	466	4,043	1,576
Marines	424,000	4,268	1,261	23,744
Air Force	1,285,000	1,200	5,884	368
Total	5,720,000	33,643	20,617	103,284

Above: Injured US Army Spec. 4 Herman E. Hofstatter receives help as he walks from an ambulance to a helicopter. Hofstatter has just been released by the North Koreans as part of a prisoner exchange program.

20 April 1953 The exchange of sick and wounded Korean POWs begins at Panmunjom, a village located just south of the 38th Parallel. The armistice ending the Korean War (1950-53) was signed here as well, on July 27, 1953. Korea was ravaged by the war, in which there were four million casualties, half of them civilian.

21 April 1953 Pvt. Carl W. Kirchenhausen of New York City, who suffers from frostbitten feet, becomes the first US soldier released in Korea under an exchange arrangement for sick and wounded prisoners. There are 64 Americans among the first 200 UN soldiers to be released under an arrangement that is to see the return of 600 Allied, 5,000 North Korean, and 700 Chinese prisoners by the end of the month.

25 May 1953 Troops from Fort Sill, Oklahoma, fire the world's first atomic artillery round at Frenchman's Flat, Nevada, at 8:30 a.m. Known as "Atomic Annie", the 280-mm (11.02 in) artillery piece (T-131) hurls her round — a Mk 19 artillery shell — 7 miles (11.25 km). The cannon (six more are made) will be retired in 1962, obsolete victims of the quick development of atomic capability in several smaller calibers.

19 June 1953 The first peacetime death sentence for espionage is carried out in Ossining, New York: Julius and Ethel Rosenberg are executed for espionage having been convicted two years earlier of passing secret information about the atomic bomb to the USSR. The Rosenberg case will remain highly controversial for deades to come, a source of public and private debate.

11 July 1953 Maj. John F. Bolt becomes the first Marine jet ace when he shoots down his fifth and sixth MiG-15s while leading an F-86 flight during an attack on four MiGs east of Sinuiju, Korea. He hits the first MiG just as it begins to gain altitude; the second when he closes to within 500 ft (150 m) and fires up

Above: A mushroom cloud formation resulting from the firing of the first atomic artillery shell in history. It was fired from the Army's new 280-mm (11-in) artillery gun and the shell hit on target with precision and accuracy.

Right: Hangar interior of the Air Force Missile and Test Center, Patrick Air Force Base, Florida. Occupied by the 1st and 69th Pilotless Bomber Squadrons, it has Martin B-61-As (foregound) and Matadors (in the back).

Above: F4U-4N Corsairs were used in Korea to help counter the slow flying aircraft of the North Koreans. An outstanding plane, it had shot down 2,140 Japanese aircraft in World War II against 189 Corsairs lost in combat.

US Army Streamers
Korean War

UN Defensive	Jun 27 — Sep 15, 1950
UN Offensive	Sep 16 — Nov 2, 1950
CCF Intervention	Nov 3, 1950 — Jan 24, 51
First UN Counteroffensive	Jan 25 — Apr 21, 1951
CCF Spring Offensive	Apr 22 — Jul 8, 1951
UN Summer-Fall Offensive	Jul 9 — Nov 27, 1951
Second Korean Winter	Nov 28, 1951 — Apr 30, 1952
Summer-Fall, 1952	May 1 — Nov 30, 1952
Third Korean Winter	Dec 1, 1952 — Apr 30, 53
Korea, Summer 1953	May 1 — Jul 27, 1953

the MiG's tailpipe. The whole show took Bolt about five minutes.

16 July 1953 Lieutenant Guy P. Berdelon destroys his fifth "Bedcheck Charlie" aircraft, thus becoming the only Navy ace of the Korean War and the only Navy nightfighter ace ever. "Bedcheck Charlie" aircraft were obsolete North Korean aircraft that flew so slowly and at such low altitudes that Air Force jets could not intercept them. F4U-4N Corsairs were used instead.

27 July 1953 The Korean armistice is signed at Panmunjon. It takes 255 meetings over two years and 17 days to reach the agreement. The armistice ended

three years of fighting that killed or maimed millions. The communist Chinese lost 900,000 men, the North Koreans 540,000. South Korean casualties were 1.3 million and US casualties exceeded 150,000. Other UN forces lost 17,000 men.

29 July 1953 Two days after the armistice ending the Korean War is signed, the Air Force announces that the Far East Air Force had shot down 839 MiG-15 jets, likely destroyed 154 more and damaged 919 others during the 37 months of the war. In all, UN air forces lost 110 aircraft in air-to-air combat, 677 to enemy ground fire and 213 to "other" causes".

12 August 1953 A fully guided Terrier surface-to-air missile is launched from the experimental missile ship *Mississippi* (EAG 1). It is the first successful shipboard launching of the missile, which closes with and destroys an F6F-5K Hellcat drone. Only eight years earlier, the Navy had set up the program from which this powered, guided, anti-aircraft missile was to emerge.

11 September 1953 The Sidewinder air-to-air missile makes the first successful interception of a drone during a test at the Naval Ordnance Test Station at Inyokern, California. The missile blows apart an F6F-5K target drone. It is not long before the missile system enters production and becomes one of the most important air-to-air weapons in the Navy and Air Force.

1 October 1953 The Air Force establishes its first "pilotless bomber squadron" at the Air Force Missile Test Center at Patrick Air Force Base, Florida. The unit will evaluate the B-61 (later to become the TM-61A Matador) surface-to-surface missile.

10 December 1953 The first Nobel Prize for peace to ever go to a professional soldier is awarded to Gen. George C. Marshall, whose Marshall Plan brought a ruined western European continent back to its feet.

21 January 1954

Above: Nautilus (SSN 571), the world's first nuclear-powered submarine is launched at Groton, Connecticut. Within a year she will be, in the words of her first captain, "Underway on nuclear power".

24 February 1954 Eisenhower approves a National Security Council recommendation to construct a Distant Early Warning — or DEW Line — which is designed to detect hostile aircraft. In 1955, following agreement with Canada, the work begins. In August 1961, the DEW line is completed and the radar network is declared operational from Greenland to the Aleutian Islands.

1 March 1954 The US explodes a deliverable hydrogen bomb in tests at Bikini atoll in the Marshall Islands. A second thermonuclear device will be tested successfully on March 20. These tests are part of Operation "Castle", and confirm the feasibility of developing lightweight, high-yield hydrogen bombs.

1 April 1954 The US Air Force Academy is created. Its temporary location is at Lowry Air Force Base, Colorado, and the first class consists of some 306 cadets, who are sworn in on 11 July, 1955. The first graduating class will have some 207 officers. The curriculum requires 1,629 hours in science, 1,548 in the humanities and 2,178 in airmanship.

1 April 1954 The first Army helicopter battalion is activated at Fort Bragg, North Carolina. The Transportation Battalion (helicopter) is put under the command of Maj. Robert Kolb and will consist of three helicopter companies and one maintenance company.

7 April 1954 Eisenhower use the term "domino principle" during a news conference as a way to describe the consequences of allowing the communists to claim victories in Indochina. Its loss, he says, would mean the loss of Burma and Thailand, the peninsula on which they are located, Japan, Formosa, the Philippines, and on down to Australia and New Zealand.

17 April 1954 The Army reveals that two battlefield artillery rockets, the Honest John (a guided missile) and the Corporal (a ballistic rocket), are being delivered to the troops for the tactical support of ground fighting.

1 April 1954 Commander H. J. Jackson, in an S2F-1 Tracker, is catapulted from the decks of the Hancock (CVA 19) in the first operational test of the

21 January 1954 The first nuclear-powered submarine, the Nautilus (SSN 571) is launched after its official christening by Mrs Dwight D. (Mamie) Eisenhower. The sixth ship to bear the name, its construction has been made possible by a group of scientists and engineers at the Naval Reactors Branch of the Atomic Energy Commission. Director of the project is Captain Hyman G. Rickover.

7 February 1954 First flight of the prototype F-104 Starfighter aircraft. Designed initially as a day fighter at the Lockheed "Skunk Works", it was later converted to a multi-role fighter with ground-mapping radar. It was the first aircraft to be armed with the M61 Vulcan Gatling gun, giving it a high rate of fire. It eventually will be built in seven countries and operated by no less than 15 air forces.

Below: Two disc antennas of the Distant Early Warning (DEW) line operating at Sondrestrom Air Base, Greenland. The line is designed to provide early warning of hostile aircraft intruding into North American air space.

Above: An Honest John rocket in flight. The field artillery era of rockets and missiles began with the firing of this particular system by the 246th Field Artillery Missile Battalion at Fort Bliss, Arkansas in 1954.

C-11 steam catapult. This is the first of a total of 254 launches that will be made this month. The Hancock was the first carrier with steam catapults capable of launching high-performance jets and was off the coast of California during the tests.

7 December 1954 The experimental X-10 remotely piloted test vehicle completes a research flight that includes a fully-automatic landing at Edwards Air Force Base, California. The twin-jet vehicle serves as a system testbed for the Navajo long-range missile

Above: The X-10 guided test vehicle is slowed to a stop by a parachute. The vehicle is used in the development of weapons. It has a modified delta-type wing and tail and landing wheels which aid in its safe recovery.

and shares its general configuration, including a canard forward surface and twin vertical fins.

11 December 1954 The aircraft carrier *Forrestal* is launched at Newport News, Virginia. It is the first aircraft carrier with an angle deck and is also the first US flattop to be constructed from the keel up since World War II. The angle-deck construction is expected to permit greater control of aircraft; simultaneous launching and landings; and to reduce the number of accidents aboard carriers.

17 January 1955 The *Nautilus* (SSN 571) sends its historic message "Underway on nuclear power", thus opening a new era in maritime propulsion. She is to serve as a way of investigating the effects of radically increased submerged speed and endurance. Anti-submarine warfare techniques are wiped out by a ship that does not need to surface, can clear an area swiftly and change depth simultaneously.

22 January 1955 The Pentagon announces that intercontinental missiles armed with nuclear missiles are being developed. The new weapons, according to the announcement, will be more than 10 times as accurate as the German V-2 rockets of World War II fame and have 25 times the range. Cited in the report are the Army's defensive Nike missile and the Air Force's Bomarc and ICBM work.

1 February 1955 US Task Force 43 is established to plan operations in the Antarctic area. More familiar by its name, Operation "Deep Freeze", the force is under the command of Rear Admiral George Dufek and will build housing, laboratories, airstrips as well as deliver necessary supplies in the Antarctic during the International Geophysical Year (1957-1958).

Above: The *Forrestal* (CVA 59) with its air group — note propeller-driven Skyraiders on the forward deck — while on maneuvers. The wide white line running diagonally across the deck is used to aid in landing aircraft.

12 February 1955 The US agrees to train the South Vietnamese Army. The Training Relations and Instruction Mission is formed to implement the training of those forces by the US military mission in Saigon.

6 May 1955 An atomic explosion detonated in the Nevada desert with a force of 35,000 tons of TNT shatters three of 10 houses near the explosion point and the others suffer broken windows and battered furnishings. The explosion was set off to test a model community and how it

Above: During an atomic test, the night sky is lit up by the flash of the explosion; the whitewash on the house burning up instantly from the heat of the fire-ball. A moment later the blast hits leaving nothing standing. It is all over in a second.

Below: Army, Navy and Air Force Military Assistance Advisory Group (MAAG) personnel pose together in Saigon-Cholon, French Indochina (as it was then known) in 1954. Within a decade, America would be deeply embroiled here and the Vietnam war would be under way.

would withstand a nuclear attack. Inhabitants of the houses who were not in bomb shelters would have been killed.

12 May 1955 All fighter aircraft in production, according to an announcement by the Navy, will be fitted with gear for inflight refueling. This establishes the techniques as a standard operational procedure.

1 June 1955 The US Navy commissions its first electronic countermeasures squadron (VQ-1) at Iwakuni, Japan. It will fly the mixed jet- and piston-engined P4M-1Q Mercator aircraft.

29 June 1955 The first B-52 bomber enters operational service with the Air Force, to become the mainstay of the bomber portion of the US strategic triad for many years. The Stratofortress was flown from the Boeing factory in Seattle, Washington, to the 93d Bomb Wing, Castle Air Force Base, California, by wing commander Brig. Gen. William E. Eubank, Jr.

11 July 1955 The US Air Force Academy is dedicated at Lowry Air Force Base, Colorado, its temporary home for the next three years. It will not be until August 29, 1958 that the $135 million academy will receive its first cadets. First commandant of the institution is Lt. Gen. Hubert R. Harmon; the first graduating class will have 207 cadets who will be commissioned in June 1959.

27 July 1955 The highest Air Force priority is assigned to the intercontinental ballistic missile program. Work had started the previous year at the direction of the Air Research and Development Command at the "little red schoolhouse", so called because work on the nation's Atlas ballistic missile had actually started in a converted schoolhouse in Inglewood, California.

1 August 1955 Under the direction of the Air Force's School of Aerospace Medicine, the first zero-gravity flights in jet aircraft begin. They are flown in a Keplerian arc, a tactic that permits the pilot to have a few seconds of weightlessness. This allows hims to test methods of drinking and other tasks that will be used in spacecraft of the future. Other tests of weightlessness had been conducted earlier.

11 August 1955 Opha Mae Johnson, who became the first enlisted woman Marine when she signed up for duty as a private on 13 August, 1918, dies in Washington, DC. Placed in charge of other female clerks in the Washington area — thus freeing other Marines for combat — she rose to the rank of sergeant. At the

Officer Ranks US Armed Forces (1900-Present)

ARMY	NAVY
Second Lieutenant	Ensign
First Lieutenant	Lieut., Jr. Grade
Captain	Lieutenant
Major	Lt. Commander
Lt. Colonel	Commander
Colonel	Captain
Brig. General	Commodore
Major General	Rear Admiral
Lt. General	Vice Admiral
General	Admiral
General of the Army	Fleet Admiral

AIR FORCE	MARINES
Second Lieut.	Second Lieut.
First Lieut.	First Lieut.
Captain	Captain
Major	Major
Lt. Colonel	Lt. Colonel
Colonel	Colonel
Brig. General	Brig. General
Major General	Major General
Lt. General	Lt. General
General	General
General of the Air Force	

Above: The first B-52 bomber. It was a "B" model, had serial number 52-8711, and was delivered from Seattle, Washington, to the 93rd Bomb Wing, Castle Air Force Base, Calif., the first wing to be equipped with B-52s.

time, this was the highest rank authorized for enlisted female Marines.

6 October 1955 Edward L. T. Lyon, a nurse anesthetist, becomes the first man to receive a commission in the Army Nurse Corps. Lt. Lyon joins 3,500 commissioned women in the Corps, a feat made possible by an amendment to Army-Navy Nurses Act of 1947 that went into effect August 1954. Prior to receiving his commission, Lyon had been the head nurse at surgical and psychiatric wards.

6 October 1955 The Department of Defense announces that the Glenn L. Martin

Below: Swordfish (SS 579). In early 1960 she became the first nuclear submarine in the western Pacific area. During this time, President Chiang Kai-shek, Republic of China, embarked on a one-day indoctrination cruise.

Company has been selected to design and build a launch vehicle to place a satellite into Earth orbit. Known as Project Vanguard, with the Navy as executive agent, the satellite is to be launched as part of the research of the upper atmosphere in connection with the International Geophysical Year, July 1957 to December 1958.

1 November 1955 The Navy commissions the *Boston* (CAG 1), the world's first guided-missile cruiser, at the Naval Shipyard in Philadelphia, Pennsylvania. Not built as a guided-missile cruiser from the keel, she had an outstanding war record, participating in the bombing of the Japanese home islands. Her after 8-in (203 mm) turret is replaced with the anti-aircraft missile launchers and she is otherwise modernized.

9 January 1956 The "Moby Dick" project is unveiled by the Air Force, which ostensibly was an effort to explore meterological problems of high-altitude circulation and the jet stream. Many balloons are sent up, with rewards offered (the offer is printed in Russian) for safe return of the packages in them. Moby Dick — according to the final report on the program — was used for reconnaissance of the USSR.

25 January 1956 The *Swordfish* (SSN 579) becomes the first atomic-powered submarine to be laid down at a naval shipyard. She will be launched on 27 August, 1957 and will steam more than 35,000 miles (56,325 km) during her first year in commission — and will be submerged more than 80 percent of the time. She was the first nuclear submarine in the Western Pacific area and the first to be overhauled on the Pacific coast.

21 February 1956 The first Redstone missile is successfully fired at White Sands Proving Grounds, New Mexico. One of the largest and most potent of US surface-to-air missiles at the time, it has a range of 175 miles (282 km) and is designed for rough handling in the field environment. It can deliver a nuclear warhead at hypersonic speed and serves as the basis for the Jupiter missile program.

12 March 1956 Attack Squadron 83 becomes the first missile-firing squadron to be deployed overseas. Equipped with F8U Crusader aircraft armed with Sparrow air-to-air missiles, the squadron deploys to the Mediterranean aboard the *Intrepid* (CVA 11) from Norfolk, Virginia.

21 May 1956 From a B-52 Stratofortress at 50,000 ft (17,070 m), Maj. David Chrichlow drops the first airborne

Above: Fireball of the first airborne drop of a hydrogen bomb. The photograph was taken from an aircraft that was 50 miles (80 km) away from the target in the Bikini atoll in the Pacific Ocean and was at 12,000 ft (3,660 m).

Above: Launch of a Redstone missile. In the mid-1960s, this was one of the largest and most potent of the operational US surface-to-surface missiles. It became fully operational overseas in June 1958.

Above: Albert Woolson lying in state in a funeral home chapel in Duluth, Minnesota, as members of the Minnesota National Guard serve as sentries of honor. At left is Sfc. Donald Anderson and at right MSgt. Leslie Kesit.

Above: This three-quarter rear view of a CH-21 helicopter of the Air Defense Command in 1967 makes it clear why the twin rotor aircraft became known as the "Flying Banana". It had gone into service 12 years earlier.

hydrogen bomb. It explodes over the Bikini atoll in the Pacific.

12 June 1956 The Army, which at this point has 181 years history and has been through seven major wars and 145 campaigns, finally adopts an official flag. It is established by presidential executive order 10,670 and signed by Eisenhower.

2 August 1956 Albert Woolson, who had answered President Abraham Lincoln's call to arms and marched off to war as a drummer boy at the age of 17, dies at the age of 109 in Duluth, Minnesota. He was the sole officially listed survivor of more than 2.2 million men who served in the Union Army. His military service started in October 1864 with the 1st Minnesota Volunteer Heavy Artillery.

14 August 1956 An Army twin-rotor H-21 helicopter is refueled from a fixed wing tanker at Fort Rucker, Alabama, in the first successful attempt to refuel a helicopter in flight. The H-21,

Above: B-58 Hustler aircraft. A three-man plane, it had a belly-mounted pod that carried nuclear weapons and fuel for the outward journey. The pod was jettisoned over the target to let the B-58 return home "clean".

Below: A Martin B-61 Matador pilotless bomber during take-off at Patrick Air Force Base, Florida. It possessed about the same size and looks as a contemporary jet fighter and carried a 3,000-lb (1,361-kg) warhead out to 620 miles (998 km).

known as the "Flying Banana" because of its shape, has the capability to carry 15 troops at about 75 mph (121 kmh). It has first gone into service with the Army in 1954.

24 August 1956 The first transcontinental helicopter flight is completed by an Army H-21 helicopter, which flies nonstop from San Diego, California, to Washington, DC, in 37 hours. It flies 2,610 miles (4,200 km) on the trip and has a crew of five on board.

21 September 1956 An F11F-1 Tiger aircraft shoots itself down while conducting firing tests over eastern Long Island, New York. The plane ran into the 20-mm projectiles it had fired moments earlier at a higher altitude. The pilot was flying at 800 mph (1,287 kmh) and at 13,000 ft (3,960 m) feet when he dove, shooting two bursts. He dove deeper and was hit a few miles from where he fired after the shells dropped. He survived the crash.

27 September 1956 Capt. Milburn Apt becomes the first pilot to fly three times faster than the speed of sound. He reaches Mach 3.196 — 2,094 mph (3,370 kmh) — in a Bell X-2 experimental aircraft over the Mojave Desert. However, Apt is killed when the plane tumbles out of control.

31 October 1956 A Navy R4D Skytrain becomes the first aircraft to land at the South Pole. The landing party is the first to stand there since Captain Robert F. Scott of the Royal Navy reached it 44 years earlier. The party remained at the Pole for 49 minutes, setting up navigational aids that will help in the future. Rear Admiral George J. Dufek with six officers and the crew made the flight.

11 November 1956 The delta-winged B-58, which is the Air Force's first supersonic bomber, makes its first flight — it lasts 40 minutes — at Fort Worth, Texas. It will go operational in

1960 and has a range of more than 5,000 miles (8,045 km) on internal fuel. The three-man bomber was made mostly of stainless steel and was retired by the Air Force in 1970.

30 November 1956 The TM-61 Matador completes its final flight rest and becomes the Air Force's first fully operational surface-to-surface tactical missile. The newer TM-61C will begin to replace it in 1957. In the later model, the range will be extended and the guidance system improved. During the same year, a more radical modification will be put into development — and its popular name changed to Mace.

3 December 1956 The Navy is authorized to proceed with development of the world's first submarine-launched ballistic missile, the solid fuel Polaris. Concurrently, the service withdraws from the liquid-fuel Jupiter missile project, which is now in the province of the Army. The first

Polaris launch will occur on July 20, 1960 from the submarine *George Washington* (SSBN 598).

1 January 1957 Lackland Air Force Base becomes the single site for all Air Force basic training. The Texas base covers an area of 6,783 acres (2,745 hectares), of which 3,972 acres (1,607 hectares) are assigned to the training annex. The base was activated in 1941 and named after Brig. Gen. Frank D. Lackland, an early commandant of the Kelly Field (Texas) Flying School. An average of 5,000 recruits per month pass through the base.

Right: The Terrier surface-to-air missile. It was one of three Navy missiles with its origins in Project "Bumblebee", set up in the waning days of World War II to develop a ramjet-powered, guided anti-aircraft weapon.

13 February 1957 The Navy announces the first successful firing of a guided missile from an American warship in the Mediterranean. The Terrier surface-to-air missile, is launched from the guided missile cruiser *Boston* (CAG 1) during that ship's first NATO cruise.

30 March 1957 The first submarine powered by a liquid-metal-cooled atomic reactor, the *Seawolf* (SS 197), is completed. The submarine's power plant, it is revealed, is enough to drive her around the world three times without refueling, and the amount of fuel used in the process would be about the size of a small grapefruit. She displaces 3,000 tons, about 750 tons more than an average destroyer.

31 May 1957 A Jupiter intermediate-range ballistic missile is successfully fired for the first time from Cape Canaveral, Florida. It flies more than the 1,500 miles (2,415 km) specified for its design range and reaches an altitude of 300 miles (483 km). Two earlier attempts had been made to fire the intermediate-range ballistic missile, but had fallen short of the test goals.

2 June 1957 Capt. Joseph W. Kittinger completes the first successful flight into the stratosphere in a Man High I balloon. Kittinger stays aloft for 6 hours 34 minutes above 92,000 ft (28,040 m) and 2 hours at 96,000 ft (29,260 m) in the plastic balloon launched from St Paul, Minnesota. Kittinger made numerous ascents in balloons that yielded a rich harvest of scientific data.

11 June 1957 The first U-2 reconnaissance aircraft is delivered to the 4080th Strategic Reconnaissance Wing, Laughlin Air Force Base, Texas. The "U" stood for "Utility", one of the steps taken to disguise the real purpose of the aircraft. Built virtually by hand, the aircraft is destined to play a key role in several major events — including the Francis Gary Powers incident and the Cuban Missile Crisis.

28 June 1957 The first all-jet tanker aircraft — a KC-135 — is delivered to the 93rd Air Refueling Squadron at Castle Air Force Base, California. Jet tankers will drastically reduce the time involved in air refueling operations. It had been estimated that total flying time for the first around-the-world flight could have been cut by 5 to 6 hours if KC-15s had been available for the effort.

19 July 1957 The first-ever firing of a nuclear-tipped air-to-air missile is successfully achieved when an F-89J Scorpion discharges an MB-1 Genie at 15,000 ft (4,570 m) above Yucca Flat, Nevada. The missile was

Above: The Lockheed U-2, built at that company's "Skunk Works", and one of the most famous of all surveillance aircraft. It was the aircraft Francis Gary Powers was piloting when he was shot down over the USSR.

made by the Douglas Aircraft Company of Santa Monica, California.

8 August 1957 The first recovery of a rocket nose cone is made. The Army rocket soars several hundred miles above Earth, travels 1,200 miles (1,930 miles) and lands within 400 yards (365 m) of its target in the Atlantic Ocean. A speed of 15,000 mph (24,140 kmh) is achieved by the nose cone of the three-stage rocket, which reenters the atmosphere without disintegrating.

27 August 1957 The *Swordfish* (SSN 579) becomes the first atomic-powered submarine to be completed at a naval shipyard when she is launched at Portsmouth, New Hampshire. Some 228 ft (69.5 m) long and with a displacement of 2,360 tons, the *Swordfish* is following in the "wake" of the L-8, which had been the first conventional submarine built in a naval shipyard (also Portsmouth) in 1917.

20 September 1957 On the fifth try, a Thor intermediate-range ballistic missile is successfully launched at Cape Canaveral, Florida. The first try in

January saw the missile topple back, crash and burn; the second went off course and was destroyed; the third "ended in failure"; and the fourth, which was also launched from the Cape, exploded 96 seconds later.

4 October 1957 The USSR launches the world's first man-made satellite — Sputnik I — From the Baikonur Cosmodrome. It orbits the Earth at altitudes between 155 and 560 miles (249 and 901 km) for 21 days. The 23-in (584 mm), 184-lb (83.5 kg) satellite becomes a symbol of a new era and has a galvanic effect on the US. The "space race" is clearly under way.

11 October 1957 For the first time, Air Force personnel launch an intercontinental missile, the XSM-62 Snark, from Cape Canaveral, Florida. The second firing of a missile from the pad during the day — a Thor had been sent on its 1,500-mile (2,415 km) way earlier — the Snark is a subsonic guided missile with a 5,000-mile (8,045 km) range. Its top speed is 600 mph (966 kmh, Mach 0.93), or slower than a fighter aircraft.

Below: The KC-135 jet tanker. In the early to mid-1950s, SAC bases became overcrowded with bombers and tankers. The first B-52 wings were typically composed of 45 bombers and 15 or 20 KC-135s, all situated at one base.

16 October 1957 The Air Force completes its first successful effort to boost a man-made object to a velocity at which it can escape from the Earth's gravitational pull. This is accomplished with a special Aerobee rocket, which — at a height of 54 miles (87 km) — manages to set off a shaped charge that boosts small metallic pellets to a speed of 33,000 mph (53,105 kmh).

19 November 1957 The Atomic Energy Commission announces the start of a nuclear-powered aircraft program to be run jointly with the Department of Defense. New head of the project office within the Commission will also be deputy to the Air Force Chief of Staff for research and development. The Air Force and the Atomic Energy Commission have each spent $230 million on the plane project in the last 8 years.

17 December 1957 At Northrop Inc, Hawthorne, California, 105 airmen, who will be assigned to the Strategic Air Command's first operational long-range missile squadron, complete training. It is the first class trained to fire intercontinental ballistic missiles. The 704th Strategic Missile Wing had been activated earlier in the year at Vandenberg Air Force Base, California, the nation's first.

11 January 1958 The first test flight of the Polaris fleet ballistic missile is conducted at Point Mugu, California. Just two years prior to the test, the Secretary of Defense had authorized the Navy to proceed with development of the missile, a submarine-launched weapon with solid propellant. At the same time, the Navy scrapped the liquid-propellant Jupiter program.

4 February 1958 The keel of the *Enterprise* (CVAN 65), the world's first nuclear-powered aircraft carrier, is laid at Newport News, Virginia. She will begin flight operations in January 1962 when an F8U Crusader aircraft becomes the first aircraft to land on her deck. She will also have a role in the space age, acting as a tracking and measuring station for John Glenn's epochal first flight.

21 February 1958 The *Gudgeon* (SS 567) becomes the first US submarine to circumnavigate the Earth. She had departed on her history-making trip on 8 July, 1957, and after exercises in Japan made her way around the world for the next six

Right: The *Arizona* Memorial. Dedicated to the servicemen killed at Pearl Harbor, it is in the form of an enclosed bridge 184 ft (56 m) long. Supported by two 250-ton concrete girders, no part of it touches the hulk of the *Arizona*.

Above: The submarine *Greyback* (SS 574), with Regulus missile aboard, enters San Diego Harbor. The Navy fired Regulus from a variety of ships and it eventually served aboard carriers, cruisers and submarines.

months. The submarine docked at Asian, African and European ports before returning to Pearl Harbor some eight months and 25,000 miles (40,235 km) later.

28 February 1958 The Department of Defense directs the Air Force to assume responsibility for developing the land-based intercontinental ballistic missile and the intermediate-range ballistic missile. The service is specifically told to begin developing the Minuteman, a solid-fuel, silo-based missile that will become an integral part of the nation's defense forces for years to come.

7 March 1958 The first submarine built from the keel up with guided missile capability — the *Grayback* (SSG 574) — is commissioned at Mare Island, California. It will serve as the platform for the first launch of a Regulus II missile at sea. Under radio command, the missile will be flown inland in simulated bombardment to Edwards Air Force Base, California.

Above: The Navy did not adopt an official flag until it was in its 185th year of operation. Approved by an executive order of President Eisenhower, its overall dimensions are 4 ft 4 in (1.32 m) hoist by 5 ft 6 in (1.68 in) fly.

15 March 1958 A permanent memorial, to be built over the wreck of the *Arizona* (BB 39) at Pearl Harbor, is authorized by the Congress. Completed on 30 May, 1962, it serves as a lasting reminder of the 1,177 men entombed there after the battleship was torn apart and sunk by the Japanese air attack on 7 December 1941.

24 April 1958 The first official Navy flag is authorized. The design — consisting of the inner pictorial portion of the seal of the US Navy within a circular yellow rope —

was submitted by Navy Secretary Thomas S. Gates, Jr, and approved by Eisenhower.

30 May 1958 Unidentified soldiers killed in World War II and the Korean War are buried at Arlington National Cemetery. A 21-gun salute is given following the interment, the processions for which are led by Eisenhower (for the Unknown of World War II) and Vice President Richard M. Nixon (Korea). The 34-minute service is concluded by Edward B. Harp, Chief of Navy Chaplains.

30 July 1958 The first submarine to travel under the North Pole from the east, the *Skate* (SSN 578), leaves her berth at New London, Connecticut under the command of Commander James Calvert. She returns to the region the following year, chooses areas of thin ice known as greenhouses from which to batter through to the surface, and takes sights that confirm locations important for navigational purposes.

1 August 1958 The *Nautilus* (SS 571) becomes the first ship to reach the North Pole. The atomic-powered submarine had submerged off the northern coast of Alaska, near Point Barrow, on August 1 and within two days will pass under the pole (at 11:15 p.m.). For four days, the *Nautilus* will cruise under the polar ice cap, covering a distance of 1,830 miles (2,945 km). At times, the ice above is 80 ft (24.4 m) thick.

8 August 1958 Eisenhower makes the first award of the Presidential Unit Citation in peacetime to the crew of the *Nautilus* (SSN 571). Capt William Anderson and his crew receive the unusual recognition for their voyage across the top of the world from 8 June to 5 August, when the ship passed submerged under the geographic North Pole.

11 August 1958 The nuclear submarine *Skate* (SSN 578) becomes the first submarine to surface at the North Pole when she breaks her way through the ice at

Above: All 116 crew members of the *Nautilus*, which made history's first undersea voyage across the North Pole, were honored with citations. They also received a New York ticker-tape parade on 27 August.

Right: Titan I intercontinental ballistic missile. Within 30 years, Air Force leaders would be proposing that versions of the Titan receive an additional stage so they could lift 8,000-lb (3,629-kg) payloads.

6:47 p.m. *Skate* had operated under the ice for 10 days, during which she surfaced nine times and navigated more than 2,400 miles (3,865 km) without surfacing. She was only the second boat to reach the North Pole and was to return to New London, Connecticut in September.

16 September 1958 In a simulated attack on Edwards Air Force Base, California, the *Grayback* (SSG 574) performs the first at-sea launch of the Regulus II missile. Even though this long-range, radio-controlled jet missile was later discontinued and funds were transferred to the more potent Polaris program, the tests point to a revolutionary advance in the power of navies to attack land bases.

16 December 1958 The first launching of a Thor intermediate range ballistic missile is made at Vandenberg Air Force Base, California, and the missile goes 1,500 miles (2,415 km) out into the Pacific Missile Range to open such use of the new facility. It is the first missile launch made under simulated combat conditions. Similar results are obtained in another launch of a Thor the same day, but is launched on the east coast.

25 December 1958 Eisenhower makes the first US voice-relay broadcast from space. "To all mankind", goes his Christmas message, "America's wish for peace on Earth and goodwill toward men everywhere." The broadcast was made possible as a result of a military communications experiment that

boosted the upper stage of an Atlas missile into orbit with a transmitter and the tape aboard.

1 January 1959 The first integration of missile and bomber forces is ordered by the Strategic Air Command. In what clearly reflects a need to organize US strategic forces in a different manner, the 702nd Strategic Missile Wing is activated and assigned to a Air Force (the 8th). This pattern of assigning missile units to numbered air forces will continue throughout the year.

6 February 1959 The Titan intercontinental ballistic missile is fired from Cape Canaveral, Florida, for the first time. Number A-3 flies downrange about 300 miles (485 km). Titan I and Titan II missiles will go on to take their places in the nation's

Below: The plotting party aboard the nuclear-powered submarine *Skate* (SSN 578) as she prepares to surface at Drift Station Alpha at the North Pole. The submarine is under the command of Commander James F. Calvert.

Left: The seven Mercury astronauts pose in front an Air Force F-106B. Project Mercury was originally established in October 1958; one of its objectives was to place a manned space capsule in orbit around the Earth.

strategic forces. Titan IIs will gain additional life as space launch vehicles placing payloads of more than 3,000 lb (1,361 kg) into polar orbit.

12 February 1959 The last operational B-36 bomber is put out to pasture, which means that Strategic Air Command has an all-jet bomber force for the first time in history. This particular B-36J had been assigned to the 95th Bomb Wing at Biggs Air Force Base, Texas, and was flown to Amon Carter Field, Fort Worth, Texas, where she was put on display as a permanent memorial.

18 February 1959 A weather reporting satellite, Vanguard II, is put into orbit from Cape Canaveral, Florida, with an Army-developed package of instruments. With an estimated lifetime of 10 years, the purpose of the phototubes aboard is to detect variations in the heat being reflected from the Earth, beam that information back, and then reconstruct it in a map of cloud covers.

6 April 1959 An announcement is made that seven pilots from the military services have been selected for Project "Mercury", established to train the first US space pilots. They are Air Force Capts. Leroy G. Cooper, Jr., Virgil I Grissom and Donald K. Slayton; Navy Lieutenant Commanders Alan B. Shepherd, Jr. and Walter M. Schirra, Jr. Navy Lieutenant M. Scott Carpenter, and Lt. Col. John H. Glenn from the Marine Corps.

10 May 1959 The first submarine with twin nuclear reactors, the *Triton* (SSN 586) is commissioned at Groton, Connecticut. Some 447 ft (136.25 m) in length and with a cruising range of 110,000 miles (177,000 km), she will serve the fleet as an early warning listening post. Fitted with high power radar and sonar gear, the boat will travel with carrier forces, running ahead of the main fleet.

3 June 1959 The Air Force Academy graduates its first class of 207 new second lieutenants. Air Force Secretary

James H. Douglas delivers the commencement address and Bradley C. Hosmer of Dunseith, North Dakota, becomes its first graduate.

8 June 1959 The first free flight of the *X-15* aircraft occurs on this date. Although the *X-15* experimental program ended in 1968, it served to bridge the gap between manned atmospheric and space flight. It also set speed and altitude records — 67 miles (107.8 km) up — that still stands today.

9 June 1959 The first US ballistic missile submarine, the *George Washington* (SSBN 589) slips into the Thames River, at Groton, Connecticut. A number of major developments are incorporated into the 380 ft (115.8 m), 5,400 ton vessel. These include the nuclear warhead, the ballistic missile, nuclear propulsion and inertial navigation, as well as radical new developments in hull design and ship control.

8 July 1959 Maj. Dale R. Buis of Imperial Beach, California, and Master Sgt. Chester M. Ovnand of Copperas Cove, Texas, became the first American soldiers to be assassinated in Vietnam. Part of an eight-man Military Assistance Advisory Group attached to the South Vietnamese Army at Bienhoa, they were sitting watching a movie in the officers' mess when communist terrorists broke in and killed them.

14 July 1959 The first atomic-powered cruiser — in fact, the world's first nuclear-powered surface warship — is launched at the Bethlehem Steel Company's Quincy, Massachusetts, shipyard. The heavy cruiser *Long Beach* (CGN 9) has a speed of more than 30 kt and a cruising range that is described as "virtually unlimited". Some 7,000 spectators are on hand to see the 14,000-ton ship join the fleet.

26 July 1959 The longest recorded parachute descent is made by Lt. Col. William H. Rankin of the Marine Corps as he ejects from his F8U Crusader jet fighter at 47,000 ft (14,325 m) in a thunderstorm over eastern North Carolina. He spends nearly 40 minutes in the air after his jet is

Left: The Air Force's famed X-15 experimental aircraft lands on Rogers dry lake bed after a successful space probing flight. At the controls is Capt. Joe Engle, the third X-15 pilot to qualify for astronaut wings.

Above: Aerial port bow view of the nuclear-powered guide missile cruiser *Long Beach* (CGN 9) underway in the Pacific. She was one of three ships to form the world's first task group of nuclear-powered ships.

Above: A Polaris missile is launched from the *Observation Island*. The Polaris first became operational in 1960 and production of 1,400 of the A1, A2 and A3 models of the missile was completed in 1968.

crippled, free falling for 7 miles (11.25 km) because his parachute has been set to open automatically at 10,000 ft (3,050 m).

7 August 1959 Two Air Force F-100F fighters land at Eielson Air Force Base, Alaska, after a 5,405 mile (8,700 km) flight that started at Wethersfield, England, 9 hours 37 minutes earlier. The first flight by jet fighter aircraft over the North Pole, the project, which was called "Julius Caesar" was used to check development routes for fighters and to test the F-100F navigational system over the Arctic.

27 August 1959 The Polaris ballistic missile is fired for the first time from a ship at sea — the *Observation Island* — off Cape Canaveral, Florida. It is the first seaborne launch of a large

solid-propellant ballistic missile. The *Observation Island* had a complete submarine-type launching and fire control system; the missile itself was launched by the force of compressed air.

4 November 1959 The astronaut escape system developed for the Mercury program is tested successfully during a launch out over the Atlantic Ocean. A 2,000-lb (907 kg) boilerplate model of the capsule is boosted to an altitude of about 7 miles (11.25 km) by a Little Joe rocket. The escape rockets are mounted on a 16 ft (4.9 m) pylon, and the entire package recovered about 5 miles (8 km) from the launch site.

19 December 1959 Civil War survivor and veteran Walter Williams dies in Houston, Texas, at the age of 117, the last of an estimated total of 3 million or more who put on a uniform during the war. He enlisted as a private in the Confederate 5th Cavalry and served as a foragemaster. This, he explained, "meant I got the grub for the others". The only thing he shot during the war was cattle.

7 January 1960 The Polaris submarine-launched ballistic missile completes its first fully guided flight of some 900 miles (1,450 km) after launch from

Cape Canaveral, Florida. The Polaris is propelled by solid fuel and is inertially guided — and it is a test of the guidance system that is successfully accomplished. The missile first became operational in late 1959.

25 January 1960 An Army Hawk downs an Honest John in the first known kill of a ballistic missile by an anti-aircraft missile. The Hawk had been developed to defend against low-flying aircraft in the late 1950s and will see service in 1962 during the Cuban missile crisis; Hawk battalions will be moved to the southeastern states closest to Cuba to supplement local air defense forces.

30 January 1960 The first M14 rifles to come from the production line are issued to units of the 101st Airborne Division at Fort Campbell, Kentucky. Contracts to procure 70,000 M14s have already been awarded. It weighs 10 lb (4.5 kg), has a 20-round magazine and can fire at a rate of 250 shots per minute —

Below: Profile of the 7.62-mm M14 rifle. Capable of firing single shots or bursts, it was used extensively in Vietnam. Some 1,500,000 in all were made and it is still in use though it is not the standard rifle for US forces.

which is faster than the Army's .30-caliber machine gun. The M14 replaces several weapons.

16 February 1960 The *Triton* (SSN 586) leaves New London, Connecticut, on an 84-day voyage that will see her become the first submarine to go around the world submerged. It crosses the equator on February 24 and completes the 41,500 mile (66,785 km) trip back in New London on May 11. The hull of the submarine was under water for the entire trip, but the upper portion broached the water twice.

25 February 1960 The Army's solid-propellant Pershing missile is successfully launched from a mobile tactical launcher. The Pershing was an outgrowth of the Army's focus on tactical problems, which in turn meant more attention for conventional and nuclear ground warfare. One of the flexible nuclear warhead carriers considered in that "mix" of weapons was the 400-mile (645 km) range Pershing.

25 March 1960 The first successful launch of a guided missile from a nuclear-powered submarine is made by the *Halibut* (SSGN 587) in exercises off Oahu, Hawaii, as the ship is underway for Australia. It launches a Regulus I, which looks like a swept-wing jet fighter and had joined the fleet in 1954. Its speed is about 600 mph (966 kmh) and range 575 miles (925 km); the last Regulus I was produced in 1958.

1 April 1960 The first weather satellite, TIROS-I (which stands for Television Infrared Observation Satellite) is launched from Cape Canaveral, Florida. Built at the direction of the Army Signal Laboratories, it takes pictures on a global scale from 450 miles (725 km) up until late June. A significant and new era in meteorological observation has been ushered in.

13 April 1960 The first navigational satellite, the 265-lb Navy Transit I-B, is placed in orbit from Cape Canaveral, Florida. The flight will demonstrate the capability to restart a satellite in space as well as the feasibility of using satellites as navigational aids. It is sent on its journey by a Thor-Able-Star rocket.

20 April 1960 The Army M60 main battle tank goes into production. This tank has proved a durable addition to the US armed forces. Major efforts to improve and upgrade the M60 have

Right: The Army's M60 main battle tank on maneuvers. Since first being brought into the inventory, the M60 has proved a reliable vehicle. The last new production of M60A3s was completed as late as August 1987.

Above: The Army's Pershing tactical missile at Cape Canaveral, Florida, just minutes before its first launch. Later in the year, the first flight test of the new guidance system for the missile is carried out successfully.

been continuous since 1971. With a full capacity of 375 gal (1,420 litres) its cruising range is 310 miles (500 km) at a steady 20 mph (32 kmh).

1 May 1960 The USSR shoots down a US U-2 reconnaissance plane near Sverdlovsk with an SA-2 missile and captures pilot Francis Gary Powers. The reconnaissance flight originated at Peshawar, Pakistan, and was denied at first by American authorities. The US later admitted its U-2s flew intelligence-gathering missions over the USSR.

24 May 1960 The Air Force puts into orbit the first successfully launched missile detection alarm system — or surveillance satellite. Launched by

Above: An Atlas-Agena launch of the Ranger VII spacecraft. The vehicle boosted the 860-lb (366 kg) spacecraft into a parking orbit around the Earth, where six television cameras took closeup pictures of the lunar surface.

Left: The original TIROS-I meteorological satellite is checked out prior to launch in the spring of 1960. It was not until she flew that man was able to view the Earth's cloud cover from above, on a global scale.

an Atlas Agena rocket combination from Cape Canaveral, Florida, Midas II has a 3,000 lb (1,361 kg) payload with infrared detecting equipment to spot the launching of missiles. This is designed to warn the nation of surprise missile attacks.

20 July 1960 The first underwater launch of a Polaris missile is accomplished. The *George Washington* (SSBN 598), off Cape Canaveral, Florida, and with the tip of a radio antenna temporarily mounted on her to receive telemetry data from the missile, serves as the platform for the successful launch.

11 August 1960 Navy frogmen recover a 300-lb (136 kg) space capsule in waters near Hawaii. This represents the first time a man-made object was recovered by the launching nation. The capsule was aboard Discoverer XIII and was on its 17th trip around the world when a signal was sent to it firing the reentry rockets and bringing the instrumented capsule back through the atmosphere.

16 August 1960 The greatest altitude from which man has fallen, and the longest delayed drop ever achieved, is accomplished by Capt. Joseph W. Kittinger. He jumps from a balloon over the New Mexico desert as part of Air Force research efforts into escape systems for jets. The 13-minute jump starts at 102,800 ft (31,335 m) with Kittinger hitting speeds up to 450 mph (725 kmh) before landing safely.

19 August 1960 The first mid-air recovery of a reentry capsule is made by an Air Force C-119J Flying Boxcar. The capsule weighs 300 lb (136 kg) and had been ejected from the Discoverer XIV satellite northwest of Hawaii and descended to 8,000 ft (2440 m) prior to being snatched in mid-air by the transport. Capsule recovery through aircraft or boat was common throughout the Discoverer program.

19 August 1960 A tribunal in Moscow convicts American U-2 pilot Francis Gary Powers of espionage and sentences him to 10 years in prison. The full sentence will not be served, however, as he will be exchanged two years later for convicted Soviet spy Rudolf Abel. Convicted of conspiring to pass defense secrets to the Kremlin, Abel had served 4½ years of a 30-year sentence when released.

7 September 1960 The first successful test firing of the Pershing ballistic missile is completed by the Army and Martin Company. Pershing is launched from a mobile unit that serves as a transporter and erector. It can be moved to the scene of battle, set up and fired in a matter of minutes. The first Pershing missile battalion will be set up at Fort Sill, Oklahoma in June 1962.

24 September 1960 The *Enterprise* (CVAN 65), the world's first nuclear-powered aircraft carrier, is launched by the Newport News Shipbuilding & Drydock Company, Newport News, Virginia. To this day, the company remains the only facility in the country capable of building nuclear aircraft carriers.

1 October 1960 The Ballistic Missile Early Warning System (BMEWS) begins operation at Thule Air Base, Greenland. It is the first of three stations designed to warn North America of any long-range ballistic-missile attack. It complements the famous DEW — or Distant Early Warning — line, which is used to detect low-flying winged missiles and aircraft in their approach to the continent.

17 January 1961 In his farewell address to the nation, President Eisenhower warns against the rise of a "military-industrial complex", a term that will be embraced by critics of the US military for years to come. Eisenhower stresses the need to guard against the "acquisition of unwarranted influence, whether sought or not, by the military-industrial complex".

Above: First submarine firing of a Polaris missile by the *George Washington* (SSNB 598). Authorization from Washington for the Navy to fully develop the Polaris missile had been received about 3½ years earlier.

Above: Photographed at the very moment of his departure by an automatic camera, Capt. Joseph W. Kittinger leaps into 100,000 ft (30,000 m) of nothing. It will take him 13 minutes to safely parachute to the ground.

Left: A C-119 makes a mid-air snatch of a Discoverer capsule over the Pacific Ocean. By the end of 1960, Air Force crews had made three capsule recoveries by this method, the last of them on 10 December.

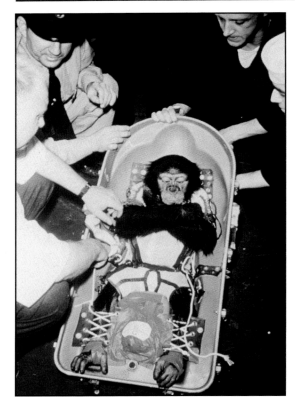

Above: One of the chimpanzees specifically trained for Mercury-Redstone 2 on the couch he will ride during his 16-minute flight. The flight will test the spacecraft's environmental control and recovery systems.

Above: Astronaut Alan B. Shepard, Jr., shown in the Project Mercury spacecraft just prior to it being sealed before his historic flight. Shepard completed the 302-mile (486-km) suborbital flight, a first for an American.

23 January 1961 Trained at the Air Force's Aeromedical Laboratory at Holloman Air Force Base, New Mexico, "Ham" becomes the first chimpanzee to go into space. On the flight, the chimpanzee's respiration and body temperature are measured — one of the first successful uses of biomedical telemetry from space. The flight lasts 3 hours, and achieves an altitude of 155 miles (142 km) and a distance of 420 miles (675 km).

1 February 1961 The first Minuteman intercontinental ballistic missile is launched from Cape Canaveral, Florida. At each given moment its three solid-fuel stages ingite perfectly and the missile is sent rocketing downrange 4,600 miles (7,400 km) with a fully operational guidance system. This is about 2,000 miles (3,220 km) short of its intended operational range. It is a significant step in the nation's ICBM program.

15 April 1961 The abortive Bay of Pigs attack on Cuba. An exile force of 1,400 anti-Castro Cubans, who are organized and equipped by the US Central Intelligence Agency, lands at the site with the benefit of air support. The invasion is crushed, however, and the result is a considerably strengthened government for Fidel Castro.

28 April 1961 A Stratolab two-man open gondola balloon lifts off from the aircraft carrier *Antietam* (CV 36) to a height of 6,000 ft (1,830 m) over the Gulf of Mexico. It becomes the first manned balloon to be launched from and return back aboard a naval vessel. The balloon is the largest ever to be used in manned flight and sets a word record altitude of 113,740 ft (34,668 m) in a flight on 4 May.

5 May 1961 Commander Alan B. Shepard, Jr, becomes the first American in space. His *Freedom 7* capsule is blasted across that frontier to an altitude of 115 miles (185 km), a maximum speed of 15,000 mph (24,140 kmh) and a distance of 302 miles (486 km) on the suborbital flight. He splashes down in the Atlantic. Delays before the launch prompted him to ask, "Why don't you fix your little problem and light this candle?"

25 May 1961 President John F. Kennedy announces the US will begin a program to land an astronaut on

Below: KC-135 on the ramp. The original C-135 Stratolifter was a KC-135A with the tanker's refueling equipment pulled — plus minor internal changes. Three of the converted KC-135As were known as C-135A "Falsies".

the moon. In what is dubbed a "second" State of the Union address, he assures the Congress the nation is ready to take on the burden and asks during the 47-minute address that non-nuclear military strength also be expanded. First year costs of the space effort: $679 million.

9 June 1961 The first C-135A Stratolifter aircraft is delivered to the Military Air Transport Service, later to become the Military Airlift Command. It represents the first step in the replacement of all piston-engined transports. Boeing Aircraft risks more than the company's net worth to build the prototype jet liner — a gamble that will pay off handsomely for it in future years.

12 June 1961 Kennedy proclaims that the US flag is to be flown day and night at the Marine (Iwo Jima) Memorial in Arlington, Virginia. The monument had been dedicated on November 10, 1954, on the 179th anniversary of the Corps. Marines, ex-Marine's and friends of the Corps, helped to underwrite the costs of Felix DeWeldon's statue of the famous flag-raising.

29 June 1961 A Navy Transit IVA satellite is launched and put into a nearly circular orbit at about 500 miles (805 km) up by a Thor-Able-Star rocket. Two satellites that were riding piggyback on the Transit IVA did not separate from each other, but worked satisfactorily. It is the

first known space vehicle to carry a nuclear generator in the form of a radioisotope-powered battery.

17 November 1961 The Air Force successfully launches the first Minuteman intercontinental ballistic missile from an underground silo at Cape Canaveral, Florida. It flies successfully down the Atlantic Missile range for 3,000 miles (4,830 km). The second-generation missile is smaller than the Atlas or Titan, but the use of multiple independently retargetable warheads (MIRVs) increases its capabilities.

25 November 1961 At Newport News, Virginia, the nuclear-powered aircraft carrier *Enterprise* (CVAN 65) is commissioned. Called the "largest moving structure ever built by man", she is 1,123 ft (342.3 m) long, displaces 85,000 tons and has a crew of 4,600 men. Her flight deck alone covers 4.5 acres (61.82 hectares).

29 November 1961 Enos becomes the first chimpanzee to orbit the Earth. He is launched from Cape Canaveral, Florida, in the last unmanned test flight of the Mercury series and completes a 3-hour flight that takes him around the world twice before he returns successfully to Earth. It is a full-stage rehearsal for the upcoming manned orbital flight by Lt. Col. John Glenn.

11 December 1961 Two Army helicopter companies arrive in South Vietnam, representing the first direct military support to that country. The USNS *Core*, a ferry-carrier, brings in the helicopter units, 33 Vertol H-21C

Above: The Marine Memorial in Arlington, Virginia. Created by Felix DeWeldon and depicting the famous flag-raising on Mount Suribachi, it was dedicated to the glory of the Corps on its 179th anniversary in 1954.

Shawnees and 400 air and ground crewmen to operate and maintain them. Their assignment will be to airlift South Vietnamese combat troops into action.

22 December 1961 Army Specialist 4 James Davis of Livingston, Tennessee is killed by the Viet Cong. President Lyndon B. Johnson will later call Davis the "first American to fall in the defense of our freedom in Vietnam".

Below: Eight in a line of ships to bear the name *Enterprise* in the Navy, the world's first nuclear-powered aircraft carrier underway. She served as a tracking station for the US' first orbital flight.

1 January 1962

Above: Rigorous training has been emphasized since the Navy SEALs were first formed. These "amphibious commandos" train continuously; here they practice making stealthy approaches and retreats by rubber boat.

Right: An Air Force C-123B on a defoliation mission over Route 1, about 48 miles (77 km) east of Saigon shortly after Operation "Ranch Hand" got under way. Herbicides were dumped over Vietnam and parts of Laos between 1962 and 1971.

Davis's death will be used to date the US involvement in that country. By the end of 1961, 14 Americans will have been killed or wounded in combat.

1 January 1962 Navy SEAL (an acronym for Sea, Air and Land) teams are established. An outgrowth of the famous frogmen and Underwater Demolition Teams of World War II, which cleared assault beaches before invasions. The reconnaissance mission is one of their skills; these special warfare units of the Navy also blow up ships, harbors, dams, bridges and power sources as well as cut rail and supply lines.

12 January 1962 Operation "Ranch Hand" is launched by the Air Force, and is labeled a "modern technological area-denial technique" to expose the trails used by the Vietnamese forces by stripping away trees and vegetation. Some 19 million gal (71.9 million litres) of the chemicals (Agent Orange — named after the color of the metal containers) are used in the operation, which will have repercussions long after the war is over.

17 January 1962 A Vought F8U Crusader piloted by Commander George Talley completes an arrested landing and catapult-assisted takeoff from the *Enterprise* (CVAN 65), the Navy's nuclear-powered aircraft carrier. The flights are considered the first of the carrier's operations with the fleet, although three other aircraft had taken off from her deck to transport personnel to the mainland after sea trials.

2 February 1962 A C-123 on a low-level training mission is lost over Southeast Asia, although the cause of its crash was

not clear. Sabotage or enemy fire was suspected, but the exact reason is never proved. The three crewmen who went down with the C-123 were the first Air Force fatalities in South Vietnam.

20 February 1962 Marine Lt. Col. John H. Glenn, in Mercury 6 becomes the first American to orbit the Earth. In a period of 5 hours, he will orbit the Earth three times. He is the first US astronaut and the third man to orbit the planet, having been preceded by the Soviets Yuri Gagarin and Gherman Titov. Glenn's successful effort makes him a national hero.

21 March 1962 A bear becomes the first living creature ejected from a supersonic aircraft, when the Air Force tests an escape capsule designed for installation on the B-58 bomber. The bear is ejected at 35,000 ft (10,670 m) from the B-58 bomber, which is flying at 870 mph (1,400 kmh); the animal returns to Earth, unharmed. A bear is selected for the test in order to simulate the size and weight of a man.

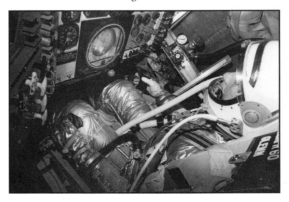

Above: Simulating what is to come. Lieutenant Colonel John H. Glenn in a centrifuge (April 1960), being subjected to the type of acceleration and low pressure time profiles he will experience on his historic flight.

Marine Corps Aircraft Losses In Southeast Asia

(August 1962 through October 1970)

Type of Loss	Number
Helicopter combat	252
Fixed wing combat	173
Helicopter operational	172
Fixed wing operational	81
Total	678

Above: The "Echo" passive communications satellite package used in the first transmission of TV pictures from space. The picture (consisting of the initials "M.I.T.") traveled between 3,000 and 4,000 miles (4,830 and 6,435 km).

Normal Complements Marine Corps Aviation Units In Vietnam

Squadron Type	Aircraft	Model
Attack Squadron (VMA) All-Weather	20	A.4
Attack Squadron (VMA) (AW)	12	A-6
Fighter Attack Squadron (VMFA)	15	F-4
Composite Reconnaissance Squadron (VMCJ)	9	EA-6A
	9	RF-4
In-Flight Refueling Squadron (VMGR)	12	KC-130
Observation Squadron (VMO)	18	OV-10A
	12	AH-1
Light Helicopter Squadron (HML)	24	U-1
Medium Helicopter Squadron (HMM)	21	CH-46
Heavy Helicopter Squadron (HMH)	18	CH-53

9 April 1962 Leading elements of a task unit designated as "Shoofly" arrive at Soc Trang, Vietnam on this Palm Sunday, which represents the start of Marine Corps aviation involvement in Vietnam. The commander of the task unit is Col. John F. Carey and initial Shoofly elements begin moving to Da Nang in the I Corps Tactical Zone. The majority of the Corps' operations would be in I Corps area.

24 April 1962 The Air Force uses an orbiting satellite for the first time to transmit television photographs from Camp Parks, California, to Westford, Massachusetts. An Echo I satellite is used to bounce photographs between the two locations.

25 April 1962 On the occasion of the 100th anniversary of the Medal of Honor, President Kennedy conducts a ceremony on the White House lawn. Joseph W. and Marshall B. Parrott attended the ceremony. They are the grandsons of Jacob Parrott, who was the first person to receive the Medal of Honor for his exploits during the Civil War. He was one of the men who engaged in the "great locomotive chase".

26 April 1962 The Ariel, the first international satellite, is launched from Cape Canaveral, Florida by the Air Force. It has six British atmospheric, solar and cosmic ray experiments aboard. Construction of the launch facilities had started less than a year earlier when Duvall Engineering of Jacksonville, Florida, was given a $258,000 contract to build the launch pad and an access road to it.

6 May 1962 The Navy launches the first known ballistic missile with a live nuclear warhead. Fired from the nuclear-powered submarine *Ethan Allen* (SSBN-608), which is submerged somewhere in the Pacific Ocean, the Polaris missile explodes as planned somewhere above the Christmas Island Pacific test area.

17 August 1962 The *High Point* (PCH 1) is launched at Seattle, Washington. She is the Navy's first hydrofoil patrol craft and is designed to evaluate this kind of propulsion. The ship has three submerged foils containing propulsion nacelles and propellers, and is capable of riding either on these or her hull, in the same fashion as a conventional ship.

22 August 1962 Kennedy announces that two US submarines had effected a rendezvous under the ice at the North Pole. The *Skate* (SSN 578) of the Atlantic Fleet and the *Seadragon* (SS 194) of the Pacific had actually surfaced through a small hole in the ice on 2 August. At the time, the two submarines were approximately 850 miles (1,370 km) from Cape Chelyuskin, the nearest Soviet territory.

14 October 1962 Air Force reconnaissance aircraft document the existence of Soviet missiles in Cuba. Photographs of a Soviet nuclear missile site under construction at San Cristobal, 100 miles (160 km) west of Havana are taken.

22 October 1962 Kennedy orders a quarantine of Cuba in reaction to proof that Soviet missiles have been spotted there. Kennedy orders a naval and air blockade of any further shipments of military equipment to the island. The Defense Department says that large force of ships and planes that is concentrating on the Caribbean area has been instructed to use force to carry out the ban.

27 October 1962 The Distinguished Service Medal is earned by Maj. Rudolf Anderson, Jr, who will receive it posthumously for action on this date. He is to become the only American casualty of the Cuban Missile Crisis. A member of the 4080th Strategic Reconnaissance Wing, he is killed when his U-2 is shot down by an anti-aircraft missile while on a special mission to gather intelligence over Cuba.

VOLGOLES ENR USSR 9 NOVEMBER

Left: The Cuban missile crisis. Soviet ship *Volgoles* leaves Cuba, an uncovered missile on her foredeck; the skintight protective casing is clearly visible. She is shadowed by the *Vesole* and a Navy patrol plane.

Above: Cuban missile crisis. High-level reconnaissance photographs taken by an Air Force U-2 aircraft. It clearly shows the missile sites on Cuba that led to the showdown between the US and the USSR.

13 March 1963 Two Soviet reconnaissance planes fly over Alaska. On 16 March, the US protests, saying "This is the first clearly established incident of a Soviet overflight of the United States." Reconnaissance planes of the USSR were flying in train (one was closely following the other) and crossed over into Alaskan territory in the vicinity of Kuskokwin Bay where the Alaskan peninsula joins the mainland.

20 June 1963 The US and USSR sign an agreement to set up an agreement to establish a "hot line" emergency communications link between Washington and Moscow to reduce the risk of accidental war. Kennedy, who had said earlier the Cuban missile crisis pointed up the need for the capitals to communicate with one another in an emergency, hailed the agreement.

5 August 1963 The US, USSR and UK sign a treaty banning nuclear tests in the atmosphere, in space and under water. The signing of the 1,500-word treaty in ceremonies at the Kremlin's Great Palace takes five minutes. Each of the signatories pledged to refrain from any further contamination of the air and the oceans with nuclear tests.

16 October 1963 Two Vela nuclear radiation detection satellites are launched from Cape Canaveral, Florida, aboard an Atlas launch vehicle. The Vela satellites were developed by TRW Systems and were the first pair in a series of satellites designed to provide information on nuclear detonations in the atmosphere or in outer space to a distance of some 100 million miles (160 million km).

22 October 1963 The first armored division to be transported by planes to a foreign country arrives in West Germany. The Air Force transports more than 15,000 men of the 2nd Armored Division and its supporting units from Fort Hood, Texas, during "Big Lift". The movement is completed in 65 hours 5 minutes and involves 223 missions, which are completed without a fatality.

21 November 1963 In his last official act as president before he is assassinated in Dallas, Texas, Kennedy dedicated a new building at the Air Force School of Aerospace Medicine, Brooks Air Force Base. 10,000 are on hand. The underlying reason for the visit by Kennedy is to reaffirm his support for the space program, a program in which the school had played a role.

6 February 1964 Except for an hour a day, Cuba shuts off water to the US naval base at Guantanamo Bay. "You do not

Above: The Washington Terminal of the direct communications link with Moscow. Housed inside the Pentagon, this sophisticated line of instant communication is meant to prevent accidental war.

Right: View of a Vela detection satellite, which would orbit the earth at 50,000-60,000 mph (80,465-96,590 kmh). Under the jurisdiction of the Advanced Research Projects Agency, the satellite was used to detect unshielded nuclear tests.

Below: President John F. Kennedy, flanked by Texas Gov. John B. Connally and Mrs Kennedy, dedicates new Air Force School of Aerospace Medicine facilities at Brooks Air Force Base, Texas. He will be assassinated the next day.

deny water even to the enemy", declares Cuban Premier Fidel Castro, who says water will flow between 8 and 9 a.m. The cutoff, says Castro, is in reprisal for seizures by the US of four fishing boats. The US views it as a pretext for reopening the entire question of a US naval base in Cuba.

5 April 1964 General of the Army MacArthur dies in Washington, D.C.,

at the age of 84. MacArthur served as Allied commander of the Southwest Pacific during World War II, as well as the administrator during the Allied occupation of Japan in the postwar era. President Truman dismissed him as commander of the UN forces in Korea in 1951, because of his views on the war.

26 June 1964 The first aerial flight to the Antarctic continent during the winter season is carried out by an LC-130 aircraft. Belonging to Air Development Squadron 6, it flew from Quonsot Point, Rhode Island, to McMurdo Sound on the unusual mission of evacuating an injured Seabee. With a New Zealand ship acting as beacon and station ship, the landing is made on a skyway, lighted by oil fires.

30 June 1964 By command of Gen. Paul Harkins, MACV (US Military Assistance Command, Vietnam), new operational terminology will now be used. From this will emerge some of the most controversial terms of the war in Vietnam, including "search and destroy", for example. Intended to describe a legitimate mission, it came into widespread use as a term for mindless brutality.

1 July 1964 Army Maj. James L. Kelly is killed in action. It will be the medical evacuation helicopter pilot's radio call sign, "Dustoff", that will become the nickname for all medical evacuation helicopters, which were one of the major medical innovations of the war in Vietnam. The more seriously wounded in the battlefield usually reached a hospital within one or two hours after being injured.

24 July 1964 President Johnson announces the successful development of the SR-71 reconnaissance aircraft. It will ultimately become known as the "Blackbird" because of its coloring. The first SR-71 will be delivered to SAC on 7 January, 1966 at Beale Air Force Base, California. It can fly at three times the speed of sound and at altitudes of more than 80,000 ft (24,385 m).

31 July 1964 The first all-nuclear naval task force that will voyage around the world without refueling, Task Force 1, departs from Norfolk, Virginia in Operation "Sea Orbit". The task force stops at 18 cities in 10 countries. It consists of the attack carrier *Enterprise* (CVAN 65), the guided missile cruiser *Long Beach* (CGN 9), and the guided missile frigate *Bainbridge* (DLGN 25).

2 August 1964 The destroyer *Maddox* (DD 731), on a routine patrol in the Gulf of Tonkin, is attacked by three communist torpedo boats. The *Maddox* fires three warning shots — to no effect. At 3:08 p.m. she opens fire and gets one with a direct hit. The others limp northward. This was the first direct clash between US and communist armed vessels since Korea.

5 August 1964 Aircraft from the carriers *Constellation* (CVA 64) and the *Ticonderoga* (CVA 14) attack naval bases, patrol boats and oil depots

Above: Helicopter evacuation of the wounded. The Army used very few helicopters for this purpose in World War II, but transported 17,700 casualties in Korea. In Vietnam, helicopters moved 900,00 sick and wounded.

— the first naval strike on North Vietnam. The strikes are in retaliation for attacks on the US destroyers *Maddox* (DD 731) and *Turner Joy* (DD 951). Two aircraft are lost; their pilots become the Navy's first pilot killed and the first POW in Vietnam.

10 August 1964 Johnson signs the Southeast Asia, or Gulf of Tonkin Resolution. It grew out of an attack by North Vietnamese torpedo boats on two US destroyers and is designed to strengthen the president's hand in dealing with the situation in Southeast Asia. Its broad charter will become the subject of fierce debate as the war in Vietnam tears apart the country.

21 September 1964 The XB-70A Valkyrie Mach 3 bomber prototype makes its first flight. Two of the futuristic delta-wing aircraft were built by North American, but the second was lost in a 1966 collision with an F-104 during a photo flight. In the face of escalating costs and a preference for nuclear-armed ballistic missiles, the program was shelved completely in 1968.

Below: North American XB-70 Valkyrie 1 on take-off during a research flight in early 1968. The DB-70 was one of the first modern aircraft to have two "verticals" (tail fins), but despite this she had a very short service life.

The Vietnam War (1964-1973)

The Vietnam War has been characterized in many ways. Fought nearly a generation ago, it continues to be measured by a different yardstick than is used for any previous American war.

It was almost the longest war in the nation's history, second only to the American Revolution. And even though the US won virtually every significant battle, it lost the war itself — a first. Easily the most divisive American conflict since brother was pitted against brother in the Civil War, it was second only to World War II in terms of its cost ($150 billion) and number of personnel involved (8,744,000 from all branches of the military services).

Like Korea — its immediate predecessor — Vietnam remained an undeclared war. It evolved that way from a complex set of decisions dating back to 1945 when President Harry S. Truman supported France's reconquest of its former colony of Indochina.

Succeeding presidents built upon these commitments, including Dwight D. Eisenhower, who helped Ngo Dinh Diem become South Vietnam's first leader after the 1954 Geneva Accords ended France's rule. The US had a limited commitment then, but it was entirely consistent with the nation's policy of containing communism throughout the world.

By the late 1950s, North Vietnamese began infiltrating the south to help the Vietcong — as the South Vietnamese insurgents were labeled. Terrorist incidents began in 1957 and intensified; Diem's inability to cope with insurgency and terrorism ultimately resulted in heavier American commitments — even though America's involvement could still be accurately described as limited.

Under President John F. Kennedy that began to change. By the end of 1962, 11,000 American service members were in Vietnam as advisers; when he was assassinated in 1963, there were 16,000, some of whom saw limited combat service.

Then came the incident of 15 August, 1964 when North Vietnamese patrol boats were involved with American destroyers. It resulted in the Tonkin Gulf Resolution, which authorized President Lyndon B. Johnson to "repel any armed attack against the forces of the United States and to prevent further aggression".

The net result was that air strikes began to be mounted against the North and US combat troops were sent to the South. At the end of 1964, 23,000 troops were in country and the pace picked up. In March 1965, two Marine brigades became the first ground troops formally committed to the country. They were followed by soldiers of the 173rd Airborne Brigade and additional Marines.

The cost of the war was $5.8 billion in 1966 and had escalated to $28.8 billion three years later. By 1967, the Army was supported by more than 1.3 million men — including the South Vietnamese Army and the troops of US allies. An average of 850,000 tons of supplies arrived monthly. These troops consumed 10 million field rations monthly, expended 80,000 tons of amunition and used 80 million gallons of gasoline.

By 1968, 550,000 Americans were in South Vietnam. This included three corps headquarters, seven Army divisions, five specialized brigades, two Marine divisions and a separate Marine regiment. In addition, the Air Force was regularly flying missions from South Vietnam, Thailand and Guam. The 7th Fleet operated along the coast and launched repeated air strikes against the North.

US allies provided support for the effort, a fact not generally recognized about the war. In fact, the total support given South Vietnam by nations other than the US (more than 30 countries sent some form of aid) was greater than that given to South Korea in the 1950s. South Korea herself lost 4,407 troops in Vietnam.

Ironically, it was the most significant US military victory — the Tet Offensive of 1968 — that proved to be the most damaging to American support for the war. More than 50,000 communists were killed in the offensive, but Americans were stunned by the ferocity of the offensive and support for the war declined greatly. President Johnson announced he would not run for reelection and halted further escalation efforts.

Concurrent with these moves, the war entered its "Vietnamization" stage — the objective of which was to build up the capabilities of the South Vietnamese Army to prosecute the war while scaling back American commitments.

In June 1969, President Richard M. Nixon announced the first major US troop withdrawals. It was never the same again, even though American and South Vietnamese troops invaded Cambodia, the Ho Chi Minh trail was raided and massive naval and air efforts were mounted. By March 1972, most US ground troops had departed and a

Below: While on a search and secure mission northwest of Bong Song, men of Co D, 503rd Infantry come under sudden sniper fire. Quickly returning that fire, they radio out for gun-ship support.

Below: A 105mm howitzer prepares to open up from its emplacement. Used extensively in Fire Support Bases this highly adaptable weapon with its crew of 8 could be transported up country by helicopter.

ceasefire agreement went into effect on 28 January, 1973.

The legacy of the war for the US was 47,253 killed in combat, another 10,449 nonbattle deaths and 313,616 wounded, of whom nearly half were classified as seriously wounded. There were 4,865 US helicopters and 3,720 other aircraft destroyed in the war. Four times the bomb tonnage (about 8 million tons) was dropped over North Vietnam, South Vietnam, Cambodia and Laos as was dropped in World War II in all theaters.

South Vietnam lost 185,528 killed, with half a million wounded. Estimates of the North Vietnam and Vietcong casualties were 924,000 combat deaths. Civilian casualties were 415,000 killed with another 935,000 wounded.

It was a war that was highly sophisticated in terms of weaponry, yet the use of land mines and punjab sticks and was common. It had all the elements of the limited wars America had fought in the past (the War of 1812, Mexico, Korea, for example), but ultimately lacked the support of the American people for its successful prosecution.

It had significant political and economic effects on the American landscape . . . the resignation of one president, a general opening of the political process within the nation, the economic problems of the early 1970s. And it resulted in problems that are still with us today — the final accounting, for example, by North Vietnam for the nation's prisoners-of-war and missing in action.

By any measure, however, it left a nation that would measure its wartime commitments more carefully in the future. As the last American commander in Vietnam put it: "The Army must have the price of involvement clear before we get involved, so that America can weigh the probable cost of involvement against the dangers of non-involvement. For there are worse things than war."

Above: The SR-71 "Blackbird" long-range reconnaissance aircraft. It is built mainly of titanium and in September 1974 flew from New York to London in less than two hours at an average speed of 1,800 mph (2,897 kmh).

US Combat Sorties Flown In Southeast Asia (1965-1972)

	Tactical Aircraft	B-52s	Other Tactical Sorties*	Total
1965	103	1	54	158
1966	254	5	135	394
1967	320	10	177	507
1968	372	21	197	590
1969	300	19	217	536
1970	193	15	177	385
1971	122	13	125	260
1972	167	28	116	311

*Other sorties include combat air patrol, escort, reconnaissance and other non-attack sorties.

5 December 1964 The Medal of Honor is presented to Army Capt. Roger H. C. Donlon for heroism in South Vietnam. The first person to receive the medal since the Korean War, he earns it for action near Nam Dong. As commanding officer of Army Special Forces Detachment A-726, he receives multiple wounds as he fights off a violent attack by a reinforced Vietcong battalion — leaving 54 of them dead.

Below: Men of the 3rd Battalion, 9th Marine Expeditionary Brigade, beach-head, Danang. They were met by sightseers, Vietnamese girls and four American soldiers. Gen. Westmoreland was reportedly "appalled".

14 December 1964 Operation "Barrel Roll" begins. The name of a plan approved by Johnson to bomb Laotian infiltration routes and military installations in the panhandle, it begins with US planes attacking "targets of opportunity". It is the beginning of tactical fighter operations in South-east Asia on a continuing basis.

22 December 1964 The SR-71 long-range reconnaissance aircraft makes its first flight. Its developer, Lockheed, and the Air Force succeeded in designing, building and completing the flight test program of this large and extremely noisy aircraft in total secrecy.

8 February 1965 The first retaliatory air strike by the Air Force in Vietnam occurs as a communications center at Vinhlinh is hit. South Vietnamese Air Vice-Marshal Nguyen Cao Ky leads the portion of the raid conducted by South Vietnamese jets, which are under Air Force escort. It is revealed after the raid that Ky, later a figure of some controversy, dropped bomb loads on an unassigned target.

18 February 1965 The first Air Force jet raids flown against an enemy concentration in Vietnam are carried out. In the first raid in which no South Vietnamese airmen have participated — which indicates there is an escalation of US involvement in the war in Vietnam — planes attack guerrillas in the Bin Dinh Province in support of South Vietnamese troops.

8 March 1965 More than 3,500 Marines land in South Vietnam to take up security duties around the large US jet airbase at Da Nang. This is the first commitment of American ground combat troops to what will become the longest war in US history. The Marine force consists of two battalion landing teams, or reinforced battalions of more than 1,500 men each from the 3rd Marine Division in Okinawa.

23 March 1965 America's first two-person space flight begins as Gemini III, nicknamed the Molly Brown, blasts off from the Eastern Test Range. The astronauts are Air Force Maj. Virgil I. (Gus) Grissom and Lieutenant Commander John W. Young. Navy frogmen pick up the astronauts at Grand Turk Island following the flight of 4 hours 53 minutes; sophisticated weightlessness and communications tests were made.

3 April 1965 The first nuclear reactor to be put into orbit, the Snap 10A, is launched from Vandenberg Air Force Base, California. The test signals the first operation in space of a light, compact propulsion system that can produce power over

long periods of time on small amounts of fuel. This is important for surveillance and patrol satellites and for manned space ships on trips to distant planets.

3 April 1965 During Operation "Rolling Thunder", US and South Vietnamese aircraft make a series of raids on bridges and roads in North Vietnam — in particular, the Hamron and Dongphuon Bridges, which are major rail links to Hanoi. The attacks are the farthest north that will be made during "Rolling Thunder"; six US aircraft are shot down during the raids, which end after three days.

30 April 1965 Announcement is made that US Coast Guard units will operate with the Navy in Vietnam. Squadron One is formed for deployment, and 17 82 ft (25 m) patrol craft arrive in Vietnam two months later; 9 more arrive in February. Coast Guard cutters patrolled the Vietnamese coast from the Demilitarized Zone to the Cambodian border, and operated from bases in Da Nang, Cat Lo and An Thoi.

3 June 1965 The launch of Gemini IV. Air Force Majs. James McDivitt and Edward H. White set an American space record for endurance of 97 hours 59 minutes. White will become the first American to walk in space when he leaves the capsule for 21 minutes. Gemini IV splashed down in the recovery area off Grand Turk Island in the Bahamas in the Atlantic on 7 June.

17 June 1965 Guam-based B-52s bomb a Vietcong concentration 30 miles (48 km) north of Saigon, the first combat use of the heavy jet bombers since they were placed in the inventory in 1952. It is the first mass bombing raid of the war under Operation "Arc Light" and is aimed at a concentration of Vietcong in Binduong province. One B-52 is lost during the operation in a collision.

10 July 1965 The first air-to-air combat victories by the Air Force in Vietnam are registered by Capts. Thomas S. Roberts and Ronald C. Anderson in one F-4, and Capts. Kenneth E. Holcombe and Arthur C. Clark in another. They are credited with knocking out two enemy MiG-17s. Navy pilots had registered their first kills the previous month, downing two enemy aircraft.

11 August 1965 An A-4E Skyhawk aircraft from the carrier *Midway* (CVA 41) becomes the first Navy plane definitely known to have been downed by a surface-to-surface missile over North Vietnam. The first Air Force aircraft to meet the same fate was

Above: Astronaut Edward H. White II outside his spacecraft. He became the first American to leave his spacecraft while in orbit — using the compressed-gas unit in his hand to move about in the weightless environment.

Below: An Air Force B-52 bomber drops 750lb (340-kg) of bombs on Vietcong targets in South Vietnam. Some 126,615 sorties were flown in B-52 bombers during the Vietnam War — six percent of them against North Vietnam.

18 August 1965

Above: Officers aboard the *Petrel* inspect the hydrogen bomb recovered by a Navy task force off the Palomares in southern Spain. The bomb fell into the sea and was lost when an Air Force bomber and tanker collided.

an F-4, which was destroyed by a surface-to-air missile some two weeks earlier on 24 July.

18 August 1965 Operation "Starlite" begins, the first major ground action of the Vietnam war that will be fought only by US troops. About 5,500 Marines destroy a Vietcong stronghold near Vantuong on a peninsula 16 miles south of Chulai. In the four-day operation, the Marines will lose 45 men and the Vietcong (most of them members of the 1st Regiment) will lose 688 killed.

14 November 1965 The 3rd Brigade, 1st Cavalry Division (Airmobile) defeats the North Vietnamese 32nd, 33rd and 36th Regiments in the Ia Drang Valley in a three-day battle that will end on 16 November. The clash represents the first major engagement of the Vietnam War between regular forces of the US and those of the NVA.

2 December 1965 The nuclear-powered carrier *Enterprise* (CVAN 65) launches 118 sorties against targets in South Vietnam, thus becoming the first nuclear ship to engage in hostilities. It carried the largest air wing (CVW-9) deployed to the western Pacific to that time, and joined in the action in Vietnam with strikes on Vietcong installations near Bien Hoa.

17 January 1966 A B-52 bomber collides with a KC-135 tanker while refueling over Spain's Mediterranean coast. Seven of the 11 men aboard the aircraft are killed. Four hydrogen bombs fall from the refueling B-52, with three of them crashing to earth where they are recovered. The fourth bomb will not be plucked from the Mediterranean Sea until three months later.

23 January 1966 The largest airlift in history of troops and equipment into a

combat zone — the effort is called Operation "Blue Light" — is completed by the Air Force's Military Airlift Command. Starting on 23 December, 1965, the operation involved 231 sorties by C-141s moving 3,000 troops and 4,700 tons of equipment of the 3rd Brigade, 25th Infantry Division from Hawaii to Pleiku, Vietnam.

4 March 1966 A flight of Air Force F-4C Phantoms is attacked by three MiG-17 jet fighters in the first air-to-air combat of the war over North Vietnam. The MiGs will make several unsuccessful passes before fleeing to the sanctuary of the communist capital area.

17 March 1966 The US midget submarine *Alvin* locates the hydrogen bomb which had been lost in the collision of an American tanker aircraft and bomber over Spain. There was no lethal leakage from the weapon, which was found, parachute still intact, some 2,500 ft (760 m) below the surface in the Sea of Palomares. The *Alvin* was one of three midget submarines used by the US in the search.

11 April 1966 Answering a call for help from the 1st Infantry Division, which is surrounded by enemy forces near Cam My, a few miles east of Saigon, Airman William H. Pitsenbarger heads off on a hazardous rescue mission. He ministers to the wounded and, in the fierce fight that continues, is killed. He becomes the first airman

Below. One of the centers of the North American Defense Command. In its various centers, it keeps track of more than 5,300 objects, which requires more than 20,000 daily observations from 24 sites worldwide.

to be awarded the Air Force Cross posthumously.

12 April 1966 B-52s of the Strategic Air Command hit targets in North Vietnam for the first time when they begin to bomb the Mu Gia Pass. The bombing will continue through 26 April, with the objective of stopping the infiltration of enemy troops. After leaving the Mu Gia Pass, Vietnamese would cross into Laos and make their way down the Ho Chi Minh Trail to South Vietnam.

20 April 1966 The combat operations center of the North American Defense Command (NORAD) moves into its Cheyenne Mountain, Colorado, complex. The nerve center of defense in North America, it can identify and track aircraft and missile threats to the entire continent. It is located in the mountain complex because of the need to ensure a fully protected underground command post.

26 April 1966 Maj. Paul J. Gilmore and 1st Lt. William T. Smith become the first pilots to destroy a MiG-21 aircraft. The F-4C pilots down the MiG with a Sidewinder missile while flying escort for F-105 Thunderchiefs when their flight is attacked near the North Vietnamese capital of Hanoi.

29 June 1966 For the first time in the Vietnamese conflict, the North Vietnamese capital of Hanoi and Haiphong, a principal port, are bombed by US jet aircraft. Navy A-4 and A-6 bombers attack a large tank farm at the edge of Hanoi; Air Force F-105s strike another tank farm 3.5 miles (5.6 km) from the center of the city that contains 20 percent of Vietnam's stores.

Below: This bomb damage photograph was taken after aircraft from the carrier *Oriskany* (CVA 34) hit oil storage areas in Vietnam. Some 7,794 combat sorties were launched from her decks during the conduct of the war.

9 October 1966 Commander Richard Bellinger records the first kill of a MiG-21 by a Navy pilot in Vietnam. Flying in his F-8 Crusader from the *Oriskany* (CVA 34), and using a Sidewinder missile, he takes out the aircraft over North Vietnam. The MiG-21 had made its first combat appearance in Vietnam earlier in the year. Only three weeks later, Bellinger takes over as the *Oriskany's* Air Wing Commander.

19 January 1967 Maj, Bernard Fisher receives the Medal of Honor, the first member of the Air Force to receive the medal for action in Southeast Asia. fisher saved the life of a fellow pilot shot down at Ashau. Against the advice of other pilots, Fisher landed and picked up the injured flier in an atmosphere described as flying inside Yankee Stadium with the people in the bleachers firing with machine guns.

22 February 1967 C-130 transports leave Bien Hoa with paratroopers from the 173rd Airborne Brigade, who will make The first and only American Battalion-size parachute assault in Vietnam. It is part of Operation "Junction City", a concerted effort to smash the Vietcong stronghold near the Cambodian border, a total of 780 men make the drop and were followed in by eight C-130Bs with 80 tons of supplies and equipment.

22 February 1967 The first land-based artillery attack of the war in Vietnam takes place when 175mm (6.89in) guns near US Camp Carrol fire 63 shells at North Vietnamese anti-aircraft Positions. They open fire at the emplacements just after a US Spotter plane had been shot at North of a buffer zone in the area.

26 February 1967 Rivers in the panhandle of North Vietnam are mined by seven A-6 Intruder aircraft flying from the *Enterprise* (CVAN 65). Led by Commander A. H. Barrie of VA-35's Black Panthers", the mines are planted at the mouths of the Song Ca and Son Giang Rivers. This air-Borne operation with aimed at Stopping coastal barges from Moving enemy supplies into the Immediate areas.

11 March 1967 The first television-guided air-to surface glide bomb (the Walleye) used in combat is fired by the aircraft of the *Oriskany* (CV34) in an attack on the barracks at Sam Son, North Vietnam.

20 April 1967 American planes bomb Haiphong, North Vietnam, for the first time, hitting two power plants inside the city. The raids are carried out by 86 planes from the carriers *Kitty Hawk* (CV63) and *Ticonderoga* (CV14). 7th Fleet aircraft follow this with attacks on Kep Airfield 37 miles (60

Above: M114A2 howitzer gets off a round. Once the enemy was located, the amount of iron that could be put on him by artillery was staggering. The idea was to pinpoint him and then hit him with artillery and bombs.

km) northeast of Hanoi. These represent the first strikes on MiG Bases in North Vietnam.

19 May 1967 The USSR ratifies a treaty with the US and UK banning nuclear weapons from outer space. Dozens of other nations sign later. The treaty bars the use of the moon, planets or other celestial bodies for military bases and also bans nuclear weapons in orbit or in space. It is the first major East-West agreement since the treaty of 1963 putting a limited ban on nuclear testing.

1 June 1967 The first nonstop transatlantic helicopter flight is completed. Supported by HC-130P tankers, two Air Force HH-3Es of the 48th Aerospace Rescue and Recovery Squadron fly a nonstop flight from New York to Parish. It follows the route taken by Charles Lindbergh 40 years earlier. It requires 30 hours 46 minutes, less time than the 33 hours 39 minutes taken by "Lucky Lindy".

Above: A-6A Intruder aircraft. Pinpoint attacks at night or in bad weather were the strong suits of this medium attack aircraft, which could carry a maximum ordnance load of 15,000 lb (6,840 kg) out to 1,077 miles (1,733 km).

8 June 1967 Israeli aircraft and patrol boats attack the American ship *Liberty* (AGTR 5) about 20 miles £32 km) off the Gaza strip. Official records say the attack was an accident in which the *Liberty* was mistaken for an *Egyptian* cargo ship. Others claim it was intentional, designed to keep the ship from intercepting key messages. Thirty-four US sailors were killed and 75 wounded.

13 August 1967 The Langson rail and highway bridge spanning the Kikung River which is about 10 miles (16 km) from the Chinese border – is hit by US planes, which also bomb rail yards at Langgai and Langdang, 19 and 26 miles (30.6 and 41.8 km) from the border. These are the closest targets to China hit by US

Below: Damage to the technical research ship *Liberty* is clearly evident after Israeli fighters and torpedo boats attacked her. More than £3 million in compensation was paid to families of the men killed in the attack.

aircraft in the Vietnam war. navy pilots will hit the targets again two months later.

9 September 1967 Airman First Class Duane D. Hackney receives the Air Force Cross for rescuing a pilot in operations in Vietnam. A parajumper with the 37th Aerospace Rescue and Recovery Squadron, Hackney became a legend in the world of rescue. He was the most decorated parajumper to serve in Vietnam and parajumpers as a group were the most decorated troops in Southeast Asia.

13 September 1967 Brigadier General Keith L. Ware is killed –he is the fourth general officer fatality in Vietnam – when his helicopter is shot down about 60 miles north of Saigon. The general was the first draftee (he was drafted on 23 November 1940) to make it to stay rank and was serving as the commander of the 1st Infantry Division when he, his staff and four helicopter crewmen go down.

24 October 1967 Some 65 US aircraft attack the huge Phuc Yen airfield 18 miles (30 km) northwest of Hanoi (it is North Vietnam's largest air base) in the first combined service strike of the war. The airfield is pounded all day and the planes return the next day to pound the MiG base again.

15 November 1967 Major Michael J. Adams becomes the first fatality of the X-15 rocket plane program when his craft crashes during a routine research flights. One of five pilots assigned to the X-15 research program, Adams had taken the plane – No. 3, which was equipped for high altitude research – up to 360,000 ft (79,250 m) before crashing in the desert.

8 December 1967 Major Robert H. Lawrence, Jr, the first black astronaut in the national space program, is killed in the crash

Below: The environmental research ship *Pueblo* underway off San Diego, California, in October 1967. In three months she will be seized by North Koreans, provoking a confrontation between that country and the US.

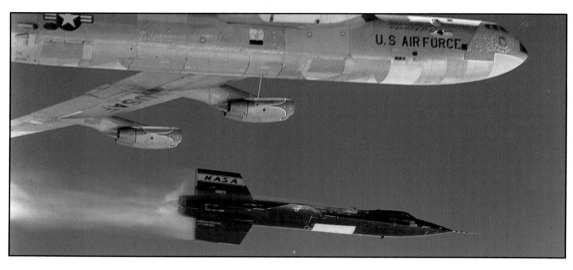

of his F-104 jet on the runway on a training flight at Edwards Air Force Base, California. The ninth astronaut to be killed in an accident, Lawrence had been picked with 15 others in June of this year to participate in training for the manned orbiting laboratory program.

23 January 1968 North Korea seizes the intelligence ship *Pueblo* (AGER 2), which represents the first time a US vessel surrenders in peacetime without putting up a fight. The capture occurs in the Sea of Japan, with North Korea claiming it violated its territorial limits of 12 miles (19.3 km). The 85-man crew will be subjected to harsh treatment, but they are released later in the year.

30 January 1968 The Vietcong launch the Tet Offensive, a major series of attacks throughout South Vietnam including one on the American Embassy. The effort is designed to destabilize he government in Saigon and provoke opposition to the war in the US. The North Vietnamese attack the nation's seven largest cities and 30 provincial capitals. Communist losses are high and by 10 February the offensive has been crushed.

23 June 1968 At midnight of the previous evening, the war in Vietnam became the longest in US history. Dated from the death of the first serviceman killed in the conflict – Army Specialist 4 James Davis – the war has lasted six years, six months

Above: An X-15 research vehicle is dropped from under the wing of a B-52. A special nickel-chromium alloy was used for the skin of this aircraft, which hit speeds approaching seven times the speed of sound.

and one day. The Revolutionary War had held the previous record, lasting six years, six months from its outbreak to the British surrender.

1 July 1968 The US, USSR, UK and 58 other nations sign the Nuclear Nonproliferation Treaty, which had been in negotiation for more than six years and which is designed to half the spread of nuclear weapons. The agreement says those signing will enter discussion sin the near future on the reduction of offensive and defensive systems and proposes a nine-point disarmament plan.

Below: The major battles and main areas of conflict during the weeks of the Tet Offensive. Most actions were short-lived except for fighting around Saigon and Hue, where it took 25 days to retake that city.

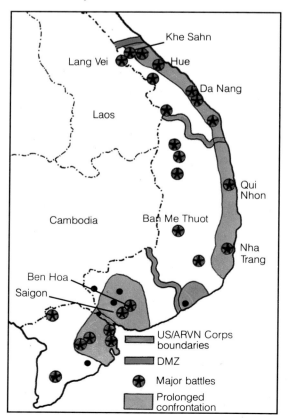

23 July 1968 Major General Robert F. Worley becomes the first Air Force general to be killed in action during the Vietnam conflict. Vice commander of the 7th Air Force, his jet reconnaissance plane is shot down by enemy ground fire. The general was at the controls of an RF-4C. Phantom jet about 65 miles (105 km) northwest of Da Nang when hit. His co-pilot manages to eject safely and is later rescued.

16 August 1968 The first Minuteman III intercontinental ballistic missile is successfully launched from Cape Canaveral, Florida. It will become the last ICBM in the US strategic force arsenal until the M-X – or Peacekeeper – is fielded in the 1980's. The land-based, silo-launched missiles are stored in individual control centers buried 50 ft (15 m) beneath the surface in capsules operated by two officers.

21 August 1968 Pfc. James Anderson, Jr, is posthumously awarded the Medal of Honor, first black Marine to receive the nation's highest honor. His platoon was the lead element in a reconnaissance patrol near Cam Lo when it came under withering automatic and small arms fire. A grenade was pitched in the middle of the platoon and he smothered it with his body, saving his comrades from injury and death.

30 September 1968 The world's only active battleship – the *New Jersey* (BB 62) – fires her first shots in battle in more than 16 years when she arrives in Vietnamese waters and goes into action. She lets loose on targets in the Demilitarized Zone, destroying two gun positions and two supply areas. She will be decommissioned

after less than 18 months with the fleet – then modernized and put in service again.

23 December 1968 The crew of the *Pueblo* is freed. The 82 survivors cross the Bridge of No Return to South Korea, preceded by the casket of Duane D. Hodges, who had been wounded during the seizure of the ship by North Koreans of 23 January. The crew, some with bruises and black eyes, leave abroad Air Force C-141 jet transports for the trip home, arriving in San Diego, California the same day.

16 January 1969 Staff Sgt. Drew D. Dix becomes the first enlisted member of the Green Berets to earn a Medal of Honor for his actions against the enemy. In Chau Doc Province in the Republic of Vietnam, he is personally responsible for 14 confirmed Vietcong killed in action (and perhaps another 25 unconfirmed), the capturing of 20 prisoners, 15 weapons and the rescue of 14 civilians during a two-day period.

10 May 1969 US and South Vietnamese forces battle the North Vietnamese for Abpia mountain (Hill 937), east of Laotian border. It is part of the sweep of the A Shua Valley. The 10-day assault is one of the bloodiest battles of the war, with Abpia (Now "Hamburger Hill") abandoned on 29 May. Since the hill had little strategic value, heavy criticism of the battle arose in the US.

8 June 1969 1st Lieutenant Sharon A. Lane dies of shrapnel wounds at Chu Lai. She is the only American service woman to be killed as a result of enemy action in Vietnam. The 25-year old native on Canton, Ohio, is killed

Above: Battleship *New Jersey* bombarding Vietnam in the mid-60's. Activated for service in Vietnam, she was decommissioned after 18 months. The *New Jersey* was recommissioned for yet a third time in December 1982.

when a rocket strikes a ward at the 312 Evacuation Hospital, some 335 miles (540 km) northeast of Saigon. The single other casualty of the same attack is a Vietnamese child.

20 July 1969 Lieutenant Colonel. Edwin Aldrin and Neil Armstrong, two crew men from Apollo 11 become the first men to step on another celestial body when the land on the moon. The lunar module *Eagle* had been launched four days earlier and entered lunar orbit on 19 July. "The Eagle has landed", says Neil Armstrong upon arriving. As he steps on the surface, he says, "One small step for a man, one giant leap for mankind." This lunar visit will last a little over two and a half hours and is the first of six landings.

14 September 1969 North Vietnamese regular army troops move into the Mekong Delta for the first time in the Vietnam War, according to reports from the US Command. The movement is reported to have taken place over

Left: The havoc of war. During the Tet Offensive even the American embassy in Saigon came under attack. This is one of the side entrances to the embassy showing the damage caused by the Vietcong insurgents.

Below: Members of the 716th MP Battalion guard the entrance to the US embassy during an attack by the Vietcong during the Tet Offensive. The Tet, or new Year, attack was aimed at 100 cities throughout the country.

the last four weeks following departure of US troops, who had left the region as part of Nixon's plan for the withdrawal of troops.

3 March 1970 The nuclear non-proliferation treaty goes into effect after 43 nations ratify it. Basic purpose of the agreement is to restrict possession of atomic weapons by forbidding nuclear powers to transfer them to other states. On the other side, the treaty forbids non-nuclear powers from acquiring the weapons. The treaty had been signed by the US and USSR in 1968.

28 March 1970 Depending on the judgment of field commanders, US troops are now permitted to cross the Cambodian border in response to enemy threats. The White House makes the announcement, stating that such crossing are to be made at the judgment of field commanders. This does not mean a widening of the war, say officials – it's a restatement of the rules already in force.

11 June 1970 Colonel Anna M. Hays, Chief of the Army Nurse Corps and Colonel Elizabeth P. Hoisington, director of the WAC, are promoted. They thus become the first women generals the Army has had in its 196-year history. Hoisington shares another distinction: her brother Perry was an Air Force general, which made them the first brother-sister generals in US history.

19 June 1970 the first flight of Minuteman III missiles becomes operational with the 741st Strategic Missile Squadron, Minot Air Force Base, North Dakota. The new missile – which replaced Minuteman I "G–series missiles – have an improved third-stage motor, more penetration aids to counter defence systems, and can carry the Mk 12 MIRV with three nuclear warheads.

5 September 1970 Operation "Jefferson Glen" is begun in Vietnam by the US 101st Airborne Division (Airmobile) in coordination with the South Vietnamese Army 1st Infantry

Division in Thua Thien Province, I Corps. The operation, which will conclude on 8 October, will be the last of the major military operations in the country in which US ground troops with participate.

21 November 1970 The raid on Son Tay prison, 23 miles (37 km) west of Hanoi, is unsuccessful. Manning on HH-3, five HH-53 and two HC-13P helicopters, the rescue team arrives shortly after the Vietcong had evacuated American prisoners. The rescuers lost an H-3 and one of the members of the party broke an ankle, but no casualties resulted from the attempt.

30 December 1970 The Navy ends its four-year role in inland waterway combat when it turns over 125 vessels to the South Vietnamese Navy. Some 650 vessels have been turned over to the South Vietnamese during the war. Around 17,000 Americans will remain in shore positions with the South Vietnamese navy, and will serve as advisers aboard their vessels.

6 January 1971 The first AV-8 Harrier aircraft is accepted at Dunsfold, England, by Marine Corps Maj. Gen. Homer S. Hill. It is the first vertical/short take-off and landing (VSTOL) fixed-wing aircraft ever accepted for use as a combat system by the US armed forces. The British-built aircraft has since proved reliable and has undergone several updates.

11 February 1971 A seabed treaty barring the installation of nuclear weapons on the ocean floor is signed by 63 nations in Washington, Moscow and London. It is the fourth in a series of disarmament moves, beginning with the 10-year-old treaty that outlaws military activity in Antarctica and including subsequent bans on nuclear activity in outer space and in Latin America.

29 March 1971 Lieutenant. William L. Calley is found guilty of murdering 22 civilians at My Lai, Vietnam, and is sentenced to life imprisonment. The incident occurred 16 March, 1968 when C Company, 1st Battalion, 20th Infantry entered the village, situated in Quang Ngai province. Some of the villagers were raped and shot in their homes; others were herded to a drainage ditch and killed.

20 April 1971 A set of figures are released by the Pentagon on this day which confirm that "fragging" incidents – which are labeled after the fragmentation grenades used against officers by soldiers – are on the increase. There were 209 such incidents in the previous year which caused the deaths of 34 men; in 1969, comparable figures of fragging were 96 incidents and 34 killed.

28 April 1971 The Navy announces that 49 new rear admirals have been selected, among them Captain Samuel Lee Gravely, Jr, the first black man to be selected for flag rank. Gravely, 48, has come up through the ranks – having seen service in World War II, Korea and Vietnam.

13 June 1971 The *New York Times* begins to publish the Pentagon Papers, a top-secret study of American involvement in Vietnam from 1945 to 1967 originally prepared for Secretary of Defense Robert S. McNamara. The 47-volume analysis is leaked to the press by Daniel Ellsberg, a military strategist, who is charged with theft, conspiracy and espionage – but the case against him is later dismissed.

Below: Brig. Gen. Elizabeth P. Hoisington, director, Women's Army Corps (left) and Brig. Gen. Anna M. Hays, chief Army Nurse Corps, hold their flags after becoming the first female generals in the history of the Army.

Below: A US mortar team at an outpost near the Cambodian border. In the early stages of this effort, operations were limited to air and artillery support; forces were committed to cross-border operations on 1 May.

16 July 1971 Jeanne M. Holm becomes the first female brigadier general commissioned in the Air Force. The 50-year old general received her stars from Air Force Secretary Robert C. Seamans, Jr Holm joined the service when she was a student in college.

10 April 1972 The US and USSR join with 70 nations and sign a biological warfare accord that binds the countries "not to develop produce, stockpile or otherwise acquire or retain" microbiological or other biological agent or toxins except for peaceful purposes. The 14-article convention also commits the signatories to make a similar effort to ban chemical weapons.

27 April 1972 Four aircraft, using Paveway I laser-guided "smart" bombs, knock down the Thanh Hoa bridge in North Vietnam. The mission proves the value of smart bombs; 871 conventional sorties had previously been flown against the bridge, with only superficial damage to the structure to show. This type of ordnance is one of the technologies that comes to maturity during the Vietnam war.

8 May 1972 The mining of all major ports in North Vietnam is ordered by Nixon. Ships in those ports have three days to leave before the mines are activated; after this, the Navy will search and seize them. The maze of 1,000 lb (454 kg) mines traps 31 vessels at Haiphong. The mines are to be removed, says Nixon, when US POWs are all returned and a supervised cease-fire begins.

10 May 1972 Lieutenant Randall F. Cunningham and Lieutenant (jg) William P. Driscoll become the first American aces of the Vietnam war – and the first US all-MiG aces. Cunningham and his radar intercept officer are in

Above: Marine AV-8 Harrier. The Marine Corps saw this aircraft as one with great potential for close support and air defense missions. it can land at relatively unprepared sites early in an amphibious assault.

an F-4J Phantom II when they shoot down three MiG 17s. As they head back to their carrier, the *Constellation*, they are forced to bail out when they take a hit; thankfully they are rescued.

11 August 1972 The US ends its Vietnam ground combat role when it deactivates the 1,043 men of the 3rd Battalion of the 21st Infantry, with supporting artillery and a medical detachment. The first American ground combat battalion landed in Vietnam on 8 March, 1965 – the 3rd Battalion, 9th Marine Regiment. At the height of US involvement, there were 112 ground combat battalions in the country.

28 August 1972 Captain. Richard S. Ritchie becomes the first Air Force ace in Vietnam and the first to destroy five MiG-21s when he records a kill over Hanoi. Based in Thailand, Ritchie and co-pilot Captain Charles DeBellevue are flying protection for other planes bombing North Vietnam and make the kill with an air-to-air missile about 30 miles (48 km) west of the North Vietnamese capital.

9 September 1972 Captain Charles DeBellevue becomes an ace when, flying in an F-4 Phantom, he bags his fifth and sixth MiGs. the leading Air Force ace of the war in Vietnam, he is the first weapon systems officer to achieve this status. This is possible because the F-4 – the primary US fighter – required a weapons system/radar intercept operator as well as a pilot – and both receive credits for kills.

22 November 1972 The first B-52 bomber to be lost to enemy action falls prey to a surface-to-air missile over North Vietnam. The aircraft limped to Thailand, where the crew ejected and were recovered. The standard SAM used by the North Vietnamese was the SA-2 "Guideline", a two-stage missile armed with a 258-lb (117 kg) warhead, which had a maximum range of 30 miles (48 km). They were usually emplaced in clusters of six.

8 January 1973 Secret peace talks between the US and the North Vietnamese resume near Paris. Just prior to the end of the war, Henry Kissinger and Le Duc Tho meet for the first time since talks broke down following an 11-day bombing attack by US forces on the Hanoi-Haiphong area.

12 January 1973 Lieutenant Walter Kovaleski and his radar intercept officer Lieutenant James Wise register the last American aerial victory of the Vietnam War. Flying in an F-4 Phantom, they destroy a MiG-17 with two Sidewinder missiles over the Gulf of Tonkin. Kovaleski will be hit with ground fire two days later and be the last American to be downed in Vietnam but he will be rescued.

27 January 1973 Lieutenant Col. William B. Nolde of Mount Pleasant Michigan, becomes the last American casualty of the Vietnam war. Colonel Nolde was killed by an artillery shell at An Loc just 11 hours before the truce took effect. A senior US adviser in the

Below: An HH-53 Jolly Green Giant refuels in midflight. Developed from the needs of the Marines for an all-weather transport helicopter, the HH-53 can carry 37 armed troops or 8,000lb (3269 kg) of cargo.

Above: The longest war in US history comes to an end as Henry Kissinger and Le Duc Tho sign the Vietnam cease-fire agreement in Paris. The US had first assumed a full combat role in Southeast Asia in 1965.

Above: Jubilant American POWs returning home on a C-141 Starlifter. They were the lucky ones. Some 2,494 servicemen and civilians were unaccounted for after the release of the prisoners was made in 1973.

An Loc province, he was just leaving the Ranger compound after saying goodnight to the province chief when the fatal round hit.

27 January 1973 The Vietnam peace accords are signed in Paris, and the longest war in US history comes to an end. Its major provisions call for a cease-fire throughout Vietnam; withdrawal of US troops and advisers; dismantling all of US bases; the release of US and other prisoners of war; that troops of North Vietnam to stay in place; and that force will not be used to reunify the country.

28 January 1973 The cease fire in the Vietnam conflict officially goes into effect, thus ending the 12-year war. Artillery fire stops at 8:05 a.m. five minutes after the cease-fire deadline. The cost to US forces involved in the conflict is 47,383 killed, 303,616 wounded, 587 captured, and 1,335 missing in action.

12 February 1973 Operation "Homecoming" – name for the operation under which US prisoners of war from Vietnam were returned – beings with the release of 142 of 588 prisoners at Hanoi's Gialam airport. The first group arrives in California two days later and is sent to homes and hospitals across the country. It will not be until 29 March that the last prisoner acknowledged by Hanoi is released.

16 March 1973 Capt. Floyd J. Thompson is freed from prison in Vietnam and is sent to Clark Air Base in the Philippines. Thompson was flying in an L-19 (9-1) plane on an aerial reconnaissance mission over Vietnam in early 1964 when his plane was hit by small arms fire, downed and he was taken prisoner. The Army officer will become the longest-held – nine years – prisoner of war in American history.

29 March 1973 The last American troops withdraw from South Vietnam as 2,501 service members leave Saigon's Ton Son Nut Air Base for the US. This marks an end to US involvement in Vietnam and leaves only the defence attaché's office. The office has cost the US 47,383 killed in action. In addition 8,611 aircraft were destroyed, 3,926 in hostile action and 4,685 by other causes.

14 May 1973 America launches Skylab I, its first manned space station. Half a million people – including 26 former American prisoners of war watch the launch at 1:30 p.m. by a two-stage Saturn lifting vehicle. Skylab stays in orbit for 28 days and obtains data on the crew for use in extending the duration of manned space flight. Other inflight experiments are also conducted.

15 August 1973 All US bombing of targets in Cambodia ceases. B-52s of the Strategic Air Command end more than eight years of conventional bombing operations in Southeast Asia. Although the truce agreement that ended the Vietnam war had been signed in Paris earlier in the year. B-52s had continued to be sent to Laos and Cambodia because of cease-fire violations.

2 February 1974 First flight of the prototype F-16 lightweight fighter aircraft. In January 1975, the Air Force announces full-scale development of the aircraft, not only as an air combat fighter, but also in the air/surface role. The program was triggered by the recognition that co-production with European allies was desirable. Four NATO allies announce orders in June 1975.

22 Febraury 1974 Lieutenant (jg) Barbara Ann Allen becomes the Navy's first designated female aviator when she receives her Gold Wings at Naval Air Station, Corpus Christi, Texas. It is announced that the 25-year old lieutenant will be assigned to fly transport aircraft. (Women are still barred from flying combat aircraft.) Allen is one of eight women who were accepted in 1973.

4 June 1974 The first woman aviator in the Army, 2nd Lieutenant Sally D. Woolfolk, graduates from the US Army Aviation Center at Fort Rucker, Alabama, as a helicopter pilot.

19 June 1974 The US Supreme Court upholds provisions of the Uniform Code of Military Justice that permit the armed services to punish "conduct unbecoming an officer and a gentleman" and conduct "of a nature to bring discredit upon the Armed Forces". It turns down Captain Howard B. Levy's challenge of his conviction at a court martial for refusing to train Vietnam-bound special forces troops.

24 October 1974 The Air Force successfully fires a Minuteman I missile after dropping it by parachute from C-5A transport aircraft. It represents a step towards a strategic missile with air and land mobility, the C-5A is flying at 20,000 ft (6,095 m) over the southern California coast when the 78,000 lb (35,380 kg) missile is dropped. It ignites at 8,000 ft (2,440 m)

23 December 1974 The B-I bomber makes its first flight. A supersonic swing-wing aircraft two-thirds the size of the bomber it is slated to replace (the

B-52), it takes off, flies a triangular course over the Mojave Desert and reaches a maximum altitude of 10,000 ft (3,050 m) before it lands. The B-1 will be scrapped by President Carter in 1977: however his successor President Reagan authorizes its production as the B-IB.

30 April 1974 The South Vietnamese capital of Saigon falls to communist forces. Thousands of South Vietnamese and all remaining Americans in the city are evacuated by helicopter and the president of South Vietnam, Duong Van Minh, announces unconditional surrender to communist forces.

12 May 1975 Cambodian communist forces seize the US merchant ship *Mayaguez* near Poulo Wai Island in the Gulf of Siam. Its 39-man crew is taken prisoner. After fruitless efforts at diplomacy in the situation, President Gerald R. Ford sends in US air, naval and Marine forces; the ship is recaptured and its crew rescued on 14 May. There are 15 Marines killed and 50 wounded in the action.

5 March 1976 The air-launched cruise missile – to become better known by its familiar acronym (ALCM) – is launched successfully from a B-52G at White Sands Missile Range, New Mexico. The missile is designed to carry a nuclear warhead into enemy defenses. Its computerized memory is correlated against the terrain it flies over, which helps direct it to the target.

28 June 1976 Women are first admitted to the Air Force Academy. Legislation signed by President Gerald R. Ford the previous fall had abolished the all-male tradition at the nation's military academies, starting with the class of 1980. Nearly 1,600 freshman started with that class at the Air Force Academy, 152 of them women. On the same day the first 38 women are enrolled at the US Coast Guard Academy at New London, Connecticut.

6 July 1976 For the first time, women are admitted to the US Naval Academy In all, 81 women are sworn in at Annapolis as members of the Academy's Class of 1980. When that class of 770 midshipmen graduates four years later, there are 55 newly-commissioned female ensigns in the ranks of the Navy.

7 July 1976 Women are enrolled as cadets at the US Military Academy at West Point for the first time. The class of 1980 numbers 1,480, of whom 119 were women. The attrition rate is such that 62 of this original number will be commissioned lieutenants with their class – the first of them being Rebecca Hollen, who finishes 10th in her class.

Above: Determined to fill the so-called "bomber gap", President Reagan ordered the production of 100 B-1B bombers. This improved version of the B-1 was redesigned to incorporate the latest stealth technology.

21 January 1977 President Jimmy Carter pardons draft evaders who refused to be inducted for the Vietnam conflict. The order's practical side is that it pardons approximately 13,000 Americans who had refused or evaded induction through flight to Canada and other parts of the world. The pardon did not address the question of 100,000 other Americans who deserted the armed forces during the war.

4 March 1977 Ensign Janna Lambine graduates from the US Naval Air Station, Whiting Field, at Milton, Florida, and becomes the first woman pilot in the Coast Guard.

18 May 1977 The US and USSR, along with 32 other nations, sign a convention that prohibits the military or other hostile use of environmental modification techniques. While modifying the weather on any large scale for military purposes is not something that has been done with any degree of success, the convention – it is agreed – does not affect any of the current capabilities of US forces in this area.

10 June 1977 Secretary of the Army Clifford L. Alexander, Jr. approves the recommendation restoring the Medal of Honor to Dr Mary Edward Walker, which a review board had revoked in 1916. The first female surgeon in the Army, Dr Walker had been imprisoned by the Confederates from 10 April through 12 August, 1864. She is the only woman to have received the Medal of Honor.

30 June 1977 President Jimmy Carter announces that production of the B-1 bomber will be halted. "My decision," says the president, "is that we should no continue with the deployment of the B-I and I am directing that we discontinue plans for production of this weapons system."

7 September 1977 The Panama Canal Treaties, calling for the US to turn over control of the waterway to Panama as well as for its perpetual neutrality, are signed by Carter and General Omar Torrijos Herrera of Panama.

2 February 1978 The Tomahawk cruise missile is successfully launched from the submarine *Barb* (SSN 596) and flies a fully guided land attack test flight, which ends at Edwards Air Force Base, California. It is the first launch of the missile from a submarine. Fired from land, air or underwater the Tomahawk is one of the most versatile missiles in history. The missile has a small cross section, the ability to fly at low altitude and gives off low heat – making it difficult to detect.

Below: A sequence shot of the Tomahawk cruise missile during an underwater launch. The Tomahawk can also be fired from surface ships. The renovated battleship *New Jersey*, for example, carries 32 of them.

Right: The F-16 Fighting Falcon aircraft. Its origins were in the Air Force's belief that there was a need for a less costly fighter than the sophisticated F-15. It was known as a "high-low" mix of fighters.

23 March 1978 Captain. Sandra M. Scott becomes the first female pilot to perform alert duty in Strategic Air Command. At the time, Scott was assigned to the 904th Air Refuelling Squadron, a KC-135 tanker unit at Mather Air Force Base, California.

11 May 1978 The first woman Marine Corps general, Margaret A. Brewer, is appointed at age 47. She had been nominated for the star on April 6 by Carter and was sworn in as director of the division of information. At the time, there was no legal provision for the routine selection and promotion of a woman to flag rank; they could, however, be designated for such a billet.

20 October 1978 A law is signed allowing women to be assigned to certain non-combatant ships. Assignment is also permitted to combat ships for temporary duty of up to 180 days, as long as no combat is forseen. Within two weeks of the time the law is signed, nine women ensigns are assigned to non-combatants, the first time women have been assigned to vessels other than hospital ships and troop transports.

6 January 1979 The first F-16 Fighting Falcon aircraft is accepted at Hill Air Force Base, Utah, by the Air Force. Developed to replace the F-4 fighter in the active force and to modernize air reserve forces, the F16 enters service with the 388th Tactical Fighter Wing. Large numbers of the aircraft are in operation throughout the world, many of them co-produced in NATO countries.

12 June 1979 Carter orders full-scale development of Missile X, which, he

Below: The trench breakout mechanism for the M-X missile being tested at Luke Air Force Base, Arizona. The missile could break out of the 10 in (25 cm) of concrete and 5ft (1.52 m) of dirt in less than a minute.

says will be based in a horizontal shelter. Missile X, or M-X, will ultimately be known as the "Peacekeeper" missile when it is deployed during the buildup of the US strategic forces in the late 1980's Peacekeeper will become, as Carter had announced, the mainstay of the nation's ICBM force.

4 November 1979 Iranian militants seize the US EMBASSY IN Tehran and capture hostages. The mob seizing the embassy is protesting the admission of the former Shah of Iran for medical treatment at an air force base in Texas. "Khomeini struggles Carter trembles", proclaims a banner. The seizure is to have long-term effects on the future of both Iran and the US.

24 November 1979 The government General Accounting Office reports that thousands of US troops were exposed to the herbicide Agent Orange in the Vietnam War, a fact previously denied by the Defense Department. Nearly 5,000 veterans had reported serious health problems related to the toxic defoliant.

28 May 1980 The first women receive commissions from military academies. Andrea Hollen, a Rhodes Scholar, is the first woman to graduate from West point Elizabeth Belzer of Westminster, Maryland, receives her commission from the Naval Academy; and Kathleen Conley of Long Beach California, finishes eighth in her class at the Air Force Academy in Colorado Springs, Colorado.

21 July 1980 In a ceremony at Hill Air Force Base, Utah, the Air Force officially names the General Dynamics F-16

fighter the Fighting Falcon. Within two years, the Fighting Falcon production line will have passed the 600 mark as the aircraft enters US tactical fighter forces. It has since seen several modifications that are designed to strengthen its capabilities.

25 January 1981 Iranian hostages return to US soil after 444 days of captivity. An Air Force CV-137, which has been dubbed "Freedom", lands at Stewart International Airport, just 17 miles (27 km) from West Point, and the first 52 passengers to debark are Marines decked out in new dress uniforms. On hand to greet them are 139 of their relatives, who have been with the president at the White House earlier in the day.

12 April 1981 The first space shuttle, *Columbia*, is launched. Despite minor malfunctions, the world's first reusable space ship will orbit the earth 36 times during a flight of 54 hours 22 minutes and touch down safely at Edwards Air Force Base in California two days later. The space shuttle program is designed to make inexpensive routine flights into space possible.

7 January 1982 Lieutenant Colleen A. Cain becomes the Coast Guard's first woman pilot to be killed in the line of duty. She dies while responding to a distress call from a sinking fishing boat with 7 people aboard. The HH-52A helicopter she is co-piloting crashes in the Wailua Valley of Molokai, Hawaii

13 November 1982 The Vietnam Memorial is dedicated in Washington, DC. Designed by a Yale architectural student by the name of Maya Ying Lin and surrounded by all sorts of

Above: American medical students wave to US troops before boarding military aircraft to leave Grenada. One reason for US action in Grenada was that US citizens like these were endangered by a "shoot-on-site" curfew.

Left: Anti-satellite test. A heat-seeking missile is launched from an Air Force F-15 fighter and will successfully home in on a six year old military satellite orbiting 290 miles (467 km) above Earth at 17,500 mph (28,165 kmh)

controversy, the two black granite walls in the form of the letter "V– list the names of the 57,939 Americans killed or missing in the war. most of the criticism is focused on the fact that there is no inscription identifying the war.

19 January 1983 An XSM-62 Snark experimental missile that was found in the jungles of Brazil by a farmer is confirmed as having been one that was launched 26 years earlier (December 5, 1956) by the Air Force. The Snark had flown too far and failed to respond to control. A Miami newspaper wrote at the time: "They shot a Snark into the air, it fell to the earth they know not where".

22 May 1983 President Ronald Reagan announces a strategic defence initiative which promptly gains the label "Star Wars" from its opponents. "I am directing," says the President, "a comprehensive and intensive effort to define a long term research and development program to begin to achieve our ultimate goal of eliminating their threat posed by strategic nuclear missiles.

17 June 1983 The 'Peacemaker' intercontinental ballistic missile makes its maiden flight. America's newest missile, it has been developed in response to the improved hardness of Soviet strategic forces. It carried the designation M-X (for Missile-Experimental) prior to being deployed in silos at the F.E. Warren Air Force Base, Wyoming. It carries up to 10 nuclear warheads.

30 August 1983 Lieutenant Col. Guion Buford a 40-year-old pilot with a doctorate in engineering, becomes the first black American in space after the shuttle *Challenger* completes liftoff from Cape Canaveral, Florida. The six-day flight, which is the eighth in the shuttle series, is on a mission to deliver a sophisticated communications and weather satellite into space.

23 October 1983 The Beirut terrorist attack. A truck loaded with TNT crashes into Marine headquarters in Beirut, Lebanon, killing 241 Marine and Navy personnel. The driver of the explosives-laden Mercedes truck was also killed by the blast which used at least 2,500 lb (11.134 kg) of explosives. It turns the four-storey building into burning rubble and is the worst disaster to befall the armed forces since Vietnam.

25 October 1983 Military action is initiated on the small Caribbean island of Grenada to evacuate American students. Called Operation "Urgent Fury", it is unleashed one week after a coup by pro-Cubans on the island results in the murder of the country's top leaders. Hostilities will end on 2 November, with US casualties at 18 dead and 115 wounded. 1,000 Americans are evacuated.

Below: Map used by Secretary Defense Caspar W. Weinberger to brief President Reagan on the Libyan strike. The circuitous route to the target was necessary because France would not permit the US to use its airspace.

10 June 1984 The Army successfully test an anti-ballistic missile that intercepts and destroys a dummy missile warhead in flight. The launch takes place from Kwajalein atoll in the central Pacific: minutes after its launch it destroys another missile that had been launched from Vandenberg Air Force Base, California. It is a key test of the technology for the Strategic Defense Initiative.

13 September 1985 The Pentagon announces that an Air Force missile, in the first test of its kind, has destroyed an orbiting satellite some 290 miles (467 km) above the Earth. Launched from an F-15 Eagle fighter, heat seeking missile homed in on the six-year old military satellite, which was orbiting the Earth at 17,500 mph (28,165 kmh). The anti-satellite test was seen by the Soviets as an acceleration of the arms race.

14 April 1984 A US air strike is launched against targets in Libya in retaliation for that country's involvement with the bombing of a West Berlin disco on April 5 and other terrorist acts. Sixteen US F-111s flying from the UK are joined by US carrier-based planes in the attacks, which hit five military bases and other centers near Tripoli and Benghazi.

22 December 1986 With 10 Peacekeeper missiles on alert on the plains of southeastern Wyoming near Francis E. Warren Air Force Base, the Air Force achieves the initial operating capability for this system. A four-stage intercontinental ballistic missile that can carry 10 reentry vehicles to separate targets 6,000 miles (9,655 km) away, it is the first American ICBM to go on line since the Minuteman III in 1970.

6 May 1987 The last Titan II intercontinental ballistic missile is taken off alert at the 308th Strategic Missile Wing, Little Rock Air Force Base, Arkansas. It marks the first time in nearly 25 years that a Titan II is not a part of the US strategic deterrent force, reflecting Reagan's announcement that Titan IIs would be retired as part of his modernization program.

26 August 1987 Navy Secretary James H. Webb, Jr – a veteran of the Vietnam conflict – announces that an Aegis guided missile cruiser will become the first American ship to carry the name of a Vietnam war battle. Known as the *Hue City*, it is named for the successful battle – it took more than a month – to retake the old Imperial capital from the North Vietnamese after the Tet offensive in 1968.

2 October 1987

Above: The Ticonderoga class guided-missile cruiser Vincennes (CG 49) firing an Asroc anti-submarine missile during trials. Equipped with an elaborate Combat Information Centre the cruiser was designed as a flagship for the US Navy.

2 October 1987 Marine Chief Warrant Officer Charles B. Russel retires at Camp Pendleton, California. he is the last of the 669,000 marines who saw active duty in World War II. Russell experienced combat in two of the decisive battles against Japan – Pelleliu and Okinawa. Russell's last eight years have been filled as an ordnance officer at Camp Pendleton.

13 October 1987 More than 7,000 active duty sailors, former seamen and family members – and thousands of spectators – gather for ceremonies dedicating the "Lone Sailor" statue in downtown Washington, D.C. The $10 million structure is dedicated to

Below: Seen here on its fourth test flight over the California desert, the Northrop B-2 Advanced Technology Bomber was beset by early technical and financial problems, which resulted in a number of delays before its maiden flight at Edwards AFB.

the navies of the US and its allies as "a living tribute to Navy personnel, past and present". It is 212 years to the day since the Navy was founded.

6 August 1988 Some 21 years after her husband died of leukaemia and 43 years after the first atomic bomb drop on Hiroshima, the widow of Master Sgt. Robert Shumard receives death benefits from the Veterans Administration. Eleanor Shumard of Detroit had been fighting for the benefit, claiming that husband Robert's death – he was a gunner on the *Enola Gay*, the B-29 that dropped the bomb – was due to radiation exposure.

8 September 1988 The first Pershing missile to be destroyed under the Intermediate-range Nuclear Forces (INF) Treaty is crushed at the Longhorn Army Ammunition Plant in Karnack, Texas. Colonel Mikolai Shabalin served as the Soviet inspection team chief as the missile was destroyed. It was static fired to burn the rocket fuel out of the motor stage and then crushed.

13 October 1988 The sole surviving B-17G to have seen combat duty in World War II (Shoo Shoo Baby") flies to the Air Force Museum, Wright-Patterson Air Force Base, Ohio from Dover Air Force Base, Delaware. Every inch of the aircraft which flew 21 missions over Germany in 1944 had been renovated by volunteers. The bomber was named after the song "Shoo Shoo Baby" made famous by the Andrews Sisters.

4 January 1989 Two US Navy F-14 Tomcat fighters on patrol over the Gulf of Tripoli shoot down two Libyan MiG-23 fighter-bombers. Both Libyan pilots are seen to use their ejector seats and parachute to the sea.

19 April 1989 Battleship USS Iowa on a firing exercise 300 miles north-east of Puerto Rico suffers a huge explosion in one of the forward 16inch turrets. 27 sailors are killed and another 20 wounded in one of the US Navy's worst peacetime disasters.

1 July 1989 US cruiser Vincennes, on patrol in the Gulf, mistakes an Iranian airliner for an attacking fighter and shoots it down. 290 people are killed and the US government issues a formal apology.

17 July 1989 First flight of B-2 'stealth' bomber at Edwards air force base, California. The program is 18 months late and over budget, resulting in constant pressure to reduce the numbers on order.

31 July 1989 Lieutenant Colonel William R Higgins, a US member of a United Nations observer mission, who was kidnapped in Beirut 17 February 1987, is shot by his captors, a pro-Iranian Shi'ite terrorist group.

10 November 1989 Crowds in West Berlin start to demolish the Berlin Wall, hated symbol of the Cold War. This leads

Below: General Colin Powell, the First African American Chairman of the Joint Chiefs of Staff, stands at the side of President George Bush at a press conference in August 1990 at the start of the Gulf War with Iraq.

Right: A US M60A3 on exercise in Egypt in preparation for war in the Gulf. By the time the allied ground forces rolled over the border into Iraq and Kuwait the Iraqi army had been depleted by thirty-eight days and nights of air bombardment.

to a change in the whole relationship between the USA and Europe, both East and West.

20 December 1989 US forces invade Panama (Operation "Just Cause") in order to remove General Noriega. 22,500 troops are involved and fatalities include 26 US soldiers, 314 Panamanian soldiers and 220 civilians. Noriega hides in the papal nunciature, but is persuaded to surrender, 3 January 1990.

2 August 1990 Iraq invades Kuwait, creating the first post-Cold War crisis. President Bush places reinforcements on stand-by to stem this unprovoked aggression. Meanwhile, the United Nations Security Council condemns the invasion (Resolution 660, 4 August) and imposes sanctions (Resolution 661, 6 August)

9 August 1990 A brigade (2,300 men) of 82nd Airborne Division arrives in Saudi Arabia, together with FB-111 bombers of the USAF. B-52s arrive in nearby Diego Garcia.

17 September 1990 USAF chief of staff, General Michael Dugan, is dismissed by Secretary of Defense, Dick Cheney, for violating standing orders banning military personnel from discussing classified matters with the Press.

29 November 1990 United Nations Security Council votes to use force to expel Iraq from Kuwait, if it does not do so voluntarily by 15 January 1991 (Resolution 678).

16 January 1991 The UN ultimatum expires and Operation Desert Storm is launched at 7pm Eastern Standard Time (EST). A series of air attacks are made on targets in Iraq, by ship-launched cruise missiles and F-117 stealth fighters.

29 January 1991 Ground operations start with an Iraqi attack on the coastal town of Kafji. After some desultory fighting the Iraqis withdraw back into Kuwaiti territory.

23 February 1991 The land element of Desert Storm begins at 4am local time, with three main thrusts. VII and VIII Corps swing around in a huge outflanking move, isolating the main battlefield from the rest of Iraq. On the right US Marines, supported by Pan-Arab elements, move along the coast, while a Pan-Arab force heads for Kuwait City. Everything goes exactly according to plan.

27 February 1991 The Gulf War ends after exactly 100 hours, with Iraq having been utterly defeated by a combination of excellent generalship and superior firepower. US casualties are 148 killed, 72 wounded.

3 March 1991 General Schwarzkopf (Commander-in-Chief Central Command) and Saudi General Prince Khalid bin Sultan (Joint Forces Commander) meet Iraqi delegation at Safwan airfield in UN-occupied Iraq. The Iraqis accept all UN demands.

Below: In defeating the Iraqi invaders, General Schwarzkopf, here in typically forceful pose, adopted the "surround and destroy" tactics of Hannibal, whose Carthaginian forces defeated a much larger Roman army in 216BC.

31 March 1991 The last US tactical nuclear weapons are removed from Europe under the INF (intermediate-range nuclear forces) Treaty. The final weapons to leave are GLCMs (ground-launched cruise missiles) from Comiso, Italy and Greenham Common, England; and Pershing 2 ballistic missiles from Germany.

19 April 1991 Following Iraqi threats to attack the Kurds in the northern part of the country, US and allied troops move in from Turkish territory.

9 June 1991 In the Philippines Mount Pinatubo, a volcano, erupts, forcing the US to evacuate Clark air force base, some 15 miles distant. The evacuation is completed by 15 June, with

10 June 1991

Right: President George Bush and Boris Yeltsin at an informal meeting in Washington, February 1992. The two men were signatories of the historic START II Treaty which confirmed Bush's earlier assertion that the Cold War was finally over.

evacuees being moved to Subic naval base; most then move on to the United States.

10 June 1991 US armed forces from the Gulf War take part in a victory parade in New York to a tumultuous welcome.

9 August 1991 General 'Stormin Norman' Schwarzkopf retires from the army, his career capped by the triumph of the Coalition Forces under his command in the Middle East.

13 August 1991 The Pentagon announces that during the Gulf War US victims of 'friendly fire' were 35 servicemen killed and 72 wounded.

5-8 September 1991 A private gathering of US Naval aviators (Tailhook Association) takes place at Las Vegas. After some social events, allegations are made that 26 women, including 14 officers, have been sexually molested.

1 October 1992 US carrier Saratoga accidentally fires two missiles at Turkish destroyer Muavenet during NATO naval maneuvers in the eastern Mediterranean. Five Turkish sailors are killed.

24 November 1992 The last US servicemen leave the Philippines, ending a presence stretching back (apart from the 1942-44 Japanese occupation) to 1898. Final evacuation is from Cubi Point naval air station, part of Subic Bay naval base.

9 December 1992 The first US troops land at Mogadishu, Somaliland, following an undertaking by President Bush that there would be a short sharp

military action to ensure that food supplies reach the starving population.

3 January 1993 Presidents Bush and Yeltsin sign the START II Treaty in Moscow, Russia, in which the two countries agree to dismantle approximately two-thirds of their strategic missile forces.

13 January 1993 The first US marine is shot dead in Somaliland, followed by the second on 27 January.

4 May 1993 The US-led multinational Unified Task Force (UNITAF) hands over to the United Nations Operation in Somalia (UNISOM).

13 May 1993 Secretary of State Les Aspin announces the termination of the Strategic Defense Initiative (SDI), also known as 'Star Wars.' Development of land-based missile interceptors is, however, to continue.

5 August 1993 Sheila Widnall, an aeronautical engineer and Assistant Provost of Massachussets Institute of Technology (MIT), receives Senate approval as Secretary of the Air Force, the first woman to be appointed as head of a branch of the US forces.

1 October 1993 General John M Shalikashvili is appointed Chairman of the Joint Chiefs of Staff. He was born in Poland and enlisted in the US Army at the age of 16, serving in Vietnam as a private.

30 April 1994 The Tailhook affair claims another victim as Admiral Frank Kelso II, the Chief of Naval Operations, requests early retirement. At one of the trials of three officers involved, the military judge dismissed the charges on the grounds that the CNO had concealed evidence that he personally witnessed some of the incidents. Admiral Kelso disputed the judges' findings but resigned in order to clear the air.

6 June 1994 President Clinton and other leaders of the World War Two Allied nations meet on the beaches of Normandy for the fiftieth anniversary of the D-day landings.

8 September 1994 The last US troops pull out of Berlin. The first US troops arrived in Berlin on 1 July 1945 as part of the victorious Allied garrison and a

Below: This artist's impression of a space-based electromagnetic rail-gun firing hypervelocity projectiles was one of many proposals put forward for the Strategic Defense Initiative. Space weaponry is, however, still a distant prospect.

Below: The Nimitz class nuclear-powered aircraft carrier USS Dwight D. Eisenhower (CVN-69), which transported the first US troops to Hait,i here transits northbound through the Suez Canal to the Mediterranean Sea.

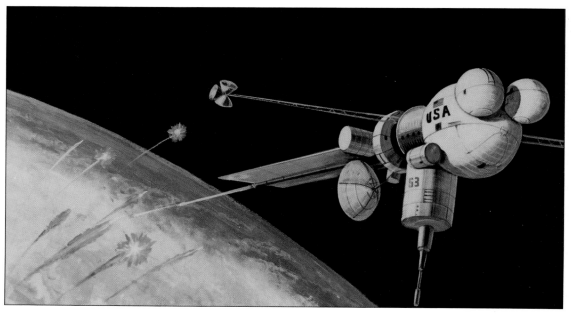

brigade was stationed there for the following 49 years, which, with its British and French allies, served as an outpost of democracy throughout the Cold War.

19 September 1994 The first wave of US troops land on the Caribbean island of Haiti, arriving by helicopter from the carrier, USS Eisenhower.

6 February 1995 Lieutenant Colonel Eileen Collins becomes the first US female shuttle pilot.

31 March 1995 US forces hand over to the United Nations Mission in Haiti (UNMIH).

1 March 1995 Final UN troops leave Somalia under protection of an 'overwhelming force' of US Marines, who returned to the country to cover the withdrawal of UNISOM II. Little has been gained by the US and UN involvement in the country, which returns to its previous obscurity.

25 May 1995 US aircraft lead NATO air forces in carrying out heavy air strikes against Bosnian Serb targets after the Bosnian Serbs have failed to react to United Nations' warnings.

2 June 1995 A USAF F-16 fighter is shot down by a Bosnian Serb SA-6 missile. The pilot, Captain Scott O'Brady, ejects, lands safely and then eludes Bosnian Serb forces for six days before being rescued by US helicopters on 8 June.

16 May 1996 Admiral Jeremy 'Mike' Boorda, aged 56, Chief of Naval Operations, is alleged to have worn two medal

Above: The USS Louisiana (SSBN-743) is the last of the Ohio-class submarines. Built to take the Trident II D-5 missiles, a more accurate missile than the Trident I, the first Ohio-class boat entered service in 1976.

pins to which he was not strictly entitled. Despite having worn them in good faith, Boorda shoots himself with a 38-caliber revolver.

3 April 1996 A USAF Boeing CT-43 transport aircraft carrying US Commerce Secretary Ron Brown crashes near Dubrovnik, Croatia. A total of 35 people are killed.

25 June 1996 Terrorist bombs explode outside a USAF barracks in Dhahran, Saudi Arabia. US casualties include 19 dead and hundreds wounded.

May 1995 The first African-American four-star admiral, Admiral Paul J Reason, takes command of the Atlantic Fleet.

13 September 1996 Nuclear attack submarine USS Cheyenne (SSN-773) is commissioned. It is the last of the Los Angeles (SSN-688) class, 56 of which have been built over 22 years. This is the longest and most successful submarine program ever.

27 July 1996 USS Louisiana (SSBN-743) is named at Electric Boat yard, Groton, Connecticut. The last of eighteen Ohio-class ballistic missile submarines, Louisiana carries 24 Trident-II missiles.

20 December 1996 In Bosnia responsibility is transferred from Implementation Force (IFOR) to Stabilisation Force (SFOR), commanded by US General William Crouch. SFOR is 31,000-strong including 8,500 US troops.

2 April 1997 Major-General Claudia Kennedy is selected for promotion to lieutenant-general, becoming US Army's first three-star female officer.

5 April 1997 The first F-22 Raptor is rolled out at Lockheed Martin's Marietta, Georgia production facility. The F-22 is intended to replace the McDonnel Douglas F-15 Eagle and will have a "first-look/ first-kill" advantage over potential opponents such as the Russian MiG-29 and Su-27 fighters.

28 April 1997 First Global Hawk unmanned aerial vehicle (UAV) is unveiled. The system has a 35.3m wingspan and flies at over 21 km (65,000ft), with a 115kg package of sensors. It can fly to a mission area 3,500 nautical miles distant and patrol for over 24 hours before returning to base.

1 May 1997 Head of UNSCOM (UN Special Commission to Iraq) Rolf Ekeus of Sweden hands over to Australian Richard Butler. The United States took the lead in establishing UNSCOM after the Gulf War, with the task of ensuring that Iraq's weapons of mass destruction are eliminated.

1 October 1997 4th Infantry Division is named as the first US Army formation to be digitized; every item in its electronic inventory will be digital as opposed to analog. This will be completed by the year 2000, making 4th Infantry Division the most capable and rapid reacting force in any army.

1 July 1997 Army General Wesley Clark is appointed NATO's Supreme Allied Commander Europe (SACEUR), succeeding General George Joulwan. The post of SACEUR has been filled by a US general officer since the fist to hold the post, General Dwight D Eisenhower was appointed in 1951.

17 February 1998 After issuing a series of warnings to Iraq over interference with UNSCOM inspection teams President Clinton issues a blunt warning to Saddam Hussein that the US is ready to go to war, if necessary.

21-23 February 1998 UN Secretary-General Kofi Annan flies to Baghdad for a last-ditch confrontation with Iraqi president, Saddam Hussein. Annan negotiates an agreement to allow the UNSCOM teams to continue with their work, which is announced on 23 February, and Annan then returns to New York to brief the Security Council on the agreement he has brokered.

Below: The F-22 Raptor – the "ultimate fighter" – combines state-of-the-art low observables, which make it hard to detect. It can supercruise at Mach 1.4 or more for extended periods and is also manouverable enough for close in-fighting.

Index

Because of the *Almanac's* wide coverage of subjects this index restricts itself to presidents; senior officers of all services; major engagements, and the Medal of Honor. Illustrations are in **bold** type.